VISUAL QUICKSTART GUIDE

SQL

Chris Fehily

 Peachpit Press

Visual QuickStart Guide

SQL

Chris Fehily

Peachpit Press

1249 Eighth Street
Berkeley, CA 94710
510/524-2178
800/283-9444
510/524-2221 (fax)
Find us on the World Wide Web at: http://www.peachpit.com
Peachpit Press is a division of Addison Wesley Longman

Editor: Becky Morgan
Production Coordinator: Lisa Brazieal
Copyeditor: Kathy Simpson
Tech Editor: Bryan Steinweg
Compositor: Maureen Forys
Indexer: Joy Dean Lee
Cover Design: The Visual Group

ISBN 0-201-11803-0

9 8 7 6 5 4 3 2

Printed and bound in the United States of America

Dedication

To my father

Special Thanks to:

Becky Morgan for picking up on the first ring.

Marjorie Baer for tossing me a "Do you know SQL?"

Kathy Simpson for sleeping 10 minutes every other day, whether she needed it or not.

Lisa Brazieal for cutting and pasting (repeatedly).

Maureen Forys for not splitting keywords.

Bryan Steinweg for continuing on next page.

Darren Pennington for getting on his soapbox.

Nancy Aldrich-Ruenzel for the seabreezes.

The data in the sample database are fictional. I lifted two book titles from Iain M. Banks's Culture novels.

CONTENTS AT A GLANCE

TABLE OF CONTENTS

Chapter 8: **Subqueries** **231**

Chapter 9: **Inserting, Updating, and
Deleting Rows** **281**

Chapter 10: **Creating, Altering, and
Dropping Tables** **301**

INTRODUCTION

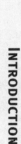

SQL is the standard programming language for creating, updating, and retrieving information that is stored in relational database management systems (DBMSes). With SQL, you can turn your ordinary questions ("Where do our customers live?") into statements that your database software can understand (`SELECT city, state FROM customers;`). You may already know how to extract this type of information by using a graphical query tool, but perhaps you've noticed that this tool becomes limiting and cumbersome as your questions grow in complexity—that's where SQL comes in.

You also can use SQL to add, change, and delete data and database objects. Most popular DBMSes—Microsoft Access, Oracle, and MySQL, for example—support SQL, although the level of support varies by product (more about that later in this chapter).

In this book, I'll teach you important relational and SQL concepts before moving on to SQL programming itself.

About SQL

SQL is:

♦ A programming language

♦ Easy to learn

♦ Nonprocedural

♦ Embedded or interactive

♦ Standardized

♦ Used to manipulate data and database objects

♦ Pronounced *es-kyu-el*

♦ Not an acronym

A programming language. SQL is a formal language in which you give instructions to—that is, program—a computer. Your database software executes your SQL program, performs the tasks you've specified, and displays the results (or an error message). Programming languages differ from spoken languages (called informal or natural languages) in that programming languages are designed for a specific purpose, have a small vocabulary, and are inflexible and utterly unambiguous. Consequently, if you don't get the results you expect, it's because your program contains an error—or bug— and not because the computer misinterpreted your instructions. (Debugging one's programs is a cardinal programming task.)

SQL, like any formal language, is defined by rules of *syntax,* which determine the words and symbols that you can use and how they can be combined, and *semantics,* which determine the actual meaning of a syntactically correct statement. Note that you can write a legal SQL statement that expresses the wrong meaning (good syntax, bad semantics). I'll introduce SQL's syntax and semantics in Chapter 3.

Listing i.1 This Microsoft Access Visual Basic routine extracts the first and last names from a table containing author information and places the results in an array.

```
Sub GetAuthorNames()
  Dim db As Database
  Dim rs As Recordset
  Dim i As Integer
  Dim au_names() As String
  Set db = CurrentDb()
  Set rs = db.OpenRecordset("authors")
  rs.MoveLast
  ReDim au_names(rs.RecordCount - 1, 1)
  With rs
    .MoveFirst
    i = 0
    Do Until .EOF
      au_names(i, 0) = ![au_fname]
      au_names(i, 1) = ![au_lname]
      i = i + 1
      .MoveNext
    Loop
  End With
  rs.Close
  db.Close
End Sub
```

Listing i.2 This single SQL statement performs the same task as the Visual Basic routine in Listing i.1. Access's internal optimizer determines the best way to extract the data.

```
SELECT au_fname, au_lname
  FROM authors;
```

Easy to learn. Easy compared with other programming languages, that is. If you've never written a program before, you'll find the transition from informal to formal language frustrating. Still, SQL's statements read like sentences to make things easy on humans. A novice programmer probably would understand the SQL statement SELECT au_fname, au_lname FROM authors ORDER BY au_lname; to mean "List the authors' first and last names, sorted by last name," whereas the same person would find the equivalent C or Perl program impenetrable.

Nonprocedural. If you've never programmed, you can skip this point without loss of continuity. If you've programmed in a language such as C or Perl, you've used a *procedural language,* in which you specify the explicit steps to follow to produce a result. SQL is a *nonprocedural language* (also called a *declarative language*), in which you describe *what* you want and not *how* to do it; your database software's optimizer will determine the "how." As such, SQL lacks traditional control constructs such as IF-THEN-ELSE, WHILE, FOR, and GO TO statements.

To demonstrate this difference, I've written programs that perform an equivalent task in Microsoft Access Visual Basic (a procedural language) and SQL. **Listing i.1** shows a VB program that extracts author names from a table that contains author information. You needn't understand the entire program, but note that it uses a Do Until loop to define explicitly how to extract data. **Listing i.2** shows how to do the same task with a single SQL statement (as opposed to around 20 lines of VB code). With SQL, you specify only what needs to be accomplished; the DBMS determines and performs internally the actual step-by-step operations needed to obtain the result. Moreover, Listing i.2 is the simplest possible SQL query. After you add common operations such as sorts, filters, and joins, you may need more than 100 lines of procedural code to accomplish what a single SQL SELECT statement can do.

Embedded or interactive. When you use *embedded* SQL, you include SQL statements in larger programs written in a procedural *host language*, which commonly is a general-purpose language (C, Java, or COBOL, for example) or a scripting language (Perl, PHP, or Python). A PHP CGI script may use embedded SQL statements to query a MySQL database, for example; MySQL will pass the query result back to a PHP variable for display or further analysis. Drawing from the preceding examples, I've embedded an SQL statement in an Access Visual Basic program in **Listing i.3**.

In *interactive* SQL (also called *dynamic* SQL), you issue SQL commands directly to your DBMS, which displays the results as soon as they're produced. DBMS servers come with graphical applications or command-line utilities that accept interactive SQL statements or text files that contain SQL programs (scripts).

This book covers only interactive SQL. Generally, any interactive SQL statement can be embedded in an application program or script. But keep in mind that interactive and embedded SQL statements may have small syntactic differences.

Standardized. SQL is not "owned" by any particular firm: It's an open standard that an ANSI committee defines and manages (**Figure i.1**). ANSI is the American National Standards Institute, a U.S. government body that facilitates the development of national standards. SQL also is an international standard because the International Organization for Standardization adopted the ANSI standard (ISO/IEC 9075:1992). Everything in this book is based on the 1992 ANSI SQL standard, so you should consider *ANSI SQL*, *SQL-92*, and *SQL* to be synonymous unless

Listing i.3 Here, Visual Basic serves as the host language for embedded SQL. I use only interactive SQL for this book's examples. Embedded SQL and interactive SQL syntax may differ slightly, depending on your DBMS.

```
listing

Sub GetAuthorNames2()
  Dim db As Database
  Dim rs As Recordset
  Set db = CurrentDb()
  Set rs = db.OpenRecordset("SELECT au_fname,
→ au_lname FROM authors;")
  ' --Do something with rs here.
  rs.Close
  db.Close
End Sub
```

Figure i.1 This is the inside cover of the 626-page ANSI document X3.135-1992, *Database Language—SQL*, which defines the SQL-92 language officially. You may purchase it in electronic format at www.ansi.org if you like. Its intended audience, however, is not SQL programmers, but people who design and implement DBMS products themselves.

I note otherwise. There *is* a newer standard named ANSI SQL-99, but most DBMS vendors won't implement it for years. SQL-99 is backward-compatible with SQL-92, so your SQL-92 programs will work with an SQL-99 database system.

All DBMS vendors add proprietary features to ANSI SQL to enhance the language. These extensions usually are additional commands, keywords, functions, data types, and control-flow constructs such as IF, WHILE, and FOR statements. Oracle and Microsoft have added so many features to standard SQL that the resulting languages—PL/SQL and Transact-SQL, respectively—can be considered to be separate languages in their own right, rather than just supersets of SQL. One vendor's extensions generally are incompatible with other vendors' products. I don't discuss proprietary SQL extensions in this book, but I do point out the "SQL parts" of an extended language that don't comply with the ANSI standard; see "Using SQL with a specific DBMS" later in this chapter.

Used to manipulate data and database objects. SQL statements generally are divided into two major categories: *data manipulation language* (DML) and *data definition language* (DDL). DML statements retrieve, reckon, insert, edit, and delete data stored in a database. This book covers DML statements (SELECT, INSERT, UPDATE, and DELETE) in Chapters 4 through 9. DDL statements create, modify, and destroy database objects such as tables, indexes, and views. I discuss DDL statements (CREATE, ALTER, and DROP) in Chapters 10 through 13.

Pronounced *es-kyu-el*. SQL isn't pronounced *sequel*; that pronunciation is a historical artifact. Avoid the error and articulate each letter: S–Q–L. I disagree with people who claim that saying *sequel* is so common that nothing's wrong with it. You shouldn't say *sequel* for the same reason that you shouldn't split infinitives when you write your novel; it may generally be accepted, but it will rasp on the ears of knowledgeable people. Also, pronounce MySQL as *my-es-kyu-el* and PostgreSQL as *post-gres-kyu-el*.

Not an acronym. It's a common misconception that *SQL* stands for *structured query language*; it stands for S–Q–L and nothing else. Why? Because ANSI says so. The official name is Database Language SQL (refer to Figure i.1). Furthermore, referring to it as a structured query language is a disservice to new SQL programmers; it amuses database professionals and academics to point out that "structured query language" is the worst possible description, as SQL:

♦ Isn't structured (because it can't be broken down into blocks or procedures)

♦ Isn't limited to only queries (that is, there's more than just the SELECT statement)

♦ Isn't a complete language (according to Turing's Thesis, which you'll study should you take Theory of Computation)

ABOUT SQL

About This Book

This book will teach you how to use the SQL programming language to maintain and query database information. After some expository material about DBMSes, the relational model, and SQL syntax in Chapters 1 through 3, I'll revert to the task-based, visual style that you're familiar with if you've read other *Visual QuickStart* books.

Although I don't assume that you've had programming experience, I do expect that you're competent with your operating system, be it Windows, Unix, Mac OS, or something else. In particular, you should be familiar with your OS's file system and know how to create, edit, delete, and organize files, folders, and directories. For some tasks, you must know how to enter commands at a command prompt or shell (also called a *DOS prompt* in older Windows versions).

This book isn't an exhaustive guide to SQL; I've limited the scope to ANSI SQL's most popular statements. For information about other SQL statements, refer to one of the many SQL reference books that covers the ANSI standard completely.

Companion Web site

At www.peachpit.com/vqs/sql, you'll find the full table of contents, corrections, updates, and all code listings (with bugs fixed). You also can write me directly at fehily@pacbell.net with questions, suggestions, corrections, and gripes related to this book.

SQL server vs. Desktop DBMSes

An *SQL server* DBMS acts as the server part of a client/server network configuration; it stores databases and responds to SQL requests made by many clients. A *client* is an application or computer that sends an SQL request to a server and accepts the server's response. If your network uses a client/server architecture, the client is the computer on your desk, and a server is a powerful, specialized machine residing in another room, building, or country. The rules that describe how client/server requests and responses are transmitted are DBMS protocols such as ODBC and JDBC.

A *desktop* DBMS is installed and runs locally. It's a stand-alone application that stores a database and does all the SQL processing itself or behaves as a client of an SQL server. A desktop DBMS can't accept requests from other clients (that is, it can't act like an SQL server).

SQL servers include Microsoft SQL Server, Oracle, MySQL, and PostgreSQL. Desktop systems include Microsoft Access and FileMaker Pro. Note that *SQL server* (not capitalized) can refer to any vendor's SQL server product, and *SQL Server* (capitalized) is Microsoft's particular SQL server product. By convention, I use *client* and *server* to refer to client and server software itself or to the machine on which the software runs, unless the distinction is important.

Audience

This book is appropriate for you if you:

◆ Lack programming experience but are familiar with computers.

◆ Are learning SQL on your own or from an instructor.

◆ Are otherwise uninterested in databases but must process large amounts of structured information because of the nature of your work. (Accountants, scientists, Web programmers, marketing analysts, sales representatives, financial planners, office managers, and managers often fall into this group.)

◆ Want to move beyond friendly but underpowered graphical query tools.

◆ Are migrating from desktop database software to SQL server software (see the sidebar in this section).

◆ Already know some SQL and want to move past simple SELECT statements.

◆ Need to create, modify, or delete database objects such as tables, indexes, and views.

◆ Need to embed SQL in programs written in languages such as Java, C, or Perl.

◆ Are a Web programmer working with MySQL or PostgreSQL.

◆ Need a desktop SQL reference book.

This book is *not* appropriate for you if you want to learn:

♦ How to design databases (although I review proper design concepts in Chapter 2).

♦ Proprietary extensions that DBMS vendors add to ANSI SQL.

♦ Advanced database programming and administration. (I don't cover installation, triggers, stored procedures, replication, backup and recovery, optimization, cursors, collations, character sets, or translations, for example.)

Typographic conventions

I use the following typographic conventions:

Italic type introduces new terms or represents replaceable identifier names in text.

`Monospace type` denotes SQL code in listings and in regular text. It also shows screen text in a command-prompt window (shell) and URLs.

`Red monospace type` denotes specific SQL code and results in listings and figures that is explained in the accompanying text. I use red highlighting to emphasize relevant portions of screen shots.

`Italic monospace type` denotes a replaceable identifier or expression whose actual value depends on the context. You'd replace `column` with an actual column name, for example.

Table i.1

Syntax Symbols	
CHARACTERS	**DESCRIPTION**
|	The vertical-bar or pipe symbol separates alternative items that may be optional or required. You may choose exactly one of the given items. (Don't type the vertical bar.) A | B | C is read "A or B or C." Don't confuse the pipe symbol with the double-pipe symbol, | |, which is SQL's string-concatenation operator.
[]	Brackets enclose one or more optional items. (Don't type the brackets.) [A | B | C] means "type A or B or C or type nothing." [D] means "type D or type nothing."
{}	Braces enclose one or more required items. (Don't type the braces.) {A | B | C} means "type A or B or C."
. . .	Ellipses mean that the preceding item(s) may be repeated any number of times.
()	Parentheses, unlike the preceding symbols, actually are part of the SQL language; type them as indicated in the syntax diagram.

Syntax conventions

I use the following conventions in SQL syntax diagrams and code listings:

◆ I use a consistent style to improve code readability and maintenance. To save space in this book, my indentation level is two spaces. In practice, indentation often is four spaces.

◆ Each SQL statement begins on a new line.

◆ As you'll learn in Chapter 3, SQL is a free-form language without restrictions on line breaks or the number of words per line. I begin each clause of a statement on a new, indented line:

```
SELECT au_fname, au_lname
  FROM authors
  ORDER BY au_lname;
```

◆ SQL is case-insensitive, which means that myname, MyName, and MYNAME are considered to be identical identifiers. I use UPPERCASE for SQL keywords such as SELECT, NULL, and CHARACTER (see "SQL Syntax" in Chapter 3), and lowercase or lower_case for all user-defined values, such as table, column, and alias names.

In some DBMSes, user-defined identifiers are case-sensitive, so it's safest to respect case when you write SQL programs.

◆ **Table i.1** shows special symbols that I use in syntax diagrams.

◆ All quote marks in SQL code are straight quotes (such as ' and "), not curly, or smart, quotes (such as ' and "). Curly quotes prevent code from working.

◆ When a column is too narrow to hold a single line of code or output, I break it into two or more segments. A gray arrow → indicates a continued line.

Using SQL with a specific DBMS

DBMS This icon indicates a vendor-specific departure from the ANSI SQL-92 standard. If you see this icon, it means that a particular vendor's version of SQL doesn't comply with ANSI SQL, and you must modify the listed SQL program to run on your DBMS. If I note, for example, that the ANSI SQL operator to combine (concatenate) two strings is || (a double pipe), but that Microsoft products use + (a plus sign) and MySQL uses the CONCAT() function instead, you'll need to change all occurrences of *a* || *b* in my SQL listing to *a* + *b* (if you're using Microsoft Access or Microsoft SQL Server) or to CONCAT(*a*,*b*) (if you're using MySQL). In most cases, my SQL programs will work as is or with minor syntactic changes. Occasionally, an SQL program won't work at all; MySQL 4.0 and earlier versions don't support subqueries, for example (although subquery support is promised for version 4.1).

This book covers these DBMSes:

- Microsoft Access 2002

- Microsoft SQL Server 2000

- Oracle Release 9i

- MySQL 4.0

- PostgreSQL 7.1

Database vs. DBMS

A database is not the same as the database software that you're running; it's incorrect to say, "Oracle is a database." Database software is called a *database management system* (DBMS). A *database,* which is just one component of a DBMS, is the data itself—that is, it's a container (one or more files) that stores structured information. Besides controlling the organization, integrity, and retrieval of data in databases, DBMSes handle tasks such as physical storage, security, replication, and error recovery.

DBMS also is abbreviated RDBMS, in which the *R* stands for *relational.* An RDBMS organizes data according to the relational model (see Chapter 2). This book covers only relational databases, so when I use DBMS, the initial *R* is implied.

What about FileMaker Pro?

FileMaker Pro is a popular desktop database application that supports the SQL SELECT statement with FROM, WHERE, and ORDER BY clauses (see Chapter 4). That may not sound like much compared with the entire SQL language but it's enough to perform the most common types of queries. You can use the SQL Query Builder tool or the Execute SQL script step to run an SQL query in FileMaker Pro; see FileMaker Pro Help or *FileMaker Pro 5/5.5 Advanced: Visual QuickPro Guide* by Cynthia L. Baron and Daniel Peck, published by Peachpit Press. You can learn about FileMaker Pro at www.filemaker.com.

I've picked these DBMSes for their popularity. I tested the SQL programs in this book with the indicated release version. The programs will work with later versions but not necessarily with earlier versions, as ANSI SQL compliance often improves in successive releases.

You still can run the SQL programs on other DBMSes, such as DB2, Sybase Adaptive Server, and Informix. If a program doesn't work, read the documentation to determine how the DBMS's SQL implementation departs from the ANSI SQL standard.

✔ Tip

■ I've included tips for Oracle 8i too. If I don't mention a specific version number then the tip applies to both Oracle 8i and 9i.

ABOUT THIS BOOK

What You'll Need

To replicate this book's examples on your own computer, you'll need:

◆ A text editor

◆ The sample database

◆ A database management system

A text editor. Although typing short or ad-hoc interactive SQL statements at a command prompt is convenient, normally you'll want to store nontrivial SQL programs in text files. By convention, my SQL file names end with the .sql suffix, but you may use .txt (or any extension) if you prefer.

A *text editor* is a utility program for creating and modifying text files. Text files contain only printable letters, numbers, and symbols—no fonts, formatting, "invisible" characters, colors, graphics, or any of the clutter usually associated with a word processor. Every operating system includes a free text editor (**Table i.2**), but you may want to explore the many excellent shareware and commercial editors (search for *text editors* at www.download.com).

✔ Tips

■ You can download all the SQL programs in this book from the companion Web site; see "About This Book" earlier in this chapter.

■ You *can* use a word processor such as Microsoft Word and save the file as text only, but that practice usually leads to maintenance problems (and professionals consider it to be bad form).

Table i.2

Common Text Editors	
ENVIRONMENT	TEXT EDITORS
Windows	Notepad
Windows command prompt	edit
Unix, Linux	vi, emacs, pico
Mac OS	TeachText, SimpleText
Mac OS X Terminal	Same as Unix

The sample database. Most of the examples in this book use the same database; see "The Sample Database" in Chapter 2. To build the sample database, run the SQL program in the Appendix or, if you're using Microsoft Access, open the file `books.mdb`. (You can download these files from the companion Web site.) If you're working with a production server DBMS, your database administrator may need to grant you permission to run SQL programs.

A database management system. How do you get SQL? You don't—you get a DBMS that understands SQL and feed it an SQL program. The DBMS will run your program and display the results. In the next chapter, I'll explain how to run SQL programs in some popular DBMSes.

WHAT YOU'LL NEED

DBMS SPECIFICS

You'll need a database management system to run SQL programs. You may have your own private copy of a DBMS running on your desktop computer, or you may have access to one over a network. In the latter case, you'll be using your desktop computer to connect to a DBMS server running on another machine. The computer where the server is running is called a *host*.

As this book is about SQL and not DBMSes, I won't rehash the instructions for installing and configuring database software. This evasion may seem like a brush-off at first glance, but setting up a DBMS varies greatly by vendor, product, version, and operating system. All DBMSes come with extensive installation, administration, reference, and tutorial documentation. (To give you an idea, just the installation manual for Oracle is around 300 pages long.)

Running SQL Programs

In this chapter, I'll describe how to run SQL programs in these DBMSes:

- Microsoft Access 2002

- Microsoft SQL Server 2000

- Oracle 9i

- MySQL 4.0

- PostgreSQL 7.1

Microsoft Access's graphical interface lets you run only one SQL statement at a time; to run multiple SQL statements, embed them in a Visual Basic program (not covered in this book). The other DBMSes let you run SQL programs in interactive mode or script mode. In *interactive mode,* you type individual SQL statements at a command prompt and view the results of each statement separately, so input and output are interleaved. In *script mode* (also called *batch mode*), you save your entire SQL program in a text file (called a *script* or a *batch file*), and a command-line utility takes the file, executes the program, and returns the results without your intervention. I'll use the sample database and the SQL program shown in **Listing 1.1** in all the examples in this chapter. I'll also describe the minimal syntax of command-line utilities; the complete syntax is given in the DBMS documentation or the command's help screen.

Listing 1.1 This file, named `listing0101.sql`, contains a simple SQL SELECT statement, which I'll use to query the sample database in subsequent DBMS examples.

```
SELECT au_fname, au_lname
  FROM authors
  ORDER BY au_lname;
```

Pathnames

A *pathname* specifies the location of a directory or file in a hierarchical file system. An *absolute pathname* specifies a location completely by listing its entire path, starting at the topmost node of the directory tree, called the *root*. A *relative pathname* specifies a location relative to the current directory. In Windows, an absolute path starts with a backslash or with a drive letter followed by a colon and a backslash. In Unix or Mac OS X Terminal, an absolute path starts with a slash.

`C:\Program Files\Microsoft SQL Server` (Windows) and `/usr/local/bin/mysql` (Unix) are absolute paths. `scripts\listing0101.sql` (Windows) and `doc/readme.txt` (Unix) are relative paths.

Pathname commonly is shortened to *path*. Although the difference is obvious from context, I'll use *pathname* to prevent confusion with the path environment variable described in the Tips in this section.

✔ Tips

■ When you specify the name of an SQL file in script mode, it may have an absolute or relative pathname; see the sidebar in this section.

■ To run a command-line utility from any particular directory, your path must list the actual directory containing the utility. A *path* is a list of directories that the OS searches for programs. For some DBMSes, the installer handles the path details; for others (such as MySQL and PostgreSQL), you'll need to add the utility's directory to your path yourself.

To view your path, type `path` (Windows) or `echo $PATH` (Unix or Mac OS X Terminal) at a command prompt, and press Enter. To change your path, add the directory in which the utility resides to the path environment variable. Search Help for *environment variable* (Windows), or modify the path command in your login initialization file, usually named `.bash_login`, `.bashrc`, `.cshrc`, `.login`, `.profile`, or `.shrc` (Unix or Mac OS X Terminal).

RUNNING SQL PROGRAMS

3

Microsoft Access

Microsoft Access is a commercial desktop DBMS. Access is appropriate for managing small and medium-size databases. You can learn about Access at www.microsoft.com/office/access/.

This book covers Microsoft Access 2002. To determine which version of Access you are running, choose Help > About Microsoft Access.

In Access 2002, the default query mode is ANSI-89. You must enable ANSI-92 SQL query mode to run many of the examples in this book.

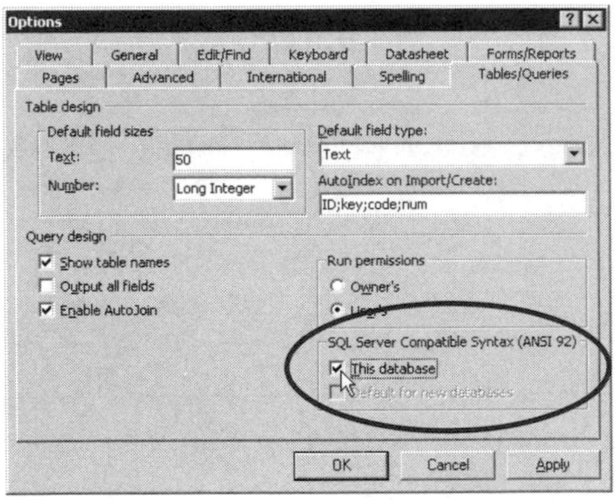

To enable ANSI-92 SQL query mode:

1. Click Tools > Options to open the Options dialog box.

2. Click the Tables/Queries tab.

3. Select the This Database checkbox (**Figure 1.1**).

✔ Tips

■ Be wary of enabling this mode in general; the two ANSI SQL query modes, ANSI-89 and ANSI-92, are not compatible. The range of data types, reserved words, and wildcard characters are different in each query mode, so your existing queries may not run or may return unexpected results.

■ For information about query modes, search Access Help for *ANSI SQL query mode*.

Figure 1.1 ANSI-92 SQL query mode allows you to run SQL statements that use ANSI-92 SQL syntax.

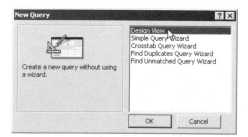

Figure 1.2 Click the New toolbar button to create a new query.

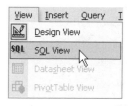

Figure 1.3 Select Design View in the New Query dialog box.

Figure 1.4 Choose SQL View to run a data manipulation language statement (SELECT, INSERT, UPDATE, or DELETE)...

If you're a casual Access user, you've probably used the query design grid to create a query. When you create a query in Design View, Access constructs the equivalent SQL statement behind the scenes for you. You can view, edit, and run the SQL statement in SQL View.

Access uses two almost-identical but separate interfaces to run data manipulation language (DML) and data definition language (DDL) SQL statements; see "About SQL" in the Introduction. DML statements include SELECT, INSERT, UPDATE, and DELETE; DDL statements include CREATE, ALTER, and DROP.

To run an SQL statement:

1. In the Database window, click Queries (below Objects), and click New in the toolbar (**Figure 1.2**).

2. In the New Query dialog box, click Design View, and click OK (**Figure 1.3**).

3. Without adding tables or queries, click Close in the Show Table dialog box.

4. To run a DML statement, choose View > SQL View (**Figure 1.4**).

   or

   To run a DDL statement, choose Query > SQL Specific > Data Definition (**Figure 1.5**).

continues on next page

Figure 1.5 ...or Data Definition to run a data definition language statement (CREATE, ALTER, or DROP).

MICROSOFT ACCESS

5. Type (or paste) an SQL statement (**Figure 1.6**).

6. Choose Query > Run to run the SQL statement (**Figure 1.7**).

Access displays the result of a SELECT statement (**Figure 1.8**) but executes other types of statements silently or displays warning dialogs, depending on your settings.

✔ Tip

■ You can run only a single SQL statement through a Query object. To run multiple statements, use multiple Query objects or a host language such as Visual Basic for Applications.

Figure 1.6 Enter an SQL statement...

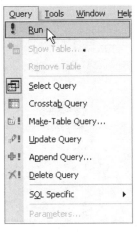

Figure 1.7 ...and run it.

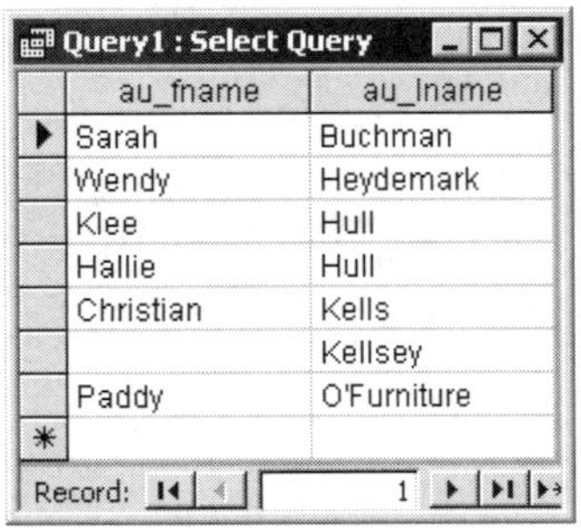

Figure 1.8 Access displays the results of a SELECT statement.

Figure 1.9 Query Analyzer uses the selected database to resolve references in your SQL statements.

Figure 1.10 The results of a SELECT statement in Query Analyzer.

Microsoft SQL Server

Whereas Microsoft Access is desktop software, Microsoft SQL Server is Microsoft's server software that supports very large databases and numbers of transactions. It runs only on Microsoft operating systems. You can learn about SQL Server at www.microsoft.com/sql/. You can download a free 120-day evaluation version of SQL Server from www.microsoft.com/sql/evaluation/.

This book covers Microsoft SQL Server 2000. To determine which version of Microsoft SQL Server you are running, type SELECT @@VERSION;, press Enter, type go, and press Enter at an osql prompt.

You can use the SQL Query Analyzer graphical tool or the osql command-line utility to run SQL programs.

To use SQL Query Analyzer:

1. Choose Start > Programs > Microsoft SQL Server > Query Analyzer.

2. Select the server and authentication mode, and click OK.

3. Select a database from the toolbar combo box (**Figure 1.9**).

4. To run SQL interactively, type an SQL statement in the query window.

   or

   To run an SQL script, choose File > Open, select a script file, and click Open.

5. Choose Query > Execute or press F5.

   The bottom pane displays the results (**Figure 1.10**).

✔ Tip

■ You also can use the isqlw command-line utility to start SQL Query Analyzer.

To use the osql command-line utility interactively:

1. At a command prompt, type:

   osql -E -d *dbname*

   -E instructs SQL Server to use a trusted connection instead of requesting a password, and *dbname* is the name of the database to use.

2. Type an SQL statement, and press Enter. The statement may span multiple lines.

3. Type *go* and press Enter to display the results (**Figure 1.11**).

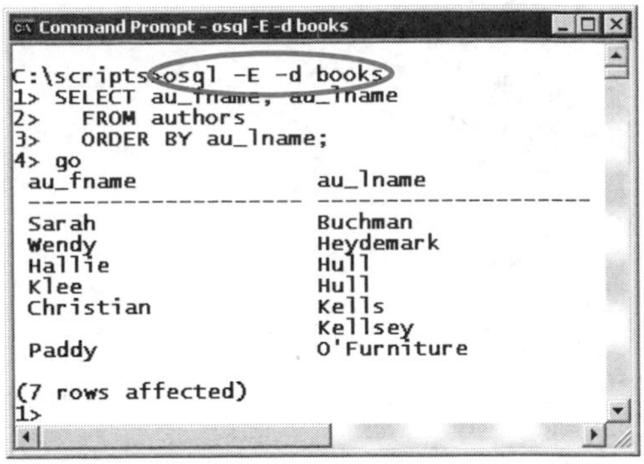

To use the osql command-line utility in script mode:

◆ At a command prompt, type:

   osql -E -d *dbname* -n -i *sql_script*

   -E instructs SQL Server to use a trusted connection instead of requesting a password, *dbname* is the name of the database to use, -n suppresses numbering and prompt symbols (>) in the output, and *sql_script* is a text file containing an SQL program and may have an absolute or relative pathname (**Figure 1.12**).

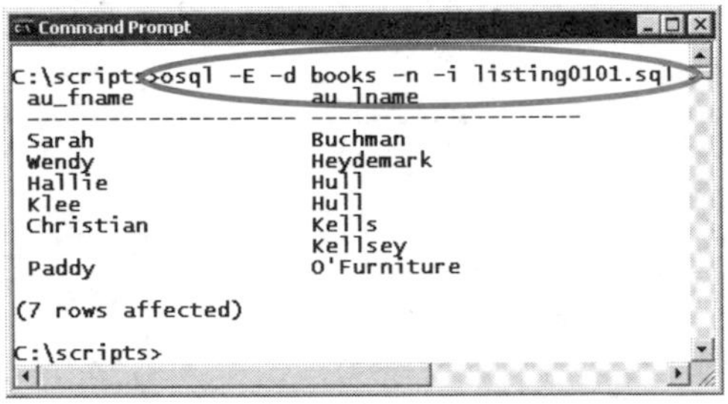

Figure 1.11 The same SELECT statement in osql interactive mode.

Figure 1.12 The same SELECT statement in osql script mode.

To exit the `osql` command-line utility:

◆ Type `exit` or `quit` and press Enter.

To display a list of `osql` command-line options:

◆ At a command prompt, type `osql -?` and press Enter.

✔ Tips

■ Your SQL Server installation may require you to specify a user name and password instead of using a trusted connection. To do so, replace the option `-E` with `-U` *login_id*, where *login_id* is your user name; `osql` will prompt you for a password.

■ If you're running `osql` from a remote computer on a network, you'll need to use the option `-S` *server* to specify the SQL Server instance to which to connect. Ask your database administrator.

MICROSOFT SQL SERVER

Oracle

Oracle is the leading commercial DBMS. It supports hideously large databases and numbers of transactions. It runs on many operating systems and hardware platforms and is so complex that a skilled database administrator must run and maintain it.

You can learn about Oracle products at www. oracle.com. The Personal Edition of Oracle is less intimidating than the Enterprise Edition. You can download a free single-user, development-only version at the Oracle Technology Network Web site (otn.oracle.com). The download file is enormous; you may order a CD Pack instead for around $40 (U.S.).

This book covers Oracle Release 9i, but I'll also include tips for 8i. The version of Oracle that you are running is displayed in the initial "Connected to" message that appears when you log on to SQL*Plus or sqlplus.

You can use the SQL*Plus graphical tool or the sqlplus command-line utility to run SQL programs.

To use SQL*Plus:

1. Start SQL*Plus.

   This procedure varies by platform. In Windows, for example, choose Start > Programs > Oracle - OraHome91 > Application Development > SQL Plus.

2. Enter your user name, password, and a database name, and click OK (**Figure 1.13**).

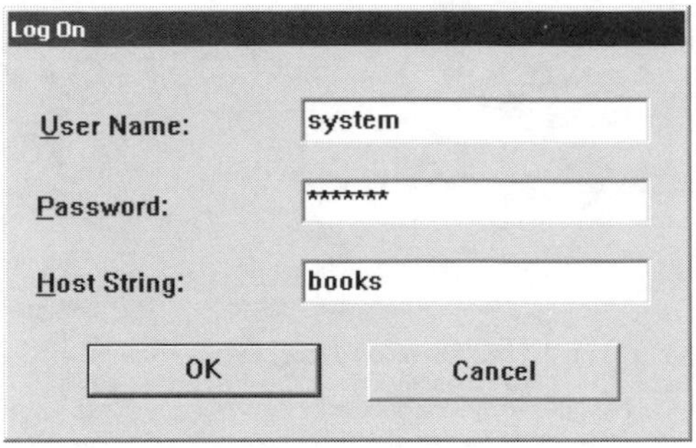

Figure 1.13 The SQL*Plus log-on screen.

ORACLE

```
Oracle SQL*Plus                          _ □ X
File  Edit  Search  Options  Help

SQL*Plus: Release 9.0.1.0.1 - Production on Su

(c) Copyright 2001 Oracle Corporation.  All ri

Connected to:
Oracle9i Enterprise Edition Release 9.0.1.1.1
JServer Release 9.0.1.1.1 - Production

SQL> SELECT au_fname, au_lname
  2     FROM authors
  3     ORDER BY au_lname;

AU_FNAME        AU_LNAME
--------------  --------------
Sarah           Buchman
Wendy           Heydemark
Hallie          Hull
Klee            Hull
Christian       Kells
                Kellsey
Paddy           O'Furniture

7 rows selected.

SQL>
```

Figure 1.14 The results of an interactive SELECT statement in SQL*Plus.

```
Oracle SQL*Plus                          _ □ X
File  Edit  Search  Options  Help

SQL*Plus: Release 9.0.1.0.1 - Production on Su

(c) Copyright 2001 Oracle Corporation.  All ri

Connected to:
Oracle9i Enterprise Edition Release 9.0.1.1.1
JServer Release 9.0.1.1.1 - Production

SQL> @C:\scripts\listing0101.sql

AU_FNAME        AU_LNAME
--------------  --------------
Sarah           Buchman
Wendy           Heydemark
Hallie          Hull
Klee            Hull
Christian       Kells
                Kellsey
Paddy           O'Furniture

7 rows selected.

SQL>
```

Figure 1.15 The same SELECT statement run as a script in SQL*Plus.

If you are connecting to a remote Oracle database, ask your database administrator for a connection identifier to enter in the Host String field.

The default database administrator's account has the user name SYSTEM and the default password manager.

3. To run SQL interactively, type an SQL statement and press Enter.

The statement may span multiple lines (**Figure 1.14**).

or

To run an SQL script, type @*sql_script* and press Enter.

sql_script is a text file containing an SQL program and may have an absolute or relative pathname (**Figure 1.15**).

ORACLE

To use the `sqlplus` command-line utility interactively:

1. At a command prompt, type:

   sqlplus *user/password@dbname*

   user is your user name, *password* is your password, and *dbname* is the name of the database to use.

2. Type an SQL statement.

   The statement may span multiple lines.

3. Press Enter to display the results (**Figure 1.16**).

To use the `sqlplus` command-line utility in script mode:

♦ At a command prompt, type:

   sqlplus *user/password@dbname*
   → @*sql_script*

   user is your user name, *password* is your password, *dbname* is the name of the database to use, and *sql_script* is a text file containing an SQL program and may have an absolute or relative pathname. Be sure to type a space between *dbname* and @*sql_script* (**Figure 1.17**).

To exit the `sqlplus` command-line utility:

♦ Type **exit** or **quit** and press Enter.

To display a list of `sqlplus` command-line options:

♦ At a command prompt, type **sqlplus -** and press Enter.

✔ Tip

■ In **sqlplus**, you can (and should) omit */password* to be prompted for your password.

Figure 1.16 The results of a SELECT statement in sqlplus interactive mode.

Figure 1.17 The same SELECT statement in sqlplus script mode.

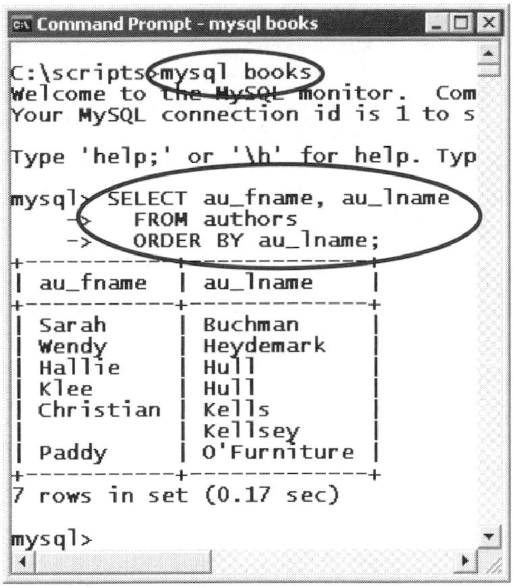

Figure 1.18 The results of a SELECT statement in mysql interactive mode.

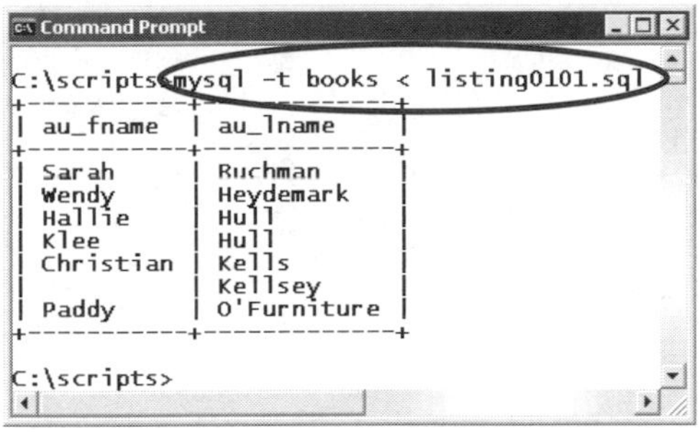

Figure 1.19 The same SELECT statement in mysql script mode.

MySQL

MySQL is a leading open-source DBMS. It is fast, stable, and supports large databases. MySQL is known for its speed but is missing some important SQL features. (Version 4.1 promises to add subqueries and foreign keys.) MySQL runs on many operating systems and hardware platforms and is free for personal use; you can download it from www.mysql.com.

This book covers MySQL 4.0. To determine which version of MySQL you are running, type SELECT VERSION(); at a mysql prompt and press Enter.

You can use the mysql command-line utility to run SQL programs.

To use the mysql command-line utility interactively:

1. At a command prompt, type:

   mysql *dbname*

   dbname is the name of the database to use.

2. Type an SQL statement.

   The statement may span multiple lines.

3. Press Enter to display the results (**Figure 1.18**).

To use the mysql command-line utility in script mode:

◆ At a command prompt, type:

   mysql -t *dbname* < *sql_script*

   -t places the results in a table (omit this option if you want tab-delimited output), *dbname* is the name of the database to use, and *sql_script* is a text file containing an SQL program and may have an absolute or relative pathname (**Figure 1.19**).

MySQL

To exit the `mysql` command-line utility:

◆ Type `exit` or `quit` and press Enter.

To display a list of `mysql` command-line options:

◆ At a command prompt, type `mysql -?` and press Enter.

This command produces a few screens of output, type `mysql -? | more`, press Enter, and press the spacebar to view one screen at a time (**Figure 1.20**).

✔ Tips

■ If you're running MySQL from a remote computer on a network, you'll need to specify a host name, user name, and password to connect to the server. To do so, type:

`mysql -h host -u user -p dbname`

host is the host name, *user* is your user name, and *dbname* is the name of the database to use. MySQL will prompt you for a password. Contact your database administrator to find out what connection parameters you should use to connect.

■ When you start the MySQL server, `mysqld`, you can specify the `--ansi` command-line option to use ANSI SQL syntax instead of MySQL syntax.

■ You can learn more about the Open Source Initiative at `www.opensource.org`.

Figure 1.20 The `mysql` help screen.

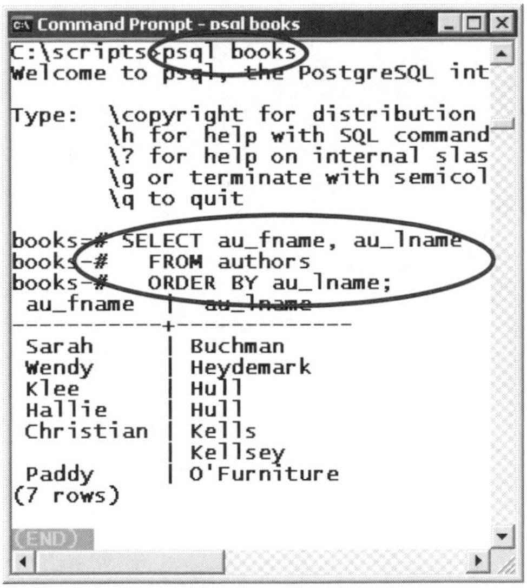

Figure 1.21 The results of a SELECT statement in psql interactive mode.

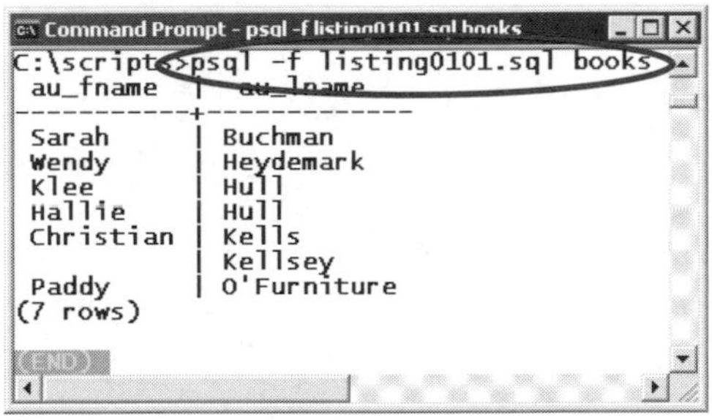

Figure 1.22 The same SELECT statement in psql script mode.

PostgreSQL

PostgreSQL is a leading open-source DBMS. It is fast, stable, and supports large databases and numbers of transactions. PostgreSQL is known for its rich feature set, and its high compliance with the ANSI SQL standard. PostgreSQL runs on many operating systems and hardware platforms and is free for personal use; you can download it from www.postgresql.org.

This book covers PostgreSQL 7.1. To determine which version of PostgreSQL you are running, type psql -V at a command prompt and press Enter.

You can use the psql command-line utility to run SQL programs.

To use the psql command-line utility interactively:

1. At a command prompt, type:

   psql *dbname*

   dbname is the database to use.

2. Type an SQL statement.

   The statement may span multiple lines.

3. Press Enter to display the results (**Figure 1.21**).

To use the psql command-line utility in script mode:

◆ At a command prompt, type:

   psql -f *sql_script dbname*

   sql_script is a text file containing an SQL program and may have an absolute or relative pathname, and *dbname* is the name of the database to use (**Figure 1.22**).

POSTGRESQL

To exit the `psql` command-line utility:

◆ Type \q and press Enter.

To display a list of `psql` command-line options:

◆ At a command prompt, type `psql -?` and press Enter (**Figure 1.23**).

✔ Tips

■ If you're running PostgreSQL from a remote computer on a network, you'll need to specify a host name, user name, and password to connect to the server. To do so, type:

`psql -h` *host* `-U` *user* `-W` *dbname*

host is the host name, *user* is your user name, and *dbname* is the name of the database to use. PostgreSQL will prompt you for a password. Contact your database administrator to find out what connection parameters you should use to connect.

■ You can learn more about the Open Source Initiative at www.opensource.org.

Figure 1.23 The psql help screen.

THE
RELATIONAL MODEL

Many good books about database design are available; this book isn't one of them. Nevertheless, to become an effective SQL programmer, you'll need to become familiar with the *relational model* (**Figure 2.1**), a data model so appealingly simple and well-suited for organizing and managing data that it squashed the competing network and hierarchical models with a satisfying Darwinian crunch.

The foundation of the relational model, mathematical *set theory*, forces you to think in terms of sets of data rather than individual items or rows of data. The model describes how to perform common algebraic operations (such as unions and intersections) on database tables in much the same way that they're performed on mathematical sets (**Figure 2.2**). Tables are analogues of sets: They're collections of distinct elements having common properties. A mathematical set would contain positive integers, for example, whereas a database table would contain information about students.

In truth, you can skip or skim most of this chapter and learn SQL programming from context and experimentation, particularly if you want to run only simple **SELECT** statements. But, as in all fields, a grasp of theory lets you *predict* results and avoid trial-and-error fixes when things go wrong.

Figure 2.1 You can read E.F. Codd's *A Relational Model of Data for Large Shared Data Banks* (*Communications of the ACM,* Vol. 13, No. 6, June 1970, pp. 377-387) at www.acm.org/classics/nov95/toc.html. Relational databases are based on the data model defined by this paper.

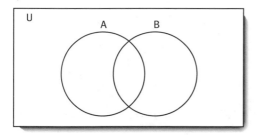

Figure 2.2 You may remember the rudiments of set theory from school. This Venn diagram expresses the results of operations on sets. The rectangle (U) represents the universe, and the circles (A and B) inside represent sets of well-defined elements. The relative position and overlap of the circles indicate relationships between sets. In the relational model, the circles are tables, and the rectangle is all the information in a database (sometimes called the *universe of discourse*).

Tables, Columns, and Rows

First, a little terminology: If you're already familiar with databases, you've heard alternative terms for the same concepts. **Table 2.1** shows how interchangeable terms are related. Formal relational-model terms are in the first column, ANSI SQL standard and DBMS documentation terms are in the second column, and the third-column terms are holdovers from traditional (nonrelational) file processing. I use SQL terms in this book (even when I'm discussing the model).

Tables

From a user's point of view, a database appears to be a collection of one or more tables (and nothing but tables). A *table:*

◆ Is the database structure that holds data.

◆ Contains data about a specific entity type. An *entity type* is a class of distinguishable real-world objects, events, or concepts with common properties—students, movies, genes, weather conditions, or appointments, for example. (Patients and appointments are different entities, so you'd store information about them in different tables).

◆ Is a two-dimensional grid characterized by *rows* and *columns* (**Figures 2.3** and **2.4**).

◆ Holds a data item called a *value* at each row–column intersection (refer to Figures 2.3 and 2.4).

◆ Has at least one column and zero or more rows. A table with no rows is an *empty table*.

◆ Has a unique name within a database.

Table 2.1

Equivalent Terms		
MODEL	**SQL**	**FILES**
Relation	Table	File
Attribute	Column	Field
Tuple	Row	Record

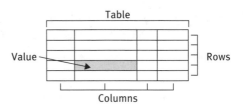

Figure 2.3 This grid is an abstract representation of a table—the fundamental storage unit in a database.

```
au_id  au_fname         au_lname
-----  ---------------  ---------------
A01    Sarah            Buchman
A02    Wendy            Heydemark
A03    Hallie           Hull
A04    Klee             Hull
```

Figure 2.4 This grid is a representation of an actual (not abstract) table, shown as a table normally appears in database software and books. This table has 3 columns, 4 rows, and 3 x 4 = 12 values. The top "row" is not a row but a header that displays column names.

```
au_lname         au_id  au_fname
---------------  -----  ---------------
Hull             A04    Klee
Buchman          A01    Sarah
Hull             A03    Hallie
Heydemark        A02    Wendy
```

Figure 2.5 Rows and columns are said to be *unordered*, meaning that their order in a table is irrelevant for informational purposes and set operations. Interchanging columns or rows does not change the meaning of the table; this table conveys the same information as the table in Figure 2.4.

Columns

Columns in a given table have these characteristics:

◆ Each column represents a specific attribute (or property) of the table's entity type. In a table `employees`, a column named `hire_date` might show when an employee was hired, for example.

◆ Each column has a domain that restricts the set of values permitted in that column. A *domain* is a set of constraints that includes restrictions on a value's data type, length, format, range, uniqueness, specific values, and nullability (whether nulls are permitted). You can't place the string value `"mimetic"` in the column `hire_date`, for example, if `hire_date` requires a valid date value.

◆ Entries in columns are single-valued (atomic); see "Normalization" later in this chapter.

◆ The order of columns (left to right) is unimportant (**Figure 2.5**).

◆ Each column has a name that uniquely identifies it within a table. (You can reuse the same column name in other tables, though.)

Rows

Rows in a given table have these characteristics:

◆ Each row describes an *entity*, which is a unique instance of an entity type—a particular student or appointment, for example.

◆ Each row contains a value or null for each of the table's columns.

◆ The order of rows (top to bottom) is unimportant (refer to Figure 2.5).

◆ No two rows in a table can be identical.

◆ Each row in a table is uniquely identified by its primary key; see "Primary Keys" later in this chapter.

✔ Tips

■ Use the SELECT statement to retrieve columns and rows; see Chapters 4 through 8. Use the INSERT, UPDATE, and DELETE statements to add, edit, and delete rows; see Chapter 9. Use the CREATE TABLE and ALTER TABLE statements to add, edit, and delete columns; see Chapter 10.

■ Tables have the attractive property of *closure*, which ensures that any operation performed on a table yields another table (**Figure 2.6**).

■ A DBMS uses two types of tables: user tables and system tables. *User tables* store user-defined data. *System tables* contain *metadata*—data about the database—such as structural information, physical details, performance statistics, and security settings. System tables collectively are called the *system catalog;* the DBMS creates and manages these tables dynamically. This scheme conforms with the relational model's requirement that *all* data be stored in tables (**Figure 2.7**).

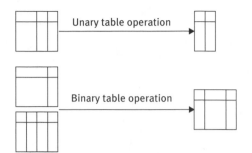

Figure 2.6 Closure guarantees that you'll get another table as a result no matter how you split or merge tables. This property allows you to nest table operations to any depth. *Monadic* or *unary table operations* operate on one table to produce a result table. *Dyadic* or *binary table operations* operate on two tables to produce a result table.

Name	Owner	Type
authors	dbo	User
publishers	dbo	User
royalties	dbo	User
title_authors	dbo	User
titles	dbo	User
dtproperties	dbo	System
syscolumns	dbo	System
syscomments	dbo	System
sysdepends	dbo	System
sysfilegroups	dbo	System
sysfiles	dbo	System
sysfiles1	dbo	System
sysforeignkeys	dbo	System
sysfulltextcatalogs	dbo	System
sysfulltextnotify	dbo	System
sysindexes	dbo	System
sysindexkeys	dbo	System
sysmembers	dbo	System
sysobjects	dbo	System
syspermissions	dbo	System
sysproperties	dbo	System
sysprotects	dbo	System
sysreferences	dbo	System
systypes	dbo	System
sysusers	dbo	System

Figure 2.7 DBMSes store system information in special tables called system tables. Here, the shaded tables are the system tables that Microsoft SQL Server creates and maintains for the sample database used in this book. You access system tables in the same way that you access user-defined tables, but don't alter them unless you know what you're doing.

- In practice, the number of rows in a table changes frequently, but the number of columns changes rarely. Database complexity makes adding or dropping columns difficult; column changes may affect keys, referential integrity, user privileges, and so on. Adding or deleting rows doesn't affect these things.

- Database designers split values into columns based on the users' needs. Phone numbers, for example, may reside in the single column `phone_number` or may be split into the columns `country_code`, `area_code`, and `subscriber_number`.

- The resemblance of spreadsheets to tables is superficial: A table doesn't depend on row and column order, doesn't perform calculations, doesn't permit free-form data entry, strictly checks each value's validity, and easily is related to other tables.

- The *relational* in *relational database* refers to relational set theory and *not* to the ability to relate tables by their common values.

- Some more terminology: The number of rows in a table is the table's *cardinality*, and the number of columns is its *degree*. In common usage, a *schema* describes a database's structure and organization, including its table definitions. According to ANSI, a schema is a collection of database objects belonging to a single user. A *catalog* is a collection of schemata.

TABLES, COLUMNS, AND ROWS

Primary Keys

Every value in a database must be accessible. As values are stored at row–column intersections in tables, it's clear that a value's location refers to a specific table, column, and row. You can identify a table or column by its unique name. Rows are unnamed, however, and require a different identification mechanism called a primary key. A *primary key* is:

- **Required.** Every table has exactly one primary key. Remember that the relational model views a table as an unordered set of rows. Because there's no concept of a "next" or "previous" row, you can't identify rows by position; without a primary key, some data would be inaccessible.

- **Unique.** Because a primary key identifies a single row in a table, no two rows in a table can have the same primary-key value.

- **Simple or composite.** A primary key comprises one or more columns in a table; a one-column key is called a *simple key*, and a multiple-column key is called a *composite key*. Database designers prefer simple keys to composite keys.

- **Not null.** A primary key value can't be empty. For composite keys, no column's value can be empty; see "Nulls" in Chapter 3.

- **Stable.** Once created, primary-key values seldom change.

- **Not reusable.** If you delete a row, you can't assign its primary-key value to a new row.

- **Minimal.** A primary key includes only the column(s) necessary for uniqueness.

A database designer designates primary keys. This process is crucial, because the consequence of a poor key choice is the inability to add data (rows) to a table. I'll review the essentials here, but read a database design book if you want to learn more about this topic.

Suppose that you need to choose a primary key for the table in **Figure 2.8**. The columns au_fname and au_lname separately won't work, because each one violates the uniqueness requirement. Combining au_fname and au_lname into a composite key won't work, because two authors may share a name. Names generally make poor keys because they're unstable (people divorce, companies merge, spellings change). The correct choice is au_id, which I invented to uniquely identify authors. Database designers invent unique identifiers when natural or obvious ones (such as names) won't work.

After a primary key is defined, your DBMS will enforce the integrity of table data. You can't insert this row, because the au_id value A02 already exists in the table:

```
A02    Christian    Kells
```

Nor can you insert this row, because au_id can't be null:

```
NULL   Christian    Kells
```

This row is legal:

```
A05    Christian    Kells
```

```
au_id au_fname        au_lname
----- --------------- ---------------
A01   Sarah           Buchman
A02   Wendy           Heydemark
A03   Hallie          Hull
A04   Klee            Hull
```

Figure 2.8 The column au_id is the primary key in this table.

✔ Tips

■ Use the PRIMARY KEY constraint to designate a primary key; see "Specifying a Primary Key with PRIMARY KEY" in Chapter 10.

■ In practice, the primary key often is placed in a table's initial column(s). When a column name contains *id* (or *key* or *code* or *num*), it's a clue that the column may be a primary key (or foreign key; see the next section).

■ Database designers often forgo common unique identifiers such as Social Security numbers for U.S. citizens or ISBN numbers for books. Instead, they use custom surrogate keys that encode information that is meaningful inside the database users' organization. An employee ID, for example, may embed the year that the person was hired.

■ Database designers may have a choice of several unique *candidate keys* in a table, one of which is designated the primary key. After designation, the remaining candidate keys become *alternate keys*.

■ You *could* use au_id and, say, au_lname as a composite key, but that combination violates the minimality criterion.

■ **DBMS** DBMSes provide data types and attributes that automatically provide unique identification values for each row (such as an integer that increments automatically for each new row). In **Microsoft Access**, it's the AutoNumber data type. In **Microsoft SQL Server**, it's the uniqueidentifier data type or the IDENTITY property. In **Oracle**, it's the ROWID data type. In **MySQL**, it's the AUTO_INCREMENT attribute. In **PostgreSQL**, it's the serial data type.

Foreign Keys

Information about different entity types is stored in different tables, so you must have a way to navigate between tables. The relational model provides a mechanism called a foreign key to associate two tables. A *foreign key* has these characteristics:

◆ It's a column (or group of columns) in a table whose values relate to, or reference, values in some other table.

◆ It ensures that rows in one table have corresponding rows in another table.

◆ The table that contains the foreign key is the *referencing* or *child* table. The other table is the *referenced* or *parent* table.

◆ A foreign key establishes a direct relationship to the parent table's primary key (or any candidate key), so foreign-key values are restricted to parent-key values that already exist. This constraint is called *referential integrity*. A particular row in a table `appointments` must have an associated row in a table `patients`, for example, or there would be appointments for patients who are nonexistent or can't be identified. An *orphan row* is a row in a child table for which no associated parent-table row exists.

◆ The values in the foreign key have the same domain as the parent key. Recall from "Tables, Columns, and Rows" earlier in this chapter that a domain is the set of all permissible values for a column.

◆ Unlike primary-key values, foreign-key values may be null (empty); see the Tips in this section.

◆ A foreign key may have a different column name than its parent key.

◆ Foreign-key values generally aren't unique in their own table.

◆ I've made a simplification in the first point: In reality, a foreign key can reference the primary key of its *own* table (rather than only some other table). A table `employees` with the primary key `employee_id` may contain a foreign key `boss_id`, for example, that references the column `employee_id`. This type of table is called *self-referencing*.

Figure 2.9 shows a primary- and foreign-key relationship between two tables.

After a foreign key is defined, your DBMS will enforce referential integrity. You can't insert this row into the table `titles`, because the `pub_id` value P05 doesn't exist in the table `publishers`:

```
T05     Exchange of Platitudes     P05
```

You can insert this row only if the foreign key permits nulls:

```
T05     Exchange of Platitudes     NULL
```

This row is legal:

```
T05     Exchange of Platitudes     P04
```

Primary key
publishers

pub_id	pub name
P01	Abatis Publishers
P02	Core Dump Books
P03	Schadenfreude Press
P04	Tenterhooks Press

Primary key   Foreign key

titles

title_id	title_name	pub_id
T01	1977!	P01
T02	200 Years of Ger...	P03
T03	Ask Your System...	P02
T04	But I Did It Unco...	P04

Figure 2.9 The column pub_id is a foreign key of the table titles that references the column pub_id of the table publishers.

✔ Tips

- Use the FOREIGN KEY constraint to specify a primary key; see "Specifying a Foreign Key with FOREIGN KEY" in Chapter 10.

- SQL lets you specify the referential-integrity action that the DBMS takes when you attempt to update or delete a key value to which foreign-key values point; see the Tips in "Specifying a Foreign Key with FOREIGN KEY" in Chapter 10.

- The decision to permit nulls in a foreign key is practical, not theoretical. Missing foreign-key values complicate enforcement of referential integrity. In practice, nulls in a foreign key often remain null temporarily, pending a real-life decision or discovery; see "Nulls" in Chapter 3.

- To prevent confusion, don't call foreign keys *links*. Links generally are understood to be pointers to places in physical memory, whereas foreign keys associate tables based on data values. Foreign keys are *logical*, not physical.

FOREIGN KEYS

Relationships

A *relationship* is an association established between common columns in two tables. A relationship can be:

◆ One-to-one

◆ One-to-many

◆ Many-to-many

One-to-one

In a one-to-one relationship, each row in table A can have *at most one* matching row in table B, and each row in table B can have *at most one* matching row in table A. Because all the information in both tables simply could be stored in just one table, one-to-one relationships are used for practical, not theoretical, reasons: They're used to segregate confidential information for security reasons, to speed queries by splitting monolithic tables, or to avoid inserting nulls into tables that contain columns with non-null values in a small subset of rows.

A one-to-one relationship is established when the primary key of one table also is a foreign key referencing the primary key of another table (**Figures 2.10** and **2.11**).

titles

title_id	title_name
T01	1977!
T02	200 Years of Ger...
T03	Ask Your System...
T04	But I Did It Unco...

royalties

title_id	advance
T01	10000
T02	1000
T03	15000
T04	20000

Figure 2.10 A one-to-one relationship. Each row in `titles` can have at most one matching row in `royalties`, and each row in `royalties` can have at most one matching row in `titles`. Here, the primary key of `royalties` also is a foreign key referencing the primary key of `titles`.

Figure 2.11 This diagram shows an alternative way to depict the one-to-one relationship in Figure 2.10. The connecting line indicates associated columns. The key symbol indicates a primary key.

publishers

pub_id	pub name
P01	Abatis Publishers
P02	Core Dump Books
P03	Schadenfreude Press
P04	Tenterhooks Press

titles

title_id	title_name	pub_id
T01	1977!	P01
T02	200 Years of Ger...	P03
T03	Ask Your System...	P02
T04	But I Did It Unco...	P04
T05	Exchange of Plati...	P04

Figure 2.12 A one-to-many relationship. Each row in publishers can have many matching rows in titles, and each row in titles has only one matching row in publishers. Here, the primary key of publishers (the *one* table) appears as a foreign key in titles (the *many* table).

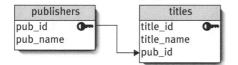

Figure 2.13 This diagram shows an alternative way to depict the one-to-many relationship in Figure 2.12. The connecting line's unadorned end indicates the *one* table, and the arrow indicates the *many* table.

One-to-many

In a one-to-many relationship, each row in table A can have *many* (zero or more) matching rows in table B, but each row in table B has *only one* matching row in table A. A publisher can publish many books, but each book is published by only one publisher, for example.

One-to-many relationships are established when the primary key of the *one* table appears as a foreign key in the *many* table (**Figures 2.12** and **2.13**).

Many-to-many

In a many-to-many relationship, each row in table A can have *many* (zero or more) matching rows in table B, and each row in table B can have *many* matching rows in table A. Each author can write many books, and each book can have many authors, for example.

A many-to-many relationships is established only by creating a third table called a *junction table*, whose composite primary key is a combination of both table's primary keys; each column in the composite key separately is a foreign key. This technique always produces a unique value for each row in the junction table and breaks the many-to-many relationship into two separate one-to-many relationships (**Figures 2.14** and **2.15**).

✔ Tips

- Joins (for performing operations on multiple tables) are covered in Chapter 7.

- You *can* establish a many-to-many relationship without creating a third table if you add repeating groups to the tables, but that method violates first normal form; see the next section.

- A one-to-many relationship also is called a *parent-child* or *master-detail* relationship.

- A junction table also is called an *associating table* or *intersection table*.

titles

title_id	title_name
T01	1977!
T02	200 Years of Ger...
T03	Ask Your System...
T04	But I Did It Unco...
T05	Exchange of Plati...

title_authors

title_id	au_id
T01	A01
T02	A01
T03	A05
T04	A03
T04	A04
T05	A04

authors

au_id	au_fname	au_lname
A01	Sarah	Buchman
A02	Wendy	Heydemark
A03	Hallie	Hull
A04	Klee	Hull

Figure 2.14 A many-to-many relationship. The junction table title_authors breaks the many-to-many relationship between titles and authors into two one-to-many relationships. Each row in titles can have many matching rows in title_authors, as can each row in authors. Here, title_id in title_authors is a foreign key that references the primary key of titles, and au_id in title_authors is a foreign key that references the primary key of authors.

Figure 2.15 This diagram shows an alternative way to depict the many-to-many relationship in Figure 2.14.

Normalization

You may have wondered why I don't consolidate all information about books (or any entity type) into a single table. It's possible, but the resulting table would be loaded with duplicate data; each book (row) would contain redundant author, publisher, and royalty details. Redundant data is the enemy of database administrators: It causes databases to grow wildly large, it slows queries, and it's a maintenance nightmare. (When someone moves, you want to change her address in one place, not thousands of places.)

Normalization is the process—a series of steps—of modifying tables to reduce redundancy and inconsistency. After each step, the database is in a particular *normal form*. The relational model defines three normal forms, named after famous ordinal numbers:

◆ First normal form (1NF)

◆ Second normal form (2NF)

◆ Third normal form (3NF)

Each normal form is stronger than its predecessors; a database in 3NF also is in 2NF and 1NF. Higher normalization levels tend to increase the number of tables relative to lower levels. *Lossless decomposition* ensures that table splitting doesn't cause information loss, and *dependency-preserving decomposition* ensures that relationships aren't lost. The matching primary- and foreign-key columns that appear when tables are split are not considered to be redundant data.

There are higher levels of normalization (4NF and 5NF, for example), but the relational model doesn't mandate them, and they're beyond the scope of this book. The types of redundancies and anomalies cured by 4NF and 5NF are rare; 3NF databases usually are in 4NF and 5NF too.

Normalization is not systematic; it's an iterative process that involves repeated table splitting and rejoining and refining until the database designer is (temporarily) happy with the result.

First normal form

A table in *first normal form:*

◆ Has columns that contain only atomic values, *and*

◆ Has no repeating groups

An *atomic* value, also called a *scalar* value, is a single value that can't be subdivided meaningfully (**Figure 2.16**). A *repeating group* is a set of two or more logically related columns (**Figure 2.17**). To fix these problems, store the data in two related tables (**Figure 2.18**).

```
title_id  title_name                        authors

--------  ------------------------------    -------------

T01       1977!                             A01

T04       But I Did It Unconsciously        A03, A04

T11       Perhaps It's a Glandular Problem  A03, A04, A06
```

Figure 2.16 In first normal form, each table's row–column intersection must contain a single value that can't be meaningfully subdivided. The column authors in this table lists multiple authors and so violates 1NF.

```
title_id  title_name                      author1  author2  author3

--------  ------------------------------  -------  -------  -------

T01       1977!                           A01

T04       But I Did It Unconsciously      A03      A04

T11       Perhaps It's a Glandular Problem A03      A04      A06
```

Figure 2.17 Redistributing the column authors into a repeating group also violates 1NF. Multiple instances of an entity shouldn't be represented as multiple columns.

title_id	title_name
T01	1977!
T04	But I Did It Unco...
T11	Perhaps It's a Gla...

title_id	au_id
T01	A01
T04	A03
T04	A04
T11	A03
T11	A04
T11	A06

Figure 2.18 The correct design solution is to move the author information to a new child table that contains one row for each author of a title. The primary key in the parent table is title_id, and the composite key in the child table is title_id and au_id.

title_authors
title_id 🔑
au_id 🔑
au_order
au_phone

Figure 2.19 au_phone depends on au_id but not title_id, so this table contains a partial functional dependency and isn't 2NF.

Second normal form

Before I give the rules for second normal form, I'll mention that a 1NF table automatically is 2NF if:

- Its primary key is a single column (that is, the key isn't composite), *or*

- All the columns in the table are part of the primary key (simple or composite)

A table in *second normal form:*

- Is in first normal form, *and*

- Has no partial functional dependencies

A table contains a *partial functional dependency* if *some* (but not all) of a composite key's values determine a nonkey column's value. A 2NF table is *fully functionally dependent,* meaning that a nonkey column's value may need to be updated if *any* column values in the composite key change.

The composite key in the table in **Figure 2.19** is title_id and au_id. The nonkey columns are au_order (the order in which authors are listed on the cover of a book with multiple authors) and au_phone (the author's phone number).

For each nonkey column, ask, "Can I determine a nonkey column value if I know only *part* of the primary-key value?" A *no* answer means the nonkey column is fully functionally dependent (good); a *yes* answer means that it's partially functionally dependent (bad).

For au_order, the questions are:

- Can I determine au_order if I know only title_id? No, because there may be more than one author for the same title.

- Can I determine au_order if I know only au_id? No, because I need to know the particular title too.

Good—au_order is fully functionally dependent and may remain in the table. This dependency is written:

{title_id, au_id} → {au_order}

and is read "title_id and au_id determine au_order" or "au_order depends on title_id and au_id". The *determinant* is the expression to the left of the arrow.

For au_phone, the questions are:

◆ Can I determine au_phone if I know only title_id? No, because there may be more than one author for the same title.

◆ Can I determine au_phone if I know only au_id? Yes! The author's phone number doesn't depend upon the title.

Bad—au_phone is partially functionally dependent and must be moved elsewhere (probably to an authors or phone_numbers table) to satisfy 2NF constraints.

Third normal form

A table in *third normal form*:

◆ Is in second normal form, *and*

◆ Has no transitive dependencies

A table contains a *transitive dependency* if a nonkey column's value determines another nonkey column's value. In 3NF tables, nonkey columns are mutually independent and dependent only on primary-key column(s). 3NF is the next logical step after 2NF.

The primary key in the table in **Figure 2.20** is title_id. The nonkey columns are price (the book's price), pub_city (the city where the book is published), and pub_id (the book's publisher).

Figure 2.20 pub_city depends on pub_id, so this table contains a transitive dependency and isn't 3NF.

For each nonkey column, ask, "Can I determine a nonkey column value if I know *any other* nonkey column value?" A *no* answer means that the column is not transitively dependent (good); a *yes* answer means that the column whose value you can determine is transitively dependent on the other column (bad).

For `price`, the questions are:

◆ Can I determine `pub_id` if I know `price`? No.

◆ Can I determine `pub_city` if I know `price`? No.

For `pub_city`, the questions are:

◆ Can I determine `price` if I know `pub_city`? No.

◆ Can I determine `pub_id` if I know `pub_city`? No, because a city may have many publishers.

For `pub_id`, the questions are:

◆ Can I determine `price` if I know `pub_id`? No.

◆ Can I determine `pub_city` if I know `pub_id`? Yes! The city where the book is published depends on the publisher.

Bad—`pub_city` is transitively dependent on `pub_id` and must be moved elsewhere (probably to a `publishers` table) to satisfy 3NF rules.

As you can see, it's not enough to ask, "Can I determine A if I know B?" to discover a transitive dependency; you also must ask, "Can I determine B if I know A?"

✔ Tip

■ If you're new to databases, the rigidness of normal forms may have you wondering why it's wrong to, say, stuff city, state, and zip into one column (after all, it makes mailing labels easier to print). The short answer is that you can't predict how you or other users will want to extract and manipulate information in the future, and 3NF is the best hedge against this uncertainty. I recommend that you normalize your database whether or not you appreciate the value of normalization. If you don't normalize, you'll eventually be in a position where you'll be splitting tables to, say, allow users to sort addresses by state. Professionals occasionally denormalize databases to speed queries, but that technique is beyond the scope of this book.

The Sample Database

Pick up an SQL or database design book, and probably you'll find a students/courses/teachers, customers/orders/products, or authors/books/publishers database. In a bow to convention, most of the SQL examples in this book use an authors/books/publishers sample database named **books**. Here are some things that you should know about **books**:

◆ Recall from "Tables, Columns, and Rows" earlier in this chapter that a database appears to the user as a collection of tables (and nothing but tables). **books** contains five tables that contain information about authors, titles they've published, their publishers, and their royalties. **Figure 2.21** depicts the tables and relationships in **books** by using the graphical conventions introduced earlier in this chapter.

◆ The SQL statements in Chapters 9 and later modify data in **books** (rather than just retrieve data). Unless I note otherwise, each new section in a chapter starts with a pristine version of **books**. In other words, assume that database changes made in one section don't carry over to the next section.

◆ Run the SQL program listed in the Appendix to create (or re-create) the database **books** on your own DMBS. You can download this program (or a fully populated Microsoft Access database) from the companion Web site; see "About This Book" in the Introduction.

◆ Some of the concepts mentioned in this section, such as data types and nulls, are covered in the next chapter.

◆ **books** is a teaching tool; its structure doesn't approach the complexity of real production databases.

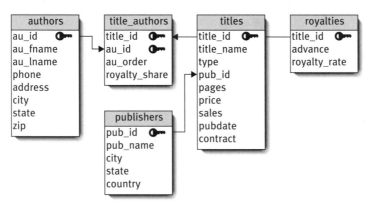

Figure 2.21 The database books.

The table *authors*

The table authors describes the books' authors. Each author has a unique identifier that's the primary key. **Table 2.2** shows the structure of the table authors, and **Figure 2.22** shows its contents.

Table 2.2

authors Table Structure

COLUMN NAME	DESCRIPTION	DATA TYPE	NULLS?	KEYS
au_id	Unique author identifier	CHAR(3)		PK
au_fname	Author first name	VARCHAR(15)		
au_lname	Author last name	VARCHAR(15)		
phone	Author telephone number	VARCHAR(12)	Yes	
address	Author address	VARCHAR(20)	Yes	
city	Author city	VARCHAR(15)	Yes	
state	Author state	CHAR(2)	Yes	
zip	Author zip (postal) code	CHAR(5)	Yes	

```
au_id au_fname   au_lname    phone        address              city           state zip
----- ---------  ----------- ------------ -------------------- -------------- ----- -----
A01   Sarah      Buchman     718-496-7223 75 West 205 St       Bronx          NY    10468
A02   Wendy      Heydemark   303-986-7020 2922 Baseline Rd     Boulder        CO    80303
A03   Hallie     Hull        415-549-4278 3800 Waldo Ave, #14F San Francisco  CA    94123
A04   Klee       Hull        415-549-4278 3800 Waldo Ave, #14F San Francisco  CA    94123
A05   Christian  Kells       212-771-4680 114 Horatio St       New York       NY    10014
A06              Kellsey     650-836-7128 390 Serra Mall       Palo Alto      CA    94305
A07   Paddy      O'Furniture 941-925-0752 1442 Main St         Sarasota       FL    34236
```

Figure 2.22 The contents of the table authors.

The table *publishers*

The table `publishers` describes the books'
publishers. Every publisher has a unique
identifier that's the primary key. **Table 2.3**
shows the structure of the table `publishers`,
and **Figure 2.23** shows its contents.

Table 2.3

publishers Table Structure				
COLUMN NAME	DESCRIPTION	DATA TYPE	NULLS	KEYS
pub_id	Unique publisher identifier	CHAR(3)		PK
pub_name	Publisher name	VARCHAR(20)		
city	Publisher city	VARCHAR(15)		
state	Publisher state/province	CHAR(2)	Yes	
country	Publisher country	VARCHAR(15)		

```
pub_id pub_name            city          state country
------ ------------------- ------------- ----- -------
P01    Abatis Publishers   New York      NY    USA
P02    Core Dump Books     San Francisco CA    USA
P03    Schadenfreude Press Hamburg       NULL  Germany
P04    Tenterhooks Press   Berkeley      CA    USA
```

Figure 2.23 The contents of the table publishers.

The table *titles*

The table `titles` describes the books. Every book has a unique identifier that's the primary key. `titles` contains a foreign key, `pub_id`, that references the table `publishers` to indicate a book's publisher. **Table 2.4** shows the structure of the table `titles`, and **Figure 2.24** shows its contents.

Table 2.4

titles Table Structure

COLUMN NAME	DESCRIPTION	DATA TYPE	NULLS?	KEYS
title_id	Unique title identifier	CHAR(3)		PK
title_name	Book title	VARCHAR(40)		
type	Subject of the book	VARCHAR(10)	Yes	
pub_id	Publisher identifier	CHAR(3)		FK publishers(pub_id)
pages	Page count	INTEGER	Yes	
price	Cover price	DECIMAL(5,2)	Yes	
sales	Lifetime number of copies sold	INTEGER	Yes	
pubdate	Date of publication	DATE	Yes	
contract	Nonzero if author(s) signed contract	SMALLINT		

title_id	title_name	type	pub_id	pages	price	sales	pubdate	contract
T01	1977!	history	P01	107	21.99	566	2000-08-01	1
T02	200 Years of German Humor	history	P03	14	19.95	9566	1998-04-01	1
T03	Ask Your System Administrator	computer	P02	1226	39.95	25667	2000-09-01	1
T04	But I Did It Unconsciously	psychology	P04	510	12.99	13001	1999-05-31	1
T05	Exchange of Platitudes	psychology	P04	201	6.95	201440	2001-01-01	1
T06	How About Never?	biography	P01	473	19.95	11320	2000-07-31	1
T07	I Blame My Mother	biography	P03	333	23.95	1500200	1999-10-01	1
T08	Just Wait Until After School	children	P04	86	10.00	4095	2001-06-01	1
T09	Kiss My Boo-Boo	children	P04	22	13.95	5000	2002-05-31	1
T10	Not Without My Faberge Egg	biography	P01	NULL	NULL	NULL	NULL	0
T11	Perhaps It's a Glandular Problem	psychology	P04	826	7.99	94123	2000-11-30	1
T12	Spontaneous, Not Annoying	biography	P01	507	12.99	100001	2000-08-31	1
T13	What Are The Civilian Applications?	history	P03	802	29.99	10467	1999-05-31	1

Figure 2.24 The contents of the table `titles`.

The table *title_authors*

Authors and books have a many-to-many relationship, because an author can write multiple books and a book can have multiple authors. `title_authors` is the junction table that associates the tables `authors` and `titles`; see "Relationships" earlier in this chapter. `title_id` and `au_id` together form a composite primary key, and each column separately is a foreign key that references `titles` and `authors`, respectively. The non-key columns indicate the order of the author's name on the book's cover (always 1 for a book with a sole author) and the fraction of total royalties that each author receives (always 1.0 for a book with a sole author). **Table 2.5** shows the structure of the table `title_authors`, and **Figure 2.25** shows its contents.

title_id	au_id	au_order	royalty_share
T01	A01	1	1.00
T02	A01	1	1.00
T03	A05	1	1.00
T04	A03	1	0.60
T04	A04	2	0.40
T05	A04	1	1.00
T06	A02	1	1.00
T07	A02	1	0.50
T07	A04	2	0.50
T08	A06	1	1.00
T09	A06	1	1.00
T10	A02	1	1.00
T11	A03	2	0.30
T11	A04	3	0.30
T11	A06	1	0.40
T12	A02	1	1.00
T13	A01	1	1.00

Figure 2.25 The contents of the table `title_authors`.

Table 2.5

title_authors Table Structure

COLUMN NAME	DESCRIPTION	DATA TYPE	NULLS?	KEYS
title_id	Title identifier	CHAR(3)		PK, FK titles(title_id)
au_id	Author identifier	CHAR(3)		PK, FK authors(au_id)
au_order	Author name order on book cover	SMALLINT		
royalty_share	Author fractional royalty share	DECIMAL(5,2)		

```
title_id advance      royalty_rate
-------- ----------- ------------

T01       10000.00         0.05
T02        1000.00         0.06
T03       15000.00         0.07
T04       20000.00         0.08
T05      100000.00         0.09
T06       20000.00         0.08
T07     1000000.00         0.11
T08           0.00         0.04
T09           0.00         0.05
T10           NULL         NULL
T11      100000.00         0.07
T12       50000.00         0.09
T13       20000.00         0.06
```

Figure 2.26 The contents of the table royalties.

The table *royalties*

The table royalties specifies the royalty rate paid to *all* the authors (not each author) of each book, including the total up-front advance against royalties paid to all authors (again, not each author) of a book. The royalties primary key is title_id. royalties has a one-to-one relationship with titles, so the royalties primary key also is a foreign key that references the titles primary key. **Table 2.6** shows the structure of the table royalties, and **Figure 2.26** shows its contents.

Table 2.6

royalties Table Structure				
COLUMN NAME	DESCRIPTION	DATA TYPE	NULLS?	KEYS
title_id	Unique title identifier	CHAR(3)		PK, FK titles(title_id)
advance	Upfront payment to author(s)	DECIMAL(9,2)	Yes	
royalty_rate	Fraction of revenue paid author(s)	DECIMAL(5,2)	Yes	

SQL Basics

You may have noticed that I barely mentioned SQL in the preceding chapter. Remember this equation:

$$SQL \neq Relational\ model$$

SQL is *based* on the relational model but isn't a faithful implementation of it. One departure from the model is that in SQL, primary keys are optional rather than mandatory. Consequently, tables without keys may have duplicate rows, rendering some data inaccessible. A complete review of the disparities is beyond the scope of this book (if you want to learn more, search the Web for SQL articles by E.F. Codd, Chris Date, or Fabian Pascal). The upshot of these discrepancies is that DBMS users, and not the DBMS itself, bear the responsibility for enforcing a relational structure. Another result is that the *Model* and *SQL* terms in Table 2.1 in Chapter 2 aren't perfectly interchangeable.

With that warning, it's time to learn SQL. An SQL program is a sequence of SQL statements executed in order. To write a program, you'll need to know the rules that govern SQL syntax. In this chapter, I'll explain the rules for forming an SQL statement. I'll also cover data types and nulls.

SQL Syntax

Figure 3.1 shows an example SQL statement. Be unconcerned about the meaning (semantics) of the statement; I'm using it to explain SQL syntax.

1. **Comment.** A *comment* is optional text that you type on a separate line of your program to explain it. Two hyphens introduce a comment, which the DBMS ignores. Comments continue to the end of the line.

2. **SQL statement.** An SQL statement is a valid combination of tokens introduced by a keyword. *Tokens* are the basic indivisible particles of the SQL language; they can't be reduced grammatically. Tokens include keywords, identifiers, operators, literals, and other symbols (all explained later).

3. **Clauses.** An SQL statement comprises one or more clauses. In general, a *clause* is a fragment of an SQL statement that is introduced by a keyword, is required or optional, and must be given in a particular order. SELECT, FROM, WHERE, and ORDER BY introduce the four clauses in this example.

4. **Keywords.** *Keywords,* also called *reserved words,* are words that SQL reserves because they have special meaning in the language. Using a keyword outside its specific context (as an identifier, for example) causes an error. **Table 3.1** lists SQL's keywords. **Table 3.2** lists SQL's potential keywords, which aren't reserved now but may be someday.

5. **Identifiers.** *Identifiers* are words that you (or the database designer) use to name database objects such as tables, columns, aliases, indexes, and views. Identifiers can't be keywords and can be up to 128 characters long. In SQL, a character can be any symbol in your character set (including Western characters and ideographs), but see the Tips in this section. au_fname, au_lname, authors, and state are the identifiers in this example.

6. **Terminating semicolon.** Every SQL statement ends with a semicolon.

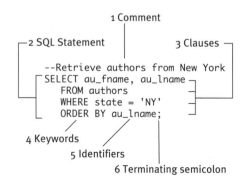

Figure 3.1 An SQL statement, with comment.

Table 3.1

SQL Keywords			
ABSOLUTE	COMMIT	ELSE	INSERT	ON
ACTION	CONNECT	END	INT	ONLY
ADD	CONNECTION	END-EXEC	INTEGER	OPEN
ALL	CONSTRAINT	ESCAPE	INTERSECT	OPTION
ALLOCATE	CONSTRAINTS	EXCEPT	INTERVAL	OR
ALTER	CONTINUE	EXCEPTION	INTO	ORDER
AND	CONVERT	EXEC	IS	OUTER
ANY	CORRESPONDING	EXECUTE	ISOLATION	OUTPUT
ARE	COUNT	EXISTS	JOIN	OVERLAPS
AS	CREATE	EXTERNAL	KEY	PAD
ASC	CROSS	EXTRACT	LANGUAGE	PARTIAL
ASSERTION	CURRENT	FALSE	LAST	POSITION
AT	CURRENT_DATE	FETCH	LEADING	PRECISION
AUTHORIZATION	CURRENT_TIME	FIRST	LEFT	PREPARE
AVG	CURRENT_TIMESTAMP	FLOAT	LEVEL	PRESERVE
BEGIN	CURRENT_USER	FOR	LIKE	PRIMARY
BETWEEN	CURSOR	FOREIGN	LOCAL	PRIOR
BIT	DATE	FOUND	LOWER	PRIVILEGES
BIT_LENGTH	DAY	FROM	MATCH	PROCEDURE
BOTH	DEALLOCATE	FULL	MAX	PUBLIC
BY	DEC	GET	MIN	READ
CASCADE	DECIMAL	GLOBAL	MINUTE	REAL
CASCADED	DECLARE	GO	MODULE	REFERENCES
CASE	DEFAULT	GOTO	MONTH	RELATIVE
CAST	DEFERRABLE	GRANT	NAMES	RESTRICT
CATALOG	DEFERRED	GROUP	NATIONAL	REVOKE
CHAR	DELETE	HAVING	NATURAL	RIGHT
CHARACTER	DESC	HOUR	NCHAR	ROLLBACK
CHAR_LENGTH	DESCRIBE	IDENTITY	NEXT	ROWS
CHARACTER_LENGTH	DESCRIPTOR	IMMEDIATE	NO	SCHEMA
CHECK	DIAGNOSTICS	IN	NOT	SCROLL
CLOSE	DISCONNECT	INDICATOR	NULL	SECOND
COALESCE	DISTINCT	INITIALLY	NULLIF	SECTION
COLLATE	DOMAIN	INNER	NUMERIC	SELECT
COLLATION	DOUBLE	INPUT	OCTET_LENGTH	SESSION
COLUMN	DROP	INSENSITIVE	OF	SESSION_USER

table continues on next page

SQL Syntax

Table 3.1 (cont.)

SQL Keywords

SET	SUM	TRAILING	UPPER	WHENEVER
SIZE	SYSTEM_USER	TRANSACTION	USAGE	WHERE
SMALLINT	TABLE	TRANSLATE	USER	WITH
SOME	TEMPORARY	TRANSLATION	USING	WORK
SPACE	THEN	TRIM	VALUE	WRITE
SQL	TIME	TRUE	VALUES	YEAR
SQLCODE	TIMESTAMP	UNION	VARCHAR	ZONE
SQLERROR	TIMEZONE_HOUR	UNIQUE	VARYING	
SQLSTATE	TIMEZONE_MINUTE	UNKNOWN	VIEW	
SUBSTRING	TO	UPDATE	WHEN	

Table 3.2

SQL Potential Keywords

AFTER	EQUALS	OLD	RETURN	TEST
ALIAS	GENERAL	OPERATION	RETURNS	THERE
ASYNC	IF	OPERATORS	ROLE	TRIGGER
BEFORE	IGNORE	OTHERS	ROUTINE	TYPE
BOOLEAN	LEAVE	PARAMETERS	ROW	UNDER
BREADTH	LESS	PENDANT	SAVEPOINT	VARIABLE
COMPLETION	LIMIT	PREORDER	SEARCH	VIRTUAL
CALL	LOOP	PRIVATE	SENSITIVE	VISIBLE
CYCLE	MODIFY	PROTECTED	SEQUENCE	WAIT
DATA	NEW	RECURSIVE	SIGNAL	WHILE
DEPTH	NONE	REF	SIMILAR	WITHOUT
DICTIONARY	OBJECT	REFERENCING	SQLEXCEPTION	
EACH	OFF	REPLACE	SQLWARNING	
ELSEIF	OID	RESIGNAL	STRUCTURE	

```
  select au_fname
  ,          AU_LNAME
             FROM
 authors WhErE      state
= 'NY' order
             bY
AU_lnamE
    ;
```

Figure 3.2 There aren't many rules about how to format an SQL statement. This statement is equivalent to the one in Figure 3.1.

SQL is a free-form language whose statements can:

- Be in uppercase or lowercase. (`SELECT` and `select` are considered to be identical keywords, for example.)

- Continue on the next line as long as you don't split words, tokens, or quoted strings in two.

- Be on the same line as other statements.

- Start in any column.

Despite this flexibility, you should adopt a consistent style (**Figure 3.2**). I use uppercase keywords and lowercase identifiers, and indent each clause on its own line; see "Typographic conventions" and "Syntax conventions" in the Introduction for information about my style.

Some common SQL programming errors are:

- Misspelling a keyword or identifier

- Omitting the terminating semicolon

- Listing clauses out of order

- Forgetting to surround string and date-time literals with quotes

- Surrounding numeric literals with quotes

- Mismatching a table and column (typing `SELECT royalty_share FROM authors;` instead of `SELECT royalty_share FROM title_authors;`, for example)

continues on next page

SQL SYNTAX

✔ Tips

- The introductory keyword of an SQL statement often is called a *verb,* as it indicates an action to perform.

- Although you can't use keywords as identifiers, you *can* embed them inside identifiers. `group` and `max` are illegal identifiers but `groups` and `max_price` are valid, for example.

- To embed spaces in an identifier, surround it with single quotes (`'last name'`). It's poor style to embed spaces in database object names; use underscores to separate words (`last_name`) or use mixed case (`LastName`).

- An *expression* is any legal combination of symbols that evaluates to a single data value. You can combine mathematical or logical operators, identifiers, constants, functions, column names, and so on. **Table 3.3** lists some common expressions and examples. I'll cover each type of expression in more detail when it arises.

- **DBMS** DBMSes place their own constraints on an identifier's length and character set; search your DBMS documentation for *identifiers* or *names.*

  DBMSes have additional keywords that can't be used as identifiers; search your DBMS documentation for *keywords* or *reserved words.*

  Microsoft SQL Server, **Oracle**, **MySQL**, and **PostgreSQL** permit inline comments and multiple-line comments between the `/*` and `*/` commenting characters; search your DBMS documentation for *comments.* **MySQL** comments can start with a `#` character.

Table 3.3

Types of Expressions	
EXPRESSION	EXAMPLE
Case	CASE WHEN n <> 0 THEN x/n ELSE 0 END
Cast	CAST(pubdate AS CHARACTER)
Datetime	start_time + '01:30'
Interval	INTERVAL '7' DAY * 2
Numeric	(sales * price) / 12
String	'Dear ' || au_fname || ','

Table 3.4

Categories of Data Types	
DATA TYPE	STORES THESE DATA
Character string	Strings of characters
Bit string	Strings of bits
Exact numeric	Integers and decimal numbers
Approximate numeric	Floating-point numbers
Datetime	Date and time values
Interval	Date and time intervals

✔ Tips

■ Use the statements **CREATE TABLE** and **ALTER TABLE** to define or change a column's data type and constraints; see Chapter 10.

■ Database designers choose data types carefully. The consequences of a poor data-type choice include the inability to add values to a column and data loss if the existing data type must be changed.

■ **DBMS** The DBMS vendor decides many data-type implementation details. Consequently, SQL data types don't directly map to specific DBMS data types, even if the data types have identical names. I'll give equivalent or similar DBMS data types in the Tips in following data-type sections. DBMSes have extended data types to store special values, such as Boolean and monetary values. For information about standard and extended data types, search your DBMS documentation for *data types*.

For information about sort order, see "Sorting Rows with **ORDER BY**" in Chapter 4.

Data Types

Recall from "Tables, Columns, and Rows" in Chapter 2 that a column's domain constrains the values that can be stored in the column. You can use a column's data type for this purpose. A *data type* has these characteristics:

◆ Each column in a table has a single data type.

◆ A data type falls into one of categories listed in **Table 3.4** (covered in the next six sections).

◆ The data type determines a column's allowable values and the operations it supports. An integer data type, for example, can represent any whole number between certain DBMS-defined limits and supports the usual arithmetic operations: addition, subtraction, multiplication, and division (among others). But an integer can't represent a nonnumeric value such as `'schadenfreude'` and doesn't support character operations such as capitalization.

◆ The data type affects the column's sort order. The integers 1, 2, and 10 are sorted arithmetically, yielding `1, 2, 10`. The character strings `'1'`, `'2'`, and `'10'` are sorted lexicographically, yielding `'1'`, `'10'`, `'2'`. *Lexicographical ordering* sorts strings by examining the values of their characters individually. Here, `'10'` comes before `'2'` because `'1'` (the first character of `'10'`) is less than `'2'` lexicographically.

◆ Literal values are stored in columns. A *literal* is a constant that is expressed as itself rather than as a result of an expression such as an arithmetic formula. Some examples: `40` and `12.34` are numeric literals, `'40'` and `'ennui'` are character literals, and `DATE '2002-05-10'` and `TIME '09:45:00'` are datetime literals.

Character String Types

Use character string data types to represent text. A *character string*, or just *string*, has these characteristics:

◆ It's an ordered sequence of zero or more characters.

◆ Its length can be fixed or varying.

◆ It's case-sensitive (`'A'` comes before `'a'` when sorted).

◆ In SQL statements, a string literal is surrounded by single quotes.

◆ It's one of the types listed in **Table 3.5**.

Table 3.5

Character String Types	
TYPE	**DESCRIPTION**
CHARACTER	Represents a fixed number of characters. A string stored in a column defined as CHARACTER(*length*) can have up to *length* characters, where *length* is a number (integer) greater than or equal to 1; the maximum *length* depends on the DBMS. When you store a string with fewer than *length* characters in a CHARACTER(*length*) column, the DBMS pads blank spaces to the end of the string to create a string that has exactly *length* characters. A CHARACTER(6) string `'Jack'` is stored as `'Jack  '`, for example. CHARACTER and CHAR are synonyms.
CHARACTER VARYING	Represents a variable number of characters. A string stored in a column defined as CHARACTER VARYING(*length*) can have up to *length* characters, where *length* is a number (integer) greater than or equal to 1; the maximum *length* depends on the DBMS. Unlike CHARACTER, when you store a string with fewer than *length* characters in a CHARACTER VARYING(*length*) column, the DBMS stores the string as-is and doesn't pad it with blank spaces. A CHARACTER VARYING(6) string `'Jack'` is stored as `'Jack'`, for example. CHARACTER VARYING, CHAR VARYING, and VARCHAR are synonyms.
NATIONAL CHARACTER	This data type is the same as CHARACTER except that it holds standardized multibyte characters or Unicode characters (see the sidebar in this section). In SQL statements, NATIONAL CHARACTER strings are written like CHARACTER strings but have an N in front of the first quote: N'ß本ä', for example. NATIONAL CHARACTER, NATIONAL CHAR, and NCHAR are synonyms.
NATIONAL CHARACTER VARYING	This data type is the same as CHARACTER VARYING except that it holds standardized multibyte characters or Unicode characters (see NATIONAL CHARACTER). NATIONAL CHARACTER VARYING, NATIONAL CHAR VARYING, and NCHAR VARYING are synonyms.

Unicode

Computers store characters (letters, digits, punctuation, control characters, and other symbols) internally by assigning them numeric values. An *encoding* determines the mapping of characters to numeric values; different languages and computer operating systems use many different native encodings. Standard U.S.-English strings use *ASCII* encoding, which assigns values to as many as 256 (2^8) different characters—not much, and not even enough to hold all the Latin characters used in modern European languages, much less all the Chinese ideographs.

Unicode is a single character set that represents the characters of almost all the world's written languages. Unicode can encode 65,536 (2^{16}) characters. The Unicode Consortium develops and maintains the Unicode standard. The actual Unicode mappings are available in the latest online or printed edition of *The Unicode Standard*, available at www.unicode.org.

✔ Tips

■ Type two adjacent single quotes to insert one single-quote character into a string. Type `'it''s'` to represent *it's*, for example. A double-quote character (") is a separate character and doesn't need this special treatment.

■ The length of a string is an integer between 0 and *length*, inclusive. A string with no characters—`''` (two single quotes with no intervening space)—is called an *empty string* or a *zero-length string*. An empty string is considered to be a VARCHAR of length zero.

■ DBMSes can sort and manipulate fixed-length strings faster than variable-length ones.

■ **DBMS** The character string data types in **Microsoft Access** are text and memo. In **Microsoft SQL Server**: char, varchar, text, nchar, nvarchar, and ntext. In **Oracle**: char, varchar, varchar2, nchar, nvarchar and nvarchar2. In **MySQL**: char, varchar, nchar, nvarchar, text, tinytext, mediumtext, and longtext. In **PostgreSQL**: char, varchar, and text.

Oracle treats empty strings as nulls; see "Nulls" later in this chapter.

Bit String Types

Use bit string data types to represent binary numbers. A *bit string* has these characteristics:

◆ It's an ordered sequence of zero or more bits.

◆ Each bit has the value 0 or 1.

◆ It typically is used to store binary data such as application files or digitized sounds and images. Long bit strings often are called *binary large objects* or *BLOBs*.

◆ In SQL statements, a bit string is surrounded by single quotes.

◆ It's one of the types listed in **Table 3.6**.

✔ Tips

■ DBMSes don't attempt to interpret bit strings; their meaning is up to the application.

■ For experienced programmers: In addition to using binary (base 2) form, you can represent bit strings in *hexadecimal,* or *hex,* (base 16) form. The hexadecimal system uses the digits 0 through 9 and the letters *A* through *F* (uppercase or lowercase). One hex character is equivalent to four bits. In SQL statements, bit strings in hexadecimal form have an X in front of the first quote. The binary string B'01001011' corresponds to hex string X'4B', for example.

■ **DBMS** The binary data types in **Microsoft Access** are yes/no, binary, and OLE object. In **Microsoft SQL Server**: binary, varbinary, and image. In **Oracle**: raw, long raw, blob, and bfile. In **MySQL**: blob, tinyblob, mediumblob, and longblob. In **PostgreSQL**: bit and varbit.

Table 3.6

Bit String Types	
TYPE	DESCRIPTION
BIT	Represents a fixed number of bits. A bit string stored in a column defined as BIT(*length*) can have up to *length* bits, where *length* is a number (integer) greater than or equal to 1; the maximum *length* depends on the DBMS. Unlike CHARACTER strings, an error usually occurs when you try to store a bit string with fewer than *length* bits in a BIT(*length*) column. In SQL statements, BIT strings are written like CHARACTER strings but have a B in front of the first quote: B'01001011' is a BIT(8) string, for example.
BIT VARYING	Represents a variable number of bits. A bit string stored in a column defined as BIT VARYING(*length*) can have up to *length* bits, where *length* is a number (integer) greater than or equal to 1; the maximum *length* depends on the DBMS. Like CHARACTER VARYING strings, when you store a bit string with fewer than *length* bits in a BIT VARYING(*length*) column, the DBMS stores the string as-is and doesn't pad it with blank spaces. A BIT VARYING(8) string B'0101' is stored as B'0101', for example.

Table 3.7

Categories of Data Types	
TYPE	DESCRIPTION
NUMERIC	Represents a decimal number. A decimal number is stored in a column defined as NUMERIC(*precision* [,*scale*]). *precision* is greater than or equal to 1; the maximum *precision* depends on the DBMS. *scale* is a value from 0 to *precision*. If *scale* is omitted, it defaults to zero (which makes the number effectively an INTEGER).
DECIMAL	This data type is similar to NUMERIC, and some DBMSes define them equivalently. The difference is that the DBMS may choose a precision greater than that specified by DECIMAL(*precision* [,*scale*]), so *precision* specifies the minimum precision, not an exact precision as in NUMERIC. DECIMAL and DEC are synonyms.
INTEGER	Represents an integer. The minimum and maximum values that can be stored in a column defined as INTEGER depend on the DBMS. INTEGER takes no arguments. INTEGER and INT are synonyms.
SMALLINT	This data type is the same as INTEGER except that it may hold a smaller range of values, depending on the DBMS. SMALLINT takes no arguments.

Exact Numeric Types

Use exact numeric data types to represent exact numerical values. An *exact numerical value* has these characteristics:

◆ It can be a negative, zero, or positive number.

◆ It's an integer or a decimal number. An *integer* is a whole number expressed without a decimal point: −39, 0, 62262. A *decimal number* has digits to the right of the decimal point: −22.06, 0.0, 0.0003, 12.34.

◆ It has a fixed precision and scale. The *precision* is the number of significant digits used to express the number; it's the total number of digits both to the right and left of the decimal point. The *scale* is the number of digits to the right of the decimal point. Obviously, the scale can't exceed the precision. To represent a whole number, set the scale equal to zero. See the Tips in this section for some examples.

◆ It's one of the types listed in **Table 3.7**.

continues on next page

✔ Tips

- **Table 3.8** shows how the number 123.89 is stored for different values of precision and scale.

- Don't enclose a numeric value in quotes.

- Store numbers as strings if the numbers are not involved in arithmetic calculations. Store telephone numbers and zip codes as strings, for example. This technique may prevent data loss: If you store the zip code `'02116'` as a number instead of as a string, you'll lose the leading zero.

- Calculations involving only integers are much faster than those involving decimal and floating-point numbers.

- **DBMS** The exact numeric data types in **Microsoft Access** are decimal, integer, byte, and long integer. In **Microsoft SQL Server**: numeric, decimal, integer, smallint, bigint, and tinyint. In **Oracle**: numeric, decimal, integer, smallint, and number. In **MySQL**: numeric, decimal, integer, smallint, bigint, mediumint, and tinyint. In **PostgreSQL**: numeric, decimal, integer, smallint, and bigint.

Table 3.8

Precision and Scale Examples for 123.89

SPECIFIED AS	STORED AS
NUMERIC(5)	124
NUMERIC(5,0)	124
NUMERIC(5,1)	123.9
NUMERIC(5,2)	123.89
NUMERIC(4,0)	124
NUMERIC(4,1)	123.9
NUMERIC(4,2)	Exceeds precision
NUMERIC(2,0)	Exceeds precision

Table 3.9

Approximate Numeric Types	
TYPE	DESCRIPTION
FLOAT	Represents a floating-point number. A floating-point number stored in a column defined as FLOAT(*precision*) has precision *precision*. *precision* is greater than or equal to 1 and expressed as the number of bits rather than a number of digits; the maximum *precision* depends on the DBMS.
REAL	This data type is the same as FLOAT except that the DBMS defines the precision. REAL numbers usually are called single-precision numbers. REAL takes no arguments.
DOUBLE PRECISION	This data type is the same as FLOAT except that the DBMS defines the precision, which must be greater than that of REAL. DOUBLE PRECISION takes no arguments.

✔ Tips

- Don't enclose a numeric value in quotes.

- **DBMS** The approximate numeric data types in **Microsoft Access** are single and double. In **Microsoft SQL Server**: float and real. In **Oracle**: float, real, double precision and number. In **MySQL**: float, real, and double precision. In **PostgreSQL**: real and double precision.

Approximate Numeric Types

Use approximate numeric data types to represent approximate numerical values. An *approximate numerical value* has these characteristics:

- ◆ It can be a negative, zero, or positive number.

- ◆ It's considered to be an approximation of a floating-point (real) number.

- ◆ It typically is used to represent very small quantities, very large quantities, or scientific calculations.

- ◆ It's expressed in scientific notation. A number in *scientific notation* is written as a decimal number multiplied by an (integer) power of 10. An uppercase E is the exponentiation symbol: $2.5E2 = 2.5 \times 10^2 = 250$, for example. The *mantissa* is the portion that expresses the significant digits (2.5 here) and the *exponent* is the power of 10 (2 here). The mantissa and exponent each may have a sign: $-2.5E-2 = -2.5 \times 10^{-2} = -0.025$.

- ◆ It has a fixed precision but no scale as such. (The sign and magnitude of the exponent determines the scale intrinsically.) The precision is the number of (binary) bits used to store the mantissa. To convert from binary to decimal precision, multiply the precision by 0.30103. To convert from decimal to binary precision, multiply the decimal precision by 3.32193. 24 bits yields 7 digits of precision, and 53 bits yields 15 digits of precision, for example.

- ◆ It's one of the types listed in **Table 3.9**.

53

Datetime Types

Use datetime data types to represent the date and time of day. *Datetime values* have these characteristics:

◆ They're specified with a relationship to UTC, or Universal Coordinated Time (formerly called Greenwich Mean Time or GMT). SQL-92 requires that every SQL session have a default offset from UTC that is used for the duration of the session. –8 hours is the normal time-zone offset of San Francisco, California, for example.

◆ The natural rules of the Gregorian calendar determine how date values are formed. DBMSes reject values that they can't recognize as dates.

◆ Time values are based on a 24-hour clock, also called military time (use 13:00, not 1:00 P.M.).

◆ Hyphens (-) separate the parts of a date, and colons (:) separate the parts of a time. A space separates a date and time when both are combined.

◆ It's one of the types listed in **Table 3.10**.

Table 3.10

Datetime Types	
TYPE	DESCRIPTION
DATE	Represents a date. A date stored in a column defined as DATE has three integer fields—YEAR, MONTH, and DAY—and is formatted *yyyy-mm-dd* (length 10). 2002-06-14, for example. **Table 3.11** lists the valid values for the fields. DATE takes no arguments.
TIME	Represents a time of day. A time stored in a column defined as TIME has three fields—HOUR, MINUTE, and SECOND—and is formatted *hh:mm:ss* (length 8). 22:06:57, for example. You optionally may define the column as TIME(*precision*) to specify fractional seconds. *precision* is the number of fractional digits and is greater than or equal to zero. The maximum *precision*, which is at least 6, depends on the DBMS. HOUR and MINUTE are integers, and SECOND is a decimal number. The format is *hh:mm:ss.ssss*... (length 9 plus the number fractional digits). '22:06:57.1333', for example. Table 3.11 lists the valid values for the fields.
TIMESTAMP	Represents a combination of DATE and TIME values separated by a space. The TIMESTAMP format is *yyyy-mm-dd hh:mm:ss* (length 19). 2002-06-14 22:06:57, for example. You also may specify fractional seconds with TIMESTAMP(*precision*). The format is *yyyy-mm-dd hh:mm:ss.ssss*... (length 20 plus the number fractional digits).
TIME WITH TIME ZONE	This data type is the same as TIME except that it adds a field, TIME_ZONE_OFFSET, to indicate the offset in hours from UTC. TIME_ZONE_OFFSET is formatted as INTERVAL HOUR TO MINUTE (see the next section) and can contain the values listed in Table 3.11. Append AT TIME ZONE *time_zone_offset* to the TIME to assign a value to the time zone. 22:06:57 AT TIME ZONE -08:00, for example. Alternatively, you may append AT LOCAL to indicate that the time zone should be the default for the session. 22:06:57 AT LOCAL, for example. If the AT clause is omitted, all times default to AT LOCAL.
TIMESTAMP WITH TIME ZONE	This data type is the same as TIMESTAMP except that it adds a field, TIME_ZONE_OFFSET, to indicate the offset in hours from UTC. The syntax rules are the same as those of TIME WITH TIME ZONE except that you must include a date. 2002-06-14 22:06:57 AT TIME ZONE -08:00, for example.

Table 3.11

Datetime Fields	
FIELD	VALID VALUES
YEAR	0001 to 9999
MONTH	01 to 12
DAY	01 to 31
HOUR	00 to 23
MINUTE	00 to 59
SECOND	00 to 61.999... (see the Tips)
TIME_ZONE_OFFSET	–12:59 to +13:00

- **DBMS** The datetime data type in **Microsoft Access** is date/time. In **Microsoft SQL Server**: datetime and smalldatetime. In **Oracle**: date and timestamp. In **MySQL**: date, time, datetime, and timestamp. In **PostgreSQL**: date, time, and timestamp.

  DBMSes allow you to enter date values in month-day-year, day-month-year, and other formats and time values based on an A.M./P.M. clock. The format in which dates and times are displayed may differ from the format in which they're entered.

  In **Microsoft Access**, surround datetime literals with # characters instead of quotes and omit the data type name prefix.

  In **Microsoft SQL Server**, omit the data type name prefix from datetime literals.

✔ Tips

- To get your system time, see "Getting the Current Date and Time" in Chapter 5.

- You can compare datetime values if they have the same fields; see "Filtering Rows with WHERE" in Chapter 4. Also see "Performing Date and Time Operations" in Chapter 5.

- The SECOND field can accept values up to 61.999... (instead of 59.999...) to allow for the (rare) insertion of *leap seconds* into a particular minute to keep Earth's clocks synchronized with sidereal time.

- To enter a datetime literal, type the date-time data type name, a space, and then the datetime value surrounded by single quotes, as in DATE '*yyyy-mm-dd*', TIME '*hh:mm:ss*', and TIMESTAMP '*yyyy-mm-dd hh:mm:ss*'.

- SQL-92 can't handle B.C.E./B.C. (Before the Common Era/Before Christ) dates, but your DBMS may be able to do so.

- In practice, timestamps often are used to build unique keys or mark events associated with the row in which they appear.

- The data type TIME WITH TIME ZONE doesn't make sense because real-world time zones have no meaning unless they're associated with a date (as the time-zone offset varies throughout the year). Favor TIMESTAMP WITH TIME ZONE.

DATETIME TYPES

Interval Types

DBMS DBMS compliance with SQL-92 intervals is spotty, so this section is meant to be used as a reference. DBMSes have their own extended data types and functions that calculate intervals and perform date and time arithmetic.

Use interval data types to represent intervals between dates and times of day. An *interval value* has these characteristics:

◆ It stores the quantity of time between two datetime values. Between 09:00 and 13:30 is an interval of 04:30 (4 hours and 30 minutes), for example. If you subtract two datetime values, you get an interval.

◆ It can be used to increment or decrement a datetime value; see "Performing Date and Time Operations" in Chapter 5.

◆ It has the same fields as datetime values (YEAR, HOUR, SECOND, and so on), but the number can have a + (forward) or – (backward) sign to indicate a direction in time. The field separators are the same as for datetime values.

◆ It comes in two categories: year-month intervals and day-time intervals. A *year-month interval* expresses an interval as years and a whole number of months. A *day-time interval* expresses an interval as days, hours, minutes, and seconds.

◆ It has a single-field or multiple-field qualifier. A single-field qualifier is specified simply as YEAR, MONTH, DAY, HOUR, MINUTE, or SECOND. A multiple-field qualifier is specified as:

start_field TO *end_field*

start_field is YEAR, DAY, HOUR, or MINUTE, and *end_field* is YEAR, MONTH, DAY, HOUR, MINUTE, or SECOND. *end_field* must be a smaller time period than *start_field*.

Table 3.12

Interval Types	
Type	**Description**
Year-month	These intervals contain only a year value, only a month value, or both. The valid column types are INTERVAL YEAR, INTERVAL YEAR(*precision*), INTERVAL MONTH, INTERVAL MONTH(*precision*), INTERVAL YEAR TO MONTH, or INTERVAL YEAR(*precision*) TO MONTH.
Day-time	These intervals may contain a day value, hour value, minute value, second value, or some combination thereof. Some of the valid column types are INTERVAL MINUTE, INTERVAL DAY(*precision*), INTERVAL DAY TO HOUR, INTERVAL DAY(*precision*) TO SECOND, or INTERVAL MINUTE(*precision*) TO SECOND(*frac_precision*).

A single-field column defined as INTERVAL HOUR could store intervals such as "4 hours" or "25 hours," for example. A multiple-field column defined as INTERVAL DAY TO MINUTE could store intervals such as "2 days, 5 hours, 10 minutes," for example.

◆ A single-field column may have a precision that specifies the length (number of positions) of the field; INTERVAL HOUR(2), for example. The precision defaults to 2 if omitted. A SECOND field may have an additional fractional precision that specifies the number of digits to the right of the decimal point—INTERVAL SECOND(5,2), for example. If fractional precision is omitted, it defaults to 6.

A multiple-field column may have a precision for *start_field* but not *end_field* (unless *end_field* is SECOND, in which case it may have a fractional precision); INTERVAL DAY(3) TO MINUTE and INTERVAL MINUTE(2) TO SECOND(4), for example.

◆ It's one of the types listed in **Table 3.12**.

✔ Tips

■ To enter an interval literal, type INTERVAL, a space, and then the interval value surrounded by single quotes, as in INTERVAL '15-3' for 15 years and 3 months or INTERVAL '-22:06:5.5' for 22 hours, 6 minutes, and 5.5 seconds ago.

■ **DBMS** **Microsoft Access**, **Microsoft SQL Server**, and **MySQL** don't support interval data types. **Oracle** and **PostgreSQL** have an interval data type.

Nulls

When your data is incomplete, you can use a null to represent a missing or unknown value. A *null* has these characteristics:

- In SQL statements, the keyword NULL represents a null.

- A null is used for a value that may never be known, may be determined later, or is inapplicable. (It's helpful to think of a null as being a marker for a missing value, rather than as a value itself.)

- A null differs from zero, a string that contains only blanks, or an empty string (' '). A null in the column price doesn't mean that an item has no price or that its price is zero; it means that the price is unknown or has not been set. (Oracle is a special case with respect to empty strings; see the DBMS Tip in this section.)

- Nulls don't belong to any data type and can be inserted into any column except ones defined as NOT NULL; see "Forbidding Nulls with NOT NULL" in Chapter 10.

- A null can be detected with IS NULL; see "Testing for Nulls with IS NULL" in Chapter 4.

- Nulls don't equal each other. You can't determine whether a null matches any other value, including another null. This situation gives rise to three-value logic; see "Combining and Negating Conditions with AND, OR, and NOT" in Chapter 4.

- Although nulls are never equal to each other by definition, DISTINCT treats all nulls in a particular column as duplicates; see "Eliminating Duplicate Rows with DISTINCT" in Chapter 4.

- When you sort a column that contains nulls, the nulls will be either greater than or less than all the non-null values, depending on the DBMS; see "Sorting Rows with ORDER BY" in Chapter 4.

- Nulls propagate through computations. The result of any expression, operation, or function that involves a null is null: (12 * NULL) / 4 = NULL; see Chapter 5.

- Aggregate functions such as SUM(), AVG(), and MAX() ignore nulls in calculations; see Chapter 6.

- If a grouping column in a GROUP BY clause contains nulls, all the nulls are put in a single group; see "Grouping Data with GROUP BY" in Chapter 6.

- Nulls affect the results of joins; see "Using Joins" in Chapter 7.

- Nulls can cause problems in subqueries; see "Nulls in Subqueries" in Chapter 8.

```
SELECT MAX(au_id)
  FROM authors
  WHERE au_lname = 'XXX';


MAX(au_id)

----------

NULL
```

Figure 3.3 Getting a null from a column that isn't nullable.

■ **DBMS** The display of nulls in results varies by DBMS. Nulls may be shown as NULL, (NULL), <NULL>, or blank, for example. Some DBMSes let you choose how nulls are displayed.

Oracle currently treats an empty string ('') as null. This treatment may not continue to be true in future releases, however, and Oracle recommends that you do not treat empty strings the same as nulls. This behavior may cause conversion problems among DBMSes. In the sample database, for example, the column au_fname in the table authors is defined as NOT NULL. In Oracle, the first name of the author Kellsey (author A06) is a single space (' '); in the other DBMSes, the first name is an empty string (''). For information about the sample database, see "The Sample Database" in Chapter 2.

✔ Tips

■ There are so many problems and complications with nulls—I've listed some of the important ones here—that some database experts urge users not to use them at all (and instead use default values or some other missing-data scheme). Nulls are necessary for some purposes, however, so professionals try to minimize their use. The moral: Use caution when interpreting results in which nulls are involved.

■ Also see "Checking for Nulls with COALESCE()" and "Comparing Expressions with NULLIF()" in Chapter 5.

■ *Nullable* means that a column is permitted to contain nulls.

■ The term *null value* is inaccurate—a null indicates the *lack* of a value.

■ Don't place the keyword NULL in quotes or your DBMS will interpret it as the character string 'NULL' rather than as a null.

■ You can get a null from a column that doesn't permit nulls. The column au_id in the table authors doesn't permit nulls, but the SELECT statement in **Figure 3.3** returns a null for the maximum au_id.

NULLS

RETRIEVING DATA FROM A TABLE

4

This chapter introduces SQL's workhorse—the **SELECT** statement. Most SQL work involves retrieving and manipulating data by using this one (albeit complex) statement. **SELECT** retrieves rows, columns, and derived values from one or more tables in a database; its syntax is:

```
SELECT columns

    FROM tables

    [JOIN joins]

    [WHERE search_condition]

    [GROUP BY grouping_columns]

    [HAVING search_condition]

    [ORDER BY sort_columns];
```

As each clause has a specific use, I'll cover the clauses individually: **SELECT, FROM, ORDER BY,** and **WHERE** in this chapter, **GROUP BY** and **HAVING** in Chapter 6, and **JOIN** in Chapter 7. (Recall that *italic type* denotes replaceable identifiers and expressions, and brackets indicate an optional clause; see "Typographic conventions" and "Syntax conventions" in the Introduction).

By convention, I call only a **SELECT** statement a *query*. (DBMS documentation and other books may refer to *any* SQL statement as a query.) Although **SELECT** is powerful, it's not dangerous: You can't use it to add, change, or delete data or database objects. (The dangerous stuff starts in Chapter 9.)

Retrieving Columns with SELECT and FROM

In its simplest form, a SELECT statement retrieves columns from a table; you can retrieve one column, multiple columns, or all columns. The SELECT clause lists the columns to display, and the FROM clause specifies the table from which to draw the columns.

To retrieve a column from a table:

◆ Type:

```
SELECT column
    FROM table;
```

column is a column name, and *table* is the name of the table that contains *column* (**Listing 4.1** and **Figure 4.1**).

To retrieve multiple columns from a table:

◆ Type:

```
SELECT columns
    FROM table;
```

columns is two or more comma-separated column names, and *table* is the name of the table that contains *columns* (**Listing 4.2** and **Figure 4.2**).

Columns are displayed in the same order in which they're listed in *columns,* not the order in which they're defined in *table.*

Listing 4.1 List the cities in which the authors live. See Figure 4.1 for the result.

```
SELECT city
    FROM authors;
```

```
city
-------------
Bronx
Boulder
San Francisco
San Francisco
New York
Palo Alto
Sarasota
```

Figure 4.1 Result of Listing 4.1.

Listing 4.2 List each author's first name, last name, city, and state. See Figure 4.2 for the result.

```
SELECT au_fname, au_lname, city, state
    FROM authors;
```

au_fname	au_lname	city	state
Sarah	Buchman	Bronx	NY
Wendy	Heydemark	Boulder	CO
Hallie	Hull	San Francisco	CA
Klee	Hull	San Francisco	CA
Christian	Kells	New York	NY
	Kellsey	Palo Alto	CA
Paddy	O'Furniture	Sarasota	FL

Figure 4.2 Result of Listing 4.2.

To retrieve all columns from a table:

◆ Type:

SELECT *

  FROM *table*;

table is the name of a table (**Listing 4.3** and **Figure 4.3**).

Columns are displayed in the order in which they're defined in *table*.

✔ Tips

■ The SELECT and FROM clauses always are required if you retrieve columns from tables; all other clauses are optional.

■ Closure guarantees that the result of every SELECT statement is a table; see the Tips in "Tables, Columns, and Rows" in Chapter 2.

■ The result in Figure 4.1 contains duplicate rows because two authors live in San Francisco. To remove duplicates, see "Eliminating Duplicate Rows with DISTINCT" later in this chapter.

continues on next page

Listing 4.3 List all the columns in the table authors. See Figure 4.3 for the result.

```
                      listing
SELECT *
  FROM authors;
```

au_id	au_fname	au_lname	phone	address	city	state	zip
A01	Sarah	Buchman	718-496-7223	75 West 205 St	Bronx	NY	10468
A02	Wendy	Heydemark	303-986-7020	2922 Baseline Rd	Boulder	CO	80303
A03	Hallie	Hull	415-549-4278	3800 Waldo Ave, #14F	San Francisco	CA	94123
A04	Klee	Hull	415-549-4278	3800 Waldo Ave, #14F	San Francisco	CA	94123
A05	Christian	Kells	212-771-4680	114 Horatio St	New York	NY	10014
A06		Kellsey	650-836-7128	390 Serra Mall	Palo Alto	CA	94305
A07	Paddy	O'Furniture	941-925-0752	1442 Main St	Sarasota	FL	34236

Figure 4.3 Result of Listing 4.3.

- The rows in your results may be ordered differently from the rows in mine; see "Sorting Rows with ORDER BY" later in this chapter.

- I use NULL to indicate a null in a table or result; see "Nulls" in Chapter 3 (**Listing 4.4** and **Figure 4.4**).

- I'll describe how to retrieve columns from multiple tables in Chapter 7.

- All results display raw, unformatted values. Monetary amounts lack currency signs, and numbers may have an inappropriate number of decimal places, for example. Reporting tools—not data-retrieval tools—format data.

- It's risky to use SELECT * in embedded SQL because the number of columns in a table may change and cause your program to fail. SELECT * is useful in interactive SQL, particularly if you don't know the names of all the columns in a table.

- An operation that selects certain columns from a table is called a *projection*.

Listing 4.4 List each publisher's city, state, and country. See Figure 4.4 for the result.

```
SELECT city, state, country
  FROM publishers;
```

```
city            state country
------------- ----- -------
New York        NY    USA
San Francisco   CA    USA
Hamburg         NULL  Germany
Berkeley        CA    USA
```

Figure 4.4 Result of Listing 4.4. The column state doesn't apply to Germany. NULL specifies a null, which is distinct from an "invisible" value such as an empty string or a string of blanks.

Creating Column Aliases with AS

In the query results so far, I've allowed the DBMS to use default values for column headings. (A column's default heading in a result is its original column name in its source table). You can use the AS clause to create a column alias. A *column alias* is an alternative name (identifier) that you specify to control how column headings are displayed in a result. Use column aliases if column names are cryptic, hard to type, too long, or too short.

Specify column aliases in the SELECT clause of a SELECT statement: Follow a column name with the AS keyword and an alias enclosed in single or double quotes, but mind the following variations:

◆ You may omit the quotes if the alias is a single word that contains only letters, digits, or underscores. Use quotes if the alias contains spaces, punctuation, or special characters.

◆ The AS keyword is optional. au_fname AS "First name" and au_fname "First name" are equivalent.

◆ If you want a particular column to retain its default heading, omit its AS clause.

To create column aliases:

◆ Type:

```
SELECT column1 AS alias1,
       column2 AS alias2,
       ...
       columnN AS aliasN
  FROM table;
```

column1, column2,..., columnN are column names, *alias1, alias2,..., aliasN* are their corresponding column aliases, and *table* is the name of the table that contains *column1, column2,....*

Listing 4.5 shows the syntactic variations of the AS clause. **Figure 4.5** shows the result of Listing 4.5.

In this book, I always include the AS keyword and surround aliases with double quotes for clarity and DBMS portability (see the DBMS Tip in this section). With these syntactic conventions, Listing 4.5 is equivalent to:

```
SELECT au_fname AS "First name",
       au_lname AS "Last name",
       city     AS "City",
       state,
       zip      AS "Postal code"
  FROM authors;
```

Listing 4.5 The AS clause specifies a column alias to display in results. This statement shows alternative constructions for AS syntax. In your programs, pick one construction and use it consistently. See Figure 4.5 for the result.

```
                        listing
SELECT au_fname AS "First name",
       au_lname AS 'Last name',
       city AS City,
       state,
       zip 'Postal code'
  FROM authors;
```

First name	Last name	City	state	Postal code
Sarah	Buchman	Bronx	NY	10468
Wendy	Heydemark	Boulder	CO	80303
Hallie	Hull	San Francisco	CA	94123
Klee	Hull	San Francisco	CA	94123
Christian	Kells	New York	NY	10014
	Kellsey	Palo Alto	CA	94305
Paddy	O'Furniture	Sarasota	FL	34236

Figure 4.5 Result of Listing 4.5.

✔ Tips

- AS also is used to name derived columns (whose values are determined by expressions other than simple column names); see "Creating Derived Columns" Chapter 5.

- You also can create table aliases with AS; see "Creating Table Aliases with AS" in Chapter 7.

- A column alias doesn't change the name of a column in a table.

- Reserved keywords can be used in quoted column headings. The query SELECT SUM(sales) AS "Sum" FROM titles; uses the reserved word SUM as a column alias, for example. For information about keywords, see "SQL Syntax" in Chapter 3.

- **DBMS** In **Microsoft Access** and **PostgreSQL**, the AS keyword is required.

  In **Oracle** and **PostgreSQL**, surround alias names with double quotes (not single quotes).

  By default, **Oracle** displays column aliases in uppercase if they are not enclosed in quotes.

  Oracle truncates column aliases to the number of characters specified in the table's column definitions. The column alias "Postal code" displays as "Posta" in a CHAR(5) column, for example.

  DBMSes may have restrictions on embedded spaces, punctuation, and special characters in aliases; search your DBMS documentation for *SELECT* or *AS*.

Eliminating Duplicate Rows with DISTINCT

Columns often contain duplicate values, and it's common to want a result that lists each duplicate only once. If I type **Listing 4.6** to list the states where the authors live, the result, **Figure 4.6**, contains unneeded duplicates. The DISTINCT keyword eliminates duplicate rows from a result.

To eliminate duplicate rows:

◆ Type:

```
SELECT DISTINCT columns
  FROM table;
```

columns is one or more comma-separated column names, and *table* is the name of the table that contains *columns* (**Listing 4.7** and **Figure 4.7**).

Listing 4.6 List the states in which the authors live. See Figure 4.6 for the result.

```
SELECT state
  FROM authors;
```

```
state
-----
NY
CO
CA
CA
NY
CA
FL
```

Figure 4.6 Result of Listing 4.6. This result contains unneeded duplicates of CA and NY.

Listing 4.7 List the distinct states in which the authors live. The DISTINCT keyword eliminates duplicate rows in the result. See Figure 4.7 for the result.

```
SELECT DISTINCT state
  FROM authors;
```

```
state
-----
NY
CO
CA
FL
```

Figure 4.7 Result of Listing 4.7. This result has no CA or NY duplicates.

Listing 4.8 List the cities and states in which the authors live. See Figure 4.8 for the result.

```
                    listing
SELECT city, state
  FROM authors;
```

```
city          state
------------- -----
Boulder       CO
Bronx         NY
New York      NY
Palo Alto     CA
San Francisco CA
San Francisco CA
Sarasota      FL
```

Figure 4.8 Result of Listing 4.8. This result contains a duplicate row for San Francisco, California.

Listing 4.9 List the distinct cities and states in which the authors live. See Figure 4.9 for the result.

```
                    listing
SELECT DISTINCT city, state
  FROM authors;
```

```
city          state
------------- -----
Boulder       CO
Bronx         NY
New York      NY
Palo Alto     CA
San Francisco CA
Sarasota      FL
```

Figure 4.9 Result of Listing 4.9. It's the city–state combination that's considered to be unique, not the value in any single column.

✔ Tips

■ If the SELECT DISTINCT clause contains more than one column, the values of *all* the columns combined determine the uniqueness of rows. The result of **Listing 4.8** is **Figure 4.8**, which contains a duplicate row that comprises two columns. The result of **Listing 4.9** is **Figure 4.9**, which eliminates the two-column duplicate.

■ Although nulls never equal each other because their values are unknown, DISTINCT considers all nulls to be duplicates of each other. SELECT DISTINCT returns only one null in a result, regardless of how many nulls it encounters; see "Nulls" in Chapter 3.

■ The SELECT statement syntax includes the optional ALL keyword. You rarely see ALL in practice because it indicates the default behavior: display all rows, including duplicates.

    SELECT columns FROM table;

is equivalent to:

    SELECT ALL columns FROM table;

The syntax diagram is:

    SELECT [ALL | DISTINCT] columns
      FROM table;

■ You can use DISTINCT with aggregate functions, see "Aggregating Distinct Values with DISTINCT" in Chapter 6.

■ If a table has a properly defined primary key, SELECT DISTINCT * FROM table; and SELECT * FROM table; return identical results because all rows are unique.

Sorting Rows with ORDER BY

Rows in a query result are unordered; you should view the order in which rows appear as being arbitrary. This situation arises because the relational model posits that row order is irrelevant for table operations. You can use the ORDER BY clause to sort rows by a specified column or columns in ascending (lowest to highest) or descending (highest to lowest) order; see the sidebar in this section. The ORDER BY clause always is the last clause in a SELECT statement.

To sort by a column:

◆ Type:

SELECT *columns*

   FROM *table*

   ORDER BY *sort_column* [ASC | DESC];

columns is one or more comma-separated column names, *sort_column* is the name of the column on which to sort the result, and *table* is the name of the table that contains *columns* and *sort_column*. (*sort_column* doesn't have to be in listed in *columns*.) Specify ASC for an ascending sort or DESC for a descending sort. If no sort direction is specified, ASC is assumed (**Listings 4.10** and **4.11**, **Figures 4.10** and **4.11**).

Listing 4.10 List the authors' first names, last names, cities, and states, sorted by ascending last name. ORDER BY performs ascending sorts by default, so the ASC keyword is optional. (In practice, ASC typically is omitted, but in this book, I'll include ASC for clarity). See Figure 4.10 for the result.

```
SELECT au_fname, au_lname, city, state
  FROM authors
  ORDER BY au_lname ASC;
```

au_fname	au_lname	city	state
Sarah	Buchman	Bronx	NY
Wendy	Heydemark	Boulder	CO
Hallie	Hull	San Francisco	CA
Klee	Hull	San Francisco	CA
Christian	Kells	New York	NY
	Kellsey	Palo Alto	CA
Paddy	O'Furniture	Sarasota	FL

Figure 4.10 Result of Listing 4.10. This result is sorted in ascending last-name order.

Sort Order

Sorting numeric and datetime values is unambiguous; sorting character strings is complex. A DBMS uses a *collating sequence,* or *collation,* to determine the order in which characters are sorted. The collation defines the order of precedence for every character in your character set. Your character set depends on the language that you're using—European languages (a Latin character set), Hebrew (the Hebrew alphabet), or Chinese (ideographs), for example. The collation also determines case sensitivity (is 'A' < 'a'?), accent sensitivity (is 'A' < 'À'?), width sensitivity (for multibyte or Unicode characters), and other factors such as linguistic practices. The SQL standard doesn't define particular collations and character sets, so each DBMS uses its own sorting strategy and default collation. DBMSes usually provide commands or tools that display the current collation and character set. Run the command **exec sp_helpsort** in Microsoft SQL Server, for example. Search your DBMS documentation for *collation* or *sort order.*

Listing 4.11 List the authors' first names, last names, cities, and states, sorted by descending first name. The DESC keyword is required. See Figure 4.11 for the result.

```
                        listing
SELECT au_fname, au_lname, city, state
  FROM authors
  ORDER BY au_fname DESC;
```

au_fname	au_lname	city	state
Wendy	Heydemark	Boulder	CO
Sarah	Buchman	Bronx	NY
Paddy	O'Furniture	Sarasota	FL
Klee	Hull	San Francisco	CA
Hallie	Hull	San Francisco	CA
Christian	Kells	New York	NY
	Kellsey	Palo Alto	CA

Figure 4.11 Result of Listing 4.11. This result is sorted in descending first-name order. The first name of the author Kellsey is an empty string (' ') and sorts last (or first in ascending order).

Listing 4.12 List the authors' first names, last names, cities, and states, sorted by descending city within ascending state. See Figure 4.12 for the result.

```
                        listing
SELECT au_fname, au_lname, city, state
  FROM authors
  ORDER BY state ASC,
           city  DESC;
```

au_fname	au_lname	city	state
Hallie	Hull	San Francisco	CA
Klee	Hull	San Francisco	CA
	Kellsey	Palo Alto	CA
Wendy	Heydemark	Boulder	CO
Paddy	O'Furniture	Sarasota	FL
Christian	Kells	New York	NY
Sarah	Buchman	Bronx	NY

Figure 4.12 Result of Listing 4.12.

To sort by multiple columns:

◆ Type:

```
SELECT columns
  FROM table
  ORDER BY sort_column1 [ASC | DESC],
           sort_column2 [ASC | DESC],
           ...
           sort_columnN [ASC | DESC];
```

columns is one or more comma-separated column names, *sort_column1, sort_column2,..., sort_columnN* are the names of the columns on which to sort the result, and *table* is the name of the table that contains *columns* and the sort columns. (The sort columns don't have to be in listed in *columns*.) Rows are sorted first by *sort_column1;* then rows that have equal values in *sort_column1* are sorted by the values in *sort_column2*, and so on. For each sort column, specify ASC for an ascending sort or DESC for a descending sort. If no sort direction is specified, ASC is assumed (**Listing 4.12** and **Figure 4.12**).

SORTING ROWS WITH ORDER BY

SQL lets you specify relative column-position numbers instead of column names in ORDER BY. The position numbers refer to the columns in the result, not the original table. Using column positions saves typing, but the resulting code is unclear and invites mistakes if you reorder the columns in the SELECT clause.

To sort by relative column positions:

◆ Type:

```
SELECT columns
  FROM table
  ORDER BY sort_num1 [ASC | DESC],
           sort_num2 [ASC | DESC],
           ...
           sort_numN [ASC | DESC];
```

columns is one or more comma-separated column names, and *sort_num1, sort_num2,..., sort_numN* are integers between 1 and the number of columns in *columns*, inclusive. Each integer specifies the relative position of a column in *columns*. *table* is the name of the table that contains *columns*. (The sort numbers can't refer to a column that's not listed in *columns*.) The sort order is the same order described in "To sort by multiple columns" earlier in this section (**Listing 4.13** and **Figure 4.13**).

Listing 4.13 List each author's first name, last name, city, and state, sorted first by ascending state (column 4 in the SELECT clause) and then by descending last name within each state (column 2). See Figure 4.13 for the result.

```
SELECT au_fname, au_lname, city, state
  FROM authors
  ORDER BY 4 ASC, 2 DESC;
```

au_fname	au_lname	city	state
	Kellsey	Palo Alto	CA
Hallie	Hull	San Francisco	CA
Klee	Hull	San Francisco	CA
Wendy	Heydemark	Boulder	CO
Paddy	O'Furniture	Sarasota	FL
Christian	Kells	New York	NY
Sarah	Buchman	Bronx	NY

Figure 4.13 Result of Listing 4.13.

Listing 4.14 Nulls in a sort column are listed first or last, depending on the DBMS. See Figure 4.14 for the result.

```
SELECT pub_id, state, country
  FROM publishers
  ORDER BY state ASC;
```

pub_id	state	country
P03	NULL	Germany
P04	CA	USA
P02	CA	USA
P01	NY	USA

Figure 4.14 Result of Listing 4.14. This result is sorted by ascending state. The DBMS in which I ran this query treats nulls as the lowest possible values, so the row with the null state is listed first. A DBMS that treats nulls as the highest possible values would list the same row last.

Listing 4.15 zip doesn't appear in the list of columns to retrieve. See Figure 4.15 for the result.

```
                        listing
SELECT city, state
   FROM authors
   ORDER BY zip ASC;
```

```
city            state
------------    -----

New York        NY
Bronx           NY
Sarasota        FL
Boulder         CO
San Francisco   CA
San Francisco   CA
Palo Alto       CA
```

Figure 4.15 Result of Listing 4.15. This result is sorted by ascending zip. Rows may appear to be in random order if you sort by an undisplayed column, confusing your end user.

Listing 4.16 This query uses column aliases in the ORDER BY clause. See Figure 4.16 for the result.

```
                        listing
SELECT au_fname AS "First name",
       au_lname AS "Last name",
       state
   FROM authors
   ORDER BY state        ASC,
            "Last name"  ASC,
            "First name" ASC;
```

```
First name  Last name    state
----------  -----------  -----

Hallie      Hull         CA
Klee        Hull         CA
            Kellsey      CA
Wendy       Heydemark    CO
Paddy       O'Furniture  FL
Sarah       Buchman      NY
Christian   Kells        NY
```

Figure 4.16 Result of Listing 4.16.

✔ Tips

- The SQL standard states that when nulls are sorted, they are either greater than or less than non-null values. Some DBMSes treat nulls as the lowest possible values, and others treat them as the highest; see the DBMS Tip later in this section and "Nulls" in Chapter 3 (**Listing 4.14** and **Figure 4.14**).

- You can sort by columns that aren't listed in the SELECT clause (**Listing 4.15** and **Figure 4.15**). This technique won't work for relative column positions.

- You can specify column aliases instead of column names in ORDER BY (**Listing 4.16** and **Figure 4.16**). See "Creating Column Aliases with AS" earlier in this chapter.

- You can specify the same column multiple times in ORDER BY (but that's silly).

- If the ORDER BY columns don't identify each row uniquely in the result, rows with duplicate values will be listed in arbitrary order. Although that's the case in some of my examples (refer to Figures 4.10, 4.12, and 4.13), you should include enough ORDER BY columns to identify rows uniquely, particularly if the result is to be displayed to an end user.

- According to the ANSI standard, the ORDER BY clause is part of a CURSOR declaration and not the SELECT statement. Cursors, which are objects defined inside application programs, are beyond the scope of this book. All popular SQL implementations allow you to use ORDER BY in a SELECT statement (because the DBMS builds a cursor invisibly).

continues on next page

SORTING ROWS WITH ORDER BY

- You can sort by the results of expressions; Chapter 5 describes how to create expressions by using functions and operators (**Listing 4.17** and **Figure 4.17**).

- You can intermingle column names, relative column positions, and expressions in ORDER BY.

- The sequence in which unordered rows appear actually is based on the physical order of rows in the DBMS table. You shouldn't rely on physical order, as it changes often, such as when rows are added, updated, or deleted or an index is created.

- Sorting by relative column position is useful in UNION queries; see "Combining Rows with UNION" in Chapter 7.

- **DBMS** For sorting purposes, **Microsoft Access**, **Microsoft SQL Server**, and **PostgreSQL** treat nulls as the lowest possible values. **Oracle** and **MySQL** treat nulls as the highest possible values.

  DBMSes restrict the columns that can appear in an ORDER BY clause, depending on data type. In **Microsoft SQL Server**, you can't sort by ntext, text, and image columns, and in **Oracle**, you can't sort by blob, clob, nclob, and bfile columns, for example. Search your DBMS documentation for *SELECT* or *ORDER BY*.

  In **Microsoft Access**, you can't use an expression's column alias in ORDER BY. To run Listing 4.17 in Access, either retype the expression in the ORDER BY clause:

  ```
  ORDER BY price * sales DESC
  ```

  or use the relative column position:

  ```
  ORDER BY 4 DESC
  ```

Listing 4.17 This query sorts by an expression. See Figure 4.17 for the result.

```
SELECT title_id,
       price,
       sales,
       price * sales AS "Revenue"
  FROM titles
  ORDER BY "Revenue" DESC;
```

title_id	price	sales	Revenue
T07	23.95	1500200	35929790.00
T05	6.95	201440	1400008.00
T12	12.99	100001	1299012.99
T03	39.95	25667	1025396.65
T11	7.99	94123	752042.77
T13	29.99	10467	313905.33
T06	19.95	11320	225834.00
T02	19.95	9566	190841.70
T04	12.99	13001	168882.99
T09	13.95	5000	69750.00
T08	10.00	4095	40950.00
T01	21.99	566	12446.34
T10	NULL	NULL	NULL

Figure 4.17 Result of Listing 4.17. This result lists titles by descending revenue (the product of price and sales).

Filtering Rows with WHERE

The result of each SELECT statement so far has included every row in the table (for the specified columns). You can use the WHERE clause to filter unwanted rows from the result. This filtering capability gives the SELECT statement its real power. In a WHERE clause, you specify a *search condition* that comprises one or more conditions that need to be satisfied by the rows of a table. A *condition,* or *predicate,* is a logical expression that evaluates to true, false, or unknown. (The unknown result arises from nulls; see the next section.) Rows for which the condition is true are included in the result; rows for which the condition is false or unknown are excluded.

SQL provides operators that express different types of conditions (**Table 4.1**). (Operators, covered in Chapter 5, are symbols or keywords that specify actions to be performed on values or other elements.) I'll cover comparisons in this section and the other conditions in the remainder of this chapter. You can combine and negate conditions by using the logical operators AND, OR, and NOT, which are covered in the next section.

SQL's *comparison operators* compare two values and evaluate to true, false, or unknown (**Table 4.2**). The data type determines how values are compared:

◆ Character strings are compared lexicographically. < means *precedes*, and > means *follows*. See "Data Types" in Chapter 3 and "Sorting Rows with ORDER BY" earlier in this chapter.

◆ Numbers are compared arithmetically. < means *smaller*, and > means *larger*.

◆ Datetimes are compared chronologically. < means *earlier*, and > means *later*. Datetimes must have the same fields (year, month, day, hour, and so on) to be compared meaningfully.

You should compare like data types. If you try to compare values that have different data types, your DBMS may:

◆ Return an error, *or*

◆ Compare the values unequally and return a result with no rows, *or*

◆ Attempt to convert the values to a common type and compare them if successful, or return an error if unsuccessful

Table 4.1

Types of Conditions	
CONDITION	SQL OPERATORS
Comparison	=, <>, <, <=, >, >=
Pattern matching	LIKE
Range filtering	BETWEEN
List filtering	IN
Null test	IS NULL

Table 4.2

Comparison Operators	
OPERATOR	DESCRIPTION
=	Equal to
<>	Not equal to
<	Less than
<=	Less than or equal to
>	Greater than
>=	Greater than or equal to

To filter rows by making a comparison:

◆ Type:

SELECT *columns*

  FROM *table*

  WHERE *test_column op value*;

columns is one or more comma-separated column names, and *table* is the name of the table that contains *columns*.

In the search condition, *test_column* is the name of a column in *table*. (*test_column* doesn't have to be listed in *columns*.) *op* is one of the comparison operators listed in Table 4.2, and *value* is a value that's compared with the value in *test_column*. (**Listings 4.18** through **4.20, Figures 4.18** through **4.20**).

✔ Tips

■ Place the WHERE clause before the ORDER BY clause in a SELECT statement in which both appear.

■ A null represents the unknown and won't match anything, not even another null. Rows in which nulls are involved in comparisons won't be in the result. To retrieve rows with nulls, see "Testing for Nulls with IS NULL" later in this chapter. For information about nulls, see "Nulls" in Chapter 3.

Listing 4.18 List the authors whose last name is not Hull. See Figure 4.18 for the result.

```
                          listing
SELECT au_id, au_fname, au_lname
  FROM authors
  WHERE au_lname <> 'Hull';
```

```
au_id au_fname  au_lname
----- --------- -----------
A01   Sarah     Buchman
A02   Wendy     Heydemark
A05   Christian Kells
A06             Kellsey
A07   Paddy     O'Furniture
```

Figure 4.18 Result of Listing 4.18.

Listing 4.19 List the titles for which there is no signed contract. See Figure 4.19 for the result.

```
                          listing
SELECT title_name, contract
  FROM titles
  WHERE contract = 0;
```

```
title_name                   contract
-------------------------    --------
Not Without My Faberge Egg          0
```

Figure 4.19 Result of Listing 4.19.

Listing 4.20 List the titles published in 2001 and later. See Figure 4.20 for the result.

```
                        listing
SELECT title_name, pubdate

  FROM titles

  WHERE pubdate >= DATE '2001-01-01';
```

```
title_name                    pubdate

----------------------------  ----------

Exchange of Platitudes         2001-01-01

Just Wait Until After School  2001-06-01

Kiss My Boo-Boo                2002-05-31
```

Figure 4.20 Result of Listing 4.20.

Listing 4.21 List the titles that generated more than $1 million in revenue. This search condition uses an arithmetic expression. See Figure 4.21 for the result.

```
                        listing
SELECT title_name,

        price * sales AS "Revenue"

  FROM titles

  WHERE price * sales > 1000000;
```

```
title_name                    Revenue

----------------------------  ----------

Ask Your System Administrator  1025396.65

Exchange of Platitudes         1400008.00

I Blame My Mother              35929790.00

Spontaneous, Not Annoying      1299012.99
```

Figure 4.21 Result of Listing 4.21.

- The right and left sides of the comparison can be more complex than I described. The general form of a comparison is:

  expr1 op expr2

  expr1 and *expr2* are expressions. An expression is any valid combination of column names, literals, functions, and operators that resolves to a single value (per row). I'll cover expressions in Chapter 5 (**Listing 4.21** and **Figure 4.21**).

- You can't use an aggregate function such as SUM() or COUNT() in a WHERE clause; see Chapter 6.

- An operation that selects certain rows from a table is called a *restriction*.

- **DBMS** Though the SQL standard states that case is significant within quoted strings, your DBMS's collating sequence determines whether string comparisons are case-insensitive ('A' = 'a') or case-sensitive ('A' ≠ 'a'). **Microsoft Access**, **Microsoft SQL Server**, and **MySQL** perform case-insensitive comparisons by default. **Oracle** and **PostgreSQL** perform case-sensitive comparisons by default.

  In **Microsoft Access** date literals, omit the DATE keyword, and surround the literal with # characters instead of quotes. To run Listing 4.20 in Access, change the date in the WHERE clause to #2001-01-01#.

  In **Microsoft SQL Server** date literals, omit the DATE keyword. To run Listing 4.20 in SQL Server, change the date in the WHERE clause to '2001-01-01'.

  In **PostgreSQL**, to compare a value in a NUMERIC or DECIMAL column with a real (floating-point) number, convert the real number to NUMERIC or DECIMAL explicitly. See "Converting Data Types with CAST()" in Chapter 5.

Combining and Negating Conditions with AND, OR, and NOT

Often, you'll need to specify multiple conditions in a single WHERE clause—to, say, retrieve rows based on the values in multiple columns. You can use the AND and OR operators to combine two or more conditions into a *compound condition*. AND, OR, and a third operator, NOT, are logical operators. *Logical operators,* or *Boolean operators,* are operators designed to work with *truth values:* true, false, and unknown.

If you've programmed in other languages (or studied propositional logic), you're familiar with the two-value logic (2VL) system. In *two-value logic,* the result of a logical expression is either true or false. 2VL assumes perfect knowledge, in which all propositions are known to be true or false. Databases model real data, however, and our knowledge of the world is imperfect—hence, the use of nulls to represent unknown values (see "Nulls" in Chapter 3).

2VL is insufficient to represent knowledge gaps, so SQL uses three-value logic (3VL). In *three-value logic,* the result of a logical expression is true, false, or unknown. If the result of a compound condition is false or unknown, the row is excluded from the result. (To retrieve rows with nulls, see "Testing for Nulls with IS NULL" later in this chapter.)

Table 4.3

AND	True	False	Unknown
True	True	False	Unknown
False	False	False	False
Unknown	Unknown	False	Unknown

Listing 4.22 List the biographies that sell for less than $20. See Figure 4.22 for the result.

```
                    listing
SELECT title_name, type, price
  FROM titles
  WHERE type = 'biography' AND price < 20;
```

```
title_name                type      price
------------------------   --------- -----
How About Never?          biography 19.95
Spontaneous, Not Annoying biography 12.99
```

Figure 4.22 Result of Listing 4.22.

Listing 4.23 List the authors whose last names begin with one of the letters *H* through *Z* and who don't live in California. See Figure 4.23 for the result.

```
                    listing
SELECT au_fname, au_lname, state
  FROM authors
  WHERE au_lname >= 'H'
    AND au_lname <= 'Zz'
    AND state <> 'CA';
```

```
au_fname   au_lname     state
--------   -----------  -----
Wendy      Heydemark    CO
Christian  Kells        NY
Paddy      O'Furniture  FL
```

Figure 4.23 Result of Listing 4.23. Remember that the results of string comparisons depend on the DBMS's collating sequence; see "Sorting Rows with ORDER BY" earlier in this chapter.

The AND operator

The AND operator's important characteristics are:

◆ AND connects two conditions and returns true only if *both* conditions are true.

◆ **Table 4.3** shows the possible outcomes when you combine two conditions with AND. The table's left column shows the truth values of the first condition, the top row shows the truth values of the second condition, and each intersection shows the AND outcome. This type of table is called a *truth table*.

◆ Any number of conditions can be connected with ANDs. All the conditions must be true for the row to be included in the result.

◆ AND is commutative (independent of order): WHERE *condition1* AND *condition2* is equivalent to WHERE *condition2* AND *condition1*.

◆ You may enclose one or both of the conditions in parentheses. (Parentheses are optional now, but see "Using AND, OR, and NOT together" later in this section to see situations in which they're required.)

See **Listings 4.22** and **4.23**, and **Figures 4.22** and **4.23,** for some AND examples.

USING AND, OR, AND NOT

The OR operator

The OR operator's important characteristics are:

◆ OR connects two conditions and returns true if *either* condition is true or if *both* conditions are true.

◆ **Table 4.4** shows the OR truth table.

◆ Any number of conditions can be connected with ORs. OR will retrieve rows that match any condition or all the conditions.

◆ Like AND, OR is commutative; the order in which you list the conditions doesn't matter.

◆ You may enclose one or both of the conditions in parentheses. (Some compound conditions require parentheses.)

See **Listings 4.24** and **4.25,** and **Figures 4.24** and **4.25,** for some OR examples.

Listing 4.25 shows the effect of nulls in conditions. You might expect the result, Figure 4.25, to display all the rows in the table `publishers`. But the row for publisher P03 is missing because it contains a null in the column `state`. The null causes the result of both of the OR conditions to be unknown, so the row is excluded from the result. To test for nulls, see "Testing for Nulls with IS NULL" later in this chapter.

Table 4.4

OR	True	False	Unknown
True	True	True	True
False	True	False	Unknown
Unknown	True	Unknown	Unknown

Listing 4.24 List the authors who live in New York State, Colorado, or San Francisco. See Figure 4.24 for the result.

```
SELECT au_fname, au_lname, city, state
  FROM authors
  WHERE (state = 'NY')
     OR (state = 'CO')
     OR (city = 'San Francisco');
```

au_fname	au_lname	city	state
Sarah	Buchman	Bronx	NY
Wendy	Heydemark	Boulder	CO
Hallie	Hull	San Francisco	CA
Klee	Hull	San Francisco	CA
Christian	Kells	New York	NY

Figure 4.24 Result of Listing 4.24.

Listing 4.25 List the publishers that are located in California or are not located in California. This example is contrived to show the effect of nulls in conditions; see Figure 4.25 for the result.

```
SELECT pub_id, pub_name, state, country
  FROM publishers
  WHERE (state = 'CA')
     OR (state <> 'CA');
```

pub_id	pub_name	state	country
P01	Abatis Publishers	NY	USA
P02	Core Dump Books	CA	USA
P04	Tenterhooks Press	CA	USA

Figure 4.25 Result of Listing 4.25.

Table 4.5

CONDITION	NOT CONDITION
True	False
False	True
Unknown	Unknown

Listing 4.26 List the authors who don't live in California. See Figure 4.26 for the result.

```
                    listing
SELECT au_fname, au_lname, state
  FROM authors
  WHERE NOT (state = 'CA');
```

```
au_fname   au_lname     state

---------  -----------  -----

Sarah      Buchman      NY

Wendy      Heydemark    CO

Christian  Kells        NY

Paddy      O'Furniture  FL
```

Figure 4.26 Result of Listing 4.26.

Listing 4.27 List the titles whose price is not less than $20 and have sold more than 15,000 copies. See Figure 4.27 for the result.

```
                    listing
SELECT title_name, sales, price
  FROM titles
  WHERE NOT (price < 20)
    AND (sales > 15000);
```

```
title_name                    sales   price

----------------------------  ------- -----

Ask Your System Administrator 25667   39.95

I Blame My Mother             1500200 23.95
```

Figure 4.27 Result of Listing 4.27.

The NOT operator

The NOT operator's important characteristics are:

◆ Unlike AND and OR, NOT doesn't connect two conditions. Instead, it negates (reverses) a single condition.

◆ **Table 4.5** shows the NOT truth table.

◆ In comparisons, place NOT before the column name or expression:

```
WHERE NOT state = 'CA'        --Correct
```

and not before the operator (even though it sounds better when read):

```
WHERE state NOT = 'CA'        --Illegal
```

◆ NOT acts upon one condition. To negate two or more conditions, repeat the NOT for each condition. To list titles that are not biographies and are not priced less than $20, for example, type:

```
SELECT title_id, type, price
  FROM titles
  WHERE NOT type = 'biography'
    AND NOT price < 20;        --Correct
```

and not:

```
SELECT title_id, type, price
  FROM titles
  WHERE NOT type = 'biography'
    AND price < 20;            --Wrong
```

The latter clause is legal but returns the wrong result. See the Tips in this section to learn ways to express equivalent NOT conditions.

◆ In comparisons, the use of NOT often is a matter of style. The following two clauses are equivalent:

```
WHERE NOT state = 'CA'
```

and

```
WHERE state <> 'CA'
```

◆ You may enclose the condition in parentheses.

See **Listings 4.26** and **4.27,** and **Figures 4.26** and **4.27,** for some NOT examples.

USING AND, OR, AND NOT

Using AND, OR, and NOT together

You can combine the three logical operators in a compound condition. Your DBMS uses SQL's precedence rules to determine which operators to evaluate first. I'll cover precedence in "Determining the Order of Evaluation" in Chapter 5, but for now, you must know that when you use multiple logical operators in a compound condition, NOT is evaluated first, then AND, and finally OR. You can override this order with parentheses: Everything in parentheses is evaluated first. Under the default precedence rules, the condition *x* AND NOT *y* OR *z* is equivalent to (*x* AND (NOT *y*)) OR *z*. It's wise to use parentheses, rather than rely on the default evaluation order, to make the evaluation order clear.

If I want to list history and biography titles priced under $20, for example, **Listing 4.28** won't work. AND is evaluated before OR, so the query is evaluated as follows:

1. Find all the biography titles under $20.

2. Find all the history titles (regardless of price).

3. List both sets of titles in the result (**Figure 4.28**).

To fix this query, I'll add parentheses to force evaluation of OR first. **Listing 4.29** is evaluated as follows:

1. Find all the biography and history titles.

2. Of the titles found in step 1, keep the ones priced under $20.

3. List the subset of titles in the result (**Figure 4.29**).

Listing 4.28 The query won't work if I want to list history and biography titles under $20, because AND has higher precedence than OR. See Figure 4.28 for the result.

```
SELECT title_id, type, price
  FROM titles
  WHERE type = 'history'
    OR type = 'biography'
    AND price < 20;
```

```
title_id type        price
-------- ---------   -----

T01      history     21.99
T02      history     19.95
T06      biography   19.95
T12      biography   12.99
T13      history     29.99
```

Figure 4.28 Result of Listing 4.28. This result contains two history titles priced over $20, which is not what I wanted.

Listing 4.29 To fix Listing 4.28, I've added parentheses to force OR to be evaluated before AND. See Figure 4.29 for the result.

```
SELECT title_id, type, price
  FROM titles
  WHERE (type = 'history'
    OR type = 'biography')
    AND price < 20;
```

```
title_id type        price
-------- ---------   -----

T02      history     19.95
T06      biography   19.95
T12      biography   12.99
```

Figure 4.29 Result of Listing 4.29. Fixed.

Table 4.6

Equivalent Conditions	
THIS CONDITION	IS EQUIVALENT TO
NOT (*p* AND *q*)	(NOT *p*) OR (NOT *q*)
NOT (*p* OR *q*)	(NOT *p*) AND (NOT *q*)
NOT (NOT *p*)	*p*

✔ Tips

- The examples in this section show the AND, OR, and NOT operators used with comparison conditions, but these operators may be used with any type of condition.

- It's a common error to type:
  ```
  WHERE state = 'NY' OR 'CA'  --Illegal
  ```
  instead of:
  ```
  WHERE state = 'NY' OR state = 'CA'
  ```

- It's easy to translate a correctly phrased spoken-language statement into an incorrect SQL statement. If you say, "List the books priced under $10 and over $30," the *and* suggests the use of the AND operator:
  ```
  SELECT title_name, price
    FROM titles
    WHERE price<10 AND price>30; --Wrong
  ```
  This query returns no rows, however, because it's impossible for a book to be priced under $10 and over $30 simultaneously, as the AND logic commands. The logical meaning of OR finds books that meet any of the criteria, not all the criteria at the same time:
  ```
  WHERE price<10 OR price>30  --Correct
  ```

- **Table 4.6** demonstrates alternative ways of expressing the same condition. The first two equivalencies are called *DeMorgan's Laws* and the third is called *double negation.*

  Slightly off-topic: With a little algebra, you can repeatedly apply equivalency rules to push NOT operators inward in a condition until they apply to individual expressions only, as in this example:
  ```
  NOT ((p AND q) OR (NOT p AND r))
  = NOT (p AND q) AND NOT (NOT p AND r)
  = (NOT p OR NOT q) AND (p OR NOT r)
  ```

- **DBMS** In **MySQL**, False AND Unknown evaluates to Unknown, not False.

Matching Patterns with LIKE

The preceding examples retrieved rows based on the exact value of a column or columns. You can use LIKE to retrieve rows based on partial information. LIKE is useful if you don't know an exact value ("The author's last name is *Kel*-something") or you want to retrieve rows with similar values ("Which authors live in the San Francisco Bay area?"). The LIKE condition's important characteristics are:

◆ LIKE works with only character strings, not numbers or datetimes.

◆ LIKE uses a pattern that values are matched against. A *pattern* is a quoted string that contains the literal characters to match and any combination of wildcards. *Wildcards* are special characters used to match parts of a value. **Table 4.7** lists the wildcard operators, and **Table 4.8** lists some example patterns.

◆ Matches may be case-insensitive or case-sensitive, depending on your DBMS; see the DBMS Tip in "Filtering Rows with WHERE" earlier in this chapter.

◆ You can negate a LIKE condition with NOT LIKE.

◆ You can combine LIKE conditions and other conditions with AND and OR.

◆ In the simplest case in which a pattern contains no wildcards, LIKE works like an = comparison (and NOT LIKE works like <>):

WHERE city LIKE 'New York'

is equivalent to:

WHERE city = 'New York'

Table 4.7

Wildcard Operators	
OPERATOR	MATCHES
%	A percent sign matches any string of zero or more characters
_	An underscore matches any one character

Table 4.8

Examples of % and _ Patterns	
PATTERN	MATCHES
'A%'	Matches a string value of length ≥ 1 that begins with *A*, including the single letter *A*. Matches 'A', 'Anonymous', and 'AC/DC'.
'%s'	Matches a string value of length ≥ 1 that ends with *s*, including the single letter *s*. A value with trailing blanks (after the *s*) won't match. Matches 's', 'Victoria Falls', and 'DBMSes'.
'%in%'	Matches a string value of length ≥ 2 that contains *in* anywhere. Matches 'in', 'inch', 'Pine', 'linchpin', and 'lynchpin'.
'____'	Matches any four-character string value. Matches 'ABCD', 'I am', and 'Jack'.
'Qua__'	Matches any five-character string value that begins with *Qua*. Matches 'Quack', 'Quaff', and 'Quake'.
'_re_'	Matches any four-character string value that has *re* as its second and third characters. Matches 'Tree', 'area', and 'fret'.
'_re%'	Matches a string value of length ≥ 3 that begins with any character and has *re* as its second and third characters. Matches 'Tree', 'area', 'fret', 'are', and 'fretful'.
'%re_'	Matches a string value of length ≥ 3 that has *re* as the second and third characters from its end, and ends with any character. Matches 'Tree', 'area', 'fret', 'red', and 'Blood red'.

Listing 4.30 List the authors whose last names begin with *Kel*. See Figure 4.30 for the result.

```
                    listing
SELECT au_fname, au_lname
  FROM authors
  WHERE au_lname LIKE 'Kel%';
```

```
au_fname  au_lname
--------- --------
Christian Kells
          Kellsey
```

Figure 4.30 Result of Listing 4.30.

Listing 4.31 List the authors whose last names have *ll* (el-el) as the third and fourth characters. See Figure 4.31 for the result.

```
                    listing
SELECT au_fname, au_lname
  FROM authors
  WHERE au_lname LIKE '__ll%';
```

```
au_fname  au_lname
--------- --------
Hallie    Hull
Klee      Hull
Christian Kells
          Kellsey
```

Figure 4.31 Result of Listing 4.31.

Listing 4.32 List the authors who live in the San Francisco Bay area. (Zip codes in that area begin with *94*.) See Figure 4.32 for the result.

```
                    listing
SELECT au_fname, au_lname, city, state, zip
  FROM authors
  WHERE zip LIKE '94___';
```

```
au_fname au_lname city          state zip
-------- -------- ------------- ----- -----
Hallie   Hull     San Francisco CA    94123
Klee     Hull     San Francisco CA    94123
         Kellsey  Palo Alto     CA    94305
```

Figure 4.32 Result of Listing 4.32.

To filter rows by matching a pattern:

◆ Type:

```
SELECT columns
  FROM table
  WHERE test_column [NOT] LIKE
        'pattern';
```

columns is one or more comma-separated column names, and *table* is the name of the table that contains *columns*.

In the search condition, *test_column* is the name of a column in *table* (*test_column* doesn't have to be listed in *columns*), and *pattern* is the pattern that's compared with the value in *test_column*. *pattern* is a string like one of the examples listed in Table 4.8. Specify NOT LIKE to retrieve rows with values that don't match *pattern* (**Listings 4.30** through **4.33, Figures 4.30** through **4.33**).

continues on next page

MATCHING PATTERNS WITH LIKE

You can search for values that contain the special wildcard characters. Use the ESCAPE keyword to specify an *escape character* that you can use to search for a percent sign or underscore as a literal character. Immediately precede a wildcard character with an escape character to strip the wildcard of its special meaning. If the escape character is !, for example, !% in a pattern searches values for a literal %. (Unescaped wildcards still have their special meaning.) The escape character can't be part of the value that you're trying to retrieve; if you're searching for '50% OFF!', choose an escape character other than !.

Table 4.9 shows some examples of escaped and unescaped patterns; the designated escape character is !.

To match a wildcard character:

◆ Type:

```
SELECT columns
  FROM table
  WHERE test_column [NOT] LIKE
        'pattern'
        ESCAPE 'escape_char';
```

The syntax is the same as the **SELECT** statement in "To filter rows by matching a pattern," except for the **ESCAPE** clause. *escape_char* is a single character. Any character in *pattern* that follows *escape_char* is interpreted literally; *escape_char* itself is not considered to be part of the search pattern (**Listing 4.34** and **Figure 4.34**).

Table 4.9

Escaped and Unescaped Patterns	
PATTERN	MATCHES
'100%'	Unescaped. Matches *100* followed by a string of zero or more characters.
'100!%'	Escaped. Matches '100%'.
'_op'	Unescaped. Matches 'top', 'hop', 'pop', and so on.
'!_op'	Escaped. Matches '_op'.

Listing 4.33 List the authors who live outside the 212, 415, and 303 area codes. This example shows three alternative patterns for excluding telephone numbers. You should favor the first alternative because single-character matches (_) are faster than multiple-character ones (%). See Figure 4.33 for the result.

```
SELECT au_fname, au_lname, phone
  FROM authors
  WHERE phone NOT LIKE '212-___-____'
    AND phone NOT LIKE '415-___-%'
    AND phone NOT LIKE '303-%';
```

```
au_fname  au_lname     phone
--------  -----------  ------------
Sarah     Buchman      718-496-7223
          Kellsey      650-836-7128
Paddy     O'Furniture  941-925-0752
```

Figure 4.33 Result of Listing 4.33.

Listing 4.34 List the titles that contain percent signs. Only the % that follows the escape character ! has its literal meaning; the other two percent signs still act as wildcards. See Figure 4.34 for the result.

```
SELECT title_name
  FROM titles
  WHERE title_name LIKE '%!%%' ESCAPE '!';
```

```
title_name
----------------------------------------
```

Figure 4.34 Result of Listing 4.34. An empty result! No title names contain a % character.

Table 4.10

Examples of [] and [^] Patterns

PATTERN	MATCHES
'[a-c]at'	Matches 'bat' and 'cat', but not 'fat'.
'[bcf]at'	Matches 'bat', 'cat', and 'fat' but not 'eat'.
'[^c]at'	Matches 'bat' and 'fat' but not 'cat'.
'se[^n]%'	Matches strings of length ≥2 that begin with *se* whose third character isn't *n*.

✔ Tips

■ *test_column* can be an expression.

■ The NOT that can precede LIKE is independent of the NOT that can precede *test_column* (see "The NOT operator" in the preceding section). This clause:

```
WHERE phone NOT LIKE '212-%'
```

is equivalent to this one:

```
WHERE NOT phone LIKE '212-%'
```

You even can write this silly double negation, which retrieves everyone with a 212 area code:

```
WHERE NOT phone NOT LIKE '212-%'
```

■ Wildcard searches are time-consuming—particularly if you use % at the start of a pattern. Don't use wildcards if another type of search will do.

■ **DBMS** **Microsoft Access** doesn't support the ESCAPE clause. Instead, surround a wildcard character with brackets to render it a literal character. To run Listing 4.34 in Access, replace the WHERE clause with:

```
WHERE title_name LIKE '%[%]%'
```

Some DBMSes, such as **Microsoft SQL Server**, support POSIX-style *regular expressions*. The [] wildcard matches any single character within a range or set, and the [^] wildcard matches any single character *not* within a range or set. **Table 4.10** lists some examples. Regular expression syntax varies by DBMS; search your DBMS documentation for *WHERE* or *LIKE*.

Some DBMSes allow you to use LIKE to search numeric and datetime columns.

Range Filtering with
BETWEEN

Use BETWEEN to determine whether a given value falls within a specified range. The BETWEEN condition's important characteristics are:

◆ BETWEEN works with character strings, numbers, and datetimes.

◆ The BETWEEN range contains a low value and a high value, separated by AND. The low value must be less than or equal to the high value.

◆ BETWEEN is a convenient, shorthand clause. You can replicate its behavior by using AND:

    WHERE test_column BETWEEN
           low_value AND high_value

is equivalent to:

    WHERE (test_column >= low_value)
      AND (test_column <= high_value)

◆ BETWEEN specifies an *inclusive range*, in which the high value and low value are included in the search. To specify an *exclusive range*, which excludes endpoints, use > and < comparisons instead of BETWEEN:

    WHERE (test_column > low_value)
      AND (test_column < high_value)

◆ String comparisons may be case-insensitive or case-sensitive, depending on your DBMS; see the DBMS Tip in "Filtering Rows with WHERE" earlier in this chapter.

◆ You can negate a BETWEEN condition with NOT BETWEEN.

◆ You can combine BETWEEN conditions and other conditions with AND and OR.

Listing 4.35 List the authors who live outside the zip range 20000–89999. See Figure 4.35 for the result.

```
                         listing
SELECT au_fname, au_lname, zip
  FROM authors
  WHERE zip NOT BETWEEN '20000' AND '89999';
```

```
au_fname   au_lname  zip

---------  --------  -----

Sarah      Buchman   10468

Hallie     Hull      94123

Klee       Hull      94123

Christian  Kells     10014

           Kellsey   94305
```

Figure 4.35 Result of Listing 4.35.

Listing 4.36 List the titles priced between $10 and $19.95, inclusive. See Figure 4.36 for the result.

```
                         listing
SELECT title_id, price
  FROM titles
  WHERE price BETWEEN 10 AND 19.95;
```

```
title_id price

-------- -----

T02      19.95

T04      12.99

T06      19.95

T08      10.00

T09      13.95

T12      12.99
```

Figure 4.36 Result of Listing 4.36.

Listing 4.37 List the titles published in 2000. See Figure 4.37 for the result.

```
                    listing
SELECT title_id, pubdate
  FROM titles
  WHERE pubdate BETWEEN DATE '2000-01-01'
                 AND     DATE '2000-12-31';
```

```
title_id pubdate
-------- ----------
T01      2000-08-01
T03      2000-09-01
T06      2000-07-31
T11      2000-11-30
T12      2000-08-31
```

Figure 4.37 Result of Listing 4.37.

Listing 4.38 List the titles priced between $10 and $19.95, exclusive. See Figure 4.38 for the result.

```
                    listing
SELECT title_id, price
  FROM titles
  WHERE (price > 10)
    AND (price < 19.95);
```

```
title_id price
-------- -----
T04      12.99
T09      13.95
T12      12.99
```

Figure 4.38 Result of Listing 4.38.

To filter rows by using a range:

◆ Type:

SELECT *columns*

　FROM *table*

　WHERE *test_column* [NOT] BETWEEN

　　　low_value AND *high_value*;

columns is one or more comma-separated column names, and *table* is the name of the table that contains *columns*.

In the search condition, *test_column* is the name of a column in *table* (*test_column* doesn't have to be listed in *columns*), and *low_value* and *high_value* specify the end-points of the range that is compared with the value in *test_column*. *low_value* must be less than or equal to *high_value*, and both values must be the same as or comparable to the data type of *test_column*. Specify NOT BETWEEN to match values that lie outside the range (**Listings 4.35** through **4.37, Figures 4.35** through **4.37**).

✔ Tips

■ *test_column* can be an expression.

■ The NOT that can precede BETWEEN is independent of the NOT that can precede *test_column;* see the Tips in "Matching Patterns with LIKE" earlier in this chapter.

■ **Listing 4.38** shows how to rewrite Listing 4.36 with an exclusive range, which doesn't include the $10 and $19.95 endpoints. See **Figure 4.38** for the result.

continues on next page

RANGE FILTERING WITH BETWEEN

- Specifying a character range requires some thought. Suppose that I want to search for last names that begin with the letter *F*. The following clause won't work because it will retrieve someone whose last name is the letter *G* (*is* the letter *G*, not *starts with* the letter *G*):

  ```
  WHERE last_name BETWEEN 'F' AND 'G'
  ```

  This next clause shows the correct way to specify the ending point (in most cases):

  ```
  WHERE last_name BETWEEN 'F' AND 'Fz'
  ```

- **DBMS** In **PostgreSQL**, convert the floating-point numbers in Listings 4.36 and 4.38 to `DECIMAL`; see "Converting Data Types with `CAST()`" in Chapter 5. To run Listings 4.36 and 4.38 in PostgreSQL, change the floating-point literals to:

  ```
  CAST(19.95 AS DECIMAL)
  ```

  In **Microsoft Access** date literals, omit the `DATE` keyword, and surround the literal with # characters instead of quotes. To run Listing 4.37 in Access, change the dates in the `WHERE` clause to `#2000-01-01#` and `#2000-12-31#`.

  In **Microsoft SQL Server** date literals, omit the `DATE` keyword. To run Listing 4.37 in SQL Server, change the dates in the `WHERE` clause to `'2000-01-01'` and `'2000-12-31'`.

  In some DBMSes, *low_value* may exceed *high_value;* search your DBMS documentation for *WHERE* or *BETWEEN*.

List Filtering with IN

Use IN to determine whether a given value matches any value in a specified list. The IN condition's important characteristics are:

◆ IN works with character strings, numbers, and datetimes.

◆ The IN list is a parenthesized listing of one or more comma-separated values. The list items needn't be in any particular order.

◆ IN is a convenient, shorthand clause. You can replicate its behavior by using OR:

```
WHERE test_column IN
      (value1, value2, value3)
```

is equivalent to:

```
WHERE (test_column = value1)
   OR (test_column = value2)
   OR (test_column = value3)
```

◆ String comparisons may be case-insensitive or case-sensitive, depending on your DBMS; see the DBMS Tip in "Filtering Rows with WHERE" earlier in this chapter.

◆ You can negate an IN condition with NOT IN.

◆ You can combine IN conditions and other conditions with AND and OR.

To filter rows by using a list:

◆ Type:

SELECT *columns*

  FROM *table*

  WHERE *test_column* [NOT] IN

      (*value1, value2,...*);

columns is one or more comma-separated column names, and *table* is the name of the table that contains *columns*.

In the search condition, *test_column* is the name of a column in *table* (*test_column* doesn't have to be listed in *columns*), and *value1, value2,...* are one or more comma-separated values that are compared with the value in *test_column*. The list values can be listed in any order and must be the same as or comparable to the data type of *test_column*. Specify NOT IN to match values that aren't in the list (**Listings 4.39** through **4.41, Figures 4.39** through **4.41**).

✔ Tips

■ *test_column* can be an expression.

■ The NOT that can precede IN is independent of the NOT that can precede *test_column;* see the Tips in "Matching Patterns with LIKE" earlier in this chapter.

■ If your list contains a large number of values, your code will be easier to read if you use one IN condition instead of many OR conditions. (Also, one IN usually runs faster than multiple ORs.)

■ A compound condition's order of evaluation is easier to read and manage if you use IN instead of multiple ORs; see "Combining and Negating Conditions with AND, OR, and NOT" earlier in this chapter.

Listing 4.39 List the authors who don't live in New York State, New Jersey, or California. See Figure 4.39 for the result.

```
SELECT au_fname, au_lname, state
  FROM authors
  WHERE state NOT IN ('NY', 'NJ', 'CA');
```

```
au_fname au_lname      state
-------- -----------   -----
Wendy    Heydemark     CO
Paddy    O'Furniture   FL
```

Figure 4.39 Result of Listing 4.39.

Listing 4.40 List the titles for which advances of $0, $1,000, or $5,000 were paid. See Figure 4.40 for the result.

```
SELECT title_id, advance
  FROM royalties
  WHERE advance IN
        (0.00, 1000.00, 5000.00);
```

```
title_id advance
-------- -------
T02      1000.00
T08         0.00
T09         0.00
```

Figure 4.40 Result of Listing 4.40.

Listing 4.41 List the titles published on the first of the year 2000, 2001, or 2002. See Figure 4.41 for the result.

```
                        listing
SELECT title_id, pubdate
  FROM titles
  WHERE pubdate IN
          (DATE '2000-01-01',
           DATE '2001-01-01',
           DATE '2002-01-01');
```

```
title_id pubdate
-------- ----------
T05      2001-01-01
```

Figure 4.41 Result of Listing 4.41.

■ You also can use IN to determine whether a given value matches any value in a sub-query; see Chapter 8.

■ NOT IN is equivalent to combining tests for inequality with AND. This statement is equivalent to Listing 4.39:

```
SELECT au_fname, au_lname, state
  FROM authors
  WHERE state <> 'NY'
    AND state <> 'NJ'
    AND state <> 'CA';
```

■ **DBMS** In **PostgreSQL**, convert the floating-point number in Listing 4.40 to DECIMAL; see "Converting Data Types with CAST()" in Chapter 5. To run Listing 4.40 in PostgreSQL, change the WHERE clause to:

```
WHERE advance IN
        (CAST(   0.00 AS DECIMAL),
         CAST(1000.00 AS DECIMAL),
         CAST(5000.00 AS DECIMAL))
```

In **Microsoft Access** date literals, omit the DATE keyword, and surround the literal with # characters instead of quotes. To run Listing 4.41 in Access, change the WHERE clause to:

```
WHERE pubdate IN
        (#1/1/2000#,
         #1/1/2001#,
         #1/1/2002#)
```

In **Microsoft SQL Server** date literals, omit the DATE keyword. To run Listing 4.41 in SQL Server, change the WHERE clause to:

```
WHERE pubdate IN
        ('2000-01-01',
         '2001-01-01',
         '2002-01-01')
```

Testing for Nulls with IS NULL

Recall from "Nulls" in Chapter 3 that nulls represent missing or unknown values. This situation causes a problem: LIKE, BETWEEN, IN, and other WHERE clause options can't find nulls because unknown values don't satisfy specific conditions. Nulls match no value—not even other nulls.

In the table publishers, for example, note that publisher P03 has a null in the column state because that column doesn't apply to Germany (**Listing 4.42** and **Figure 4.42**). I can't use complementary comparisons to select the null, because null is neither California nor not-California; it's undefined (**Listings 4.43** and **4.44, Figures 4.43** and **4.44**).

To avert disaster, SQL provides IS NULL to determine whether a given value is null. The IS NULL condition's important characteristics are:

◆ IS NULL works for columns of any data type.

◆ You can negate an IS NULL condition with IS NOT NULL.

◆ You can combine IS NULL conditions and other conditions with AND and OR.

To retrieve rows with nulls or non-null values:

◆ Type:
SELECT *columns*

   FROM *table*

   WHERE *test_column* IS [NOT] NULL;
columns is one or more comma-separated column names, and *table* is the name of the table that contains *columns*.

Listing 4.42 List the locations of all the publishers. See Figure 4.42 for the result.

```
SELECT pub_id, city, state, country
  FROM publishers;
```

pub_id	city	state	country
P01	New York	NY	USA
P02	San Francisco	CA	USA
P03	Hamburg	NULL	Germany
P04	Berkeley	CA	USA

Figure 4.42 Result of Listing 4.42. The column state doesn't apply to the publisher located in Germany.

Listing 4.43 List the publishers located in California. See Figure 4.43 for the result.

```
SELECT pub_id, city, state, country
  FROM publishers
  WHERE state = 'CA';
```

pub_id	city	state	country
P02	San Francisco	CA	USA
P04	Berkeley	CA	USA

Figure 4.43 Result of Listing 4.43. This result doesn't include publisher P03.

Listing 4.44 List the publishers located outside California (the wrong way—see Listing 4.45 for the correct way). See Figure 4.44 for the result.

```
SELECT pub_id, city, state, country
  FROM publishers
  WHERE state <> 'CA';
```

```
pub_id city      state country
------ -------- ----- -------
P01    New York NY    USA
```

Figure 4.44 Result of Listing 4.44. This result doesn't include publisher P03 either. The conditions state = 'CA' and state <> 'CA' aren't complementary after all; nulls don't match any value and so can't be selected by using the types of conditions I've covered so far.

Listing 4.45 List the publishers located outside California (the correct way). See Figure 4.45 for the result.

```
                       listing
SELECT pub_id, city, state, country
  FROM publishers
  WHERE state <> 'CA'
    OR state IS NULL;
```

```
pub_id city      state country
------ -------- ----- -------
P01    New York NY    USA
P03    Hamburg  NULL  Germany
```

Figure 4.45 Result of Listing 4.45. Now publisher P03 is in the result.

Listing 4.46 List the biographies whose (past or future) publication dates are known. See Figure 4.46 for the result.

```
                       listing
SELECT title_id, type, pubdate
  FROM titles
  WHERE type = 'biography'
    AND pubdate IS NOT NULL;
```

```
title_id type      pubdate
-------- --------- ----------
T06      biography 2000-07-31
T07      biography 1999-10-01
T12      biography 2000-08-31
```

Figure 4.46 Result of Listing 4.46. Without the IS NOT NULL condition, this result would have included title T10.

In the search condition, *test_column* is the name of a column in *table*. (*test_column* doesn't have to be listed in *columns*.) Specify NOT NULL to match non-null values (**Listings 4.45** and **4.46**, **Figures 4.45** and **4.46**).

✔ Tips

- *test_column* can be an expression.

- The NOT that can precede NULL is independent of the NOT that can precede *test_column*; see the Tips in "Matching Patterns with LIKE" earlier in this chapter.

- Nulls cause rows to be excluded from results only if a column containing nulls is a test column in a WHERE condition. The following statement, for example, retrieves all the rows in the table publishers (refer to Figure 4.42) because the null in the column state isn't compared with anything:

  ```
  SELECT pub_id, city, state, country
    FROM publishers
    WHERE country <> 'Canada';
  ```

- It bears repeating that a null isn't the same as an empty string (''). In the table authors, for example, the column au_fname contains an empty string for author A06 (last name of Kellsey). The WHERE condition to find the first name is:

  ```
  WHERE au_fname = ''
  ```

  and not:

  ```
  WHERE au_fname IS NULL
  ```

  But see the warning about **Oracle** in the DBMS Tip in "Nulls" in Chapter 3.

- To forbid nulls in a column, see "Forbidding Nulls with NOT NULL" in Chapter 10.

TESTING FOR NULLS WITH IS NULL

OPERATORS AND FUNCTIONS

Operators and functions permit you to calculate results derived from column data, system-determined values, and constant expressions. You can perform:

◆ Arithmetic operations—Cut everyone's salary by 10 percent.

◆ String operations—Concatenate personal information into a mailing address.

◆ Datetime operations—Compute the time interval between two dates.

◆ System operations—Find out what time your DBMS thinks it is.

An *operator* is a symbol or keyword indicating an operation that acts on one or more elements. The elements, called *operands,* are SQL expressions. Recall from the "SQL Syntax" Tips in Chapter 3 that an expression is any legal combination of symbols and tokens that evaluates to a single value (or null). In `price * 2`, for example, `*` is the operator, and `price` and `2` are its operands.

A *function* is a built-in, named routine that performs a specialized task. Most functions take parenthesized *arguments,* which are values you pass to the function that the function then uses to perform its task. Arguments can be column names, constants, nested functions, or more-complex expressions. In `UPPER(au_lname)`, for example, `UPPER` is the function name, and `au_lname` is the argument.

Creating Derived Columns

You can use operators and functions to create derived columns. A *derived column* is the result of a calculation and is created with a SELECT-clause expression that is something other than a simple reference to a column. Derived columns don't become permanent columns in a table; they're for display purposes only.

The values in a derived column often are computed from values in existing columns, but you also can create a derived column by using a constant expression (such as a string, number, or date) or system value (such as the system time). **Listing 5.1** shows a SELECT statement that yields a trivial arithmetic calculation; it needs no FROM clause because it doesn't retrieve data from a table. **Figure 5.1** shows the result.

Recall from "Tables, Columns, and Rows" in Chapter 2 that closure guarantees that every result is a table, so even this simple result is a table: a 1 x 1 table that contains the value 5. If I retrieve a column along with a constant, the constant appears in every row of the result (**Listing 5.2** and **Figure 5.2**).

Your DBMS will assign a default name to a derived column unless you name the column with an AS clause; see "Creating Column Aliases with AS" in Chapter 4 (**Listing 5.3** and **Figure 5.3**). In this book, I'll name derived columns explicitly.

Listing 5.1 A constant expression in a SELECT clause. No FROM clause is needed, because I'm not retrieving data from a table. See Figure 5.1 for the result.

```
SELECT 2 + 3;
```

```
2 + 3
-----
    5
```

Figure 5.1 Result of Listing 5.1. This result is a table with one row and one column.

Listing 5.2 Here, I've retrieved a column and a constant expression. See Figure 5.2 for the result.

```
SELECT au_id, 2 + 3
  FROM authors;
```

```
au_id 2 + 3
----- -----
A01       5
A02       5
A03       5
A04       5
A05       5
A06       5
A07       5
```

Figure 5.2 Result of Listing 5.2. The constant is repeated in each row.

Listing 5.3 List the book prices discounted by 10 percent. The derived columns would have DBMS-specific default names if the AS clauses were removed. See Figure 5.3 for the result.

```
                      listing
SELECT title_id,
       price,
       0.10 AS "Discount",
       price * (1 - 0.10) AS "New price"
  FROM titles;
```

title_id	price	Discount	New price
T01	21.99	0.10	19.79
T02	19.95	0.10	17.95
T03	39.95	0.10	35.96
T04	12.99	0.10	11.69
T05	6.95	0.10	6.25
T06	19.95	0.10	17.95
T07	23.95	0.10	21.56
T08	10.00	0.10	9.00
T09	13.95	0.10	12.56
T10	NULL	0.10	NULL
T11	7.99	0.10	7.19
T12	12.99	0.10	11.69
T13	29.99	0.10	26.99

Figure 5.3 Result of Listing 5.3.

✔ **Tip**

■ **DBMS** **Oracle** requires a FROM clause in a SELECT statement and so creates the dummy table DUAL automatically to be used for SELECTing a constant expression; search Oracle documentation for *DUAL table*. To run Listing 5.1 in Oracle, add a FROM clause that selects the constant value from DUAL:

```
SELECT 2 + 3
  FROM DUAL;
```

In **PostgreSQL**, convert the floating-point number in Listing 5.3 to DECIMAL; see "Converting Data Types with CAST()" later in this chapter. To run Listing 5.3 in PostgreSQL, change the New price calculation in the SELECT clause to:

```
price * CAST((1 - 0.10) AS DECIMAL)
```

CREATING DERIVED COLUMNS

Performing Arithmetic Operations

A *monadic arithmetic operator* performs a mathematical operation on a single numeric operand to produce a result. The - (negation) operator changes the sign of its operand, and the not very useful + (identity) operator leaves its operand unchanged. A *dyadic arithmetic operator* performs a mathematical operation on two numeric operands to produce a result. These operators include the usual ones: + (addition), - (subtraction), * (multiplication), and / (division). **Table 5.1** lists SQL's arithmetic operators (*expr* is a numeric expression).

To change the sign of a number:

♦ Type -*expr*

expr is a numeric expression (**Listing 5.4** and **Figure 5.4**).

To add, subtract, multiply, or divide:

♦ Type *expr1* + *expr2* to add, *expr1* - *expr2* to subtract, *expr1* * *expr2* to multiply, or *expr1* / *expr2* to divide.

expr1 and *expr2* are numeric expressions (**Listing 5.5** and **Figure 5.5**).

Listing 5.4 The negation operator changes the sign of a number. See Figure 5.4 for the result.

```
SELECT title_id,
       -advance AS "Advance"
  FROM royalties;
```

```
title_id Advance
-------- -----------

T01        -10000.00
T02         -1000.00
T03        -15000.00
T04        -20000.00
T05       -100000.00
T06        -20000.00
T07      -1000000.00
T08             0.00
T09             0.00
T10             NULL
T11       -100000.00
T12        -50000.00
T13        -20000.00
```

Figure 5.4 Result of Listing 5.4. Note that zero has no sign (is neither positive nor negative).

Listing 5.5 List the biographies by descending revenue (= price x sales). See Figure 5.5 for the result.

```
SELECT title_id,
       price * sales AS "Revenue"
  FROM titles
  WHERE type = 'biography'
  ORDER BY price * sales DESC;
```

```
title_id Revenue
-------- -----------

T07      35929790.00
T12       1299012.99
T06        225834.00
T10             NULL
```

Figure 5.5 Result of Listing 5.5.

Table 5.1

Arithmetic Operators

Operator	What it does
-*expr*	Reverses the sign of *expr*
+*expr*	Leaves *expr* unchanged
expr1 + *expr2*	Sums *expr1* and *expr2*
expr1 - *expr2*	Subtracts *expr2* from *expr1*
expr1 * *expr2*	Multiplies *expr1* and *expr2*
expr1 / *expr2*	Divides *expr1* by *expr2*

PERFORMING ARITHMETIC OPERATIONS

Listing 5.6 This query's first derived column divides pages by the integer constant 10, and the second derived column divides pages by the floating-point constant 10.0. In the result, you'd expect identical values to be in both derived columns. See Figures 5.6a and 5.6b for the results.

```
SELECT title_id,
       pages,
       pages/10   AS "pages/10",
       pages/10.0 AS "pages/10.0"
  FROM titles;
```

```
title_id pages pages/10 pages/10.0
-------- ----- -------- ----------
T01        107     10.7       10.7
T02         14      1.4        1.4
T03       1226    122.6      122.6
T04        510     51.0       51.0
T05        201     20.1       20.1
T06        473     47.3       47.3
T07        333     33.3       33.3
T08         86      8.6        8.6
T09         22      2.2        2.2
T10       NULL     NULL       NULL
T11        826     82.6       82.6
T12        507     50.7       50.7
T13        802     80.2       80.2
```

Figure 5.6a Result of Listing 5.6 for Microsoft Access, Oracle, and MySQL. Dividing two integers yields a floating-point number (as you'd expect).

```
title_id pages pages/10 pages/10.0
-------- ----- -------- ----------
T01        107       10       10.7
T02         14        1        1.4
T03       1226      122      122.6
T04        510       51       51.0
T05        201       20       20.1
T06        473       47       47.3
T07        333       33       33.3
T08         86        8        8.6
T09         22        2        2.2
T10       NULL     NULL       NULL
T11        826       82       82.6
T12        507       50       50.7
T13        802       80       80.2
```

Figure 5.6b Result of Listing 5.6 for Microsoft SQL Server and PostgreSQL. Dividing two integers yields an integer; the fractional part of the result is discarded (not as you'd expect).

✔ Tips

- The result of any arithmetic operation that involves a null is null.

- If you use multiple operators in a single expression, you may need to use parentheses to control the calculation order; see "Determining the Order of Evaluation" later in this chapter.

- Monadic operators also are called *unary operators,* and dyadic operators also are called *binary operators.*

- **DBMS** All DBMSes provide additional arithmetic operators and functions. These extensions include statistical, financial, scientific, trigonometric, and conversion functions; search your DBMS documentation for *operators* and *functions.*

  If you mix numeric data types in an arithmetic expression, your DBMS converts, or *coerces,* all the numbers to the data type of the expression's most complex operand and returns the result in this type. This conversion process is called *promotion.* If you add an INTEGER and a FLOAT, for example, the DBMS converts the integer to a float, adds the numbers, and returns the sum as a float. In some cases, you may need to convert a data type to another data type explicitly; see "Converting Data Types with CAST()" later in this chapter.

  Be careful when dividing integers by integers. If an integer dividend is divided by an integer divisor, the result may be an integer that has any fractional part of the result truncated. You might expect the two derived columns in **Listing 5.6** to contain the same values, because the column **pages** (an INTEGER) is divided by two equal constants: 10 (an integer) and 10.0 (a float). **Microsoft Access**, **Oracle**, and **MySQL** return the result you'd expect (**Figure 5.6a**), but **Microsoft SQL Server** and **PostgreSQL** truncate the result of an integer division (**Figure 5.6b**).

PERFORMING ARITHMETIC OPERATIONS

Determining the Order of Evaluation

Precedence determines the priority of various operators when more than one operator is used in an expression. Operators with higher precedence are evaluated first. Arithmetic operators (+, -, *, and so on) have higher precedence than comparison operators (<, = , >, and so on), which have higher precedence than logical operators (NOT, AND , OR), so this expression:

```
a or b * c >= d
```

is equivalent to this one:

```
a or ((b * c) >= d)
```

Operators with lower precedence are less *binding* than those with higher precedence. **Table 5.2** lists operator precedences from most to least binding. Operators in the same row have equal precedence.

Associativity determines the order of evaluation in an expression when adjacent operators have equal precedence. SQL uses left-to-right associativity.

You don't need to memorize all this information. You can use parentheses to override precedence and associativity rules (**Listing 5.7** and **Figure 5.7**).

✔ Tips

- **DBMS** Table 5.2 is incomplete; it omits some standard (such as IN and EXISTS) and nonstandard (DBMS-specific) operators. To determine the complete order of evaluation that your DBMS uses, search your DBMS documentation for *precedence*.

  To run Listing 5.7 in **Oracle**, add a FROM DUAL clause; see the DBMS Tip in "Creating Derived Columns" earlier in this chapter.

Table 5.2

Order of Evaluation (Highest to Lowest)

OPERATOR	DESCRIPTION
+, -	Monadic identity, monadic negation
*, /	Multiplication, division
+, -	Addition, subtraction
=, <>, <, <=, >, >=	Comparison operators
NOT	Logical NOT
AND	Logical AND
OR	Logical OR

Listing 5.7 The first and second columns show how to use parentheses to override precedence rules. The third and fourth columns show how to use parentheses to override associativity rules. See Figure 5.7 for the result.

```
                        listing
SELECT 2 + 3 * 4    AS "2+3*4",
       (2 + 3) * 4 AS "(2+3)*4",
       6 / 2 * 3   AS "6/2*3",
       6 / (2 * 3) AS "6/(2*3)";
```

```
2+3*4 (2+3)*4 6/2*3 6/(2*3)
----- ------- ----- -------
   14      20     9       1
```

Figure 5.7 Result of Listing 5.7.

- It's good programming style to add parentheses (even when they're unnecessary) to complex expressions to ensure your intended evaluation order and improve readability.

Concatenating Strings with ||

Use the || (concatenation) operator to combine, or *concatenate*, strings. The || operator's important characteristics are:

◆ The || operator is two consecutive vertical-bar, or pipe, characters.

◆ Concatenation doesn't add a space between strings.

◆ ||, a dyadic operator, combines two strings into a single string: `'formal'` || `'dehyde'` is `'formaldehyde'`.

◆ You can chain concatenations to combine multiple strings into a single string: `'a'` || `'b'` || `'c'` || `'d'` is `'abcd'`.

◆ Concatenation with an empty string (`''`) leaves a string unchanged: `'a'` || `''` || `'b'` is `'ab'`.

◆ The result of any concatenation operation that involves a null is null: `'a'` || NULL || `'b'` is NULL. (But see the Oracle exception in the DBMS Tip in this section.)

◆ To concatenate a string and a nonstring (such as a numeric or datetime value), you must convert the nonstring to a string if your DBMS doesn't convert it implicitly; see "Converting Data Types with CAST()" later in this chapter.

To concatenate strings:

◆ Type:

string1 || *string2*

string1 and *string2* are the strings to be combined. Each operand is a string expression such as a column that contains character strings, a string literal, or the result of an operation or function that returns a string (**Listings 5.8** through **5.11**, **Figures 5.8** through **5.11**).

✔ Tips

■ You can use || in SELECT, WHERE, and ORDER BY clauses or anywhere an expression is allowed.

■ You can concatenate bit strings: B'0100' || B'1011' is B'01001011'.

■ You can use the TRIM() function to remove unwanted spaces from concatenated strings. Recall from "Character String Types" in Chapter 3 that CHAR values are padded with trailing spaces, which sometimes creates long, ugly stretches of spaces in concatenated strings. TRIM() will remove the extra space in front of the name *Kellsey* in Figure 5.8, for example; see "Trimming Characters with TRIM()" later in this chapter.

Listing 5.8 List the authors' first and last names, concatenated into a single column and sorted by last name/first name. See Figure 5.8 for the result.

```
SELECT au_fname || ' ' || au_lname
        AS "Author name"
  FROM authors
  ORDER BY au_lname ASC, au_fname ASC;
```

```
Author name
-----------------
Sarah Buchman
Wendy Heydemark
Hallie Hull
Klee Hull
Christian Kells
 Kellsey
Paddy O'Furniture
```

Figure 5.8 Result of Listing 5.8.

Listing 5.9 List biography sales by descending sales order. Here, I need to convert sales from an integer to a string. See Figure 5.9 for the result.

```
SELECT CAST(sales AS CHAR(7))
        || ' copies sold of title '
        || title_id
          AS "Biography sales"
  FROM titles
  WHERE type = 'biography'
    AND sales IS NOT NULL
  ORDER BY sales DESC;
```

```
Biography sales
-------------------------------
1500200 copies sold of title T07
100001  copies sold of title T12
11320   copies sold of title T06
```

Figure 5.9 Result of Listing 5.9.

Listing 5.10 List biographies by descending publication date. Here, I need to convert *pubdate* from a datetime to a string. See Figure 5.10 for the result.

```
                      listing
SELECT 'Title '
      || title_id
      || ' published on '
      || CAST(pubdate AS CHAR(10))
         AS "Biography publication dates"
  FROM titles
  WHERE type = 'biography'
    AND pubdate IS NOT NULL
  ORDER BY pubdate DESC;
```

```
Biography publication dates
----------------------------------
Title T12 published on 2000-08-31
Title T06 published on 2000-07-31
Title T07 published on 1999-10-01
```

Figure 5.10 Result of Listing 5.10.

Listing 5.11 List all the authors named *Klee Hull*. See Figure 5.11 for the result.

```
                      listing
SELECT au_id, au_fname, au_lname
  FROM authors
  WHERE au_fname || ' ' || au_lname
        = 'Klee Hull';
```

```
au_id au_fname au_lname
----- -------- --------
A04   Klee     Hull
```

Figure 5.11 Result of Listing 5.11.

■ **DBMS** In **Microsoft Access**, the concatenation operator is +, and the conversion function is Format(*string*). To run Listings 5.8 through 5.11 in Access, change the concatenation and conversion expressions to (Listing 5.8):

au_fname + ' ' + au_lname

and (Listing 5.9):

Format(sales)

→ + ' copies sold of title '

→ + title_id

and (Listing 5.10):

'Title '

→ + title_id

→ + ' published on '

→ + Format(pubdate)

and (Listing 5.11):

au_fname + ' ' + au_lname

→ = 'Klee Hull';

In **Microsoft SQL Server**, the concatenation operator is +. To run Listings 5.8 through 5.11 in SQL Server, change the concatenation expressions to (Listing 5.8):

au_fname + ' ' + au_lname

and (Listing 5.9):

CAST(sales AS CHAR(7))

→ + ' copies sold of title '

→ + title_id

and (Listing 5.10):

'Title '

→ + title_id

→ + ' published on '

→ + CAST(pubdate AS CHAR(10))

and (Listing 5.11):

au_fname + ' ' + au_lname

→ = 'Klee Hull';

continues on next page

CONCATENATING STRINGS WITH ||

In **MySQL**, the concatenation function is CONCAT() (| | is legal, but it means logical OR in MySQL by default). CONCAT() takes any number of arguments and converts nonstrings to strings as necessary (so CAST() isn't needed). To run Listings 5.8 through 5.11 in MySQL, change the concatenation expressions to (Listing 5.8):

```
CONCAT(au_fname, ' ', au_lname)
```

and (Listing 5.9):

```
CONCAT(sales,
→ ' copies sold of title ',
→ title_id)
```

and (Listing 5.10):

```
CONCAT('Title ',
→ title_id,
→ ' published on ',
→ pubdate)
```

and (Listing 5.11):

```
CONCAT(au_fname, ' ', au_lname)
→ = 'Klee Hull';
```

Oracle treats an empty string as null: 'a' | | NULL | | 'b' returns 'ab'. See the DBMS Tip in "Nulls" in Chapter 3.

Oracle, **MySQL**, and **PostgreSQL** convert nonstrings to strings implicitly in concatenations; Listings 5.9 and 5.10 still will run on these DBMSes if you omit CAST(). Search your DBMS documentation for *concatenation* or *conversion*.

Listing 5.12 Split the publisher IDs into alphabetic and numeric parts. The alphabetic part of a publisher ID is the first character, and the remaining characters are the numeric part. See Figure 5.12 for the result.

```
                          listing
SELECT pub_id,
        SUBSTRING(pub_id FROM 1 FOR 1)
          AS "Alpha part",
        SUBSTRING(pub_id FROM 2)
          AS "Num part"
   FROM publishers;
```

```
pub_id Alpha part Num part
------ ---------- --------
P01    P          01
P02    P          02
P03    P          03
P04    P          04
```

Figure 5.12 Result of Listing 5.12.

Listing 5.13 List the first initial and last name of the authors from New York State and Colorado. See Figure 5.13 for the result.

```
                          listing
SELECT SUBSTRING(au_fname FROM 1 FOR 1)
        || '. '
        || au_lname
          AS "Author name",
        state
   FROM authors
   WHERE state IN ('NY', 'CO');
```

```
Author name   state
------------  -----
S. Buchman    NY
W. Heydemark  CO
C. Kells      NY
```

Figure 5.13 Result of Listing 5.13.

Extracting a Substring with SUBSTRING()

Use the SUBSTRING() function to extract part of a string. The SUBSTRING() function's important characteristics are:

◆ A *substring* is any sequence of contiguous characters from the source string, including an empty string or the entire source string itself.

◆ SUBSTRING() extracts part of a string starting at a specified position and continuing for a specified number of characters.

◆ A substring of an empty string is an empty string.

◆ If any argument is null, SUBSTRING() returns null. (But see the Oracle exception in the DBMS Tip in this section.)

To extract a substring:

◆ Type:
SUBSTRING(*string* FROM *start* [FOR *length*])
string is the source string from which to extract the substring. *string* is a string expression such as a column that contains character strings, a string literal, or the result of an operation or function that returns a string. *start* is an integer that specifies where the substring begins, and *length* is an integer that specifies the length of the substring (the number of characters to return). If FOR *length* is omitted, SUBSTRING() returns all the characters from *start* to the end of *string*. (**Listings 5.12** through **5.14**, **Figures 5.12** through **5.14**).

✔ Tips

- You can use SUBSTRING() in SELECT, WHERE, and ORDER BY clauses or anywhere an expression is allowed.

- You can extract substrings from bit strings: SUBSTRING(B'01001011', 5, 4) returns B'1011'.

- **DBMS** In **Microsoft Access**, the substring function is Mid(*string*, *start* [,*length*]). Use + to concatenate strings. To run Listings 5.12 through 5.14 in Access, change the substring expressions to (Listing 5.12):

  Mid(pub_id, 1, 1)

  Mid(pub_id, 2)

  and (Listing 5.13):

  Mid(au_fname, 1, 1) + '. ' + au_lname

  and (Listing 5.14):

  Mid(phone, 1, 3)='415'

  In **Microsoft SQL Server**, the substring function is SUBSTRING(*string*, *start*, *length*). Use + to concatenate strings. To run Listings 5.12 through 5.14 in SQL Server, change the substring expressions to (Listing 5.12):

  SUBSTRING(pub_id, 1, 1)

  SUBSTRING(pub_id, 2, LEN(pub_id) - 1)

  and (Listing 5.13):

  SUBSTRING(au_fname, 1, 1)

  → + '. '

  → + au_lname

  and (Listing 5.14):

  SUBSTRING(phone, 1, 3)='415'

  In **Oracle**, the substring function is SUBSTR(*string*, *start* [,*length*]). To run Listings 5.12 through 5.14 in Oracle, change the substring expressions to (Listing 5.12):

  SUBSTR(pub_id, 1, 1)

  SUBSTR(pub_id, 2)

Listing 5.14 List the authors whose area code is 415. See Figure 5.14 for the result.

```
SELECT au_fname, au_lname, phone
  FROM authors
  WHERE SUBSTRING(phone FROM 1 FOR 3)='415';
```

```
au_fname au_lname phone
-------- -------- ------------
Hallie   Hull     415-549-4278
Klee     Hull     415-549-4278
```

Figure 5.14 Result of Listing 5.14.

and (Listing 5.13):

SUBSTR(au_fname, 1, 1)

→ || '. '

→ || au_lname

and (Listing 5.14):

SUBSTR(phone, 1, 3)='415'

In **MySQL**, use CONCAT() to run Listing 5.13 (see "Concatenating Strings with ||" earlier in this chapter). Change the concatenation expression to:

CONCAT(

→ SUBSTRING(au_fname FROM 1 FOR 1),

→ '. ',

→ au_lname)

Oracle treats an empty string as null: SUBSTR(NULL, 1, 2) returns ''. See the DBMS Tip in "Nulls" in Chapter 3.

Your DBMS implicitly may constrain *start* and *length* arguments that are too small or too large to sensible values. The DBMS may replace a negative *start* with 1 or a too-long *length* with the length of *string*, for example. Search your DBMS documentation for *substring* or *substr*.

Changing String Case with UPPER() and LOWER()

Use the UPPER() function to return a string with lowercase letters converted to uppercase, and use the LOWER() function to return a string with uppercase letters converted to lowercase. The UPPER() and LOWER() functions' important characteristics are:

◆ A *cased* character is a letter that can be lowercase (*a*) or uppercase (*A*).

◆ Case changes affect only letters; digits, punctuation, and whitespace are left unchanged.

◆ UPPER() and LOWER() typically are used to format results and make case-insensitive comparisons in a WHERE clause.

◆ Case changes have no effect on empty strings.

◆ If its argument is null, UPPER() and LOWER() return null. (But see the Oracle exception in the DBMS Tip in this section.)

To convert a string to uppercase or lowercase:

◆ To convert a string to uppercase, type:

UPPER(*string*)

or

To convert a string to lowercase, type:

LOWER(*string*)

string is a string expression such as a column that contains character strings, a string literal, or the result of an operation or function that returns a string (**Listings 5.15** and **5.16**, **Figures 5.15** and **5.16**).

✔ Tips

■ You can use UPPER() and LOWER() in SELECT, WHERE, and ORDER BY clauses or anywhere an expression is allowed.

■ UPPER() and LOWER() don't affect character sets with no concept of case (such as Hebrew).

■ UPPER() and LOWER() affect accented characters: UPPER('ö') returns 'Ö', for example.

■ **DBMS** In **Microsoft Access**, the upper- and lowercase functions are UCase(*string*) and LCase(*string*). To run Listings 5.15 and 5.16 in Access, change the case expressions to (Listing 5.15):

LCase(au_fname)

UCase(au_lname)

and (Listing 5.16):

UCase(title_name) LIKE '%MO%'

Oracle treats an empty string as null: UPPER(NULL) and LOWER(NULL) return ''. See the DBMS Tip in "Nulls" in Chapter 3.

Your DBMS may provide other string-casing functions to, say, invert case or convert strings to sentence or title case. Search your DBMS documentation for *character functions*.

Listing 5.15 List the authors' first names in lowercase and last names in uppercase. See Figure 5.15 for the result.

```
SELECT LOWER(au_fname) AS "Lower",
       UPPER(au_lname) AS "Upper"
  FROM authors;
```

```
Lower       Upper

---------   -----------

sarah       BUCHMAN
wendy       HEYDEMARK
hallie      HULL
klee        HULL
christian   KELLS
            KELLSEY
paddy       O'FURNITURE
```

Figure 5.15 Result of Listing 5.15.

Listing 5.16 List the titles that contain the characters *MO*, regardless of case. All the letters in the LIKE pattern must be uppercase for this query to work. See Figure 5.16 for the result.

```
SELECT title_name
  FROM titles
  WHERE UPPER(title_name) LIKE '%MO%';
```

```
title_name

------------------------

200 Years of German Humor
I Blame My Mother
```

Figure 5.16 Result of Listing 5.16.

Listing 5.17 This query strips leading, trailing, and both leading and trailing spaces from the string ' AAA '. The < and > characters show the extent of the trimmed strings. See Figure 5.17 for the result.

```
SELECT
  '<' || '  AAA  ' || '>'
    AS "Untrimmed",
  '<' || TRIM(LEADING FROM '  AAA  ') || '>'
    AS "Leading",
  '<' || TRIM(TRAILING FROM '  AAA  ') || '>'
    AS "Trailing",
  '<' || TRIM('  AAA  ') || '>'
    AS "Both";
```

```
Untrimmed  Leading    Trailing   Both
---------  ---------  ---------  -----
<  AAA  >  <AAA  >    <  AAA>    <AAA>
```

Figure 5.17 Result of Listing 5.17.

Trimming Characters with TRIM()

Use the TRIM() function to remove unwanted characters from the ends of a string. The TRIM() function's important characteristics are:

- You can trim leading characters, trailing characters, or both. (You can't use TRIM() to remove characters from *within* a string.)

- By default, TRIM() trims spaces, but you can strip off any unwanted characters, such as leading and trailing zeros or asterisks.

- TRIM() typically is used to format results and make comparisons in a WHERE clause.

- TRIM() is useful for trimming trailing spaces from CHAR values. Recall from "Character String Types" in Chapter 3 that DBMSes automatically add spaces to the end of CHAR values to create strings of exactly a specified length.

- Trimming has no effect on empty strings.

- If any argument is null, TRIM() returns null. (But see the Oracle exception in the DBMS Tip in this section.)

To trim spaces from a string:

- Type:

  TRIM([[LEADING | TRAILING | BOTH] FROM] *string*)

  string is a string expression such as a column that contains character strings, a string literal, or the result of an operation or function that returns a string. Specify LEADING to remove leading spaces, TRAILING to remove trailing spaces, or BOTH to remove leading and trailing spaces. If this specifier is omitted, BOTH is assumed (**Listing 5.17** and **Figure 5.17**).

To trim characters from a string:

◆ Type:

TRIM([LEADING | TRAILING | BOTH] 'trim_chars' FROM string)

string is the string to trim, and *trim_chars* is one or more characters to remove from *string*. Each argument is a string expression such as a column that contains character strings, a string literal, or the result of an operation or function that returns a string. Specify LEADING to remove leading characters, TRAILING to remove trailing characters, or BOTH to remove leading and trailing characters. If this specifier is omitted, BOTH is assumed (**Listings 5.18** and **5.19**, **Figures 5.18** and **5.19**).

✔ Tips

■ You can use TRIM() in SELECT, WHERE, and ORDER BY clauses or anywhere an expression is allowed.

■ In Listing 5.8 earlier in this chapter, I concatenated authors' first and last names into a single column. The result, Figure 5.8, contains a single extra space before the author named Kellsey. This space—which separates the first and last names in the other rows—appears because Kellsey has no first name. You can use TRIM() to remove this leading space. Change the concatenation expression in Listing 5.8 to:

TRIM(au_fname || ' ' || au_lname)

Listing 5.18 Strip the leading *H* from the authors' last names that begin with *H*. See Figure 5.18 for the result.

```
listing
SELECT au_lname,
       TRIM(LEADING 'H' FROM au_lname)
         AS "Trimmed name"
  FROM authors;
```

```
au_lname     Trimmed name
----------   ------------
Buchman      Buchman
Heydemark    eydemark
Hull         ull
Hull         ull
Kells        Kells
Kellsey      Kellsey
O'Furniture  O'Furniture
```

Figure 5.18 Result of Listing 5.18.

Listing 5.19 List the three-character title IDs that start with *T1*, ignoring leading and trailing spaces. See Figure 5.19 for the result.

```
listing
SELECT title_id
  FROM titles
  WHERE TRIM(title_id) LIKE 'T1_';
```

```
title_id
--------
T10
T11
T12
T13
```

Figure 5.19 Result of Listing 5.19.

■ **DBMS** In **Microsoft Access**, the trimming functions are `LTrim(`*`string`*`)` to trim leading spaces, `RTrim(`*`string`*`)`to trailing spaces, and `Trim(`*`string`*`)` to trim both leading and trailing spaces. Use the `Replace(`*`string`*`,` *`find`*`,` *`replacement`* `[,`*`start`*`] [,`*`count`*`] [,`*`compare`*`])` function to trim nonspace characters (actually, to replace nonspaces with empty strings). Use + to concatenate strings. To run Listings 5.17 and 5.18 in Access, change the trim expressions to (Listing 5.17):

```
'<' + '  AAA  ' + '>'
'<' + LTRIM( '  AAA  ') + '>'
'<' + RTRIM( '  AAA  ') + '>'
'<' + TRIM('  AAA  ') + '>'
```

and (Listing 5.18):

```
Replace(au_lname, 'H', '', 1, 1)
```

In **Microsoft SQL Server**, the trimming functions are `LTRIM(`*`string`*`)` to leading spaces and `RTRIM(`*`string`*`)` to trim trailing spaces. Use + to concatenate strings. To run Listing 5.19 in SQL Server, change the trim expressions to:

```
'<' + '  AAA  ' + '>'
'<' + LTRIM('  AAA  ') + '>'
'<' + RTRIM('  AAA  ') + '>'
'<' + LTRIM(RTRIM('  AAA  ')) + '>'
```

SQL Server's `LTRIM()` and `RTRIM()` functions remove spaces but not arbitrary *trim_chars* characters. You can nest and combine SQL Server's `CHARINDEX()`, `LEN()`, `PATINDEX()`, `REPLACE()`, `STUFF()`, `SUBSTRING()`, and other character functions to replicate arbitrary-character

trimming. To run Listing 5.18 in SQL Server, change the trim expression to:

```
REPLACE(
→ SUBSTRING(au_lname, 1, 1),'H','')
→ + SUBSTRING(au_lname, 2,
→ LEN(au_lname))
```

To run Listing 5.19 in SQL Server, change the trim expression to:

```
LTRIM(RTRIM(title_id)) LIKE 'T1_'
```

In **Oracle**, add a `FROM DUAL` clause to run Listing 5.17; see the DBMS Tip in "Creating Derived Columns" earlier in this chapter. Oracle forbids multiple characters in *trim_chars*.

In **MySQL**, use `CONCAT()` to run Listing 5.17 (see "Concatenating Strings with ||" earlier in this chapter). Change the concatenation expressions to:

```
CONCAT('<','  AAA  ','>')
CONCAT('<',
→ TRIM(LEADING FROM '  AAA  '),
→ '>')
CONCAT('<',
→ TRIM(TRAILING FROM '  AAA  '),
→ '>')
CONCAT('<',TRIM('  AAA  '),'>')
```

Oracle treats an empty string as null: `TRIM(NULL)` returns `''`. See the DBMS Tip in "Nulls" in Chapter 3.

Your DBMS may provide padding functions to *add* spaces or other characters to strings. The **Oracle** padding functions are `LPAD()` and `RPAD()`, for example. Search your DBMS documentation for *character functions*.

TRIMMING CHARACTERS WITH TRIM()

Finding the Length of a String with CHARACTER_LENGTH()

Use the CHARACTER_LENGTH() function to return the number of characters in a string. The CHARACTER_LENGTH() function's important characteristics are:

◆ CHARACTER_LENGTH() returns an integer greater than or equal to zero.

◆ CHARACTER_LENGTH() counts characters, not bytes. A multibyte or Unicode character represents one character. (To count bytes, see the Tips in this section.)

◆ The length of an empty string is zero.

◆ If its argument is null, CHARACTER_LENGTH() returns null. (But see the Oracle exception in the DBMS Tip in this section.)

To find the length of a string:

◆ Type:

CHARACTER_LENGTH(*string*)

string is a string expression such as a column that contains character strings, a string literal, or the result of an operation or function that returns a string (**Listings 5.20** and **5.21**, **Figures 5.20** and **5.21**).

✔ Tips

■ You can use CHARACTER_LENGTH() in SELECT, WHERE, and ORDER BY clauses or anywhere an expression is allowed.

■ CHARACTER_LENGTH and CHAR_LENGTH are synonyms.

Listing 5.20 List the lengths of the authors' first names. See Figure 5.20 for the result.

```
SELECT au_fname,
       CHARACTER_LENGTH(au_fname) AS "Len"
  FROM authors;
```

```
au_fname   Len
---------  ---
Sarah        5
Wendy        5
Hallie       6
Klee         4
Christian    9
             0
Paddy        5
```

Figure 5.20 Result of Listing 5.20.

Listing 5.21 List the books whose titles contain fewer than 30 characters, sorted by ascending title length. See Figure 5.21 for the result.

```
SELECT title_name,
       CHARACTER_LENGTH(title_name) AS "Len"
  FROM titles
  WHERE CHARACTER_LENGTH(title_name) < 30
  ORDER BY CHARACTER_LENGTH(title_name) ASC;
```

title_name	Len
1977!	5
Kiss My Boo-Boo	15
How About Never?	16
I Blame My Mother	17
Exchange of Platitudes	22
200 Years of German Humor	25
Spontaneous, Not Annoying	25
But I Did It Unconsciously	26
Not Without My Faberge Egg	26
Just Wait Until After School	28
Ask Your System Administrator	29

Figure 5.21 Result of Listing 5.21.

- SQL also defines the `BIT_LENGTH()` and `OCTET_LENGTH()` functions. `BIT_LENGTH(expr)` returns the number of bits in an expression; `BIT_LENGTH(B'01001011')` returns 8. `OCTET_LENGTH(expr)` returns the number of bytes in an expression; `OCTET_LENGTH(B'01001011')` returns 1, and `OCTET_LENGTH('ABC')` returns 3. Octet length equals bit-length/8 (rounded up to the nearest integer, if necessary). See the DBMS Tip in this section for information about DBMS bit- and byte-length functions.

- **DBMS** In **Microsoft Access** and **Microsoft SQL Server**, the string-length function is `LEN(string)`. To run Listings 5.20 and 5.21 in Access and SQL Server, change the length expressions to (Listing 5.20):

  `LEN(au_fname)`

  and (Listing 5.21):

  `LEN(title_name)`

  In **Oracle**, the string-length function is `LENGTH(string)`. To run Listings 5.20 and 5.21 in Oracle, change the length expressions to (Listing 5.20):

  `LENGTH(au_fname)`

  and (Listing 5.21):

  `LENGTH(title_name)`

  Bit- and byte-count functions vary by DBMS. **Microsoft Access** has `Len()`. **Microsoft SQL Server** has `DATALENGTH()`. **Oracle** has `LENGTHB()`. **MySQL** has `BIT_COUNT()` and `OCTET_LENGTH()`. **PostgreSQL** has `OCTET_LENGTH()`.

  Oracle treats an empty string as null: `LENGTH(NULL)` returns `''`. Figure 5.20 will show 1 (not 0) in the next-to-last row because the author's first name is `' '` (a space) in the Oracle database. See the DBMS Tip in "Nulls" in Chapter 3.

USING CHARACTER_LENGTH()

Finding Substrings with POSITION()

Use the POSITION() function to locate a particular substring within a given string. The POSITION() function's important characteristics are:

◆ POSITION() returns an integer (≥ 0) that indicates the starting position of a substring's first occurrence within a string.

◆ If the string doesn't contain the substring, POSITION() returns zero.

◆ String comparisons may be case-insensitive or case-sensitive, depending on your DBMS; see the DBMS Tip in "Filtering Rows with WHERE" in Chapter 4.

◆ The position of any substring within an empty string is zero.

◆ If any argument is null, POSITION() returns null. (But see the Oracle exception in the DBMS Tip in this section.)

To find a substring:

◆ Type:

POSITION(*substring* IN *string*)

substring is the string to search for, and *string* is the string to search. Each argument is a string expression such as a column that contains character strings, a string literal, or the result of an operation or function that returns a string. POSITION() returns the lowest (integer) position in *string* in which *substring* occurs, or zero if *substring* isn't found (**Listings 5.22** and **5.23**, **Figures 5.22** and **5.23**).

Listing 5.22 List the position of the substring *e* in the authors' first names and the position of the substring *ma* in the authors' last names. See Figure 5.22 for the result.

```
SELECT
    au_fname,
    POSITION('e' IN au_fname) AS "Pos e",
    au_lname,
    POSITION('ma' IN au_lname) AS "Pos ma"
FROM authors;
```

au_fname	Pos e	au_lname	Pos ma
Sarah	0	Buchman	5
Wendy	2	Heydemark	6
Hallie	6	Hull	0
Klee	3	Hull	0
Christian	0	Kells	0
	0	Kellsey	0
Paddy	0	O'Furniture	0

Figure 5.22 Result of Listing 5.22.

Listing 5.23 List the books whose titles contain the letter *u* somewhere within the first 10 characters, sorted by descending position of the *u*. See Figure 5.23 for the result.

```
                     listing
SELECT title_name,
       POSITION('u' IN title_name) AS "Pos"
  FROM titles
  WHERE POSITION('u' IN title_name)
        BETWEEN 1 AND 10
  ORDER BY POSITION('u' IN title_name) DESC;
```

```
title_name                     Pos
---------------------------    ---
Not Without My Faberge Egg      10
Spontaneous, Not Annoying       10
How About Never?                 8
Ask Your System Administrator    7
But I Did It Unconsciously       2
Just Wait Until After School     2
```

Figure 5.23 Result of Listing 5.23.

✔ Tips

■ You can use POSITION() in SELECT, WHERE, and ORDER BY clauses or anywhere an expression is allowed.

■ **DBMS** In **Microsoft Access**, the position function is InStr(*start_position*, *string*, *substring*). To run Listings 5.22 and 5.23 in Access, change the position expressions to (Listing 5.22):

InStr(1, au_fname, 'e')

InStr(1, au_lname, 'ma')

and (Listing 5.23):

InStr(1, title_name, 'u')

In **Microsoft SQL Server**, the position function is CHARINDEX(*substring*, *string*). To run Listings 5.22 and 5.23 in SQL Server, change the position expressions to (Listing 5.22):

CHARINDEX('e', au_fname)

CHARINDEX('ma', au_lname)

and (Listing 5.23):

CHARINDEX('u', title_name)

In **Oracle**, the position function is INSTR(*string*, *substring*). To run Listings 5.22 and 5.23 in Oracle, change the position expressions to (Listing 5.22):

INSTR(au_fname, 'e')

INSTR(au_lname, 'ma')

and (Listing 5.23):

INSTR(title_name, 'u')

Oracle treats an empty string as null: POSITION(NULL) returns ''. See the DBMS Tip in "Nulls" in Chapter 3.

You can nest and combine substring and position functions to find substring occurrences beyond the first occurrence, but DBMSes provide enhanced position functions to do that. **Microsoft Access** has InStr(). **Microsoft SQL Server** has CHARINDEX(). **Oracle** has INSTR(). **MySQL** has LOCATE().

Performing Date and Time Operations

DBMS DBMS compliance with SQL-92 datetime/interval operators and functions is spotty, so this section is meant to be used as a reference. DBMSes have their own extended operators and functions that perform date and time arithmetic. For information about datetime and interval data types, see "Datetime Types" and "Interval Types" in Chapter 3.

Use the same operators introduced in "Performing Arithmetic Operations" earlier in this chapter to perform datetime and interval arithmetic. The common temporal operations are:

◆ Subtracting two dates to calculate the interval between them

◆ Adding or subtracting an interval and a date to calculate a future or past date

◆ Adding or subtracting two intervals to get a new interval

◆ Multiplying or dividing an interval by a number to get a new interval

Some operations are undefined; adding two dates makes no sense, for example. **Table 5.3** lists the valid SQL operators involving datetimes and intervals. The sidebar in this section explains why you can use the same operator to perform different operations.

Table 5.3

Datetime and Interval Operations	
OPERATION	RESULT
Datetime − Datetime	Interval
Datetime + Interval	Datetime
Datetime − Interval	Datetime
Interval + Datetime	Datetime
Interval + Interval	Interval
Interval − Interval	Interval
Interval * Numeric	Interval
Interval / Numeric	Interval
Numeric * Interval	Interval

Operator Overloading

Recall that the +, −, *, and / operators also are used for numeric operations and that Microsoft DBMSes use + for string concatenation as well. *Operator overloading* is the assignment of more than one function to a particular operator. The operation performed depends on the data types of the operands involved. Here, the +, −, *, and / operators behave differently with numbers than they do with datetimes and intervals (as well as strings, in Microsoft's case). Your DBMS may overload other operators and functions as well. *Function overloading* is the assignment of more than one behavior to a particular function, depending on the data types of the arguments involved. The MySQL CONCAT() function (see the DBMS Tip in "Concatenating Strings with ||" earlier in this chapter), for example, takes nonstring as well as string arguments. Nonstrings cause CONCAT() to perform additional conversions that it doesn't need to perform on strings.

Listing 5.24 List the books published in the first half of the years 2001 and 2002, sorted by descending publication date. See Figure 5.24 for the result.

```
                      listing
SELECT
    title_id,
    pubdate
FROM titles
WHERE EXTRACT(YEAR FROM pubdate)
         BETWEEN 2001 AND 2002
    AND EXTRACT(MONTH FROM pubdate)
         BETWEEN 1 AND 6
ORDER BY pubdate DESC;
```

```
title_id  pubdate
--------  ----------

T09       2002-05-31
T08       2001-06-01
T05       2001-01-01
```

Figure 5.24 Result of Listing 5.24.

■ You can use temporal operators and functions in SELECT, WHERE, and ORDER BY clauses or anywhere an expression is allowed.

■ If any operand or argument is null, an expression returns null.

The SQL EXTRACT() function isolates a single field of a datetime or interval and returns it as a number. EXTRACT() typically is used in comparison expressions or for formatting results.

To extract part of a datetime or interval:

◆ Type:

EXTRACT(*field* FROM *datetime_or_interval*)

field is the part of *datetime_or_interval* to return. *field* is YEAR, MONTH, DAY, HOUR, MINUTE, SECOND, TIMEZONE_HOUR, or TIMEZONE_MINUTE (refer to Table 3.11 in Chapter 3). *datetime_or_interval* is a datetime or interval expression such as a column that contains datetime or interval values, a datetime or interval literal, or the result of an operation or function that returns a datetime or interval. If *field* is SECOND, EXTRACT() returns a NUMERIC value; otherwise, it returns an INTEGER (**Listing 5.24** and **Figure 5.24**).

✔ Tips

■ **DBMS** In **Microsoft Access** and **Microsoft SQL Server**, the extraction function is DATEPART(*datepart*, *date*). To run Listing 5.24 in Access and SQL Server, change the extraction expressions to:

DATEPART("yyyy", pubdate)

DATEPART("m", pubdate)

Oracle, **MySQL**, and **PostgreSQL** accept different or additional values for the *field* argument of EXTRACT().

DBMSes also provide functions that add intervals to dates. Some examples: DATEDIFF() in **Microsoft Access** and **Microsoft SQL Server**, ADD_MONTHS() in **Oracle**, and DATE_ADD() and DATE_SUB() in **MySQL**.

Complex date and time arithmetic is so common in SQL programming that all DBMSes provide lots of temporal extensions. Search your DBMS documentation for *date and time functions* or *datetime functions*.

Getting the Current Date and Time

Use the CURRENT_DATE, CURRENT_TIME, and CURRENT_TIMESTAMP functions to get the current date and time from the system clock of the particular computer where the DBMS is running.

To get the current date and time:

◆ To get the current date, type:

CURRENT_DATE

or

To get the current time, type:

CURRENT_TIME

or

To get the current time stamp, type:

CURRENT_TIMESTAMP

CURRENT_DATE returns a DATE, CURRENT_TIME returns a TIME, and CURRENT_TIMESTAMP returns a TIMESTAMP; see "Datetime Types" in Chapter 3 (**Listings 5.25** and **5.26**, **Figures 5.25** and **5.26**).

Listing 5.25 Print the current date, time, and time stamp. See Figure 5.25 for the result.

```
SELECT
    CURRENT_DATE AS "Date",
    CURRENT_TIME AS "Time",
    CURRENT_TIMESTAMP AS "Timestamp";
```

```
Date        Time     Timestamp
----------  -------- -------------------
2002-03-10 10:09:24 2002-03-10 10:09:24
```

Figure 5.25 Result of Listing 5.25.

Listing 5.26 List the books whose publication date falls within 90 days of the current date or is unknown, sorted by descending publication date (refer to Figure 5.25 for the "current" date of this query). See Figure 5.26 for the result.

```
SELECT title_id, pubdate
  FROM titles
  WHERE pubdate
        BETWEEN CURRENT_TIMESTAMP
                - INTERVAL 90 DAY
            AND CURRENT_TIMESTAMP
                + INTERVAL 90 DAY
    OR pubdate IS NULL
  ORDER BY pubdate DESC;
```

```
title_id pubdate
-------- ----------
T09      2002-05-31
T10      NULL
```

Figure 5.26 Result of Listing 5.26.

✔ Tips

- You can use datetime functions in SELECT, WHERE, and ORDER BY clauses or anywhere an expression is allowed.

- CURRENT_TIME and CURRENT_TIMESTAMP each take a *precision* argument that specifies the decimal fractions of a second to be included in the time. CURRENT_TIME(6), for example, returns the current time with six digits of precision in the SECOND field. For information about precision, see "Datetime Types" in Chapter 3.

- **DBMS** In **Microsoft Access**, the datetime system functions are Date(), Time(), and Now(). To run Listing 5.25 in Access, change the datetime expressions to:

```
Date() AS "Date"
Time() AS "Time"
Now() AS "Timestamp"
```

To run Listing 5.26 in Access, change the BETWEEN clause to:

```
BETWEEN NOW() - 90
    AND NOW() + 90
```

In **Microsoft SQL Server**, the datetime system function is CURRENT_TIMESTAMP (or its synonym, GETDATE()). CURRENT_DATE and CURRENT_TIME aren't supported. To run Listing 5.25 in SQL Server, omit the CURRENT_DATE and CURRENT_TIME expressions. To run Listing 5.26 in SQL Server, change the BETWEEN clause to:

```
BETWEEN CURRENT_TIMESTAMP - 90
    AND CURRENT_TIMESTAMP + 90
```

In **Oracle**, the datetime system function is SYSDATE. Oracle 9i and later versions support CURRENT_DATE and CURRENT_TIMESTAMP (but not CURRENT_TIME). Listing 5.25 also requires a FROM DUAL clause; see the DBMS Tip in "Creating Derived Columns" earlier in this chapter. To run Listing 5.25 in Oracle, change the statement to:

```
SELECT SYSDATE AS "Date"
  FROM DUAL;
```

SYSDATE returns the system date and time but doesn't display the time unless formatted to do so with the function TO_CHAR():

```
SELECT TO_CHAR(SYSDATE,
 'YYYY-MM-DD HH24:MI:SS')
  FROM DUAL;
```

To run listing 5.26 in Oracle, change the BETWEEN clause to:

```
BETWEEN SYSDATE - 90
    AND SYSDATE + 90
```

To run listing 5.26 in **PostgreSQL**, change the WHERE clause to:

```
BETWEEN CURRENT_TIMESTAMP - 90
    AND CURRENT_TIMESTAMP + 90
```

For information about datetime system functions, search your DBMS documentation for *date and time functions* or *system functions*.

Getting User Information

Use the CURRENT_USER function to identify the active user within the database server.

To get the current user:

◆ Type:

CURRENT_USER

(**Listing 5.27** and **Figure 5.27**).

✔ Tips

■ You can use user functions in SELECT, WHERE, and ORDER BY clauses or anywhere an expression is allowed.

■ SQL also defines the SESSION_USER and SYSTEM_USER functions. The *current user* indicates the *authorization identifier* under whose privileges SQL statements currently are run. (The current user may have permission to run, say, only SELECT statements.) The *session user* indicates the authorization ID associated with the current session. The *system user* is the user as identified by the host operating system. The DBMS determines user values, and these three values may or may not be identical. For information about users, sessions, and privileges, search your DBMS documentation for *authorization, session, user,* or *role.*

■ **DBMS** To run Listing 5.27 in **Microsoft Access**, change the statement to:

SELECT CurrentUser AS "User";

To run Listing 5.27 in **Oracle**, change the statement to:

SELECT USER AS "User" FROM DUAL;

To run Listing 5.27 in **MySQL**, change the statement to:

SELECT USER() AS "User";

Listing 5.27 Print the current user. See Figure 5.27 for the result.

```
SELECT CURRENT_USER AS "User";
```

```
User
-------
cfehily
```

Figure 5.27 Result of Listing 5.27.

Microsoft SQL Server supports SESSION_USER and SYSTEM_USER. **MySQL** supports SESSION_USER() and SYSTEM_USER(). **Oracle's** SYS_CONTEXT() returns a session's user attributes. **PostgreSQL** supports SESSION_USER.

For information about user system functions, search your DBMS documentation for *user* or *system functions.*

Converting Data Types with CAST()

In many situations, your DBMS will convert, or *cast*, data types automatically. It may allow you to use numbers and dates in character expressions such as concatenation, for example, or it will promote numbers automatically in mixed arithmetic expressions (see the DBMS Tip in "Performing Arithmetic Operations" earlier in this chapter). Use the CAST() function to convert an expression of one data type to another data type when your DBMS doesn't perform the conversion automatically. For information about data types, see "Data Types" in Chapter 3.

The CAST() function's important characteristics are:

◆ *Implicit conversions* are those conversions that occur without specifying CAST(). *Explicit conversions* are those conversions that require CAST() to be specified. In some cases, conversion isn't allowed; you can't convert a FLOAT to a TIMESTAMP, for example.

◆ The data type being converted is the *source data type*, and the result data type is the *target data type*.

◆ You can convert any numeric or datetime data type to any character data type.

◆ You can convert any character data type to any other data type if the character string represents a valid literal value of the target data type. (DBMSes remove leading and trailing spaces when converting strings to numeric or datetime values.)

◆ Some numeric conversions, such as DECIMAL-to-INTEGER, round or truncate values. (Whether the value is rounded or truncated depends on the DBMS.)

continues on next page

◆ A VARCHAR-to-CHAR conversion may truncate strings.

◆ Some conversions may cause an error if the new data type doesn't have enough room to display the converted value. A FLOAT-to-SMALLINT conversion will fail if the floating-point number falls outside the range your DBMS permits for SMALLINT values (typically, –32,768 through 32,767).

◆ A NUMERIC-to-DECIMAL conversion may require an explicit cast to prevent the loss of precision or scale that might occur in an implicit conversion.

◆ In a DATE-to-TIMESTAMP conversion, the time part of the result will be 00:00:00 (midnight).

◆ If any argument is null, CAST() returns null. (But see the Oracle exception in the DBMS Tip in this section.)

To convert one data type to another:

◆ Type:

CAST(*expr* AS *data_type*)

expr is the expression to convert, and *data_type* is the target data type. *data_type* is one of the data types described in Tables 3.5, 3.6, 3.7, 3.9, 3.10, and 3.12 in Chapter 3 and may include *length, precision,* or *scale* arguments where applicable. Acceptable *data_type* values include CHAR(10), VARCHAR(25), NUMERIC(5,2), INTEGER, FLOAT, and DATE, for example. An error occurs if the data type or value of *expr* is incompatible with *data_type* (**Listings 5.28** and **5.29**, **Figures 5.28a**, **5.28b**, and **5.29**).

Listing 5.28 Convert the book prices from the DECIMAL data type to INTEGER and CHAR(8) data types. The < and > characters show the extent of the CHAR(8) strings. Your result will be either Figure 5.28a or 5.28b, depending on whether your DBMS truncates or rounds integers.

```
                         listing
SELECT
    price
      AS "price(DECIMAL)",
    CAST(price AS INTEGER)
      AS "price(INTEGER)",
    '<' || CAST(price AS CHAR(8)) || '>'
      AS "price(CHAR(8))"
FROM titles;
```

price(DECIMAL)	price(INTEGER)	price(CHAR(8))
21.99	21	<21.99 >
19.95	19	<19.95 >
39.95	39	<39.95 >
12.99	12	<12.99 >
6.95	6	<6.95 >
19.95	19	<19.95 >
23.95	23	<23.95 >
10.00	10	<10.00 >
13.95	13	<13.95 >
NULL	NULL	NULL
7.99	7	<7.99 >
12.99	12	<12.99 >
29.99	29	<29.99 >

Figure 5.28a Result of Listing 5.28. You'll get this result if your DBMS *truncates* decimal numbers to convert them to integers.

price(DECIMAL)	price(INTEGER)	price(CHAR(8))
21.99	22	<21.99 >
19.95	20	<19.95 >
39.95	40	<39.95 >
12.99	13	<12.99 >
6.95	7	<6.95 >
19.95	20	<19.95 >
23.95	24	<23.95 >
10.00	10	<10.00 >
13.95	14	<13.95 >
NULL	NULL	NULL
7.99	8	<7.99 >
12.99	13	<12.99 >
29.99	30	<29.99 >

Figure 5.28b Result of Listing 5.28. You'll get this result if your DBMS *rounds* decimal numbers to convert them to integers.

Listing 5.29 List history and biography book sales with a portion of the book title, sorted by descending sales. The CHAR(20) conversion shortens the title to make the result more readable. See Figure 5.29 for the result.

```
                      listing
SELECT
    CAST(sales AS CHAR(8))
    || ' copies sold of '
    || CAST(title_name AS CHAR(20))
      AS "History and biography sales"
  FROM titles
 WHERE sales IS NOT NULL
   AND type IN ('history', 'biography')
 ORDER BY sales DESC;
```

```
History and biography sales
-------------------------------------------
1500200  copies sold of I Blame My Mother
100001   copies sold of Spontaneous, Not Ann
11320    copies sold of How About Never?
10467    copies sold of What Are The Civilia
9566     copies sold of 200 Years of German
566      copies sold of 1977!
```

Figure 5.29 Result of Listing 5.29.

✔ Tips

- You can use CAST() in SELECT, WHERE, and ORDER BY clauses or anywhere an expression is allowed.

- *Widening conversions* are those conversions in which there is no possibility of data loss or incorrect results. SMALLINT-to-INTEGER, for example, is a widening conversion because the INTEGER data type can accommodate every possible value of the SMALLINT data type. The reverse operation, called a *narrowing conversion,* may cause data loss because some INTEGER values can't be represented by a SMALLINT. Widening conversions always are allowed, but narrowing conversions may cause your DBMS to issue a warning or error.

- **DBMS** **Microsoft Access** has a family of type-conversion functions rather than a single CAST() function: CStr(*expr*), CInt(*expr*), and CDec(*expr*) convert *expr* to a string, integer, and decimal number, for example. You can use Space(*number*) to add spaces to strings and Left(*string, length*) to truncate strings. Use + to concatenate strings. To run Listings 5.28 and 5.29 in Access, change the cast expressions to (Listing 5.28):

  CInt(price)

  '<' + CStr(price) + '>'

  and (Listing 5.29):

  CStr(sales)

  → + Space(8 - Len(CStr(sales)))

  → + ' copies sold of '

  → + Left(title_name, 20)

  continues on next page

CONVERTING DATA TYPES WITH CAST()

In **Microsoft SQL Server**, use + to concatenate strings (Listing 5.28):

```
'<' + CAST(price AS CHAR(8)) + '>'
```

and (Listing 5.29):

```
CAST(sales AS CHAR(8))
→ + ' copies sold of '
→ + CAST(title_name AS CHAR(20))
```

Oracle doesn't permit character conversions to CHAR(*length*) if *length* is shorter than the source string. Instead, use SUBSTR() to truncate strings; see the DBMS Tip in "Extracting a Substring with SUBSTRING()" earlier in this chapter. To run Listing 5.29 in Oracle, change the CAST() expression to:

```
CAST(sales AS CHAR(8))
→ || ' copies sold of '
→ || SUBSTR(title_name, 1, 20)
```

In **MySQL**, the CAST() function is limited to binary, datetime, and integer target data types. (Use SIGNED instead of INTEGER for *data_type*.) You can use RPAD(*string*, *length*, *padstring*) to add spaces to strings and LEFT(*string*, *length*) to truncate strings. Use CONCAT() to concatenate strings. To run Listings 5.28 and 5.29 in MySQL, change the CAST() expressions to (Listing 5.28):

```
CAST(price AS SIGNED)
CONCAT('<', RPAD(price, 8, ' '), '>')
```

and (Listing 5.29):

```
CONCAT(
→ RPAD(sales, 8, ' '),
→ ' copies sold of ',
→ LEFT(title_name, 20))
```

In **PostgreSQL**, use SUBSTRING() to truncate strings and use TO_CHAR(*number*, *format*) to convert a number to a string. To run Listings 5.28 and 5.29 in PostgreSQL, change the CAST() expressions to (Listing 5.28):

```
CAST(price AS INTEGER)
'<'|| TO_CHAR(price, '99.99 ') ||'>'
```

and (Listing 5.29):

```
SUBSTRING(title_name FROM 1 FOR 20)
```

Oracle treats an empty string as null: CAST(NULL AS CHAR) returns ''. See the DBMS Tip in "Nulls" in Chapter 3.

In **PostgreSQL**, to compare a value in a NUMERIC or DECIMAL column with a real (floating-point) number, you must convert the real number to NUMERIC or DECIMAL explicitly. The following statement, for example, fails in PostgreSQL, because the data type of the column price is DECIMAL(5,2):

```
SELECT price
  FROM titles
  WHERE price < 20.00;
```

This statement fixes the problem:

```
SELECT price
  FROM titles
  WHERE price < CAST(20.00 AS
    DECIMAL);
```

DBMSes have additional conversion and formatting functions. Some examples: CONVERT() in **Microsoft SQL Server** and **MySQL**; TO_CHAR(), TO_DATE(), TO_TIMESTAMP(), and TO_NUMBER() in **Oracle** and **PostgreSQL**. Search your DBMS documentation for *conversion*, *cast*, or *formatting functions*.

Evaluating Conditional Values with CASE

Before SQL-92, programmers complained that SQL's lack of conditional constructs forced them to rely on the host language to take certain actions based on a condition's truth value (true, false, or unknown). To attenuate this criticism, SQL-92 introduced the CASE expression and its shorthand equivalents, COALESCE() and NULLIF(). I'll cover CASE in this section and the other constructs in the remainder of this chapter.

The CASE expression's important characteristics are:

◆ If you've programmed before, you'll recognize that CASE provides SQL the equivalent of the if-then-else, case, or switch statements used in procedural languages, except that CASE is an expression, not a statement.

◆ CASE is used to evaluate several conditions and return a single value for the first true condition.

◆ CASE allows you to display an alternative value to the actual value in a column. CASE makes no changes to the underlying data.

◆ A common use of CASE is to replace codes or abbreviations with more-readable values. If the column marital_status contains the integer codes 1, 2, 3, or 4—meaning single, married, divorced, or widowed—your human readers will prefer to see explanatory text rather than cryptic codes. (Database designers prefer to use codes, because it's more efficient to store and manage abbreviated codes than explanatory text.)

continues on next page

- CASE has two formats: simple and searched. The *simple* CASE expression compares an expression to a set of simple expressions to determine the result. The *searched* CASE expression evaluates a set of logical (Boolean) expressions to determine the result.

- CASE returns an optional ELSE result as the default value if no test condition is true.

To use a simple CASE expression:

- Type:

    CASE *comparison_value*
        WHEN *value1* THEN *result1*
        WHEN *value2* THEN *result2*
        ...
        WHEN *valueN* THEN *resultN*
        [ELSE *default_result*]
    END

    value1, value2,..., valueN are expressions. *result1, result2,..., resultN* are expressions returned when the corresponding value matches the expression *comparison_value*. All expressions must be of the same type or must be implicitly convertible to the same type.

    Each value is compared to *comparison_value* in order. First, *value1* is compared. If it matches *comparison_value*, *result1* is returned; otherwise, *value2* is compared to *comparison_value*. If *value2* matches *comparison_value*, *result2* is returned, and so on. If no matches occur, *default_result* is returned. If ELSE *default_result* is omitted, ELSE NULL is assumed (**Listing 5.30** and **Figure 5.30**).

Listing 5.30 Raise the price of history books by 10 percent and psychology books by 20 percent, and leave the prices of other books unchanged. See Figure 5.30 for the result.

```
SELECT
    title_id,
    type,
    price,
    CASE type
        WHEN 'history'
            THEN price * 1.10
        WHEN 'psychology'
            THEN price * 1.20
        ELSE price
    END
        AS "New price"
FROM titles
ORDER BY type ASC, title_id ASC;
```

title_id	type	price	New price
T06	biography	19.95	19.95
T07	biography	23.95	23.95
T10	biography	NULL	NULL
T12	biography	12.99	12.99
T08	children	10.00	10.00
T09	children	13.95	13.95
T03	computer	39.95	39.95
T01	history	21.99	24.19
T02	history	19.95	21.95
T13	history	29.99	32.99
T04	psychology	12.99	15.59
T05	psychology	6.95	8.34
T11	psychology	7.99	9.59

Figure 5.30 Result of Listing 5.30.

Listing 5.31 List the books categorized by different sales ranges, sorted by ascending sales. See Figure 5.31 for the result.

```
                      listing
SELECT
    title_id,
    CASE
      WHEN sales IS NULL
        THEN 'Unknown'
      WHEN sales <= 1000
        THEN 'Not more than 1,000'
      WHEN sales <= 10000
        THEN 'Between 1,001 and 10,000'
      WHEN sales <= 100000
        THEN 'Between 10,001 and 100,000'
      WHEN sales <= 1000000
        THEN 'Between 100,001 and 1,000,000'
      ELSE 'Over 1,000,000'
    END
      AS "Sales category"
  FROM titles
  ORDER BY sales ASC;
```

```
title_id Sales category
-------- -----------------------------
T10      Unknown
T01      Not more than 1,000
T08      Between 1,001 and 10,000
T09      Between 1,001 and 10,000
T02      Between 1,001 and 10,000
T13      Between 10,001 and 100,000
T06      Between 10,001 and 100,000
T04      Between 10,001 and 100,000
T03      Between 10,001 and 100,000
T11      Between 10,001 and 100,000
T12      Between 100,001 and 1,000,000
T05      Between 100,001 and 1,000,000
T07      Over 1,000,000
```

Figure 5.31 Result of Listing 5.31.

To use a searched CASE expression:

◆ Type:
CASE

WHEN *condition1* THEN *result1*

WHEN *condition2* THEN *result2*

. . .

WHEN *conditionN* THEN *resultN*

[ELSE *default_result*]

END

condition1, condition2,..., conditionN are search conditions. (Search conditions comprise one or more logical expressions, with multiple expressions linked by AND or OR; see "Filtering Rows with WHERE" in Chapter 4.) *result1, result2,..., resultN* are expressions returned when the corresponding condition evaluates to true. All expressions must be of the same type or must be implicitly convertible to the same type.

Each condition is evaluated in order. First, *condition1* is evaluated. If it's true, *result1* is returned; otherwise, *condition2* is evaluated. If *condition2* is true, *result2* is returned, and so on. If no conditions are true, *default_result* is returned. If ELSE *default_result* is omitted, ELSE NULL is assumed (**Listing 5.31** and **Figure 5.31**).

✔ Tips

■ You can use CASE in SELECT, WHERE, and ORDER BY clauses or anywhere an expression is allowed.

■ When a result is returned, CASE may or may not evaluate the expressions in any remaining WHEN clauses, depending on the DBMS. For this reason, you should watch for undesirable side effects, such as the evaluation of any expression resulting in a division-by-zero error.

continues on next page

EVALUATING CONDITIONAL VALUES WITH CASE

■ This CASE expression can help you prevent division-by-zero errors:

```
CASE
  WHEN n <> 0 THEN expr/n
  ELSE 0
END
```

■ The simple CASE expression is just shorthand for this searched CASE expression:

```
CASE
  WHEN comparison_value = value1
    THEN result1
  WHEN comparison_value = value2
    THEN result2
  ...
  WHEN comparison_value = valueN
    THEN resultN
  [ELSE default_result]
END
```

■ **DBMS** **Microsoft Access** doesn't support CASE, use the Switch (*condition1*, *result1*, *condition2*, *result2*,...) function instead. To run Listings 5.30 and 5.31 in Access, change the CASE expressions to (Listing 5.30):

```
Switch(
→ type IS NULL, NULL,
→ type = 'history', price * 1.10,
→ type = 'psychology', price *1.20,
→ type IN ('biography',
→ 'children', 'computer'), price)
```

and (Listing 5.31):

```
Switch(
→ sales IS NULL,
→ 'Unknown',
→ sales <= 1000,
→ 'Not more than 1,000',
→ sales <= 10000,
→ 'Between 1,001 and 10,000',
→ sales <= 100000,
→ 'Between 10,001 and 100,000',
→ sales <= 1000000,
→ 'Between 100,001 and 1,000,000',
→ sales > 1000000,
→ 'Over 1,000,000')
```

Oracle 9i and later versions support simple CASE expressions and will run Listing 5.30 as is. In Oracle 8i, translate the simple CASE expression to a searched CASE expression or use the function DECODE(*comparison_value*, *value1*, *result1*, *value2*, *result2*,..., *default_result*). To run Listing 5.30 in Oracle 8i, change the CASE expression to:

```
DECODE(type,
→ NULL,         NULL,
→ 'history',    price * 1.10,
→ 'psychology', price * 1.20,
→ price)
```

In **PostgreSQL**, convert the floating-point numbers in Listing 5.30 to DECIMAL; see "Converting Data Types with CAST()" earlier in this chapter. To run Listing 5.30 in PostgreSQL, change new-price calculations in the CASE expression to:

```
price * CAST((1.10) AS DECIMAL)
price * CAST((1.20) AS DECIMAL)
```

Listing 5.32 List the publishers' locations. If the state is null, print *N/A*. See Figure 5.32 for the result.

```
                         listing
SELECT
    pub_id,
    city,
    COALESCE(state, 'N/A') AS "state",
    country
  FROM publishers;
```

```
pub_id  city          state  country
------  ------------  -----  -------
P01     New York      NY     USA
P02     San Francisco CA     USA
P03     Hamburg       N/A    Germany
P04     Berkeley      CA     USA
```

Figure 5.32 Result of Listing 5.32.

✔ Tips

■ You can use COALESCE() in SELECT, WHERE, and ORDER BY clauses or anywhere an expression is allowed.

■ **DBMS** **Microsoft Access** doesn't support COALESCE(); use the Switch() function instead. To run Listing 5.32 in Access, change the COALESCE() expression to:

Switch(state IS NOT NULL, state,
→ state IS NULL, 'N/A')

Oracle 9i and later versions support COALESCE() and will run Listing 5.32 as is. Oracle 8i doesn't support COALESCE(); use the NVL(*expr1*, *expr2*) function instead. (NVL() takes only two expressions; use CASE for three or more expressions.) To run Listing 5.32 in Oracle 8i, change the COALESCE() expression to:

NVL(state, 'N/A')

Checking for Nulls with COALESCE()

The COALESCE() function returns the first non-null expression among its arguments. COALESCE() often is used to display a specific value instead of a null in a result, which is helpful if your users find nulls confusing. COALESCE() is just shorthand for a common form of the searched CASE expression:

COALESCE(*expr1*, *expr2*, *expr3*)

is equivalent to:

```
CASE
   WHEN expr1 IS NOT NULL THEN expr1
   WHEN expr2 IS NOT NULL THEN expr2
   ELSE expr3
END
```

To return the first non-null value:

◆ Type:
COALESCE(*expr1*, *expr2*,...)

expr1, expr2,..., represent one or more comma-separated expressions. All expressions must be of the same type or must be implicitly convertible to the same type. Each expression is evaluated in order until one evaluates to non-null and is returned. If all the expressions are null, COALESCE() returns null (**Listing 5.32** and **Figure 5.32**).

Comparing Expressions with NULLIF()

The NULLIF() function compares two expressions and returns null if they are equal, or the first expression otherwise. NULLIF() typically is used to convert a user-defined missing, unknown, or inapplicable value to null.

Rather than use a null, some people prefer to represent a missing value with, say, the number −1 or the string 'N/A'. DBMSes have clear rules for operations that involve nulls, so it's sometimes desirable to convert user-defined missing values to nulls. If you want to calculate the average of the values in a column, for example, you'd get the wrong answer if you had −1 values intermingled with the real, nonmissing values. Instead you can use NULLIF() to convert the −1 values to nulls, which your DBMS will ignore during calculations.

NULLIF() is just shorthand for a common form of the searched CASE expression:

```
NULLIF(expr1, expr2)
```

is equivalent to:

```
CASE
  WHEN expr1 = expr2 THEN NULL
  ELSE expr1
END
```

Listing 5.33 In the table `titles`, the column `contract` contains zero if no book contract exists. This query changes the value zero to null. Nonzero values aren't affected. See Figure 5.33 for the result.

```
listing
SELECT
    title_id,
    contract,
    NULLIF(contract, 0) AS "Null contract"
  FROM titles;
```

```
title_id contract Null contract
-------- -------- -------------
T01         1            1
T02         1            1
T03         1            1
T04         1            1
T05         1            1
T06         1            1
T07         1            1
T08         1            1
T09         1            1
T10         0         NULL
T11         1            1
T12         1            1
T13         1            1
```

Figure 5.33 Result of Listing 5.33.

To return a null if two expressions are equivalent:

◆ Type:

`NULLIF(expr1, expr2)`

expr1 and *expr2* are expressions. `NULLIF()` compares *expr1* and *expr2*. If they are equal, the function returns null. If they're unequal, the function returns *expr1*. You can't specify the literal `NULL` for *expr1* (**Listing 5.33** and **Figure 5.33**).

✔ Tips

■ You can use `NULLIF()` in `SELECT`, `WHERE`, and `ORDER BY` clauses or anywhere an expression is allowed.

■ **DBMS** **Microsoft Access** doesn't support `NULLIF()`; use the expression `IIf(expr1 = expr2, NULL, expr1)` instead. To run Listing 5.33 in Access, change the `NULLIF()` expression to:

`IIf(contract = 0, NULL, contract)`

Oracle 9i and later versions support `NULLIF()` and will run Listing 5.33 as is. Oracle 8i doesn't support `NULLIF()`; use `CASE` instead. To run Listing 5.33 in Oracle 8i, change the `NULLIF()` expression to:

```
CASE
    WHEN contract = 0 THEN NULL
    ELSE contract
END
```

SUMMARIZING AND GROUPING DATA

The preceding chapter described *scalar functions,* which operate on individual row values. This chapter introduces SQL's *aggregate functions,* or *set functions,* which operate on a group of values to produce a single, summarizing value. You apply an aggregate to a set of rows, which may be:

◆ All the rows in a table

◆ Only those rows specified by a WHERE clause

◆ Those rows created by a GROUP BY clause

No matter how many rows the set contains, an aggregate function returns a single statistic: a sum, minimum, or average, for example.

In this chapter, I'll also cover the SELECT statement's GROUP BY clause, which groups rows, and HAVING clause, which filters groups.

Using Aggregate Functions

Table 6.1 lists SQL's standard aggregate functions. The important characteristics of the aggregate functions are:

◆ In Table 6.1, *expr* often is a column name, but it also can be a literal, function, or any combination of column names, literals, and functions coupled by operators.

◆ SUM() and AVG() work with only numeric data types. MIN() and MAX() work with characters, numeric, and datetime data types. COUNT(*expr*) and COUNT(*) work with all data types.

◆ All aggregate functions except COUNT(*) ignore nulls. (You can use COALESCE() in an aggregate function argument to substitute a value for a null; see "Checking for Nulls with COALESCE()" in Chapter 5.)

◆ COUNT(*expr*) and COUNT(*) never return null but return either a positive integer or zero. The other aggregate functions return null if the set contains no rows or contains rows with only nulls.

◆ Use the DISTINCT keyword to aggregate distinct values; see "Aggregating Distinct Values with DISTINCT" later in this chapter.

◆ Aggregate functions often are used with the GROUP BY clause; see "Grouping Rows with GROUP BY" later in this chapter.

◆ Use a WHERE clause to restrict the rows used in aggregate calculations; see "Filtering Rows with WHERE" in Chapter 4.

◆ Default column headings for aggregate expressions vary by DBMS; use AS to name the result column. See "Creating Column Aliases with AS" in Chapter 4.

Table 6.1

Aggregate Functions	
FUNCTION	RETURNS
MIN(*expr*)	Minimum value in *expr*
MAX(*expr*)	Maximum value in *expr*
SUM(*expr*)	Sum of the values in *expr*
AVG(*expr*)	Average (arithmetic mean) of the values in *expr*
COUNT(*expr*)	The number of non-null values in *expr*
COUNT(*)	The number of rows in a table or set

USING AGGREGATE FUNCTIONS

◆ An aggregate expression *can't* appear in a WHERE clause. If you want to find the title of the book with the highest sales, you *can't* use:

```
SELECT title_id          --Illegal
  FROM titles
  WHERE sales = MAX(sales);
```

◆ You *can't* mix nonaggregate (row-by-row) and aggregate expressions in a SELECT clause. A SELECT clause must contain either all nonaggregate expressions or all aggregate expressions. If you want to find the title of the book with the highest sales, you *can't* use:

```
SELECT title_id, MAX(sales)
  FROM titles;              --Illegal
```

The one exception to this rule is that you *can* mix nonaggregate and aggregate expressions for grouping columns (see "Grouping Rows with GROUP BY" later in this chapter):

```
SELECT type, SUM(sales)
  FROM titles
  GROUP BY type;           --Legal
```

◆ You *can* use more than one aggregate expression in a SELECT clause:

```
SELECT MIN(sales), MAX(sales)
  FROM titles;             --Legal
```

◆ You *can't* nest aggregate functions:

```
SELECT SUM(AVG(sales))
  FROM titles;             --Illegal
```

◆ You *can* use aggregate expressions in subqueries. This statement finds the title of the book with the highest sales:

```
SELECT title_id, price      --Legal
  FROM titles
  WHERE sales =
    (SELECT MAX(sales) FROM titles);
```

◆ You *can't* use subqueries (see Chapter 8) in aggregate expressions: AVG(SELECT price FROM titles) is illegal.

✔ Tip

■ **DBMS** **Oracle** lets you nest aggregate expressions in GROUP BY queries. The following example calculates the average of the maximum sales of all book types. Oracle evaluates the inner aggregate MAX(sales) for the grouping column type and then aggregates the results again:

```
SELECT AVG(MAX(sales))
  FROM titles
  GROUP BY type;    --Legal in Oracle
```

MySQL 4.0 and earlier versions don't support subqueries.

DBMSes provide additional aggregate functions to calculate other statistics, such as the standard deviation; search your DBMS documentation for *aggregate functions* or *group functions*.

Finding a Minimum with MIN()

Use the aggregate function MIN() to find the minimum of a set of values.

To find the minimum of a set of values:

◆ Type:

MIN(*expr*)

expr is a column name, literal, or expression. The result has the same data type as *expr*.

Listing 6.1 and **Figure 6.1** show some queries that involve MIN(). The first query returns the price of the lowest-priced book. The second query returns the earliest publication date. The third query returns the number of pages in the shortest history book.

✔ Tips

■ MIN() works with character, numeric, and datetime data types.

■ With character data columns, MIN() finds the value that is lowest in the sort sequence; see "Sorting Rows with ORDER BY" in Chapter 4.

■ DISTINCT isn't meaningful with MIN(); see "Aggregating Distinct Values with DISTINCT" later in this chapter.

■ **DBMS** String comparisons may be case-insensitive or case-sensitive, depending on your DBMS; see the DBMS Tip in "Filtering Rows with WHERE" in Chapter 4.

When comparing two VARCHAR strings for equality, your DBMS may right-pad the shorter string with spaces and compare the strings position by position. In this case, the strings 'Jack' and 'Jack ' are equal. Refer to your DBMS documentation (or experiment) to determine which string MIN() returns.

Listing 6.1 Some MIN() queries. See Figure 6.1 for the results.

```
                          listing
SELECT MIN(price) AS "Min price"
  FROM titles;


SELECT MIN(pubdate) AS "Earliest pubdate"
  FROM titles;


SELECT MIN(pages) AS "Min history pages"
  FROM titles
  WHERE type = 'history';
```

```
Min price
---------
     6.95


Earliest pubdate
----------------
1998-04-01


Min history pages
----------------
              14
```

Figure 6.1 Results of Listing 6.1.

Listing 6.2 Some MAX() queries. See Figure 6.2 for the results.

```
                    listing
SELECT MAX(au_lname) AS "Max last name"
   FROM authors;

SELECT
    MIN(price) AS "Min price",
    MAX(price) AS "Max price",
    MAX(price) - MIN(price) AS "Range"
  FROM titles;

SELECT MAX(price * sales)
          AS "Max history revenue"
   FROM titles
   WHERE type = 'history';
```

```
Max last name
-------------
O'Furniture

Min price Max price Range
--------- --------- -----
     6.95     39.95 33.00

Max history revenue
-------------------
          313905.33
```

Figure 6.2 Results of Listing 6.2.

Finding a Maximum with MAX()

Use the aggregate function MAX() to find the maximum of a set of values.

To find the maximum of a set of values:

◆ Type:

MAX(*expr*)

expr is a column name, literal, or expression. The result has the same data type as *expr*.

Listing 6.2 and **Figure 6.2** show some queries that involve MAX(). The first query returns the author's last name that is last alphabetically. The second query returns the prices of the cheapest and most expensive books, and the price range. The third query returns the highest revenue (= price × sales) among the history books.

✔ Tips

■ MAX() works with character, numeric, and datetime data types.

■ With character data columns, MAX() finds the value that is highest in the sort sequence; see "Sorting Rows with ORDER BY" in Chapter 4.

■ DISTINCT isn't meaningful with MAX(); see "Aggregating Distinct Values with DISTINCT" later in this chapter.

■ **DBMS** String comparisons may be case-insensitive or case-sensitive, depending on your DBMS; see the DBMS Tip in "Filtering Rows with WHERE" in Chapter 4.

When comparing two VARCHAR strings for equality, your DBMS may right-pad the shorter string with spaces and compare the strings position-by-position. In this case, the strings 'Jack' and 'Jack ' are equal. Refer to your DBMS documentation (or experiment) to determine which string MAX() returns.

Calculating a Sum with SUM()

Use the aggregate function SUM() to find the sum (total) of a set of values.

To calculate the sum of a set of values:

◆ Type:

SUM(*expr*)

expr is a column name, literal, or numeric expression. The result's data type is at least as precise as the most precise data type used in *expr*.

Listing 6.3 and **Figure 6.3** show some queries that involve SUM(). The first query returns the total advances paid to all authors. The second query returns the total sales of books published in 2000. The third query returns the total price, sales, and revenue (= price × sales) of all books. Note a mathematical chestnut in action here: "The sum of the products doesn't (necessarily) equal the product of the sums."

✔ Tips

■ SUM() works with only numeric data types.

■ The sum of no rows is null—not zero as you might expect.

■ **DBMS** In **Microsoft Access** date literals, omit the DATE keyword, and surround the literal with # characters instead of quotes. To run Listing 6.3 in Access, change the date literals in the second query to #2000-01-01# and #2000-12-31#.

In **Microsoft SQL Server** date literals, omit the DATE keyword. To run Listing 6.3 in SQL Server, change the date literals to '2000-01-01' and '2000-12-31'.

Listing 6.3 Some SUM() queries. See Figure 6.3 for the results.

```
                        listing
SELECT SUM(advance) AS "Total advances"
  FROM royalties;


SELECT SUM(sales)
         AS "Total book sales for 2000"
  FROM titles
  WHERE pubdate
    BETWEEN DATE '2000-01-01'
        AND DATE '2000-12-31';


SELECT
    SUM(price) AS "Total price",
    SUM(sales) AS "Total sales",
    SUM(price * sales) AS "Total revenue"
  FROM titles;
```

```
Total advances
--------------
    1336000.00


Total book sales for 2000
-------------------------
                   231677


Total price Total sales Total revenue
----------- ----------- -------------
    220.65      1975446    41428860.77
```

Figure 6.3 Results of Listing 6.3.

Listing 6.4 Some AVG() queries. See Figure 6.4 for the results.

```
                    listing
SELECT AVG(price * 2) AS "AVG(price * 2)"
  FROM titles;


SELECT AVG(sales) AS "AVG(sales)",
       SUM(sales) AS "SUM(sales)"
  FROM titles
  WHERE type = 'business';


SELECT title_id, sales
  FROM titles
  WHERE sales >
       (SELECT AVG(sales) FROM titles)
  ORDER BY sales DESC;
```

```
AVG(price * 2)
--------------
      36.775000


AVG(sales) SUM(sales)
---------- ----------
NULL       NULL


title_id sales
-------- -------
T07      1500200
T05       201440
```

Figure 6.4 Results of Listing 6.4.

Finding an Average with AVG()

Use the aggregate function **AVG()** to find the average, or arithmetic mean, of a set of values. The *arithmetic mean* is the sum of a set of quantities divided by the number of quantities in the set.

To calculate the average of a set of values:

◆ Type:

AVG(*expr*)

expr is a column name, literal, or numeric expression. The result's data type is at least as precise as the most precise data type used in *expr*.

Listing 6.4 and **Figure 6.4** shows some queries that involve **AVG()**. The first query returns the average price of all books if prices were doubled. The second query returns the average and total sales for business books; both calculations are null (not zero), because the table contains no business books. The third query uses a subquery (see Chapter 8) to list the books with above-average sales.

✔ Tips

■ AVG() works with only numeric data types.

■ The average of no rows is null—not zero, as you might expect.

■ If you've used, say, 0 or –1 instead of null to represent missing values, the inclusion of those numbers in AVG() calculations yields an incorrect result. Use NULLIF() to convert the missing-value numbers to nulls, so they'll be excluded from calculations; see "Comparing Expressions with NULLIF()" in Chapter 5.

■ **DBMS** **MySQL** 4.0 and earlier versions lack subquery support and won't run the third query in Listing 6.4.

Counting Rows with COUNT()

Use the aggregate function COUNT() to count the number of rows in a set of values. COUNT() has two forms:

◆ COUNT(*expr*) returns the number of rows in which *expr* is not null.

◆ COUNT(*) returns the count of all rows in a set, including nulls and duplicates.

To count non-null rows:

◆ Type:

COUNT(*expr*)

expr is a column name, literal, or expression. The result is an integer greater than or equal to zero.

To count all rows, including nulls:

◆ Type:

COUNT(*)

COUNT(*) returns an integer greater than or equal to zero.

Listing 6.5 and **Figure 6.5** show some queries that involve COUNT(*expr*) and COUNT(*). The three queries count rows in the table **titles** and are identical except for the WHERE clause. The row counts in the first query differ because the column **price** contains a null. In the second query, the row counts are identical because the WHERE clause eliminates the row with the null price before the count. The third query shows the row-count differences between the results of first two queries.

✔ Tips

■ COUNT(*expr*) and COUNT(*) work with all data types.

■ COUNT(*expr*) and COUNT(*) never return null.

■ DISTINCT isn't meaningful with COUNT(*); see "Aggregating Distinct Values with DISTINCT" later in this chapter.

Listing 6.5 Some COUNT() queries. See Figure 6.5 for the results.

```
SELECT
    COUNT(title_id) AS "COUNT(title_id)",
    COUNT(price) AS "COUNT(price)",
    COUNT(*) AS "COUNT(*)"
  FROM titles;

SELECT
    COUNT(title_id) AS "COUNT(title_id)",
    COUNT(price) AS "COUNT(price)",
    COUNT(*) AS "COUNT(*)"
  FROM titles
  WHERE price IS NOT NULL;

SELECT
    COUNT(title_id) AS "COUNT(title_id)",
    COUNT(price) AS "COUNT(price)",
    COUNT(*) AS "COUNT(*)"
  FROM titles
  WHERE price IS NULL;
```

```
COUNT(title_id) COUNT(price) COUNT(*)
--------------- ------------ --------
             13           12       13

COUNT(title_id) COUNT(price) COUNT(*)
--------------- ------------ --------
             12           12       12

COUNT(title_id) COUNT(price) COUNT(*)
--------------- ------------ --------
              1            0        1
```

Figure 6.5 Results of Listing 6.5.

Aggregating Distinct Values with DISTINCT

You can use DISTINCT to eliminate duplicate values in aggregate function calculations; see "Eliminating Duplicate Rows with DISTINCT" in Chapter 4. The general syntax of an aggregate function is:

agg_func([ALL | DISTINCT] *expr*)

agg_func is MIN, MAX, SUM, AVG, or COUNT. *expr* is a column name, literal, or expression. ALL applies the aggregate function to all values, and DISTINCT specifies that each unique value is considered. ALL is the default and rarely is seen in practice.

With SUM(), AVG(), and COUNT(*expr*), DISTINCT eliminates duplicate values before the sum, average, or count is calculated. DISTINCT isn't meaningful with MIN() and MAX(); you can use it, but it won't change the result. You can't use DISTINCT with COUNT(*).

To calculate the sum of a set of distinct values:

◆ Type:

SUM(DISTINCT *expr*)

expr is a column name, literal, or numeric expression. The result's data type is at least as precise as the most precise data type used in *expr*.

continues on next page

To calculate the average of a set of distinct values:

◆ Type:

AVG(DISTINCT *expr*)

expr is a column name, literal, or numeric expression. The result's data type is at least as precise as the most precise data type used in *expr*.

To count distinct non-null rows:

◆ Type:

COUNT(DISTINCT *expr*)

expr is a column name, literal, or expression. The result is an integer greater than or equal to zero.

The queries in **Listing 6.6** return the count, sum, and average of book prices. The non-DISTINCT and DISTINCT results in **Figure 6.6** differ because the DISTINCT results eliminate the duplicates of prices $12.99 and $19.95 from calculations.

✔ Tips

■ DISTINCT in a SELECT clause and DISTINCT in an aggregate function don't return the same result.

The three queries in **Listing 6.7** count the author IDs in the table title_authors. **Figure 6.7** shows the results. The first query counts all the author IDs in the table. The second query returns the same result as the first query because COUNT() already has done its work and returned a value in single row before DISTINCT is applied. In the third query, DISTINCT is applied to the author IDs before COUNT() starts counting.

Listing 6.6 Some DISTINCT aggregate queries. See Figure 6.6 for the results.

```
SELECT
    COUNT(*)      AS "COUNT(*)",
    COUNT(price)  AS "COUNT(price)",
    SUM(price)    AS "SUM(price)",
    AVG(price)    AS "AVG(price)"
  FROM titles;

SELECT
    COUNT(DISTINCT price)
      AS "COUNT(DISTINCT)",
    SUM(DISTINCT price)
      AS "SUM(DISTINCT)",
    AVG(DISTINCT price)
      AS "AVG(DISTINCT)"
  FROM titles;
```

COUNT(*)	COUNT(price)	SUM(price)	AVG(price)
13	12	220.65	18.3875

COUNT(DISTINCT)	SUM(DISTINCT)	AVG(DISTINCT)
10	187.71	18.7710

Figure 6.6 Results of Listing 6.6.

Listing 6.7 DISTINCT in a SELECT clause and DISTINCT in an aggregate function differ in meaning. See Figure 6.7 for the results.

```
                        listing
SELECT COUNT(au_id)
        AS "COUNT(au_id)"
  FROM title_authors;


SELECT DISTINCT COUNT(au_id)
        AS "DISTINCT COUNT(au_id)"
  FROM title_authors;


SELECT COUNT(DISTINCT au_id)
        AS "COUNT(DISTINCT au_id)"
  FROM title_authors;
```

```
COUNT(au_id)
------------
          17


DISTINCT COUNT(au_id)
--------------------
                  17


COUNT(DISTINCT au_id)
--------------------
                   6
```

Figure 6.7 Results of Listing 6.7.

■ Mixing non-DISTINCT and DISTINCT aggregates in the same SELECT clause can produce misleading results.

The four queries in **Listing 6.8** (following page) show the four combinations of non-DISTINCT and DISTINCT sums and counts. Of the four results in **Figure 6.8** (following page), only the first result (no DISTINCTs) and final result (all DISTINCTs) are consistent mathematically, which you can verify with AVG(price) and AVG(DISTINCT price). In the second and third queries (mixed non-DISTINCTs and DISTINCTs), you can't calculate a valid average by dividing the sum by the count.

■ **DBMS** **Microsoft Access** doesn't support DISTINCT aggregate functions. This statement, for example, is illegal in Access:

```
SELECT SUM(DISTINCT price)
  FROM titles;    --Illegal in Access
```

But you can replicate it with this subquery (see the Tips in "Using Subqueries as Column Expressions" in Chapter 8):

```
SELECT SUM(price)
  FROM (SELECT DISTINCT price
          FROM titles);
```

This Access workaround won't let you mix non-DISTINCT and DISTINCT aggregates, however, as in the second and third queries in Listing 6.8.

In **Microsoft SQL Server**, if you use DISTINCT, *expr* must be a column name only. It can't include an arithmetic expression:

```
SELECT COUNT(DISTINCT price * sales)
  FROM titles; --Illegal in SQL Server
```

MySQL supports COUNT(DISTINCT *expr*) but not SUM(DISTINCT *expr*) and AVG(DISTINCT *expr*). Listings 6.6 and 6.8 won't run in MySQL.

continues on next page

Listing 6.8 Mixing non-DISTINCT and DISTINCT aggregates in the same SELECT clause can produce misleading results. See Figure 6.8 for the results.

```listing
SELECT
    COUNT(price)
        AS "COUNT(price)",
    SUM(price)
        AS "SUM(price)"
  FROM titles;


SELECT
    COUNT(price)
        AS "COUNT(price)",
    SUM(DISTINCT price)
        AS "SUM(DISTINCT price)"
  FROM titles;


SELECT
    COUNT(DISTINCT price)
        AS "COUNT(DISTINCT price)",
    SUM(price)
        AS "SUM(price)"
  FROM titles;


SELECT
    COUNT(DISTINCT price)
        AS "COUNT(DISTINCT price)",
    SUM(DISTINCT price)
        AS "SUM(DISTINCT price)"
  FROM titles;
```

```
COUNT(price) SUM(price)
------------ ----------
          12     220.65


COUNT(price) SUM(DISTINCT price)
------------ -------------------
          12              187.71


COUNT(DISTINCT price) SUM(price)
--------------------- ----------
                   10     220.65


COUNT(DISTINCT price) SUM(DISTINCT price)
--------------------- -------------------
                   10              187.71
```

Figure 6.8 Results of Listing 6.8. The differences in the counts and sums indicate duplicate prices. Averages (sum/count) obtained from the second (187.71/12) or third query (220.65/10) are incorrect. The first (220.65/12) and fourth (187.71/10) queries produce consistent averages.

Listing 6.9 List the number of books each author wrote (or co-wrote). See Figure 6.9 for the result.

```
             listing
SELECT
    au_id,
    COUNT(*) AS "num_books"
  FROM title_authors
  GROUP BY au_id;
```

```
au_id num_books
----- ---------
A01          3
A02          4
A03          2
A04          4
A05          1
A06          3
```

Figure 6.9 Result of Listing 6.9.

Grouping Rows with
GROUP BY

To this point, I've used aggregate functions to summarize all the values in a column or just those values that matched a WHERE search condition. You can use the GROUP BY clause to divide a table into logical *groups* (categories) and calculate aggregate statistics for each group.

An example will clarify the concept. **Listing 6.9** uses GROUP BY to count the number of books that each author wrote (or co-wrote). In the SELECT clause, the column au_id identifies each author, and the derived column num_books counts each author's books. The GROUP BY clause causes num_books to be calculated for every unique au_id instead of only once for the entire table. **Figure 6.9** shows the result. In this example, au_id is called the *grouping column*.

The GROUP BY clause's important characteristics are:

◆ The GROUP BY clause comes after the WHERE clause and before the ORDER BY clause.

◆ Grouping columns can be column names or derived columns.

◆ Every nonaggregate column in the SELECT clause must appear in the GROUP BY clause. This statement is illegal because pub_id isn't in the GROUP BY clause:

```
SELECT type, pub_id, COUNT(*)
  FROM titles
  GROUP BY type;        --Illegal
```

Because the GROUP BY can return only one row for each value of type, there's no way to return multiple values of pub_id that are associated with any particular value of type.

continues on next page

◆ If the SELECT clause contains a complex nonaggregate expression (more than just a simple column name), the GROUP BY expression must match the SELECT expression exactly.

◆ Specify multiple grouping columns in the GROUP BY clause to nest groups. Data is summarized at the last specified group.

◆ If a grouping column contains a null, that row becomes a group in the result. If a grouping column contains more than one null, the nulls are put into a single group. A group that contains multiple nulls doesn't imply that the nulls equal one another.

◆ Use a WHERE clause in a query containing a GROUP BY clause to eliminate rows before grouping occurs.

◆ You can't use a column alias in the GROUP BY clause, though table aliases are allowed as qualifiers; see "Creating Table Aliases with AS" in Chapter 7.

◆ Without an ORDER BY clause, groups returned by GROUP BY aren't in any particular order. To sort the result of Listing 6.9 by the descending number of books, for example, add the clause ORDER BY "num_books" DESC.

To group rows:

◆ Type:

```
SELECT columns
    FROM table
    [WHERE search_condition]
    GROUP BY grouping_columns
    [HAVING search_condition]
    [ORDER BY sort_columns];
```

columns and *grouping_columns* are one or more comma-separated column names, and *table* is the name of the table that contains *columns* and *grouping_columns*. The nonaggregate columns that appear in *columns* also must appear in *grouping_columns*. The order of the column names in *grouping_columns* determines the grouping levels, from the highest to the lowest level of grouping.

The GROUP BY clause restricts the rows of the result; only one row appears for each distinct value in the grouping column or columns. Each row in the result contains summary data related to the specific value in its grouping columns.

If the statement includes a WHERE clause, the DBMS groups values after it applies *search_condition* to the rows in *table*. If the statement includes an ORDER BY clause, the columns in *sort_columns* must be drawn from those in *columns*. The WHERE and ORDER BY clauses are covered in "Filtering Rows with WHERE" and "Sorting Rows with ORDER BY" in Chapter 4. HAVING, which filters grouped rows, is covered in the next section.

Listing 6.10 and **Figure 6.10** show the difference between COUNT(*expr*) and COUNT(*) in a query that contains GROUP BY. The table publishers contains one null in the column state (for publisher P03 in Germany). Recall from "Counting Rows with COUNT()" earlier in this chapter that COUNT(*expr*) counts non-null values and COUNT(*) counts all values, including nulls. In the result, GROUP BY recognizes the null and creates a null group for it. COUNT(*) finds (and counts) the one null in the column state. But COUNT(state) contains a zero for the null group because

COUNT(state) finds only a null in the null group, which it excludes from the count—hence, the zero.

If a nonaggregate column contains nulls, using COUNT(*) rather than COUNT(expr) can produce misleading results. **Listing 6.11** and **Figure 6.11** show summary sales statistics for each type of book. The sales value for one of the biographies is null, so COUNT(sales)

and COUNT(*) differ by 1. The average calculation in the fifth column, SUM/COUNT(sales), is consistent mathematically, whereas the sixth-column average, SUM/COUNT(*), is not. I've verified the inconsistency with AVG(sales) in the final column. (Recall a similar situation in Listing 6.8 in "Aggregating Distinct Values with DISTINCT" earlier in this chapter.)

continues on next page

Listing 6.10 This query illustrates the difference between COUNT(expr) and COUNT(*) in a GROUP BY query. See Figure 6.10 for the result.

```
SELECT
    state,
    COUNT(state) AS "COUNT(state)",
    COUNT(*)    AS "COUNT(*)"
  FROM publishers
  GROUP BY state;
```

```
state COUNT(state) COUNT(*)
----- ------------ --------
NULL            0        1
CA              2        2
NY              1        1
```

Figure 6.10 Result of Listing 6.10.

Listing 6.11 For mathematically consistent results, use COUNT(expr), rather than COUNT(*), if expr contains nulls. See Figure 6.11 for the result.

```
SELECT
    type,
    SUM(sales)   AS "SUM(sales)",
    COUNT(sales) AS "COUNT(sales)",
    COUNT(*)     AS "COUNT(*)",
    SUM(sales)/COUNT(sales)
      AS "SUM/COUNT(sales)",
    SUM(sales)/COUNT(*)
      AS "SUM/COUNT(*)",
    AVG(sales)   AS "AVG(sales)"
  FROM titles
  GROUP BY type;
```

type	SUM(sales)	COUNT(sales)	COUNT(*)	SUM/COUNT(sales)	SUM/COUNT(*)	AVG(sales)
biography	1611521	3	4	537173.67	402880.25	537173.67
children	9095	2	2	4547.50	4547.50	4547.50
computer	25667	1	1	25667.00	25667.00	25667.00
history	20599	3	3	6866.33	6866.33	6866.33
psychology	308564	3	3	102854.67	102854.67	102854.67

Figure 6.11 Result of Listing 6.11.

Listing 6.12 and **Figure 6.12** show a simple GROUP BY query that calculates the total sales, average sales, and number of titles for each type of book. In **Listing 6.13** and **Figure 6.13**, I've added a WHERE clause to eliminate books priced under $13 before grouping. I've also added an ORDER BY clause to sort the result by descending total sales of each book type.

Listing 6.14 and **Figure 6.14** use multiple grouping columns to count the number of titles of each type that each publisher publishes.

In **Listing 6.15** and **Figure 6.15**, I revisit Listing 5.31 in "Evaluating Conditional Values with CASE" in Chapter 5. But instead of listing each book categorized by its sales range, I use GROUP BY to list the number of books in each sales range.

continues on page 152

Listing 6.12 This simple GROUP BY query calculates a few summary statistics for each type of book. See Figure 6.12 for the result.

```
SELECT
    type,
    SUM(sales)   AS "SUM(sales)",
    AVG(sales)   AS "AVG(sales)",
    COUNT(sales) AS "COUNT(sales)"
  FROM titles
  GROUP BY type;
```

TYPE	SUM(sales)	AVG(sales)	COUNT(sales)
biography	1611521	537173.67	3
children	9095	4547.50	2
computer	25667	25667.00	1
history	20599	6866.33	3
psychology	308564	102854.67	3

Figure 6.12 Result of Listing 6.12.

Listing 6.13 Here, I've added WHERE and ORDER BY clauses to Listing 6.12 to cull books priced under $13 and sort the result by descending total sales. See Figure 6.13 for the result.

```
SELECT
    type,
    SUM(sales)   AS "SUM(sales)",
    AVG(sales)   AS "AVG(sales)",
    COUNT(sales) AS "COUNT(sales)"
  FROM titles
  WHERE price >= 13
  GROUP BY type
  ORDER BY "SUM(sales)" DESC;
```

type	SUM(sales)	AVG(sales)	COUNT(sales)
biography	1511520	755760.00	2
computer	25667	25667.00	1
history	20599	6866.33	3
children	5000	5000.00	1

Figure 6.13 Result of Listing 6.13.

Listing 6.14 List the number of books of each type for each publisher, sorted by descending count within ascending publisher ID. See Figure 6.14 for the result.

```
SELECT
    pub_id,
    type,
    COUNT(*) AS "COUNT(*)"
  FROM titles
  GROUP BY pub_id, type
  ORDER BY pub_id ASC, "COUNT(*)" DESC;
```

pub_id	type	COUNT(*)
P01	biography	3
P01	history	1
P02	computer	1
P03	history	2
P03	biography	1
P04	psychology	3
P04	children	2

Figure 6.14 Result of Listing 6.14.

Listing 6.15 List the number of books in each calculated sales range, sorted by ascending sales. See Figure 6.15 for the result.

```
SELECT
    CASE
      WHEN sales IS NULL
        THEN 'Unknown'
      WHEN sales <= 1000
        THEN 'Not more than 1,000'
      WHEN sales <= 10000
        THEN 'Between 1,001 and 10,000'
      WHEN sales <= 100000
        THEN 'Between 10,001 and 100,000'
      WHEN sales <= 1000000
        THEN 'Between 100,001 and 1,000,000'
      ELSE 'Over 1,000,000'
    END
      AS "Sales category",
    COUNT(*) AS "Num titles"
  FROM titles
  GROUP BY
    CASE
      WHEN sales IS NULL
        THEN 'Unknown'
      WHEN sales <= 1000
        THEN 'Not more than 1,000'
      WHEN sales <= 10000
        THEN 'Between 1,001 and 10,000'
      WHEN sales <= 100000
        THEN 'Between 10,001 and 100,000'
      WHEN sales <= 1000000
        THEN 'Between 100,001 and 1,000,000'
      ELSE 'Over 1,000,000'
    END
  ORDER BY MIN(sales) ASC;
```

Sales category	Num titles
Unknown	1
Not more than 1,000	1
Between 1,001 and 10,000	3
Between 10,001 and 100,000	5
Between 100,001 and 1,000,000	2
Over 1,000,000	1

Figure 6.15 Result of Listing 6.15.

GROUPING ROWS WITH GROUP BY

✔ Tips

- Use the WHERE clause to exclude rows that you don't want grouped, and use the HAVING clause to filter rows after they have been grouped. For information about HAVING, see the next section.

- If used without an aggregate function, GROUP BY acts like DISTINCT (**Listing 6.16** and **Figure 6.16**). For information about DISTINCT, see "Eliminating Duplicate Rows with DISTINCT" in Chapter 4.

- You can use GROUP BY to look for patterns in your data. In **Listing 6.17** and **Figure 6.17**, I'm looking for a relationship between price categories and average sales.

- Don't rely on GROUP BY to sort your result. I recommend that you include ORDER BY whenever you use GROUP BY (even though I've omitted ORDER BY in some examples). In some DBMSes, a GROUP BY implies an ORDER BY.

- The multiple values returned by an aggregate function in a GROUP BY query are called *vector aggregates*. In a query that lacks a GROUP BY clause, the single value returned by an aggregate function is a *scalar aggregate*.

- **DBMS** In **Microsoft Access**, use the Switch() function instead of the CASE expression in Listing 6.15. See the DBMS Tip in "Evaluating Conditional Values with CASE" in Chapter 5.

  MySQL doesn't allow CASE in a GROUP BY clause. Listing 6.15 won't run in MySQL.

  Some DBMSes, such as **MySQL** and **PostgreSQL**, permit column aliases in the GROUP BY clause.

Listing 6.16 Both of these queries return the same result. See Figure 6.16 for the result.

```
                  listing
SELECT type
  FROM titles
  GROUP BY type;

SELECT DISTINCT type
  FROM titles;
```

```
type
----------
biography
children
computer
history
psychology
```

Figure 6.16 Either statement in Listing 6.16 returns this result.

Listing 6.17 List the average sales for each price, sorted by ascending price. See Figure 6.17 for the result.

```
                  listing
SELECT price, AVG(sales) AS "AVG(sales)"
  FROM titles
  WHERE price IS NOT NULL
  GROUP BY price
  ORDER BY price ASC;
```

```
price    AVG(sales)
-------  ----------
  6.95    201440.0
  7.99     94123.0
 10.00      4095.0
 12.99     56501.0
 13.95      5000.0
 19.95     10443.0
 21.99       566.0
 23.95   1500200.0
 29.99     10467.0
 39.95     25667.0
```

Figure 6.17 Result of Listing 6.17. Ignoring the statistical outlier at $23.95, a weak inverse relationship between price and sales is apparent.

Filtering Groups
with HAVING

The HAVING clause sets conditions on the GROUP BY clause similar to the way that WHERE interacts with SELECT. The HAVING clause's important characteristics are:

◆ The HAVING clause comes after the GROUP BY clause and before the ORDER BY clause.

◆ Just as WHERE limits the number of rows displayed by SELECT, HAVING limits the number of groups displayed by GROUP BY.

◆ The WHERE search condition is applied *before* grouping occurs, and the HAVING search condition is applied *after*.

◆ HAVING syntax is similar to the WHERE syntax, except that HAVING can contain aggregate functions.

◆ A HAVING clause can reference any of the items that appear in the SELECT list.

The sequence in which the WHERE, GROUP BY, and HAVING clauses are applied is:

1. The WHERE clause filters the rows that result from the operations specified in the FROM and JOIN clauses.

2. The GROUP BY clause groups the output of the WHERE clause.

3. The HAVING clause filters rows from the grouped result.

To filter groups:

◆ Following the GROUP BY clause, type:

HAVING *search_condition*

search_condition is a search condition used to filter groups. *search_condition* can contain aggregate functions but otherwise is identical to the WHERE search condition, described in "Filtering Rows with WHERE" and subsequent sections in Chapter 4. You may combine and negate multiple HAVING conditions with the logical operators AND, OR, and NOT.

The HAVING search condition is applied to the rows in the output produced by grouping. Only the groups that meet the search condition appear in the result. You can apply a HAVING clause only to columns that appear in the GROUP BY clause or in an aggregate function.

In **Listing 6.18** and **Figure 6.18**, I revisit Listing 6.9 earlier in this chapter, but instead of listing the number of books that each author wrote (or co-wrote), I use HAVING to list only the authors who have written three or more books.

In **Listing 6.19** and **Figure 6.19**, the HAVING condition also is an aggregate expression in the SELECT clause. This query still works if you remove the AVG() expression from the SELECT list (**Listing 6.20** and **Figure 6.20**).

Listing 6.18 List the number of books written (or co-written) by each author who has written three or more books. See Figure 6.18 for the result.

```
SELECT
    au_id,
    COUNT(*) AS "num_books"
  FROM title_authors
  GROUP BY au_id
  HAVING COUNT(*) >= 3;
```

```
au_id num_books
----- ---------
A01         3
A02         4
A04         4
A06         3
```

Figure 6.18 Result of Listing 6.18.

Listing 6.19 List the number of titles and average revenue for the types with average revenue over $1 million. See Figure 6.19 for the result.

```
SELECT
    type,
    COUNT(price) AS "COUNT(price)",
    AVG(price * sales) AS "AVG revenue"
  FROM titles
  GROUP BY type
  HAVING AVG(price * sales) > 1000000;
```

```
type        COUNT(price) AVG revenue
----------  ------------ -----------
biography              3 12484879.00
computer               1  1025396.65
```

Figure 6.19 Result of Listing 6.19.

Listing 6.20 Listing 6.19 still works without AVG(price * sales) in the SELECT list. See Figure 6.20 for the result.

```
SELECT
    type,
    COUNT(price) AS "COUNT(price)"
  FROM titles
  GROUP BY type
  HAVING AVG(price * sales) > 1000000;
```

```
type          COUNT(price)
----------    ------------
biography               3
computer                1
```

Figure 6.20 Result of Listing 6.20.

Listing 6.21 List the number of books of each type for each publisher, for publishers with more than one title of a type. See Figure 6.21 for the result.

```
SELECT
    pub_id,
    type,
    COUNT(*) AS "COUNT(*)"
  FROM titles
  GROUP BY pub_id, type
  HAVING COUNT(*) > 1
  ORDER BY pub_id ASC, "COUNT(*)" DESC;
```

```
pub_id type          COUNT(*)
------ ----------    --------
P01    biography            3
P03    history              2
P04    psychology           3
P04    children             2
```

Figure 6.21 Result of Listing 6.21.

In **Listing 6.21** and **Figure 6.21**, multiple grouping columns count the number of titles of each type that each publisher publishes. The HAVING condition removes groups in which the publisher has one or fewer titles of a particular type. This query retrieves a subset of the result of Listing 6.14 earlier in this chapter.

In **Listing 6.22** and **Figure 6.22**, the WHERE clause first removes all rows except for books from publishers P03 and P04. Then the GROUP BY clause groups the output of the WHERE clause by type. Finally, the HAVING clause filters rows from the grouped result.

continues on next page

Listing 6.22 For books from publishers P03 and P04, list the total sales and average price by type, for types with more than $10,000 total sales and less than $20 average price. See Figure 6.22 for the result.

```
SELECT
    type,
    SUM(sales) AS "SUM(sales)",
    AVG(price) AS "AVG(price)"
  FROM titles
  WHERE pub_id IN ('P03', 'P04')
  GROUP BY type
  HAVING SUM(sales) > 10000
    AND AVG(price) < 20;
```

```
type          SUM(sales) AVG(price)
----------    ---------- ----------
psychology        308564       9.31
```

Figure 6.22 Result of Listing 6.22.

✔ Tip

- Generally, HAVING clauses should involve only aggregates. The only conditions that should be specified in the HAVING clause are those conditions that must be applied *after* the grouping operation has been performed. It's more efficient to specify conditions that can be applied before the grouping operation in the WHERE clause. The following statements, for example, are equivalent, but the first statement is preferable because it reduces the number of rows that have to be grouped:

```
SELECT pub_id, SUM(sales) --Faster
  FROM titles
  WHERE pub_id IN ('P03', 'P04')
  GROUP BY pub_id
  HAVING SUM(sales) > 10000;

SELECT pub_id, SUM(sales) --Slower
  FROM titles
  GROUP BY pub_id
  HAVING SUM(sales) > 10000
    AND pub_id IN ('P03', 'P04');
```

RETRIEVING DATA FROM MULTIPLE TABLES

7

All the queries so far have retrieved rows from a single table. Now I'll explain how to use joins to retrieve rows from multiple tables simultaneously. Recall from "Relationships" in Chapter 2 that a relationship is an association established between common columns in two tables. A *join* is a table operation that uses related columns to combine rows from two input tables into one result table. You can chain joins to retrieve rows from an unlimited number of tables.

Why do joins matter? The most important database information isn't so much stored in the rows of individual tables; rather, it is the implied relationships between sets of related rows. In the sample database, for example, the individual rows of the tables authors, publishers, and titles contain important values, of course, but it's the implied relationships that allow you to understand and analyze your data in its entirety: Who wrote what? Who published what? To whom do we send royalty checks? And so on.

In this chapter, I'll explain the different types of joins, why they're used, and how to create a SELECT statement that uses them.

Qualifying Column Names

Recall from "Tables, Columns, and Rows" in Chapter 2 that column names must be unique within a table but can be reused in other tables. The tables authors and publishers in the sample database both contain a column named city, for example.

To identify an otherwise-ambiguous column uniquely in a query that involves multiple tables, use its qualified name. A *qualified name* is a table name followed by a dot and the name of the column in the table. Because tables must have different names within a database, a qualified name uniquely identifies a single column within the entire database.

To qualify a column name:

◆ Type:

table.column

column is a column name, and *table* is name of the table that contains *column* (**Listing 7.1** and **Figure 7.1**).

✔ Tips

■ You can mix qualified and unqualified names within the same statement.

■ Qualified names aren't required if there's no chance of ambiguity—that is, if the query's tables have no common column names. To improve system performance, however, qualify *all* columns in a query with joins.

■ Another good reason to use qualified names is to ensure that changes to a table's structure don't introduce ambiguities. If someone adds the column zip to the table publishers, any unqualified references to zip in a query that selects from the tables authors (which already contains a column zip) and publishers would be ambiguous.

Listing 7.1 Here, the qualified names resolve otherwise-ambiguous references to the column city in the tables authors and publishers. See Figure 7.1 for the result.

```
SELECT au_id, authors.city
  FROM authors
  INNER JOIN publishers
    ON authors.city = publishers.city;
```

```
au_id city
----- -------------
A03   San Francisco
A04   San Francisco
A05   New York
```

Figure 7.1 Result of Listing 7.1. This result lists authors who live in the same city as some publisher; I'll explain the join syntax later in this chapter.

■ Qualification still works in queries that involve a single table. In fact, every column has an implicit qualifier. The following two statements are equivalent:

```
SELECT
    au_fname,
    au_lname
  FROM authors;
```

and

```
SELECT
    authors.au_fname,
    authors.au_lname
  FROM authors;
```

■ **DBMS** DBMSes may require still more qualifiers, depending on where your query resides in the DBMS hierarchy. You may need to qualify a table with a server name, database name, and owner name. Table aliases are useful in SQL statements that require lengthy qualified names; see the next section. A fully qualified table name in **Microsoft SQL Server**, for example, is:

server_name.db_name.owner_name.
→ *table_name*

Oracle 8i requires WHERE join syntax; see "Creating Joins with JOIN or WHERE" later in this chapter. Oracle 9i and later versions support JOIN syntax and will run Listing 7.1 as is. To run Listing 7.1 in Oracle 8i, type:

```
SELECT au_id, authors.city
  FROM authors, publishers
  WHERE authors.city =
    publishers.city;
```

QUALIFYING COLUMN NAMES

Creating Table Aliases with AS

You can create table aliases by using **AS** just as you can create column aliases; see "Creating Column Aliases with **AS**" in Chapter 4. Table aliases:

- Save typing

- Reduce statement clutter

- Exist only for the duration of a statement

- Don't appear in the result (unlike column aliases)

- Don't change the name of a table in the database

- Also are called *correlation names* in the context of subqueries (see Chapter 8)

To create a table alias:

- In a **FROM** clause or **JOIN** clause, type:

  table [AS] *alias*

  table is a table name, and *alias* is its alias name. *alias* is a single, unquoted word that contains only letters, digits, or underscores; don't use spaces, punctuation, or special characters. The **AS** keyword is optional (**Listing 7.2** and **Figure 7.2**).

Listing 7.2 Tables aliases make queries shorter and easier to read. Note that you can use an alias in the SELECT clause before it's actually defined later in the statement. See Figure 7.2 for the result.

```
listing
SELECT au_fname, au_lname, a.city
  FROM authors a
  INNER JOIN publishers p
    ON a.city = p.city;
```

au_fname	au_lname	city
Hallie	Hull	San Francisco
Klee	Hull	San Francisco
Christian	Kells	New York

Figure 7.2 Result of Listing 7.2.

✔ Tips

- In this book, I omit the AS keyword for DBMS portability (see the DBMS Tip in this section).

- In practice, table aliases are short (typically, one or two characters), but names of any length are valid.

- If you want to use the actual name of any particular table, omit its alias.

- An alias name hides a table name. If you alias a table, you must use its alias in all qualified references. The following statement is illegal; the table name authors doesn't exist because its alias *a* is defined:

```
SELECT authors.au_id
    FROM authors a;          --Illegal
```

- Each table's alias must be unique within the same SQL statement.

- Table aliases are required to refer to the same table more than once in a self-join; see "Creating a Self-Join" later in this chapter

- You also can use AS to assign aliases to views; see Chapter 12.

- You can't use keywords as table aliases; see "SQL Syntax" in Chapter 3.

- **DBMS** In **Oracle**, you must omit the AS keyword when you create a table alias.

  Oracle 8i requires WHERE join syntax; see "Creating Joins with JOIN or WHERE" later in this chapter. Oracle 9i and later versions support JOIN syntax and will run Listing 7.2 as is. To run Listing 7.2 in Oracle 8i, type:

```
SELECT a.au_fname, a.au_lname,
    a.city
  FROM authors a, publishers p
  WHERE a.city = p.city;
```

Using Joins

A query that extracts data from more than one table must perform a join. In the following sections, I'll explain the different types of joins (**Table 7.1**), why they're used, and how to create SELECT statements that use them.

The important characteristics of joins are:

◆ The two join operands (input tables) usually are called the first table and the second table, but they are called the left table and the right table in outer joins, in which table order matters.

◆ The tables always are joined row by row and side by side by satisfying whatever join condition(s) you specify in the query.

◆ Rows that don't match may be included or excluded, depending on the type of join.

◆ Values in joined columns usually are compared for equality (=), but you also can compare values by using the other comparison operators (<>, <, <=, >, or >=).

◆ An *equijoin* is a join condition that uses the = operator to combine rows that have equivalent values in the joined columns.

◆ An equijoin is a special case of the more general *theta join*, which compares values using not only the = operator, but also any of the other comparison operators.

◆ A join's connecting columns often are associated key columns, but you can join any columns with compatible data types (except for cross joins, which require no specific join columns).

Table 7.1

Types of Joins	
JOIN	DESCRIPTION
Cross join	Returns all rows from the first table in which each row from the first table is combined with all rows from the second table.
Natural join	A join that compares, for equality, all the columns in the first table with corresponding columns that have the same name in the second table.
Inner join	A join that uses a comparison operator to match rows from two tables based on the values in common columns from each table. Inner joins are the most common type of join.
Left outer join	Returns *all* the rows from the left table, not just the ones in which the joined columns match. If a row in the left table has no matching rows in the right table, the associated result row contains nulls for all SELECT-clause columns coming from the right table.
Right outer join	The reverse of a left outer join. All rows from the right table are returned. Nulls are returned for the left table if a right-table row has no matching left-table row.
Full outer join	Returns all rows in both the left and right tables. If a row has no match in the other table, the SELECT-clause columns from the other table contain nulls. If there is a match between the tables, the entire result row contains values from both tables.
Self-join	A join of a table to itself.

Table 7.2

Set Operations	
OPERATION	RETURNS
Union	All the rows returned by both queries, with duplicates removed.
Intersect	All rows common to both queries (that is, all distinct rows retrieved by both queries).
Except	All rows from the first query, without the rows that appear in the second query. Duplicates are removed from the result.

◆ To ensure that a join is meaningful, compare values in columns defined over the same domain. It's possible to join the columns `titles.price` and `royalties.advance`, for example, but the result will be meaningless. A typical join condition specifies a foreign key in one table and the associated primary key in the other table (see "Primary Keys" and "Foreign Keys" in Chapter 2).

◆ If a key is composite (comprises multiple columns), you can join all the key's columns.

◆ Joined columns needn't have the same column name (except for natural joins).

◆ You can nest, chain, and combine joins to join more than two tables, but understand that the DBMS works its way through your query by executing joins on exactly two tables at a time. The two tables in each join can be two base tables from the database, a base table and a table that is the result of a previous join, or two tables that are the results of previous joins.

◆ The SQL standard doesn't limit the number of tables (or joins) that may appear in a query, but your DBMS will have built-in limits, or your database administrator may set limits that are lower than the built-in limits. It's unlikely that you'll need more than five or six tables in a query; two or three tables are more usual.

◆ If a join's connecting columns contain nulls, the nulls never join. Nulls represent unknown values that aren't considered to be equal (or unequal) to one another. Nulls in a column from one of the joined tables can be returned only by using a cross join or an outer join (unless a `WHERE` clause excludes null values explicitly). For information about nulls, see "Nulls" in Chapter 3.

◆ Joins exist only for the duration of a query and aren't part of the database or DBMS.

◆ The data types of the join columns must be compatible, meaning that the DBMS can convert values to a common type for comparisons. For most DBMSes, numeric data types (`INTEGER`, `FLOAT`, and `NUMERIC`, for example), character data types (`CHAR`, `VARCHAR`), and datetime data types (`DATE`, `TIMESTAMP`) are compatible.

Conversions require computational over-head. For the best performance, the join columns should have *identical* data types, including whether nulls are allowed. For information about data types, see "Data Types" in Chapter 3.

◆ For faster queries, index the join columns (see Chapter 11).

◆ You can join views to tables or to other views (see Chapter 12).

◆ You can use either `JOIN` syntax or `WHERE` syntax to create a join; see the next section.

◆ At the end of this chapter, I'll cover SQL set operations (**Table 7.2**). The set operations aren't joins, but they let you combine rows from two query results into one result.

Creating Joins with JOIN or WHERE

You have two alternative ways of specifying a join: by using JOIN syntax or WHERE syntax. The ANSI SQL-92 standard prescribes JOIN syntax, but older SQL standards prescribe WHERE; hence, both JOIN and WHERE syntax are legal in most DBMSes.

Both types of syntax are used widely, so I'll give examples that show how to implement equivalent JOIN and WHERE queries. JOIN queries will be in the main text, and the equivalent WHERE queries will be in the Tips.

In this section, I'll show you the general syntax for JOIN and WHERE joins that involve two tables. The actual syntax that you'll use in real queries will vary by the join type, the number of columns joined, the number of tables joined, and the syntax requirements of your DBMS. The syntax diagrams and examples in the following sections will show you how to create specific joins.

To create a join by using JOIN:

◆ Type:

```
SELECT columns
    FROM table1 join_type table2
      ON join_conditions
    [WHERE search_condition]
    [GROUP BY grouping_columns]
    [HAVING search_condition]
    [ORDER BY sort_columns];
```

columns is one or more comma-separated expressions or column names from *table1* or *table2*. If *table1* and *table2* have a column name in common, you must qualify all references to these columns throughout the query to prevent ambiguity; see "Qualifying Column Names" earlier in this chapter.

table1 and *table2* are the names of the joined tables. You can alias the table names; see "Creating Table Aliases with AS" earlier in this chapter.

join_type specifies what kind of join is performed: CROSS JOIN, NATURAL JOIN, INNER JOIN, LEFT OUTER JOIN, RIGHT OUTER JOIN, or FULL OUTER JOIN.

join_conditions specifies one or more join conditions to be evaluated for each pair of joined rows. (The ON clause isn't allowed in cross joins and natural joins.) A join condition takes this form:

[*table1*.]*column* op [*table2*.]*column*

op usually is = but can be any comparison operator: =, <>, <, <=, >, or >= (refer to Table 4.2 in Chapter 4). You may combine multiple join conditions with AND or OR; see "Combining and Negating Conditions with AND, OR, and NOT" in Chapter 4.

The WHERE and ORDER BY clauses are covered in Chapter 4; GROUP BY and HAVING are covered in Chapter 6.

Listing 7.3a A join that uses JOIN syntax. See Figure 7.3 for the result.

```
                    listing
SELECT au_fname, au_lname, a.city
  FROM authors a
  INNER JOIN publishers p
    ON a.city = p.city;
```

Listing 7.3b The same join, using WHERE syntax. See Figure 7.3 for the result.

```
                    listing
SELECT au_fname, au_lname, a.city
  FROM authors a, publishers p
  WHERE a.city = p.city;
```

```
au_fname   au_lname  city
---------  --------  -------------
Hallie     Hull      San Francisco
Klee       Hull      San Francisco
Christian  Kells     New York
```

Figure 7.3 Result of Listings 7.3a and 7.3b.

To create a join by using WHERE:

◆ Type:

```
SELECT columns
    FROM table1, table2
    WHERE join_conditions
    [GROUP BY grouping_columns]
    [HAVING search_condition]
    [ORDER BY sort_columns];
```

columns, table1, and *table2* have the same meaning as in "To create a join by using JOIN" earlier in this section.

join_conditions also has the same meaning as in "To create a join by using JOIN," except that *op* may be a special symbol that indicates the join type. The WHERE clause also can include (nonjoin) search conditions to filter rows; see "Filtering Rows with WHERE" in Chapter 4.

The ORDER BY clause is covered in Chapter 4; GROUP BY and HAVING are covered in Chapter 6.

Listings 7.3a and **7.3b** show equivalent queries that use JOIN and WHERE syntax. See **Figure 7.3** for the result.

Query Execution Sequence

When your DBMS processes joins, it uses a logical sequence to execute the entire query. The DBMS:

1. Applies the join conditions in the JOIN clause.

2. Applies the join conditions and search conditions in the WHERE clause.

3. Groups rows according to the GROUP BY clause.

4. Applies the search conditions in the HAVING clause to the groups.

5. Sorts the result according to the ORDER BY clause.

✔ Tips

- It may seem odd to use a WHERE clause to specify join conditions, but the join condition *does* act as a filter. When you join two tables, the DBMS internally pairs every row in the left table with every row in the right table, forming a cross join (see the next section). The DBMS then uses the join condition to filter rows from the cross join (conceptually, anyway; DBMS optimizers don't actually create enormous cross-joined tables for every join).

- The compelling reason to prefer JOIN to WHERE syntax is that JOIN makes the join type explicit. A LEFT OUTER JOIN B is clearer than, say, A *= B. For the most common type of joins—simple inner joins—I think WHERE syntax is easier to understand, however. Both JOIN and WHERE syntax are popular, so you'll have to learn both to read queries created by other people.

- In a three-table join, only one table can be used to bridge from one of the other tables to the third table. I'll give specific examples of this rule in the following sections.

- The SELECT-clause list for a join can reference all the columns in the joined tables or any subset of the columns. The list isn't required to contain columns from every table in the join. In a three-table join, for example, none of the columns from the middle table has to be referenced in the list.

- Joined columns don't have to have the same name.

- Joined columns don't have to have the same data type. If the data types aren't identical, they must be compatible or must be data types that your DBMS can convert implicitly. If the data types can't be converted implicitly, the join condition must convert the data type explicitly by using the CAST() function. For information about implicit and explicit conversions, see "Converting Data Types with CAST()" in Chapter 5.

- If you're using WHERE syntax with two or more join conditions, you'll almost always want to combine all the join conditions with AND. Combining join conditions with OR is legal, but the result is hard to interpret. For more information about AND and OR, see "Combining and Negating Conditions with AND, OR, and NOT" in Chapter 4.

- Most queries that use joins can be rewritten by using a subquery (a query nested within another query), and most subqueries can be rewritten as joins. For information about subqueries, see Chapter 8.

- **DBMS** **Oracle** 8i and earlier versions don't support JOIN syntax; use WHERE joins instead. Oracle 9i and later versions support JOIN syntax.

  Your DBMS may prohibit joins on columns with particular data types (especially binary data types). **Microsoft SQL Server** prohibits joins on ntext, text, and image columns, and **Oracle** prohibits joins on LOB columns, for example. Search your DBMS documentation for *joins*.

The USING Clause

For JOIN syntax, the SQL standard also defines a USING clause that can be used instead of the ON clause if the joined columns have the same name and are compared for equality:

```
FROM table1 join_type table2
  USING (columns)
```

columns is a comma-separated list of one or more column names. The parentheses are required. The query performs an equijoin on the named pair(s) of columns. The type of join is called a *named columns join*. Rewriting Listing 7.3a with USING:

```
SELECT au_fname, au_lname, a.city
  FROM authors a
  INNER JOIN publishers p
    USING (city);
```

The USING clause acts like a natural join, except that you can use it if you don't want to join *all* pairs of columns with the same name in both tables. Note that the preceding USING example joins only on the column city in both tables, whereas a natural join would join on both the columns city and state common to the tables. See "Creating a Natural Join with NATURAL JOIN" later in this chapter.

USING is a syntactic convenience that doesn't add extra functionality to SQL. A USING clause always can be replicated with an ON clause in JOIN syntax or with a WHERE clause in WHERE syntax. I won't mention USING again except in "Creating a Natural Join with NATURAL JOIN" later in this chapter.

DBMS **Microsoft Access** and **Microsoft SQL Server** don't support USING. **Oracle** 9i doesn't permit qualified column names in the SELECT clause of joins that contain a USING clause. To run the preceding USING example in Oracle 9i, change *a.city* to city in the SELECT clause.

Creating a Cross Join with CROSS JOIN

A cross join:

◆ Returns all possible combinations of rows of two tables. The result contains all rows from the first table; *each* row from the first table is combined with *all* rows from the second table.

◆ Doesn't use a join condition. To create a cross join, omit the ON clause if you're using JOIN syntax, or omit the WHERE clause if you're using WHERE syntax.

◆ Seldom is used in practice, as the result is hard to interpret.

◆ Can produce a huge result, even with small tables. If one table contains m rows and the other contains n rows, the result contains $m \times n$ rows.

◆ Is a computationally expensive and time-consuming query.

◆ Also is called a *Cartesian product* or *cross product*.

To create a cross join:

◆ Type:

```
SELECT columns
  FROM table1
  CROSS JOIN table2
```

columns is one or more comma-separated expressions or column names from *table1* or *table2*. *table1* and *table2* are the names of the joined tables. If the tables have some column names in common, qualify those column names with names of the tables (**Listing 7.4** and **Figure 7.4**).

Listing 7.4 A cross join displays all possible combinations of rows from two tables. See Figure 7.4 for the result.

```
SELECT
    au_id,
    pub_id,
    a.state AS "au_state",
    p.state AS "pub_state"
  FROM authors a
  CROSS JOIN publishers p;
```

au_id	pub_id	au_state	pub_state
A01	P01	NY	NY
A02	P01	CO	NY
A03	P01	CA	NY
A04	P01	CA	NY
A05	P01	NY	NY
A06	P01	CA	NY
A07	P01	FL	NY
A01	P02	NY	CA
A02	P02	CO	CA
A03	P02	CA	CA
A04	P02	CA	CA
A05	P02	NY	CA
A06	P02	CA	CA
A07	P02	FL	CA
A01	P03	NY	NULL
A02	P03	CO	NULL
A03	P03	CA	NULL
A04	P03	CA	NULL
A05	P03	NY	NULL
A06	P03	CA	NULL
A07	P03	FL	NULL
A01	P04	NY	CA
A02	P04	CO	CA
A03	P04	CA	CA
A04	P04	CA	CA
A05	P04	NY	CA
A06	P04	CA	CA
A07	P04	FL	CA

Figure 7.4 Result of Listing 7.4.

✔ Tips

- Using WHERE syntax, Listing 7.4 is equivalent to:

```
SELECT au_id, pub_id,
    a.state AS "au_state",
    p.state AS "pub_state"
  FROM authors a, publishers p;
```

- Use SELECT * to retrieve all columns from both tables (see "Retrieving Columns with SELECT and FROM" in Chapter 4). This query retrieves all columns from the tables authors and publishers:

```
SELECT *
  FROM authors
  CROSS JOIN publishers;
```

Equivalently, using WHERE syntax:

```
SELECT *
  FROM authors, publishers;
```

- Use SELECT table.* to retrieve all columns from just one of the tables. The following query retrieves all columns from the table authors and only the column pub_id from the table publishers:

```
SELECT authors.*, p.pub_id
  FROM authors
  CROSS JOIN publishers p;
```

Equivalently, using WHERE syntax:

```
SELECT authors.*, p.pub_id
  FROM authors, publishers p;
```

- To find the cross product of n tables by using JOIN syntax, type:

```
SELECT columns
  FROM table1
  CROSS JOIN table2
  ...
  CROSS JOIN tableN
```

Equivalently, using WHERE syntax:

```
SELECT columns
  FROM table1, table2,..., tableN
```

- Cross products often are produced mistakenly. If your result contains an unexpectedly large number of rows, you may have omitted a join condition from your query accidentally.

- Although a cross product rarely is the result you want in practice, your DBMS (theoretically) generates a cross product internally as the first step in processing every join. After the DBMS has the cross product, it uses the SELECT-clause list to delete columns and the join and search conditions to delete rows.

- The join

```
t1 CROSS JOIN t2
```

is equivalent to any of the following joins:

```
t1 INNER JOIN t2 ON 1 = 1
t1 LEFT OUTER JOIN t2 ON 1 = 1
t1 RIGHT OUTER JOIN t2 ON 1 = 1
t1 FULL OUTER JOIN t2 ON 1 = 1
```

t1 and *t2* are tables, and 1 = 1 represents any condition that always is true. Inner and outer joins are covered later in this chapter.

- For programmers: One practical use of cross joins is to produce data sets for testing software. Suppose that you have a function that takes n arguments, and each argument assumes m representative test values. You can generate all $m \times n$ test cases by finding the cross product of n tables (one table for each argument), in which each table has one column and m rows (one row that contains each test value). This method still works if m differs for each argument.

- **DBMS** **Microsoft Access** supports only WHERE syntax for cross joins. To run Listing 7.4 in Access, use the statement given in the first Tip in this section.

  Oracle 8i and earlier versions don't support JOIN syntax; use WHERE joins instead. Oracle 9i and later versions support JOIN syntax.

Creating a Natural Join with NATURAL JOIN

A natural join:

♦ Is a special case of an equijoin; it compares all the columns in one table with corresponding columns that have the *same name* in the other table for equality.

♦ Works only if the input tables have one or more pairs of meaningfully comparable, identically named columns.

♦ Performs joins implicitly. Don't specify an ON or USING clause in a natural join.

♦ Is a syntactic convenience that always can be replicated explicitly with an ON clause in JOIN syntax or a WHERE clause in WHERE syntax.

To create a natural join:

♦ Type:

SELECT *columns*

    FROM *table1*

    NATURAL JOIN *table2*

columns is one or more comma-separated expressions or column names from *table1* or *table2*. Your DBMS may require identical column names to be qualified with the names of the tables (see the DBMS Tip in this section). *table1* and *table2* are the names of the joined tables.

The columns in *table1* are joined with the identically named columns in *table2* and compared for equality. NATURAL JOIN creates natural inner joins; to create natural outer joins, see the Tips in this section.

Listing 7.5 List each book's publisher. See Figure 7.5 for the result.

```
SELECT
    t.title_id,
    t.pub_id,
    p.pub_name
  FROM publishers p
  NATURAL JOIN titles t;
```

title_id	pub_id	pub_name
T01	P01	Abatis Publishers
T02	P03	Schadenfreude Press
T03	P02	Core Dump Books
T04	P04	Tenterhooks Press
T05	P04	Tenterhooks Press
T06	P01	Abatis Publishers
T07	P03	Schadenfreude Press
T08	P04	Tenterhooks Press
T09	P04	Tenterhooks Press
T10	P01	Abatis Publishers
T11	P04	Tenterhooks Press
T12	P01	Abatis Publishers
T13	P03	Schadenfreude Press

Figure 7.5 Result of Listing 7.5.

Listing 7.6 List each book's publisher and advance, for books with advances less than $20,000. See Figure 7.6 for the result.

```
                        listing
SELECT
    t.title_id,
    t.pub_id,
    p.pub_name,
    r.advance
  FROM publishers p
  NATURAL JOIN titles t
  NATURAL JOIN royalties r
 WHERE r.advance < 20000;
```

title_id	pub_id	pub_name	advance
T01	P01	Abatis Publishers	10000
T02	P03	Schadenfreude Press	1000
T03	P02	Core Dump Books	15000
T08	P04	Tenterhooks Press	0
T09	P04	Tenterhooks Press	0

Figure 7.6 Result of Listing 7.6.

When your DBMS runs **Listing 7.5**, it will join rows in the table publishers with rows in the table titles that have equal values in the columns publishers.pub_id and titles.pub_id—the two columns that have the same name in both tables. See **Figure 7.5** for the result.

In **Listing 7.6**, I've added another join to Listing 7.5 to retrieve the advance for each book. The WHERE condition retrieves books with advances less than $20,000. When your DBMS runs Listing 7.6, it will join the pub_id columns in the tables publishers and titles, *and* it will join the title_id columns in the tables titles and royalties. See **Figure 7.6** for the result.

✔ Tips

- To replicate a natural join by using WHERE syntax, use an equijoin with a WHERE clause that uses AND operators to combine join conditions. Each join condition equates each pair of columns with the same name in the input tables. The equivalent WHERE queries are (Listing 7.5):

  ```
  SELECT t.title_id, t.pub_id,
      p.pub_name
    FROM publishers p, titles t
   WHERE p.pub_id = t.pub_id;
  ```
  and (Listing 7.6):
  ```
  SELECT t.title_id, t.pub_id,
      p.pub_name, r.advance
    FROM publishers p, titles t,
      royalties r
   WHERE p.pub_id = t.pub_id
     AND t.title_id = r.title_id
     AND r.advance < 20000;
  ```

continues on next page

CREATING A NATURAL JOIN WITH NATURAL JOIN

■ To replicate a natural join by using inner or outer JOIN syntax, use an equijoin with an ON clause that uses AND operators to combine join conditions. Each join condition equates each pair of columns with the same name in both input tables. The equivalent JOIN queries are (Listing 7.5):

```
SELECT t.title_id, t.pub_id,
    p.pub_name
  FROM publishers p
  INNER JOIN titles t
    ON p.pub_id = t.pub_id;
```

and (Listing 7.6):

```
SELECT t.title_id, t.pub_id,
    p.pub_name, r.advance
  FROM publishers p
  INNER JOIN titles t
    ON p.pub_id = t.pub_id
  INNER JOIN royalties r
    ON t.title_id = r.title_id
  WHERE r.advance < 20000;
```

■ You also can replicate a natural join by using JOIN syntax with a USING clause (see the sidebar in "Creating Joins with JOIN or WHERE" earlier in this chapter). NATURAL JOIN is a shorthand form of USING; it forms a USING list consisting of exactly those column names that appear in both tables. The equivalent USING queries are (Listing 7.5):

```
SELECT t.title_id, t.pub_id,
    p.pub_name
  FROM publishers p
  INNER JOIN titles t
    USING (pub_id);
```

and (Listing 7.6):

```
SELECT t.title_id, t.pub_id,
    p.pub_name, r.advance
  FROM publishers p
  INNER JOIN titles t
    USING (pub_id)
  INNER JOIN royalties r
    USING (title_id)
  WHERE r.advance < 20000;
```

■ The syntax NATURAL JOIN actually creates an inner join: NATURAL JOIN is equivalent to NATURAL INNER JOIN. You can create natural outer joins with:

```
NATURAL LEFT [OUTER] JOIN
NATURAL RIGHT [OUTER] JOIN
NATURAL FULL [OUTER] JOIN
```

Inner and outer joins are described later in this chapter.

■ If you use a natural join, be certain that all related (joinable) columns have the same name in both tables and that all unrelated columns have unique names.

■ The meaning of *natural join* differs slightly in the relational model (Chapter 2) and the SQL standard. In the model, a natural join always is a join from a foreign key to its parent key. In SQL, a natural join is a join of two tables over *all* columns that have the same name (not just key columns). See Listing 7.9 later in this chapter for an example of a natural join that doesn't involve key columns.

To make the model and the SQL definitions of natural join agree, a database designer will ensure that all the foreign keys have the same names as their parent keys and that all other columns have unique names.

■ **DBMS** **Microsoft Access** and **Microsoft SQL Server** don't support NATURAL JOIN syntax. To run Listings 7.5 and 7.6 in Access and SQL Server, use either WHERE syntax (given in the first Tip in this section) or JOIN syntax (given in the second Tip in this section).

Oracle 8i and earlier versions don't support JOIN syntax; use WHERE joins instead. Oracle 9i and later versions support JOIN syntax. Oracle 9i doesn't permit qualified column names in the SELECT clause of natural joins. To run Listings 7.5 and 7.6 in Oracle 9i, omit the qualifiers (Listing 7.5):

```
SELECT title_id, pub_id, pub_name
  FROM publishers
  NATURAL JOIN titles;
```

and (Listing 7.6):

```
SELECT title_id, pub_id,
    pub_name, advance
  FROM publishers
  NATURAL JOIN titles
  NATURAL JOIN royalties
  WHERE advance < 20000;
```

Oracle 9i doesn't permit qualified column names in the SELECT clause of joins that contain a USING clause. To run the USING examples in the earlier Tip in Oracle 9i, change t.title_id to title_id, t.pub_id to pub_id, and so on.

MySQL requires ambiguous column names to be qualified, even in natural joins.

In **PostgreSQL**, the use of qualifiers with ambiguous column names is optional in natural joins.

Creating an Inner Join with INNER JOIN

An inner join:

◆ Uses a comparison operator (=, <>, <, <=, >, or >=) to match rows from two tables based on the values in common columns from each table. You can retrieve all rows in which the author identifier (the column au_id) is the same in both the tables authors and title_authors, for example.

◆ Returns a result that contains only joined rows that satisfy the join condition(s).

◆ Is the most common type of join; I'll give many examples.

To create an inner join:

◆ Type:

```
SELECT columns
  FROM table1
  INNER JOIN table2
    ON join_conditions
```

columns is one or more comma-separated expressions or column names from table1 or table2. table1 and table2 are the names of the joined tables. If the tables have some column names in common, qualify those column names with names of the tables.

join_conditions specifies one or more join conditions to be evaluated for each pair of joined rows. A join condition takes this form:

[table1.]column op [table2.]column

op usually is = but can be any comparison operator: =, <>, <, <=, >, or >= (refer to Table 4.2 in Chapter 4). You may combine multiple join conditions with AND or OR; see "Combining and Negating Conditions with AND, OR, and NOT" in Chapter 4.

✔ Tips

■ To create an inner join of three or more tables by using JOIN syntax, type:

```
SELECT columns
  FROM table1
  INNER JOIN table2
    ON join_condition1
  INNER JOIN table3
    ON join_condition2
  ...
```

Using WHERE syntax, type:

```
SELECT columns
  FROM table1, table2,...
  WHERE join_condition1
    AND join_condition2
    ...
```

■ By default, JOIN (without CROSS, NATURAL, OUTER, or any other modifiers) is equivalent to INNER JOIN.

■ **DBMS** **Oracle** 8i and earlier versions don't support JOIN syntax; use WHERE joins instead. Oracle 9i and later versions support JOIN syntax.

You can use WHERE syntax or JOIN syntax in **Microsoft Access**, but if you use JOIN syntax in joins that involve three or more tables, Access requires you to nest joins by using the following general syntax:

```
SELECT columns
  FROM table1
  INNER JOIN (table2
  INNER JOIN (table3
  INNER JOIN (table4
  INNER JOIN ...)
  ON table3.column3 op table4.column4)
  ON table2.column2 op table3.column3)
  ON table1.column1 op table2.column2;
```

(Other DBMSes also allow you to nest joins by using parentheses, but Access requires it.)

Listing 7.7 List the books that each author wrote (or co-wrote). See Figure 7.7 for the result.

```
                    listing
SELECT
    a.au_id,
    a.au_fname,
    a.au_lname,
    ta.title_id
  FROM authors a
  INNER JOIN title_authors ta
    ON a.au_id = ta.au_id
  ORDER BY a.au_id ASC, ta.title_id ASC;
```

au_id	au_fname	au_lname	title_id
A01	Sarah	Buchman	T01
A01	Sarah	Buchman	T02
A01	Sarah	Buchman	T13
A02	Wendy	Heydemark	T06
A02	Wendy	Heydemark	T07
A02	Wendy	Heydemark	T10
A02	Wendy	Heydemark	T12
A03	Hallie	Hull	T04
A03	Hallie	Hull	T11
A04	Klee	Hull	T04
A04	Klee	Hull	T05
A04	Klee	Hull	T07
A04	Klee	Hull	T11
A05	Christian	Kells	T03
A06		Kellsey	T08
A06		Kellsey	T09
A06		Kellsey	T11

Figure 7.7 Result of Listing 7.7.

Listing 7.7 joins two tables on the column au_id to list the books that each author wrote (or co-wrote). Each author's au_id in the table authors matches zero or more rows in the table title_authors. See **Figure 7.7** for the result. Note that author A07 (Paddy O'Furniture) is omitted from the result because he has written no books and so has no matching rows in title_authors.

✔ Tip

■ Using WHERE syntax, Listing 7.7 is equivalent to:

```
SELECT a.au_id, a.au_fname,
    a.au_lname, ta.title_id
  FROM authors a, title_authors ta
  WHERE a.au_id = ta.au_id
  ORDER BY a.au_id ASC,
    ta.title_id ASC;
```

CREATING AN INNER JOIN WITH INNER JOIN

Listing 7.8 joins two tables on the column `pub_id` to list each book's title name and ID, and each book's publisher name and ID. Note that the join is necessary to retrieve only the publisher name (the fourth column in the result), all the other three columns are available in the table `titles`. See **Figure 7.8** for the result.

✔ Tip

- Using WHERE syntax, Listing 7.8 is equivalent to:

```
SELECT t.title_id, t.title_name,
    t.pub_id, p.pub_name
  FROM titles t, publishers p
  WHERE p.pub_id = t.pub_id
  ORDER BY t.title_name ASC;
```

Listing 7.8 List each book's title name and ID, and each book's publisher name and ID. See Figure 7.8 for the result.

```
SELECT
    t.title_id,
    t.title_name,
    t.pub_id,
    p.pub_name
  FROM titles t
  INNER JOIN publishers p
    ON p.pub_id = t.pub_id
  ORDER BY t.title_name ASC;
```

title_id	title_name	pub_id	pub_name
T01	1977!	P01	Abatis Publishers
T02	200 Years of German Humor	P03	Schadenfreude Press
T03	Ask Your System Administrator	P02	Core Dump Books
T04	But I Did It Unconsciously	P04	Tenterhooks Press
T05	Exchange of Platitudes	P04	Tenterhooks Press
T06	How About Never?	P01	Abatis Publishers
T07	I Blame My Mother	P03	Schadenfreude Press
T08	Just Wait Until After School	P04	Tenterhooks Press
T09	Kiss My Boo-Boo	P04	Tenterhooks Press
T10	Not Without My Faberge Egg	P01	Abatis Publishers
T11	Perhaps It's a Glandular Problem	P04	Tenterhooks Press
T12	Spontaneous, Not Annoying	P01	Abatis Publishers
T13	What Are The Civilian Applications?	P03	Schadenfreude Press

Figure 7.8 Result of Listing 7.8.

Listing 7.9 List the authors who live in the same city and state in which a publisher is located. See Figure 7.9 for the result.

```
                      listing
SELECT
    a.au_id,
    a.au_fname,
    a.au_lname,
    a.city,
    a.state
  FROM authors a
  INNER JOIN publishers p
    ON a.city = p.city
    AND a.state = p.state
  ORDER BY a.au_id ASC;
```

```
au_id au_fname  au_lname city          state
----- --------- -------- ------------- -----
A03   Hallie    Hull     San Francisco CA
A04   Klee      Hull     San Francisco CA
A05   Christian Kells    New York      NY
```

Figure 7.9 Result of Listing 7.9.

Listing 7.9 uses two join conditions to list the authors who live in the same city and state as some publisher (any publisher). See **Figure 7.9** for the result. Note that this query is a natural join on the identically named, nonkey columns `city` and `state` in the two tables (see "Creating a Natural Join with `NATURAL JOIN`" earlier in this chapter). An equivalent query is:

```
SELECT a.au_id, a.au_fname, a.au_lname,
    a.city, a.state
  FROM authors a
  NATURAL JOIN publishers p
  ORDER BY a.au_id ASC;
```

✔ Tip

- Using `WHERE` syntax, Listing 7.9 is equivalent to :

```
SELECT a.au_id, a.au_fname,
    a.au_lname, a.city, a.state
  FROM authors a, publishers p
  WHERE a.city = p.city
    AND a.state = p.state
  ORDER BY a.au_id ASC;
```

CREATING AN INNER JOIN WITH INNER JOIN

Listing 7.10 combines an inner join with WHERE conditions to list books published in California or outside the large North American countries; see "Filtering Rows with WHERE" in Chapter 4. See **Figure 7.10** for the result.

✔ Tip

- Using WHERE syntax, Listing 7.10 is equivalent to):

```
SELECT t.title_id, t.title_name,
    p.state, p.country
  FROM titles t, publishers p
  WHERE t.pub_id = p.pub_id
    AND (p.state = 'CA'
    OR p.country NOT IN
       ('USA', 'Canada', 'Mexico'))
  ORDER BY t.title_id ASC;
```

Listing 7.10 List the books published in California or outside the large North American countries. See Figure 7.10 for the result.

```
SELECT
    t.title_id,
    t.title_name,
    p.state,
    p.country
  FROM titles t
  INNER JOIN publishers p
    ON t.pub_id = p.pub_id
  WHERE p.state = 'CA'
    OR p.country NOT IN
       ('USA', 'Canada', 'Mexico')
  ORDER BY t.title_id ASC;
```

title_id	title_name	state	country
T02	200 Years of German Humor	NULL	Germany
T03	Ask Your System Administrator	CA	USA
T04	But I Did It Unconsciously	CA	USA
T05	Exchange of Platitudes	CA	USA
T07	I Blame My Mother	NULL	Germany
T08	Just Wait Until After School	CA	USA
T09	Kiss My Boo-Boo	CA	USA
T11	Perhaps It's a Glandular Problem	CA	USA
T13	What Are The Civilian Applications?	NULL	Germany

Figure 7.10 Result of Listing 7.10.

Listing 7.11 List the number of books that each author wrote (or co-wrote). See Figure 7.11 for the result.

```
                    listing
SELECT
    a.au_id,
    COUNT(ta.title_id) AS "Num books"
FROM authors a
INNER JOIN title_authors ta
    ON a.au_id = ta.au_id
GROUP BY a.au_id
ORDER BY a.au_id ASC;
```

```
au_id Num books
----- ---------
A01         3
A02         4
A03         2
A04         4
A05         1
A06         3
```

Figure 7.11 Result of Listing 7.11.

Listing 7.11 combines an inner join with the aggregate function COUNT() and a GROUP BY clause to list the number of books that each author wrote (or co-wrote). For information about aggregate functions and GROUP BY, see Chapter 6. See **Figure 7.11** for the result. Note that, as in Figure 7.7, author A07 (Paddy O'Furniture) is omitted from the result because he has written no books and so has no matching rows in title_authors. See Listing 7.30 in "Creating Outer Joins with OUTER JOIN" later in this chapter for an example that lists authors who have written no books.

✔ Tip

- Using WHERE syntax, Listing 7.11 is equivalent to:
```
SELECT a.au_id,
    COUNT(ta.title_id)
        AS "Num books"
  FROM authors a, title_authors ta
  WHERE a.au_id = ta.au_id
  GROUP BY a.au_id
  ORDER BY a.au_id ASC;
```

Listing 7.12 uses WHERE conditions to list the advance paid for each biography. See **Figure 7.12** for the result.

✔ Tip

- Using WHERE syntax, Listing 7.12 is equivalent to:

```
SELECT t.title_id, t.title_name,
    r.advance
  FROM royalties r, titles t
  WHERE r.title_id = t.title_id
    AND t.type = 'biography'
    AND r.advance IS NOT NULL
  ORDER BY r.advance DESC;
```

Listing 7.12 List the advance paid for each biography. See Figure 7.12 for the result.

```
                    listing
SELECT
    t.title_id,
    t.title_name,
    r.advance
  FROM royalties r
  INNER JOIN titles t
    ON r.title_id = t.title_id
  WHERE t.type = 'biography'
    AND r.advance IS NOT NULL
  ORDER BY r.advance DESC;
```

title_id	title_name	advance
T07	I Blame My Mother	1000000.00
T12	Spontaneous, Not Annoying	50000.00
T06	How About Never?	20000.00

Figure 7.12 Result of Listing 7.12.

Listing 7.13 List the count and total advance paid for each type of book. See Figure 7.13 for the result.

```
                        listing
SELECT
    t.type,
    COUNT(r.advance)
      AS "COUNT(r.advance)",
    SUM(r.advance)
      AS "SUM(r.advance)"
  FROM royalties r
  INNER JOIN titles t
    ON r.title_id = t.title_id
  WHERE r.advance IS NOT NULL
  GROUP BY t.type
  ORDER BY t.type ASC;
```

type	COUNT(r.advance)	SUM(r.advance)
biography	3	1070000.00
children	2	0.00
computer	1	15000.00
history	3	31000.00
psychology	3	220000.00

Figure 7.13 Result of Listing 7.13.

Listing 7.13 uses aggregate functions and a GROUP BY clause to list the count and total advance paid for each type of book. See **Figure 7.13** for the result.

✔ Tip

- Using WHERE syntax, Listing 7.13 is equivalent to:

```
SELECT t.type,
    COUNT(r.advance)
      AS "COUNT(r.advance)",
    SUM(r.advance)
      AS "SUM(r.advance)"
  FROM royalties r, titles t
  WHERE r.title_id = t.title_id
    AND r.advance IS NOT NULL
  GROUP BY t.type
  ORDER BY t.type ASC;
```

Listing 7.14 is similar to Listing 7.13, except that it uses an additional grouping column to list the count and total advance paid for each type of book by publisher. See **Figure 7.14** for the result.

✔ Tip

- Using WHERE syntax, Listing 7.14 is equivalent to:

```
SELECT t.type, t.pub_id,
    COUNT(r.advance)
        AS "COUNT(r.advance)",
    SUM(r.advance)
        AS "SUM(r.advance)"
    FROM royalties r, titles t
    WHERE r.title_id = t.title_id
        AND r.advance IS NOT NULL
    GROUP BY t.type, t.pub_id
    ORDER BY t.type ASC, t.pub_id ASC;
```

Listing 7.14 List the count and total advance paid for each type of book, by publisher. See Figure 7.14 for the result.

```
SELECT
    t.type,
    t.pub_id,
    COUNT(r.advance) AS "COUNT(r.advance)",
    SUM(r.advance) AS "SUM(r.advance)"
FROM royalties r
INNER JOIN titles t
    ON r.title_id = t.title_id
WHERE r.advance IS NOT NULL
GROUP BY t.type, t.pub_id
ORDER BY t.type ASC, t.pub_id ASC;
```

type	pub_id	COUNT(r.advance)	SUM(r.advance)
biography	P01	2	70000.00
biography	P03	1	1000000.00
children	P04	2	0.00
computer	P02	1	15000.00
history	P01	1	10000.00
history	P03	2	21000.00
psychology	P04	3	220000.00

Figure 7.14 Result of Listing 7.14.

Listing 7.15 List the number of co-authors of each book written by two or more authors. See Figure 7.15 for the result.

```
                    listing
SELECT
    ta.title_id,
    COUNT(ta.au_id) AS "Num authors"
  FROM authors a
  INNER JOIN title_authors ta
    ON a.au_id = ta.au_id
  GROUP BY ta.title_id
  HAVING COUNT(ta.au_id) > 1
  ORDER BY ta.title_id ASC;
```

```
title_id Num authors
-------- -----------
T04                2
T07                2
T11                3
```

Figure 7.15 Result of Listing 7.15.

Listing 7.15 uses a HAVING clause to list the number of co-authors of each book written by two or more authors. For information about HAVING, see "Filtering Groups with HAVING" in Chapter 6. See **Figure 7.15** for the result.

✔ Tip

■ Using WHERE syntax, Listing 7.15 is equivalent to:

```
SELECT ta.title_id,
    COUNT(ta.au_id) AS "Num authors"
  FROM authors a, title_authors ta
  WHERE a.au_id = ta.au_id
  GROUP BY ta.title_id
  HAVING COUNT(ta.au_id) > 1
  ORDER BY ta.title_id ASC;
```

You also can join values in two columns that aren't equal. **Listing 7.16** uses greater-than (>) join to find each book whose revenue (= price × sales) is at least 10 times greater than the advance paid to the author(s). See **Figure 7.16** for the result. The use of <, <=, >, and >= joins is common, but not-equal joins (<>) are used rarely. Generally, not-equal joins make sense only when used with a self-join; see "Creating a Self-Join" later in this chapter.

✔ Tip

■ Using WHERE syntax, Listing 7.16 is equivalent to:

```
SELECT t.title_id, t.title_name,
    r.advance,
    t.price * t.sales AS "Revenue"
  FROM titles t, royalties r
  WHERE t.price * t.sales >
        r.advance * 10
    AND t.title_id = r.title_id
  ORDER BY t.price * t.sales DESC;
```

Listing 7.16 List each book whose revenue (= price x sales) is at least 10 times greater than its advance. See Figure 7.16 for the result.

```
SELECT
    t.title_id,
    t.title_name,
    r.advance,
    t.price * t.sales AS "Revenue"
FROM titles t
INNER JOIN royalties r
  ON t.price * t.sales > r.advance * 10
  AND t.title_id = r.title_id
ORDER BY t.price * t.sales DESC;
```

title_id	title_name	advance	Revenue
T07	I Blame My Mother	1000000.00	35929790.00
T05	Exchange of Platitudes	100000.00	1400008.00
T12	Spontaneous, Not Annoying	50000.00	1299012.99
T03	Ask Your System Administrator	15000.00	1025396.65
T13	What Are The Civilian Applications?	20000.00	313905.33
T06	How About Never?	20000.00	225834.00
T02	200 Years of German Humor	1000.00	190841.70
T09	Kiss My Boo-Boo	.00	69750.00
T08	Just Wait Until After School	.00	40950.00

Figure 7.16 Result of Listing 7.16.

Complicated queries can arise from simple questions. In **Listing 7.17**, I must join three tables to list the author names and the names of the books that each author wrote (or co-wrote). See **Figure 7.17** for the result.

✔ Tips

- Using WHERE syntax, Listing 7.17 is equivalent to:

```
SELECT a.au_fname, a.au_lname,
    t.title_name
```

Listing 7.17 List the author names and the names of the books that each author wrote (or co-wrote). See Figure 7.17 for the result.

```
                    listing
SELECT
    a.au_fname,
    a.au_lname,
    t.title_name
FROM authors a
INNER JOIN title_authors ta
  ON a.au_id = ta.au_id
INNER JOIN titles t
  ON t.title_id = ta.title_id
ORDER BY a.au_lname ASC, a.au_fname ASC,
    t.title_name ASC;
```

```
FROM authors a, title_authors ta,
    titles t
WHERE a.au_id = ta.au_id
    AND t.title_id = ta.title_id
ORDER BY a.au_lname ASC,
    a.au_fname ASC,
    t.title_name ASC;
```

- **DBMS** To run Listing 7.17 in **Microsoft Access**, type:

```
SELECT a.au_fname, a.au_lname,
    t.title_name
  FROM titles AS t
  INNER JOIN (authors AS a
    INNER JOIN title_authors AS ta
      ON a.au_id = ta.au_id)
    ON t.title_id = ta.title_id
  ORDER BY a.au_lname ASC,
    a.au_fname ASC,
    t.title_name ASC;
```

```
au_fname   au_lname   title_name
---------  ---------  -----------------------------------
Sarah      Buchman    1977!
Sarah      Buchman    200 Years of German Humor
Sarah      Buchman    What Are The Civilian Applications?
Wendy      Heydemark  How About Never?
Wendy      Heydemark  I Blame My Mother
Wendy      Heydemark  Not Without My Faberge Egg
Wendy      Heydemark  Spontaneous, Not Annoying
Hallie     Hull       But I Did It Unconsciously
Hallie     Hull       Perhaps It's a Glandular Problem
Klee       Hull       But I Did It Unconsciously
Klee       Hull       Exchange of Platitudes
Klee       Hull       I Blame My Mother
Klee       Hull       Perhaps It's a Glandular Problem
Christian  Kells      Ask Your System Administrator
           Kellsey    Just Wait Until After School
           Kellsey    Kiss My Boo-Boo
           Kellsey    Perhaps It's a Glandular Problem
```

Figure 7.17 Result of Listing 7.17.

CREATING AN INNER JOIN WITH INNER JOIN

Expanding on Listing 7.17, **Listing 7.18** requires a four-table join to list the publisher names along with names of the authors and books. See **Figure 7.18** for the result.

Listing 7.18 List the author names, the names of the books that each author wrote (or co-wrote), and the publisher names. See Figure 7.18 for the result.

```
SELECT
    a.au_fname,
    a.au_lname,
    t.title_name,
    p.pub_name
FROM authors a
INNER JOIN title_authors ta
    ON a.au_id = ta.au_id
INNER JOIN titles t
    ON t.title_id = ta.title_id
INNER JOIN publishers p
    ON p.pub_id = t.pub_id
ORDER BY a.au_lname ASC, a.au_fname ASC,
    t.title_name ASC;
```

```
au_fname    au_lname   title_name                          pub_name
---------   ---------  ----------------------------------  -------------------
Sarah       Buchman    1977!                               Abatis Publishers
Sarah       Buchman    200 Years of German Humor           Schadenfreude Press
Sarah       Buchman    What Are The Civilian Applications? Schadenfreude Press
Wendy       Heydemark  How About Never?                    Abatis Publishers
Wendy       Heydemark  I Blame My Mother                   Schadenfreude Press
Wendy       Heydemark  Not Without My Faberge Egg          Abatis Publishers
Wendy       Heydemark  Spontaneous, Not Annoying           Abatis Publishers
Hallie      Hull       But I Did It Unconsciously          Tenterhooks Press
Hallie      Hull       Perhaps It's a Glandular Problem    Tenterhooks Press
Klee        Hull       But I Did It Unconsciously          Tenterhooks Press
Klee        Hull       Exchange of Platitudes              Tenterhooks Press
Klee        Hull       I Blame My Mother                   Schadenfreude Press
Klee        Hull       Perhaps It's a Glandular Problem    Tenterhooks Press
Christian   Kells      Ask Your System Administrator       Core Dump Books
            Kellsey    Just Wait Until After School        Tenterhooks Press
            Kellsey    Kiss My Boo-Boo                     Tenterhooks Press
            Kellsey    Perhaps It's a Glandular Problem    Tenterhooks Press
```

Figure 7.18 Result of Listing 7.18.

✔ Tips

■ Using WHERE syntax, Listing 7.18 is equivalent to:

```
SELECT a.au_fname, a.au_lname,
    t.title_name, p.pub_name
  FROM authors a, title_authors ta,
    titles t, publishers p
  WHERE a.au_id = ta.au_id
    AND t.title_id = ta.title_id
    AND p.pub_id = t.pub_id
  ORDER BY a.au_lname ASC,
    a.au_fname ASC,
    t.title_name ASC;
```

■ **DBMS** To run Listing 7.18 in **Microsoft Access**, type:

```
SELECT a.au_fname, a.au_lname,
    t.title_name, p.pub_name
  FROM (publishers AS p
    INNER JOIN titles AS t
      ON p.pub_id = t.pub_id)
    INNER JOIN (authors AS a
      INNER JOIN title_authors AS ta
        ON a.au_id = ta.au_id)
      ON t.title_id = ta.title_id
  ORDER BY a.au_lname ASC,
    a.au_fname ASC,
    t.title_name ASC;
```

CREATING AN INNER JOIN WITH INNER JOIN

Listing 7.19 calculates the total royalties for all books. The gross royalty of a book is the book's revenue (= sales × price) times the royalty rate (the fraction of revenue paid to the author). In most cases, the author receives an initial advance against royalties. The publisher deducts the advance from the gross royalty to get the net royalty. If the net royalty is positive, the publisher must pay the author; if the net royalty is negative or zero, the author gets nothing, because he or she still haven't "earned out" the advance. See **Figure 7.19** for the result. Gross royalties are labeled "Total royalties," gross advances are labeled "Total advances," and net royalties are labeled "Total due to authors."

Listing 7.19 calculates total royalties for all books; the subsequent examples in this section will show you how to break down royalties by author, book, publisher, and other groups.

✔ Tip

- Using WHERE syntax, Listing 17.19 is equivalent to:

```
SELECT
    SUM(t.sales * t.price *
      r.royalty_rate)
      AS "Total royalties",
    SUM(r.advance)
      AS "Total advances",
    SUM((t.sales * t.price *
      r.royalty_rate) - r.advance)
      AS "Total due to authors"
  FROM titles t, royalties r
 WHERE r.title_id = t.title_id
   AND t.sales IS NOT NULL;
```

Listing 7.19 Calculate the total royalties for all books. See Figure 7.19 for the result.

```
                                    listing

SELECT
    SUM(t.sales * t.price * r.royalty_rate) AS "Total royalties",
    SUM(r.advance) AS "Total advances",
    SUM((t.sales * t.price * r.royalty_rate) - r.advance) AS "Total due to authors"
  FROM titles t
  INNER JOIN royalties r
    ON r.title_id = t.title_id
  WHERE t.sales IS NOT NULL;
```

```
Total royalties  Total advances  Total due to authors
---------------  --------------  --------------------
    4387219.55      1336000.00             3051219.55
```

Figure 7.19 Result of Listing 7.19.

Listing 7.20 uses a three-table join to calculate the royalty earned by each author for each book that the author wrote (or co-wrote). Because a book may have multiple authors, per-author royalty calculations involve each author's share of a book's royalty (and advance). The author's royalty share for each book is given in the table `title_authors` in the column `royalty_share`. For a book with a sole author, `royalty_share` is 1.0 (100 percent). For a book with multiple authors, the `royalty_share` of each author is a fractional amount between 0 and 1 (inclusive); all the `royalty_share` values for a particular book must sum to 1.0 (100 percent). See **Figure 7.20** for the result. The sum of the values in each of the last three columns in the result equals the corresponding total in Figure 7.19.

✔ Tips

■ Using `WHERE` syntax, Listing 17.20 is equivalent to:

```
SELECT ta.au_id, t.title_id,
    t.pub_id,
    t.sales * t.price *
      r.royalty_rate *
      ta.royalty_share
      AS "Royalty share",
    r.advance * ta.royalty_share
      AS "Advance share",
    (t.sales * t.price *
      r.royalty_rate *
      ta.royalty_share) -
    (r.advance *
      ta.royalty_share)
      AS "Due to author"
```

code continues on next page

Listing 7.20 Calculate the royalty earned by each author for each book that the author wrote (or co-wrote). See Figure 7.20 for the result.

```
                              listing
SELECT
    ta.au_id,
    t.title_id,
    t.pub_id,
    t.sales * t.price * r.royalty_rate * ta.royalty_share AS "Royalty share",
    r.advance * ta.royalty_share AS "Advance share",
    (t.sales * t.price * r.royalty_rate * ta.royalty_share) -
      (r.advance * ta.royalty_share) AS "Due to author"
  FROM title_authors ta
  INNER JOIN titles t
    ON t.title_id = ta.title_id
  INNER JOIN royalties r
    ON r.title_id = t.title_id
  WHERE t.sales IS NOT NULL
  ORDER BY ta.au_id ASC, t.title_id ASC;
```

```
FROM title_authors ta,
   titles t, royalties r
WHERE t.title_id = ta.title_id
   AND r.title_id = t.title_id
   AND t.sales IS NOT NULL
ORDER BY ta.au_id ASC,
   t.title_id ASC;
```

■ **DBMS** To run Listing 7.20 in **Microsoft Access**, type:

```
SELECT ta.au_id, t.title_id,
   t.pub_id,
   t.sales * t.price *
     r.royalty_rate *
     ta.royalty_share
     AS "Royalty share",
   r.advance * ta.royalty_share
     AS "Advance share",
   (t.sales * t.price *
     r.royalty_rate *
     ta.royalty_share) -
   (r.advance * ta.royalty_share)
     AS "Due to author"
FROM (titles AS t
   INNER JOIN royalties AS r
     ON t.title_id = r.title_id)
INNER JOIN title_authors AS ta
   ON t.title_id = ta.title_id
WHERE t.sales IS NOT NULL
ORDER BY ta.au_id ASC,
   t.title_id ASC;
```

```
au_id title_id pub_id Royalty share Advance share Due to author
----- -------- ------ ------------- ------------- -------------
A01   T01      P01          622.32      10000.00      -9377.68
A01   T02      P03        11450.50       1000.00      10450.50
A01   T13      P03        18834.32      20000.00      -1165.68
A02   T06      P01        18066.72      20000.00      -1933.28
A02   T07      P03      1976138.45     500000.00    1476138.45
A02   T12      P01       116911.17      50000.00      66911.17
A03   T04      P04         8106.38      12000.00      -3893.62
A03   T11      P04        15792.90      30000.00     -14207.10
A04   T04      P04         5404.26       8000.00      -2595.74
A04   T05      P04       126000.72     100000.00      26000.72
A04   T07      P03      1976138.45     500000.00    1476138.45
A04   T11      P04        15792.90      30000.00     -14207.10
A05   T03      P02        71777.77      15000.00      56777.77
A06   T08      P04         1638.00           .00       1638.00
A06   T09      P04         3487.50           .00       3487.50
A06   T11      P04        21057.20      40000.00     -18942.80
```

Figure 7.20 Result of Listing 7.20.

Listing 7.21 is similar to Listing 7.20 except that it adds a join to the table authors to print the author names and includes a WHERE condition to retrieve rows with only positive royalties. See **Figure 7.21** for the result.

Listing 7.21 List only positive royalties earned by each author for each book that the author wrote (or co-wrote). See Figure 7.21 for the result.

```
SELECT
    a.au_id,
    a.au_fname,
    a.au_lname,
    t.title_name,
    (t.sales * t.price * r.royalty_rate * ta.royalty_share) -
      (r.advance * ta.royalty_share) AS "Due to author"
FROM authors a
INNER JOIN title_authors ta
  ON a.au_id = ta.au_id
INNER JOIN titles t
  ON t.title_id = ta.title_id
INNER JOIN royalties r
  ON r.title_id = t.title_id
WHERE t.sales IS NOT NULL
  AND (t.sales * t.price * r.royalty_rate * ta.royalty_share) -
    (r.advance * ta.royalty_share) > 0
ORDER BY a.au_id ASC, t.title_id ASC;
```

CREATING AN INNER JOIN WITH INNER JOIN

✔ Tips

- Using WHERE syntax, Listing 7.21 is equivalent to:

```
SELECT a.au_id, a.au_fname,
    a.au_lname, t.title_name,
    (t.sales * t.price *
      r.royalty_rate *
      ta.royalty_share) -
    (r.advance * ta.royalty_share)
    AS "Due to author"
FROM authors a, title_authors ta,
  titles t, royalties r
WHERE a.au_id = ta.au_id
  AND t.title_id = ta.title_id
  AND r.title_id = t.title_id
  AND t.sales IS NOT NULL
  AND (t.sales * t.price *
      r.royalty_rate *
      ta.royalty_share) -
      (r.advance *
      ta.royalty_share) > 0
ORDER BY a.au_id ASC,
  t.title_id ASC;
```

- **DBMS** To run Listing 7.21 in **Microsoft Access**, type:

```
SELECT a.au_id, a.au_fname,
    a.au_lname, t.title_name,
    (t.sales * t.price *
      r.royalty_rate *
      ta.royalty_share) -
    (r.advance * ta.royalty_share)
    AS "Due to author"
FROM (titles AS t
  INNER JOIN royalties AS r
    ON t.title_id = r.title_id)
INNER JOIN (authors AS a
    INNER JOIN title_authors AS ta
    ON a.au_id = ta.au_id)
  ON t.title_id = ta.title_id
WHERE t.sales IS NOT NULL
  AND (t.sales * t.price *
      r.royalty_rate *
      ta.royalty_share) -
      (r.advance * ta.royalty_share)
      > 0
ORDER BY a.au_id ASC,
  t.title_id ASC;
```

```
au_id au_fname   au_lname   title_name                       Due to author
----- ---------  ---------  -----------------------------    -------------
A01   Sarah      Buchman    200 Years of German Humor             10450.50
A02   Wendy      Heydemark  I Blame My Mother                   1476138.45
A02   Wendy      Heydemark  Spontaneous, Not Annoying             66911.17
A04   Klee       Hull       Exchange of Platitudes                26000.72
A04   Klee       Hull       I Blame My Mother                   1476138.45
A05   Christian  Kells      Ask Your System Administrator         56777.77
A06              Kellsey    Just Wait Until After School           1638.00
A06              Kellsey    Kiss My Boo-Boo                        3487.50
```

Figure 7.21 Result of Listing 7.21.

Listing 7.22 uses a GROUP BY clause to calculate the total royalties paid by each publisher. The aggregate function COUNT() computes the total number of books for which each publisher pays royalties. Note that each author's royalty share is unnecessary here, because no per-author calculations are involved. See **Figure 7.22** for the result. The sum of the values in each of the last three columns in the result equals the corresponding total in Figure 7.19.

✔ Tip

- Using WHERE syntax, Listing 7.22 is equivalent to:

```
SELECT t.pub_id,
```

```
COUNT(t.sales) AS "Num books",
SUM(t.sales * t.price *
  r.royalty_rate)
  AS "Total royalties",
SUM(r.advance)
  AS "Total advances",
SUM((t.sales * t.price *
  r.royalty_rate) -
  r.advance)
  AS "Total due to authors"
FROM titles t, royalties r
WHERE r.title_id = t.title_id
  AND t.sales IS NOT NULL
GROUP BY t.pub_id
ORDER BY t.pub_id ASC;
```

Listing 7.22 Calculate the total royalties paid by each publisher. See Figure 7.22 for the result.

```
SELECT
    t.pub_id,
    COUNT(t.sales) AS "Num books",
    SUM(t.sales * t.price * r.royalty_rate) AS "Total royalties",
    SUM(r.advance) AS "Total advances",
    SUM((t.sales * t.price * r.royalty_rate) - r.advance) AS "Total due to authors"
FROM titles t
INNER JOIN royalties r
  ON r.title_id = t.title_id
WHERE t.sales IS NOT NULL
GROUP BY t.pub_id
ORDER BY t.pub_id ASC;
```

pub_id	Num books	Total royalties	Total advances	Total due to authors
P01	3	135600.21	80000.00	55600.21
P02	1	71777.77	15000.00	56777.77
P03	3	3982561.72	1021000.00	2961561.72
P04	5	197279.85	220000.00	-22720.15

Figure 7.22 Result of Listing 7.22.

Listing 7.23 is similar to Listing 7.22 except that it calculates the total royalties earned by each author for all books written (or co-written). See **Figure 7.23** for the result. The sum of the values in each of the last three columns in the result equals the corresponding total in Figure 7.19.

✔ Tips

■ Using WHERE syntax, Listing 7.23 is equivalent to:
   SELECT

```
    ta.au_id,
    COUNT(sales) AS "Num books",
    SUM(t.sales * t.price *
      r.royalty_rate *
      ta.royalty_share)
      AS "Total royalties share",
    SUM(r.advance *
      ta.royalty_share)
      AS "Total advances share",
```
code continues on next page

Listing 7.23 Calculate the total royalties earned by each author for all books written (or co-written). See Figure 7.23 for the result.

```
                              listing
SELECT
    ta.au_id,
    COUNT(sales) AS "Num books",
    SUM(t.sales * t.price * r.royalty_rate * ta.royalty_share) AS "Total royalties share",
    SUM(r.advance * ta.royalty_share) AS "Total advances share",
    SUM((t.sales * t.price * r.royalty_rate * ta.royalty_share) -
      (r.advance * ta.royalty_share)) AS "Total due to author"
  FROM title_authors ta
  INNER JOIN titles t
    ON t.title_id = ta.title_id
  INNER JOIN royalties r
    ON r.title_id = t.title_id
  WHERE t.sales IS NOT NULL
  GROUP BY ta.au_id
  ORDER BY ta.au_id ASC;
```

au_id	Num books	Total royalties share	Total advances share	Total due to author
A01	3	30907.14	31000.00	-92.86
A02	3	2111116.34	570000.00	1541116.34
A03	2	23899.28	42000.00	-18100.72
A04	4	2123336.32	638000.00	1485336.32
A05	1	71777.77	15000.00	56777.77
A06	3	26182.70	40000.00	-13817.30

Figure 7.23 Result of Listing 7.23.

```
    SUM((t.sales * t.price *
      r.royalty_rate *
      ta.royalty_share) -
      (r.advance *
      ta.royalty_share))
      AS "Total due to author"
FROM title_authors ta, titles t,
  royalties r
WHERE t.title_id = ta.title_id
  AND r.title_id = t.title_id
  AND t.sales IS NOT NULL
GROUP BY ta.au_id
ORDER BY ta.au_id ASC;
```

■ **DBMS** To run Listing 7.23 in **Microsoft Access**, type:

```
SELECT ta.au_id,
    COUNT(sales) AS "Num books",
    SUM(t.sales * t.price *
      r.royalty_rate *
      ta.royalty_share)
      AS "Total royalties share",
    SUM(r.advance *
      ta.royalty_share)
      AS "Total advances share",
    SUM((t.sales * t.price *
      r.royalty_rate *
      ta.royalty_share) -
      (r.advance *
      ta.royalty_share))
      AS "Total due to author"
FROM (title_authors AS ta
  INNER JOIN titles AS t
    ON t.title_id = ta.title_id)
INNER JOIN royalties AS r
  ON r.title_id = t.title_id
WHERE t.sales IS NOT NULL
GROUP BY ta.au_id
ORDER BY ta.au_id ASC;
```

Listing 7.24 uses two grouping columns to calculate the total royalties to be paid by each U.S. publisher to each author for all books written (or co-written) by the author. The HAVING condition returns retrieve rows with only positive net royalties, and the WHERE condition retrieves only U.S. publishers. See **Figure 7.24** for the result.

Listing 7.24 Calculate the positive net royalties to be paid by each U.S. publisher to each author for all books written (or co-written) by the author. See Figure 7.24 for the result.

```
SELECT
    t.pub_id,
    ta.au_id,
    COUNT(*) AS "Num books",
    SUM(t.sales * t.price * r.royalty_rate * ta.royalty_share) AS "Total royalties share",
    SUM(r.advance * ta.royalty_share) AS "Total advances share",
    SUM((t.sales * t.price * r.royalty_rate * ta.royalty_share) -
      (r.advance * ta.royalty_share)) AS "Total due to author"
FROM title_authors ta
INNER JOIN titles t
  ON t.title_id = ta.title_id
INNER JOIN royalties r
  ON r.title_id = t.title_id
INNER JOIN publishers p
  ON p.pub_id = t.pub_id
WHERE t.sales IS NOT NULL
  AND p.country IN ('USA')
GROUP BY t.pub_id, ta.au_id
HAVING SUM((t.sales * t.price * r.royalty_rate * ta.royalty_share) -
  (r.advance * ta.royalty_share)) > 0
ORDER BY t.pub_id ASC, ta.au_id ASC;
```

pub_id	au_id	Num books	Total royalties share	Total advances share	Total due to author
P01	A02	2	134977.89	70000.00	64977.89
P02	A05	1	71777.77	15000.00	56777.77
P04	A04	3	147197.87	138000.00	9197.87

Figure 7.24 Result of Listing 7.24.

✔ Tips

- Using WHERE syntax, Listing 7.24 is equivalent to:

```
SELECT t.pub_id, ta.au_id,
    COUNT(*) AS "Num books",
    SUM(t.sales * t.price *
      r.royalty_rate *
      ta.royalty_share)
      AS "Total royalties share",
    SUM(r.advance *
      ta.royalty_share)
      AS "Total advances share",
    SUM((t.sales * t.price *
      r.royalty_rate *
      ta.royalty_share) -
      (r.advance *
      ta.royalty_share))
      AS "Total due to author"
  FROM title_authors ta, titles t,
    royalties r, publishers p
  WHERE t.title_id = ta.title_id
    AND r.title_id = t.title_id
    AND p.pub_id = t.pub_id
    AND t.sales IS NOT NULL
    AND p.country IN ('USA')
  GROUP BY t.pub_id, ta.au_id
  HAVING SUM((t.sales * t.price *
    r.royalty_rate *
    ta.royalty_share) -
    (r.advance * ta.royalty_share))
    > 0
  ORDER BY t.pub_id ASC,
    ta.au_id ASC;
```

- **DBMS** To run Listing 7.24 in **Microsoft Access**, type:

```
SELECT t.pub_id,
    ta.au_id,
    COUNT(*) AS "Num books",
    SUM(t.sales * t.price *
      r.royalty_rate *
      ta.royalty_share)
      AS "Total royalties share",
    SUM(r.advance *
      ta.royalty_share)
      AS "Total advances share",
    SUM((t.sales * t.price *
      r.royalty_rate *
      ta.royalty_share) -
      (r.advance *
      ta.royalty_share))
      AS "Total due to author"
  FROM ((publishers AS p
    INNER JOIN titles AS t
      ON p.pub_id = t.pub_id)
        INNER JOIN royalties AS r
          ON t.title_id =
            r.title_id)
    INNER JOIN title_authors AS ta
      ON t.title_id = ta.title_id
  WHERE t.sales IS NOT NULL
    AND p.country IN ('USA')
  GROUP BY t.pub_id, ta.au_id
  HAVING SUM((t.sales * t.price *
    r.royalty_rate *
    ta.royalty_share) -
    (r.advance * ta.royalty_share))
    > 0
  ORDER BY t.pub_id ASC,
    ta.au_id ASC;
```

CREATING AN INNER JOIN WITH INNER JOIN

Creating Outer Joins with OUTER JOIN

In the preceding section, you learned that inner joins return rows only if at least one row from both tables satisfies the join condition(s). An inner join eliminates the rows that don't match with a row from the other table, whereas an *outer join* returns *all* rows from at least one of the tables (provided that those rows meet any WHERE or HAVING search conditions).

Outer joins are useful for answering questions that involve missing quantities: authors who have written no books or classes with no enrolled students, for example. Outer joins also are helpful for creating reports in which you want to list all the rows of one table along with matching rows from another table: all authors and any books that sold more than a given number of copies or all products with order quantities, including products no one ordered, for example.

Unlike other joins, the order in which you specify the tables in outer joins is important, so the two join operands are called the left table and the right table. Outer joins come in three flavors:

◆ **Left outer join.** The result of a left outer join includes all the rows from the left table specified in the LEFT OUTER JOIN clause, not just the rows in which the joined columns match. If a row in the left table has no matching rows in the right table, the associated row in the result contains nulls for all SELECT-list columns coming from the right table.

◆ **Right outer join.** A right outer join is the reverse of a left outer join. All rows from the right table are returned. Nulls are returned for the left table if a right table row has no matching row in the left table.

◆ **Full outer join.** A full outer join, which is a combination of left and right outer joins, returns all rows in both the left and right tables. If a row has no match in the other table, the SELECT-list columns from the other table contain nulls. If a match occurs between the tables, the entire row in the result contains data values from both tables.

To summarize, all rows are retrieved from the left table referenced in a left outer join, all rows are retrieved from the right table referenced in a right outer join, and all rows from both tables are retrieved in a full outer join. In all cases, unmatched rows are padded with nulls. In the result, you can't distinguish the nulls (if any) that were in the input tables originally from the nulls inserted by the outer join operation. Remember that the condition NULL = NULL is unknown and not a match; see "Nulls" in Chapter 3.

To create a left outer join:

◆ Type:

```
SELECT columns
   FROM left_table
   LEFT [OUTER] JOIN right_table
     ON join_conditions
```

columns is one or more comma-separated expressions or column names from *left_table* or *right_table*. *left_table* and *right_table* are the names of the joined tables. If the tables have some column names in common, qualify those column names with names of the tables.

join_conditions specifies one or more join conditions to be evaluated for each pair of joined rows. A join condition takes this form:

```
[left_table.]column op
```

→ `[right_table.]column`

op usually is = but can be any comparison operator: =, <>, <, <=, >, or >= (refer to Table 4.2 in Chapter 4). You may combine multiple join conditions with **AND** or **OR**; see "Combining and Negating Conditions with **AND**, **OR**, and **NOT**" in Chapter 4.

The keyword **OUTER** is optional.

To create a right outer join:

◆ Type:

```
SELECT columns
   FROM left_table
   RIGHT [OUTER] JOIN right_table
     ON join_conditions
```

columns, *left_table*, *right_table*, and *join_conditions* have the same meaning as in "To create a left outer join."

The keyword **OUTER** is optional.

To create a full outer join:

◆ Type:

```
SELECT columns
   FROM left_table
   FULL [OUTER] JOIN right_table
     ON join_conditions
```

columns, *left_table*, *right_table*, and *join_conditions* have the same meaning as in "To create a left outer join."

The keyword **OUTER** is optional.

✔ Tips

■ For outer joins, you should use **JOIN** syntax instead of **WHERE** syntax when possible, because **JOIN** syntax is more precise. SQL lacks standardized **WHERE** syntax for outer joins, so syntax varies by DBMS. A DBMS also may place restrictions on **WHERE** outer joins that don't exist for **JOIN** outer joins. See the DBMS Tip later in this section for specific information.

continues on next page

CREATING OUTER JOINS WITH OUTER JOIN

- Be wary of the order in which tables appear in outer joins. Unlike other joins, outer joins aren't associative—that is, the result of a query that involves an outer join depends on the order in which the tables are grouped and joined (associated). The following two three-table inner joins are equivalent (except for the column order in the result):

```
SELECT * FROM table1
  INNER JOIN table2
  INNER JOIN table3
```

and:

```
SELECT * FROM table2
  INNER JOIN table3
  INNER JOIN table1
```

But the following two three-table outer joins yield different results:

```
SELECT * FROM table1
  LEFT OUTER JOIN table2
  LEFT OUTER JOIN table3
```

and:

```
SELECT * FROM table2
  LEFT OUTER JOIN table3
  LEFT OUTER JOIN table1
```

- The SQL standard defines a *union join,* which doesn't actually match rows from two tables but returns a full outer join with matching rows removed. Every row in a union join comprises the columns of one table joined with nulls for the columns of the other table. The result of the statement *t1* UNION JOIN *t2* looks like this table:

All rows of *t1*	Nulls
Nulls	All rows of *t2*

I haven't devoted an entire section to UNION JOIN because it has few practical uses and many DBMSes don't support it. You can simulate a union join by using a full outer join.

t1 UNION JOIN *t2*

is equivalent to:

t1 FULL OUTER JOIN *t2* ON 1 = 2

t1 and *t2* are tables, and 1 = 2 represents any condition that always is false. Note that UNION JOIN differs from UNION, which is a set operation and not a join; see "Combining Rows with UNION" later in this chapter.

- **DBMS** **Microsoft SQL Server** uses the outer join operator * in WHERE syntax to create outer joins. Attach * to the left or right of the comparison operator to create a left or right outer join. For outer joins, WHERE syntax is less precise than OUTER JOIN syntax and may yield an ambiguous query. The *= and =* operators may not be supported in a future version of SQL Server, so I'll give just a few examples later in this section.

  Oracle 8i and earlier versions don't support JOIN syntax; use WHERE joins instead. Oracle 9i and later versions support JOIN syntax. Oracle uses the outer join operator (+) in WHERE syntax to create outer joins. Add (+) after the table that must be expanded (filled with nulls). See the examples later in this section.

Listing 7.25 List the cities of the authors and the cities of the publishers. See Figure 7.25 for the result.

```
┌─────────────────── listing ───────────────────┐
SELECT a.au_fname, a.au_lname, a.city
  FROM authors a;


SELECT p.pub_name, p.city
  FROM publishers p;
```

For reference in the following four examples, **Listing 7.25** and **Figure 7.25** show the city for each author and publisher.

au_fname	au_lname	city
Sarah	Buchman	Bronx
Wendy	Heydemark	Boulder
Hallie	Hull	San Francisco
Klee	Hull	San Francisco
Christian	Kells	New York
	Kellsey	Palo Alto
Paddy	O'Furniture	Sarasota

pub_name	city
Abatis Publishers	New York
Core Dump Books	San Francisco
Schadenfreude Press	Hamburg
Tenterhooks Press	Berkeley

Figure 7.25 Result of Listing 7.25.

CREATING OUTER JOINS WITH OUTER JOIN

Listing 7.26 performs an inner join of the tables authors and publishers on their city columns. The result, **Figure 7.26**, lists only the authors who live in cities in which a publisher is located. You can compare the result of this inner join with the results of the outer joins in the following three examples.

✔ Tip

■ Using WHERE syntax, Listing 7.26 is equivalent to:
```
SELECT a.au_fname, a.au_lname,
    p.pub_name
  FROM authors a, publishers p
  WHERE a.city = p.city;
```

Listing 7.26 List the authors who live in cities in which a publisher is located. See Figure 7.26 for the result.

```
SELECT a.au_fname, a.au_lname, p.pub_name
  FROM authors a
  INNER JOIN publishers p
    ON a.city = p.city;
```

```
au_fname   au_lname  pub_name
---------  --------  -----------------
Hallie     Hull      Core Dump Books
Klee       Hull      Core Dump Books
Christian  Kells     Abatis Publishers
```

Figure 7.26 Result of Listing 7.26.

Listing 7.27 This left outer join includes all rows in the table authors in the result, whether or not there's a match in the column city in the table publishers. See Figure 7.27 for the result.

```
██████████████      listing      ██████████
SELECT a.au_fname, a.au_lname, p.pub_name
  FROM authors a
  LEFT OUTER JOIN publishers p
    ON a.city = p.city
  ORDER BY p.pub_name ASC,
    a.au_lname ASC, a.au_fname ASC;
```

```
au_fname    au_lname     pub_name
---------   -----------  -----------------

Sarah       Buchman      NULL

Wendy       Heydemark    NULL

            Kellsey      NULL

Paddy       O'Furniture  NULL

Christian   Kells        Abatis Publishers

Hallie      Hull         Core Dump Books

Klee        Hull         Core Dump Books
```

Figure 7.27 Result of Listing 7.27. Note that there's no matching data for four of the listed authors, so these rows contain null in the column pub_name.

Listing 7.27 uses a left outer join to include all authors in the result, regardless of whether a publisher is located in the same city. See **Figure 7.27** for the result.

✔ Tip

■ **DBMS** To run Listing 7.27 in **Microsoft SQL Server** by using WHERE syntax, type:

```
SELECT a.au_fname, a.au_lname,
    p.pub_name
  FROM authors a, publishers p
  WHERE a.city *= p.city
  ORDER BY p.pub_name ASC,
    a.au_lname ASC, a.au_fname ASC;
```

To run Listing 7.27 in **Oracle** 8i, type:

```
SELECT a.au_fname, a.au_lname,
    p.pub_name
  FROM authors a, publishers p
  WHERE a.city = p.city (+)
  ORDER BY p.pub_name ASC,
    a.au_lname ASC, a.au_fname ASC;
```

CREATING OUTER JOINS WITH OUTER JOIN

Listing 7.28 uses a right outer join to include all publishers in the result, regardless of whether an author lives in the publisher's city. See **Figure 7.28** for the result.

✔ Tip

- **DBMS** To run Listing 7.28 in **Microsoft SQL Server** by using WHERE syntax, type:

```
SELECT a.au_fname, a.au_lname,
    p.pub_name
  FROM authors a, publishers p
  WHERE a.city =* p.city
  ORDER BY p.pub_name ASC,
    a.au_lname ASC, a.au_fname ASC;
```

To run Listing 7.28 in **Oracle** 8i, type:

```
SELECT a.au_fname, a.au_lname,
    p.pub_name
  FROM authors a, publishers p
  WHERE a.city (+) = p.city
  ORDER BY p.pub_name ASC,
    a.au_lname ASC, a.au_fname ASC;
```

Listing 7.28 This right outer join includes all rows in the table publishers in the result, whether or not there's a match in the column city in the table authors. See Figure 7.28 for the result.

```
SELECT a.au_fname, a.au_lname, p.pub_name
  FROM authors a
  RIGHT OUTER JOIN publishers p
    ON a.city = p.city
  ORDER BY p.pub_name ASC,
    a.au_lname ASC, a.au_fname ASC;
```

au_fname	au_lname	pub_name
Christian	Kells	Abatis Publishers
Hallie	Hull	Core Dump Books
Klee	Hull	Core Dump Books
NULL	NULL	Schadenfreude Press
NULL	NULL	Tenterhooks Press

Figure 7.28 Result of Listing 7.28. Note that there's no matching data for two of the listed publishers, so these rows contain nulls in the columns au_fname and au_lname.

Listing 7.29 uses a full outer join to include all publishers and all authors in the result, regardless of whether a publisher and author are located in the same city. See **Figure 7.29** for the result.

Listing 7.29 This full outer join includes all rows in the tables authors and publishers in the result, whether or not there's a match in the city columns. See Figure 7.29 for the result.

```
                          listing
SELECT a.au_fname, a.au_lname, p.pub_name
  FROM authors a
  FULL OUTER JOIN publishers p
    ON a.city = p.city
  ORDER BY p.pub_name ASC,
    a.au_lname ASC, a.au_fname ASC;
```

au_fname	au_lname	pub_name
Sarah	Buchman	NULL
Wendy	Heydemark	NULL
	Kellsey	NULL
Paddy	O'Furniture	NULL
Christian	Kells	Abatis Publishers
Hallie	Hull	Core Dump Books
Klee	Hull	Core Dump Books
NULL	NULL	Schadenfreude Press
NULL	NULL	Tenterhooks Press

Figure 7.29 Result of Listing 7.29. This result contains nine rows: four rows for authors who have no matching rows in the table publishers, three rows in which the author and publisher coexist in the same city, and two rows for publishers who have no matching city in the table authors.

✔ Tips

- **DBMS** In **Microsoft SQL Server**, you can't place the * operator on both sides of the comparison operator to form a full outer join. Instead, form the union of a left and right outer join; see "Combining Rows with UNION" later in this chapter. To run Listing 7.29 in SQL Server by using WHERE syntax, type:

  ```
  SELECT a.au_fname, a.au_lname,
    p.pub_name
   FROM authors a, publishers p
   WHERE a.city *= p.city
  UNION ALL
  SELECT a.au_fname, a.au_lname,
    p.pub_name
   FROM authors a, publishers p
   WHERE a.city =* p.city
    AND a.city IS NULL;
  ```

  In **Oracle**, you can't place the (+) operator on both sides of the comparison operator to form a full outer join. Instead, form the union of a left and right outer join; see "Combining Rows with UNION" later in this chapter. To run Listing 7.29 in Oracle 8i, type:

  ```
  SELECT a.au_fname, a.au_lname,
    p.pub_name
   FROM authors a, publishers p
   WHERE a.city = p.city (+)
  UNION ALL
  SELECT a.au_fname, a.au_lname,
    p.pub_name
   FROM authors a, publishers p
   WHERE a.city (+) = p.city
    AND a.city IS NULL;
  ```

  continues on next page

Microsoft Access and **MySQL** don't support full outer joins, but you can replicate one by taking the union of left and right outer joins; see "Combining Rows with UNION" later in this chapter. In the following example, the first UNION table is a left outer join restricted to return all the rows in authors as well as the matched rows in publishers based on city. The second UNION table is a right outer join restricted to return only the unmatched rows in **publishers**. To run Listing 7.29 in Access or MySQL, type:

```
SELECT a.au_fname, a.au_lname,
    p.pub_name
  FROM authors a
  LEFT OUTER JOIN publishers p
    ON a.city = p.city
UNION ALL
SELECT a.au_fname, a.au_lname,
    p.pub_name
  FROM authors a
  RIGHT OUTER JOIN publishers p
    ON a.city = p.city
  WHERE a.city IS NULL;
```

Listing 7.30 List the number of books that each author wrote (or co-wrote), including authors who have written no books. See Figure 7.30 for the result.

```
                    listing
SELECT
    a.au_id,
    COUNT(ta.title_id) AS "Num books"
  FROM authors a
  LEFT OUTER JOIN title_authors ta
    ON a.au_id = ta.au_id
  GROUP BY a.au_id
  ORDER BY a.au_id ASC;
```

```
au_id Num books
----- ---------
A01         3
A02         4
A03         2
A04         4
A05         1
A06         3
A07         0
```

Figure 7.30 Result of Listing 7.30.

Listing 7.30 uses a left outer join to list the number of books that each author wrote (or co-wrote). See **Figure 7.30** for the result. Note that in contrast to Listing 7.11 in "Creating an Inner Join with INNER JOIN" earlier in this chapter, the author A07 (Paddy O'Furniture) appears in the result even though he has written no books.

✔ Tip

- **DBMS** To run Listing 7.30 in **Oracle** 8i, type:

```
SELECT a.au_id,
    COUNT(ta.title_id)
      AS "Num books"
  FROM authors a, title_authors ta
  WHERE a.au_id = ta.au_id (+)
  GROUP BY a.au_id
  ORDER BY a.au_id ASC;
```

Listing 7.31 uses a WHERE condition to test for null and list *only* the authors who haven't written a book. See **Figure 7.31** for the result.

✔ Tip

- **DBMS** To run Listing 7.31 in **Oracle** 8i, type:

```
SELECT a.au_id, a.au_fname,
     a.au_lname
  FROM authors a, title_authors ta
  WHERE a.au_id = ta.au_id (+)
    AND ta.au_id IS NULL;
```

Listing 7.31 List the authors who haven't written (or co-written) a book. See Figure 7.31 for the result.

```
SELECT a.au_id, a.au_fname, a.au_lname
  FROM authors a
  LEFT OUTER JOIN title_authors ta
    ON a.au_id = ta.au_id
  WHERE ta.au_id IS NULL;
```

```
au_id au_fname au_lname
----- -------- -----------
A07   Paddy    O'Furniture
```

Figure 7.31 Result of Listing 7.31.

Listing 7.32 combines an inner join and a left outer join to list all authors and any books they wrote (or co-wrote) that sold more than 100,000 copies. In this example, first I created a filtered INNER JOIN result and then OUTER JOINed it with the table authors, from which I wanted all rows. See **Figure 7.32** for the result.

Listing 7.32 List all authors and any books written (or co-written) that sold more than 100,000 copies. See Figure 7.32 for the result.

```listing
SELECT a.au_id, a.au_fname, a.au_lname,
    tta.title_id, tta.title_name, tta.sales
  FROM authors a
  LEFT OUTER JOIN
  (SELECT ta.au_id, t.title_id,
      t.title_name, t.sales
    FROM title_authors ta
    INNER JOIN titles t
      ON t.title_id = ta.title_id
    WHERE sales > 100000) tta
    ON a.au_id = tta.au_id
  ORDER BY a.au_id ASC, tta.title_id ASC;
```

✔ **Tip**

■ **DBMS** To run Listing 7.32 in **Oracle** 8i, type:

```
SELECT a.au_id, a.au_fname,
    a.au_lname,
    tta.title_id, tta.title_name,
    tta.sales
  FROM authors a,
    (SELECT ta.au_id, t.title_id,
        t.title_name, t.sales
      FROM title_authors ta,
        titles t
      WHERE t.title_id =
          ta.title_id
      AND sales > 100000) tta
  WHERE a.au_id = tta.au_id (+)
  ORDER BY a.au_id ASC,
    tta.title_id ASC;
```

continues on next page

au_id	au_fname	au_lname	title_id	title_name	sales
A01	Sarah	Buchman	NULL	NULL	NULL
A02	Wendy	Heydemark	T07	I Blame My Mother	1500200
A02	Wendy	Heydemark	T12	Spontaneous, Not Annoying	100001
A03	Hallie	Hull	NULL	NULL	NULL
A04	Klee	Hull	T05	Exchange of Platitudes	201440
A04	Klee	Hull	T07	I Blame My Mother	1500200
A05	Christian	Kells	NULL	NULL	NULL
A06		Kellsey	NULL	NULL	NULL
A07	Paddy	O'Furniture	NULL	NULL	NULL

Figure 7.32 Result of Listing 7.32.

MySQL 4.0 and earlier versions don't support subqueries; see the DBMS Tip in "Understanding Subqueries" in Chapter 8. For complicated queries, you often can create a temporary table to hold the subquery; see "Creating a Temporary Table with CREATE TEMPORARY TABLE" in Chapter 10. To run Listing 7.32 in MySQL, type:

```
CREATE TEMPORARY TABLE tta
  SELECT ta.au_id, t.title_id,
      t.title_name, t.sales
    FROM title_authors ta
    INNER JOIN titles t
      ON t.title_id = ta.title_id
    WHERE sales > 100000;

SELECT a.au_id, a.au_fname,
    a.au_lname, tta.title_id,
    tta.title_name, tta.sales
  FROM authors a
  LEFT OUTER JOIN tta
    ON a.au_id = tta.au_id
  ORDER BY a.au_id ASC,
    tta.title_id ASC;

DROP TABLE tta;
```

Creating a Self-Join

A *self-join* is a normal SQL join that joins a table to itself and retrieves rows from a table by comparing values in one or more columns in the same table. Self-joins often are used in tables with a *reflexive relationship,* which is a primary-key/foreign-key relationship from a column or combination of columns in a table to other columns in that same table. For information about keys, see "Primary Keys" and "Foreign Keys" in Chapter 2.

No tables in the sample database have a reflexive relationship, so I'll show you an example that's used in many SQL books and tutorials. Suppose that you have the following table, named `employees`:

```
emp_id emp_name          boss_id

------ ----------------- -------

E01    Lord Copper       NULL

E02    Jocelyn Hitchcock E01

E03    Mr. Salter        E01

E04    William Boot      E03

E05    Mr. Corker        E03
```

`emp_id` is a primary key that uniquely identifies the employee, and `boss_id` is an employee ID that identifies the employee's manager. Each manager also is an employee, so to ensure that each manager ID that is added to the table matches an existing employee ID, `boss_id` is defined as a foreign key of `emp_id`. **Listing 7.33** uses this reflexive relationship to compare rows within the table and retrieve the *name* of the manager of each employee. (You wouldn't need a join at all to get just the manager's ID.) See **Figure 7.33** for the result.

The same table (`employees`) appears twice in Listing 7.33 with two different aliases (`e1` and `e2`) that are used to qualify column names in the join condition:

```
e1.boss_id = e2.emp_id
```

As with any join, a self-join requires two tables, but instead of adding a second table to the join, you add a second *instance* of the same table. That way, you can compare a column in the first instance of the table to a column in the second instance. As with all joins, your DBMS combines and returns rows of the table that satisfy the join condition. You really aren't creating another copy of the table—you're joining the table to itself—but the effect may be easier to understand if you think about it as being two tables.

Listing 7.33 List the name of each employee and the name of his or her manager. See Figure 7.33 for the result.

```
                    listing
SELECT
    e1.emp_name AS "Employee name",
    e2.emp_name AS "Boss name"
FROM employees e1
INNER JOIN employees e2
  ON e1.boss_id = e2.emp_id;
```

```
Employee name      Boss name

----------------- -----------

Jocelyn Hitchcock Lord Copper

Mr. Salter        Lord Copper

William Boot      Mr. Salter

Mr. Corker        Mr. Salter
```

Figure 7.33 Result of Listing 7.33. Note that Lord Copper, who has no boss, is excluded from the result because his null `boss_id` doesn't satisfy the join condition.

To create a self-join:

◆ Type:

```
SELECT columns
  FROM table [AS] alias1
  INNER JOIN table [AS] alias2
    ON join_conditions
```

columns is one or more comma-separated expressions or column names from *table*. *alias1* and *alias2* are different alias names that are used to refer to *table* in *join_conditions*. See "Creating Table Aliases with **AS**" earlier in this chapter.

join_conditions specifies one or more join conditions to be evaluated for each pair of joined rows. A join condition takes this form:

alias1.column op alias2.column

op can be any comparison operator: =, <>, <, <=, >, or >= (refer to Table 4.2 in Chapter 4). You may combine multiple join conditions with **AND** or **OR**; see "Combining and Negating Conditions with **AND, OR,** and **NOT**" in Chapter 4.

✔ Tips

■ You can join a table to itself even if no reflexive relationship exists. A common type of self-join compares a column in the first instance of the table to the *same* column in the second instance. This join condition allows you to compare the values in a column to one another, as shown in the subsequent examples in this section.

■ **DBMS** **Oracle** 8i and earlier versions don't support **JOIN** syntax; use **WHERE** joins instead. Oracle 9i and later versions support **JOIN** syntax.

Listing 7.34 List the authors who live in the same state as author A04 (Klee Hull). See Figure 7.34 for the result.

```
                    listing
SELECT a1.au_id, a1.au_fname,
    a1.au_lname, a1.state
  FROM authors a1
  INNER JOIN authors a2
    ON a1.state = a2.state
  WHERE a2.au_id = 'A04';
```

```
au_id au_fname au_lname state
----- -------- -------- -----
A03   Hallie   Hull     CA
A04   Klee     Hull     CA
A06            Kellsey  CA
```

Figure 7.34 Result of Listing 7.34.

Listing 7.34 uses a WHERE search condition and self-join from the column **state** to itself to find all authors who live in the same state as author A04 (Klee Hull). See **Figure 7.34** for the result.

✔ Tips

■ Using WHERE syntax, Listing 7.34 is equivalent to:

```
SELECT a1.au_id, a1.au_fname,
    a1.au_lname, a1.state
  FROM authors a1, authors a2
  WHERE a1.state = a2.state
    AND a2.au_id = 'A04';
```

■ Self-joins often can be restated as subqueries (see Chapter 8). Using a subquery, Listing 7.34 is equivalent to:

```
SELECT au_id, au_fname,
    au_lname, state
  FROM authors
  WHERE state IN
    (SELECT state
       FROM authors
       WHERE au_id = 'A04');
```

For every biography, **Listing 7.35** lists the other biographies that outsold it. Note that the WHERE search condition requires type = 'biography' for both tables t1 and t2 because the join condition considers the column type to be two separate columns. See **Figure 7.35** for the result.

✔ Tip

- Using WHERE syntax, Listing 7.35 is equivalent to:

```
SELECT t1.title_id, t1.sales,
    t2.title_id AS "Better seller",
    t2.sales AS "Higher sales"
  FROM titles t1, titles t2
  WHERE t1.sales < t2.sales
    AND t1.type = 'biography'
    AND t2.type = 'biography'
  ORDER BY t1.title_id ASC,
    t2.sales ASC;
```

Listing 7.35 For every biography, list the title ID and sales of the other biographies that outsold it. See Figure 7.35 for the result.

```
SELECT t1.title_id, t1.sales,
    t2.title_id AS "Better seller",
    t2.sales AS "Higher sales"
  FROM titles t1
  INNER JOIN titles t2
    ON t1.sales < t2.sales
  WHERE t1.type = 'biography'
    AND t2.type = 'biography'
  ORDER BY t1.title_id ASC, t2.sales ASC;
```

title_id	sales	Better seller	Higher sales
T06	11320	T12	100001
T06	11320	T07	1500200
T12	100001	T07	1500200

Figure 7.35 Result of Listing 7.35.

Listing 7.36 List all pairs of authors who live in New York State. See Figure 7.36 for the result.

```
SELECT
    a1.au_fname, a1.au_lname,
    a2.au_fname, a2.au_lname
 FROM authors a1
 INNER JOIN authors a2
   ON a1.state = a2.state
 WHERE a1.state = 'NY'
 ORDER BY a1.au_id ASC, a2.au_id ASC;
```

au_fname	au_lname	au_fname	au_lname
Sarah	Buchman	Sarah	Buchman
Sarah	Buchman	Christian	Kells
Christian	Kells	Sarah	Buchman
Christian	Kells	Christian	Kells

Figure 7.36 Result of Listing 7.36.

Listing 7.36 is a self-join to find all pairs of authors within New York State. See **Figure 7.36** for the result.

✔ Tip

■ Using WHERE syntax, Listing 7.36 is equivalent to:

```
SELECT
    a1.au_fname, a1.au_lname,
    a2.au_fname, a2.au_lname
 FROM authors a1, authors a2
 WHERE a1.state = a2.state
   AND a1.state = 'NY'
 ORDER BY a1.au_id ASC,
    a2.au_id ASC;
```

The first and fourth rows of Figure 7.36 are unnecessary because they indicate that Sarah Buchman lives in the same state as Sarah Buchman, and likewise for Christian Kells. To eliminate these rows, I'll add another join condition to retain only those rows in which the two authors differ (**Listing 7.37** and **Figure 7.37**).

✔ Tip

- Using WHERE syntax, Listing 7.37 is equivalent to:

```
SELECT
    a1.au_fname, a1.au_lname,
    a2.au_fname, a2.au_lname
  FROM authors a1, authors a2
  WHERE a1.state = a2.state
    AND a1.au_id <> a2.au_id
    AND a1.state = 'NY'
  ORDER BY a1.au_id ASC,
    a2.au_id ASC;
```

Listing 7.37 List all different pairs of authors who live in New York State. See Figure 7.37 for the result.

```
SELECT
    a1.au_fname, a1.au_lname,
    a2.au_fname, a2.au_lname
  FROM authors a1
  INNER JOIN authors a2
    ON a1.state = a2.state
    AND a1.au_id <> a2.au_id
  WHERE a1.state = 'NY'
  ORDER BY a1.au_id ASC, a2.au_id ASC;
```

au_fname	au_lname	au_fname	au_lname
Sarah	Buchman	Christian	Kells
Christian	Kells	Sarah	Buchman

Figure 7.37 Result of Listing 7.37.

Listing 7.38 List all different pairs of authors who live in New York State, with no redundancies. See Figure 7.38 for the result.

```
                          listing
SELECT
    a1.au_fname, a1.au_lname,
    a2.au_fname, a2.au_lname
  FROM authors a1
  INNER JOIN authors a2
    ON a1.state = a2.state
    AND a1.au_id < a2.au_id
  WHERE a1.state = 'NY'
  ORDER BY a1.au_id ASC, a2.au_id ASC;
```

```
au_fname  au_lname  au_fname   au_lname
--------  --------  ---------  --------
Sarah     Buchman   Christian  Kells
```

Figure 7.38 Result of Listing 7.38.

Figure 7.37 still isn't quite what I want, because the two result rows are redundant. The first row states that Sarah Buchman lives in the same state as Christian Kells, and the second row gives the same information. To eliminate this redundancy, I'll change the second join condition's comparison operator from not-equal to less-than (**Listing 7.38** and **Figure 7.38**).

✔ Tip

■ Using WHERE syntax, Listing 7.38 is equivalent to:

```
SELECT
    a1.au_fname, a1.au_lname,
    a2.au_fname, a2.au_lname
  FROM authors a1, authors a2
  WHERE a1.state = a2.state
    AND a1.au_id < a2.au_id
    AND a1.state = 'NY'
  ORDER BY a1.au_id ASC,
    a2.au_id ASC;
```

CREATING A SELF-JOIN

Combining Rows
with UNION

In the next three sections, I'll cover the UNION, INTERSECT, and EXCEPT set operators, which combine the results of two SELECT statements into a single result. These operators can be mixed and chained to combine more than two tables. The UNION operator is supported widely; the other two operators, less so.

A UNION operation combines the results of two queries into a single result that comprises the rows returned by both queries. (This operation differs from a join, which combines columns from two tables.) A UNION expression removes duplicate rows from the result; a UNION ALL expression doesn't remove duplicates.

Unions are simple, but they have some restrictions:

◆ The SELECT-clause lists in the two queries must have the same number of columns (column names, arithmetic expressions, aggregate functions, and so on).

◆ The corresponding columns in the two queries must be listed in the same order in the two queries.

◆ The corresponding columns must have the same data type or must be implicitly convertible to the same type.

◆ If the names of corresponding columns match, that column name is used in the result. If the corresponding column names differ, it's up to the DBMS to determine the column name in the result. Most DBMSes take the result's column names from the first individual query in the UNION statement. If you want to rename a column in the result, use an AS clause in the first query; see "Creating Column Aliases with AS" in Chapter 4.

◆ An ORDER BY clause can appear in only the final query in the UNION statement. The sort is applied to the final, combined result. Because the result's column names depend on the DBMS, it's often easiest to use relative column positions to specify the sort order; see "Sorting Rows with ORDER BY" in Chapter 4.

◆ GROUP BY and HAVING can be specified in the individual queries only; they can't be used to affect the final result.

To combine rows:

◆ Type:

    select_statement1
    UNION [ALL]
    select_statement2;

select_statement1 and select_statement2 are SELECT statements. The number and the order of the columns must be identical in both statements, and the data types of corresponding columns must be compatible. Duplicate rows are eliminated from the result unless ALL is specified.

Listing 7.39 List the states where authors and publishers are located. See Figure 7.39 for the result.

```
                        listing
SELECT state FROM authors

UNION

SELECT state FROM publishers;
```

```
state
-----
NULL
CA
CO
FL
NY
```

Figure 7.39 Result of Listing 7.39.

Listing 7.39 lists the states where authors and publishers are located. By default, UNION removes duplicate rows from the result. See **Figure 7.39** for the result.

Listing 7.40 is the same as Listing 7.39 except that it includes the ALL keyword, so all rows are included in the results, and duplicates aren't removed. See **Figure 7.40** for the result.

Listing 7.40 List the states where authors and publishers are located, including duplicates. See Figure 7.40 for the result.

```
SELECT state FROM authors
UNION ALL
SELECT state FROM publishers;
```

```
state
-----
NY
CO
CA
CA
NY
CA
FL
NY
CA
NULL
CA
```

Figure 7.40 Result of Listing 7.40.

Listing 7.41 List the names of all the authors and publishers. See Figure 7.41 for the result.

```
                    listing
SELECT au_fname || ' ' || au_lname AS "Name"
  FROM authors
UNION
SELECT pub_name
  FROM publishers
  ORDER BY 1 ASC;
```

```
Name
-------------------
 Kellsey
Abatis Publishers
Christian Kells
Core Dump Books
Hallie Hull
Klee Hull
Paddy O'Furniture
Sarah Buchman
Schadenfreude Press
Tenterhooks Press
Wendy Heydemark
```

Figure 7.41 Result of Listing 7.41.

Listing 7.41 lists the names of all the authors and publishers. The AS clause in the first query names the column in the result. The ORDER BY clause uses a relative column position instead of a column name to sort the result. See **Figure 7.41** for the result.

COMBINING ROWS WITH UNION

Listing 7.42 expands on Listing 7.41 and defines the extra column Type to identify which table each row came from. The WHERE conditions retrieve the authors and publishers from New York State only. See **Figure 7.42** for the result.

Listing 7.42 List the names of all the authors and publishers located in New York State, sorted by type and then by name. See Figure 7.42 for the result.

```
SELECT
    'author' AS "Type",
    au_fname || ' ' || au_lname AS "Name",
    state
  FROM authors
  WHERE state = 'NY'
UNION
SELECT
    'publisher',
    pub_name,
    state
  FROM publishers
  WHERE state = 'NY'
  ORDER BY 1 ASC, 2 ASC;
```

```
Type       Name               state
---------  -----------------  -----
author     Christian Kells    NY
author     Sarah Buchman      NY
publisher  Abatis Publishers  NY
```

Figure 7.42 Result of Listing 7.42.

Listing 7.43 List the names of all the authors and publishers located in New York State, and the titles of books published in New York State, sorted by type and then by name. See Figure 7.43 for the result.

```
                     listing
SELECT
    'author' AS "Type",
    au_fname || ' ' || au_lname AS "Name"
  FROM authors
  WHERE state = 'NY'
UNION
SELECT
    'publisher',
    pub_name
  FROM publishers
  WHERE state = 'NY'
UNION
SELECT
    'title',
    title_name
  FROM titles t
  INNER JOIN publishers p
    ON t.pub_id = p.pub_id
  WHERE p.state = 'NY'
  ORDER BY 1 ASC, 2 ASC;
```

```
Type       Name
---------  --------------------------
author     Christian Kells
author     Sarah Buchman
publisher  Abatis Publishers
title      1977!
title      How About Never?
title      Not Without My Faberge Egg
title      Spontaneous, Not Annoying
```

Figure 7.43 Result of Listing 7.43.

Listing 7.43 adds a third query to Listing 7.42 to retrieve the titles of books published in New York State also. See **Figure 7.43** for the result.

COMBINING ROWS WITH UNION

Listing 7.44 is similar to Listing 7.43 except that it lists the counts of each author, publisher, and book, instead of their names. See **Figure 7.44** for the result.

Listing 7.44 List the counts of all the authors and publishers located in New York State, and the titles of books published in New York State, sorted by type. See Figure 7.44 for the result.

```
SELECT
    'author' AS "Type",
    COUNT(au_id) AS "Count"
  FROM authors
  WHERE state = 'NY'
UNION
SELECT
    'publisher',
    COUNT(pub_id)
  FROM publishers
  WHERE state = 'NY'
UNION
SELECT
    'title',
    COUNT(title_id)
  FROM titles t
  INNER JOIN publishers p
    ON t.pub_id = p.pub_id
  WHERE p.state = 'NY'
  ORDER BY 1 ASC;
```

```
Type       Count
---------  -----
author        2
publisher     1
title         4
```

Figure 7.44 Result of Listing 7.44.

Listing 7.45 Raise the price of history books by 10 percent and psychology books by 20 percent, and leave the prices of other books unchanged. See Figure 7.45 for the result.

```
                      listing

SELECT title_id, type, price,
    price * 1.10 AS "New price"
  FROM titles
  WHERE type = 'history'
UNION
SELECT title_id, type, price, price * 1.20
  FROM titles
  WHERE type = 'psychology'
UNION
SELECT title_id, type, price, price
  FROM titles
  WHERE type NOT IN ('psychology','history')
  ORDER BY type ASC, title_id ASC;
```

```
title_id type        price   New price
-------- ----------  ------- ---------
T06      biography    19.95      19.95
T07      biography    23.95      23.95
T10      biography     NULL       NULL
T12      biography    12.99      12.99
T08      children     10.00      10.00
T09      children     13.95      13.95
T03      computer     39.95      39.95
T01      history      21.99      24.19
T02      history      19.95      21.95
T13      history      29.99      32.99
T04      psychology   12.99      15.59
T05      psychology    6.95       8.34
T11      psychology    7.99       9.59
```

Figure 7.45 Result of Listing 7.45.

In **Listing 7.45**, I revisit Listing 5.30 in "Evaluating Conditional Values with CASE" in Chapter 5. But instead of using CASE to change book prices and simulate if-then logic, I use multiple UNION queries. See **Figure 7.45** for the result.

✔ Tips

- UNION is a commutative operation: A UNION B is the same as B UNION A.

- The SQL standard gives INTERSECT higher precedence than UNION and EXCEPT, but the actual precedence used by your DBMS may differ. Use parentheses to specify order of evaluation in queries with mixed set operators; see "Determining the Order of Evaluation" in Chapter 5.

- If you mix UNION and UNION ALL in a single statement, use parentheses to specify order of evaluation. Take these two statements, for example:

```
SELECT * FROM table1
UNION ALL
(SELECT * FROM table2
UNION
SELECT * FROM table3);
```

and:

```
(SELECT * FROM table1
UNION ALL
SELECT * FROM table2)
UNION
SELECT * FROM table3;
```

The first statement eliminates duplicates in the union of *table2* and *table3* but doesn't eliminate duplicates in the union of that result and *table1*. The second statement includes duplicates in the union of *table1* and *table2* but eliminates duplicates in the subsequent union with *table3*, so ALL has no effect on the final result of this statement.

- The result of a UNION operation may be sorted even if you don't specify an ORDER BY clause, because your DBMS performs an internal sort to identify and exclude duplicate rows. (UNION ALL results aren't sorted internally.)

- **DBMS** In **Microsoft Access** and **Microsoft SQL Server**, use + to concatenate strings (see "Concatenating Strings with ||" in Chapter 5). To run Listings 7.41 through 7.43 in Access and SQL Server, change the concatenation expressions to:

```
au_fname + ' ' + au_lname
```

In **MySQL**, use CONCAT() to concatenate strings (see "Concatenating Strings with ||" in Chapter 5). To run Listings 7.41 through 7.43 in MySQL, change the concatenation expressions to:

```
CONCAT(au_fname, ' ', au_lname)
```

In **PostgreSQL**, convert the floating-point numbers in Listing 7.45 to DECIMAL; see "Converting Data Types with CAST()" in Chapter 5. To run Listing 7.45 in PostgreSQL, change new-price calculations to:

```
price * CAST((1.10) AS DECIMAL)
price * CAST((1.20) AS DECIMAL)
```

Listing 7.46 List the cities in which both an author and a publisher are located. See Figure 7.46 for the result.

```
                    listing
SELECT city
  FROM authors
INTERSECT
SELECT city
  FROM publishers;
```

```
city
-------------
New York
San Francisco
```

Figure 7.46 Result of Listing 7.46.

Finding Common Rows with INTERSECT

An INTERSECT operation combines the results of two queries into a single result that comprises all the rows common to both queries. Intersections have the same restrictions as unions; see "Combining Rows with UNION" earlier in this chapter.

To find common rows:

◆ Type:

select_statement1

INTERSECT

select_statement2;

select_statement1 and *select_statement2* are SELECT statements. The number and the order of the columns must be identical in both statements, and the data types of corresponding columns must be compatible. Duplicate rows are eliminated from the result.

Listing 7.46 uses INTERSECT to list the cities in which both an author and a publisher are located. See **Figure 7.46** for the result.

✔ Tips

- **INTERSECT** is a commutative operation: **A INTERSECT B** is the same as **B INTERSECT A**.

- The SQL standard gives **INTERSECT** higher precedence than **UNION** and **EXCEPT**, but the actual precedence used by your DBMS may differ. Use parentheses to specify order of evaluation in queries with mixed set operators; see "Determining the Order of Evaluation" in Chapter 5.

- It's helpful to think of **UNION** as logical **OR** and **INTERSECTION** as logical **AND**; see "Combining and Negating Conditions with **AND**, **OR**, and **NOT**" in Chapter 4. If you want to know, for example, which products are supplied by vendor A *or* vendor B, type:

```
SELECT product_id
  FROM vendor_a_product_list
UNION
SELECT product_id
  FROM vendor_b_product_list;
```

If you want to know which products are supplied by vendor A *and* vendor B, type:

```
SELECT product_id
  FROM vendor_a_product_list
INTERSECT
SELECT product_id
  FROM vendor_b_product_list;
```

- If your DBMS doesn't support **INTERSECT**, you can replicate it with an **INNER JOIN** or an **EXISTS** subquery (see Chapter 8). Each of the following statements is equivalent to Listing 7.46 (inner join):

```
SELECT DISTINCT authors.city
  FROM authors
  INNER JOIN publishers
    ON authors.city =
       publishers.city;
```

or (**EXISTS** subquery):

```
SELECT DISTINCT city
  FROM authors
  WHERE EXISTS
    (SELECT *
      FROM publishers
      WHERE authors.city =
            publishers.city)
```

- **DBMS** **Microsoft Access**, **Microsoft SQL Server**, and **MySQL** don't support **INTERSECT**. To run Listing 7.46 in Access, SQL Server, and MySQL, use the equivalent **INNER JOIN** query given in the preceding Tip.

Listing 7.47 List the cities in which an author lives but a publisher isn't located. See Figure 7.47 for the result.

```
                        listing
SELECT city
  FROM authors
EXCEPT
SELECT city
  FROM publishers;
```

```
city
---------
Boulder
Bronx
Palo Alto
Sarasota
```

Figure 7.47 Result of Listing 7.47.

Finding Different Rows with EXCEPT

An EXCEPT operation, also called a *difference*, combines the results of two queries into a single result that comprises the rows that belong only to the first query. To contrast INTERSECT and EXCEPT, A INTERSECT B contains rows from table A that *are* duplicated in table B, whereas A EXCEPT B contains rows from table A that *aren't* duplicated in table B. Differences have the same restrictions as unions; see "Combining Rows with UNION" earlier in this chapter.

To find different rows:

◆ Type:

select_statement1

EXCEPT

select_statement2;

select_statement1 and *select_statement2* are SELECT statements. The number and the order of the columns must be identical in both statements, and the data types of corresponding columns must be compatible. Duplicate rows are eliminated from the result.

Listing 7.47 uses EXCEPT to list the cities in which an author lives but a publisher isn't located. See **Figure 7.47** for the result.

✔ Tips

- Unlike UNION and INTERSECT, EXCEPT is not commutative: A EXCEPT B isn't the same as B EXCEPT A.

- The SQL standard gives INTERSECT higher precedence than UNION and EXCEPT, but the actual precedence used by your DBMS may differ. Use parentheses to specify order of evaluation in queries with mixed set operators; see "Determining the Order of Evaluation" in Chapter 5.

- If your DBMS doesn't support EXCEPT, you can replicate it with an outer join, a NOT EXISTS subquery, or a NOT IN subquery (see Chapter 8). Each of the following statements is equivalent to Listing 7.47 (outer join):

```
SELECT DISTINCT a.city
  FROM authors a
  LEFT OUTER JOIN publishers p
    ON a.city = p.city
  WHERE p.city IS NULL;
```

or (NOT EXISTS subquery):

```
SELECT DISTINCT city
  FROM authors
  WHERE NOT EXISTS
    (SELECT *
      FROM publishers
      WHERE authors.city =
            publishers.city);
```

or (NOT IN subquery):

```
SELECT DISTINCT city
  FROM authors
  WHERE city NOT IN
    (SELECT city
      FROM publishers);
```

- **DBMS** **Microsoft Access**, **Microsoft SQL Server**, and **MySQL** don't support EXCEPT. To run Listing 7.47 in Access, SQL Server, and MySQL, use the equivalent OUTER JOIN query given in the preceding Tip.

  In **Oracle**, the EXCEPT operator is called MINUS. To run Listing 7.47 in Oracle, type:

```
SELECT city FROM authors
MINUS
SELECT city FROM publishers;
```

SUBQUERIES

To this point, I've used a single SELECT statement to retrieve data from one or more tables. In this chapter, I'll describe nested queries, which allow you to retrieve or modify data based on another query's result.

A *subquery* is a SELECT statement embedded in another SQL statement. You can nest a subquery in:

- The SELECT, FROM, WHERE, or HAVING clause of another SELECT statement

- Another subquery

- An INSERT, UPDATE, or DELETE statement

In general, you can use a subquery anywhere an expression is allowed, but your DBMS may place specific restrictions on where subqueries may appear. I'll cover subqueries nested in a SELECT statement or another subquery in this chapter, and subqueries embedded in INSERT, UPDATE, and DELETE statements in Chapter 9.

Understanding Subqueries

In this section, I'll define some terms and introduce subqueries by giving an example of a SELECT statement that contains a simple subquery. In subsequent sections, I'll explain the types of subqueries and their syntax and semantics.

Suppose that you want to list the names of the publishers of biographies. The naive approach is to write two queries: one query to retrieve the IDs of all the biography publishers (**Listing 8.1** and **Figure 8.1**), and a second query that uses the first query's result to list the publisher names (**Listing 8.2** and **Figure 8.2**).

A better way is to use an inner join (**Listing 8.3** and **Figure 8.3**); see "Creating an Inner Join with INNER JOIN" in Chapter 7.

Another alternative is to use a subquery (**Listing 8.4** and **Figure 8.4**). The subquery in Listing 8.4 is shown in red. A subquery also is called an *inner query*, and the statement containing a subquery is called an *outer query*. In other words, an enclosed subquery is an inner query of an outer query. Remember that a subquery may be nested in another subquery, so *inner* and *outer* are relative terms in statements with multiple nested subqueries.

I'll explain how a DBMS executes subqueries in "Simple and Correlated Subqueries" later in this chapter, but for now, all that you need to know is that in Listing 8.4, the DBMS processes the inner query (in red) first and

Listing 8.1 List the biography publishers. See Figure 8.1 for the result.

```
                      listing
SELECT pub_id
  FROM titles
  WHERE type = 'biography';
```

```
pub_id
------
P01
P03
P01
P01
```

Figure 8.1 Result of Listing 8.1. You can add DISTINCT to the SELECT clause of Listing 8.1 to list the publishers only once; see "Eliminating Duplicate Rows with DISTINCT" in Chapter 4.

Listing 8.2 This query uses the result of Listing 8.1 to list the names of the biography publishers. See Figure 8.2 for the result.

```
                      listing
SELECT pub_name
  FROM publishers
  WHERE pub_id IN ('P01', 'P03');
```

```
pub_name
------------------
Abatis Publishers
Schadenfreude Press
```

Figure 8.2 Result of Listing 8.2.

Listing 8.3 List the names of the biography publishers by using an inner join. See Figure 8.3 for the result.

```
                           listing
SELECT DISTINCT pub_name
  FROM publishers p
  INNER JOIN titles t
    ON p.pub_id = t.pub_id
  WHERE t.type = 'biography';
```

```
pub_name
-------------------
Abatis Publishers
Schadenfreude Press
```

Figure 8.3 Result of Listing 8.3.

Listing 8.4 List the names of the biography publishers by using a subquery. See Figure 8.4 for the result.

```
                           listing
SELECT pub_name
  FROM publishers
  WHERE pub_id IN
    (SELECT pub_id
      FROM titles
      WHERE type = 'biography');
```

```
pub_name
-------------------
Abatis Publishers
Schadenfreude Press
```

Figure 8.4 Result of Listing 8.4.

then uses its interim result to run the outer query (in black) and get the final result. The IN keyword that introduces the subquery tests for list membership and works like IN in "List Filtering with IN" in Chapter 4. Note that the inner query in Listing 8.4 is the same query as Listing 8.1, and the outer query is the same query as Listing 8.2.

✔ Tips

- Sometimes you'll see the term *subquery* used to refer to an *entire* SQL statement that contains one or more subqueries. To prevent confusion, I won't use that terminology in this book.

- **DBMS** **MySQL** 4.0 and earlier versions don't support subqueries (although MySQL 4.1 is slated to support them). The subquery examples in this chapter won't run in MySQL 4.0 and earlier versions. You have three choices to work around this lack of subquery support, in order of preference: Recast the subquery as a join (see "Subqueries vs. Joins" later in this chapter), create a temporary table to hold the result of a subquery (see "Creating a Temporary Table with CREATE TEMPORARY TABLE" in Chapter 10 and the temporary-table example in the DBMS Tip in "Creating Outer Joins with OUTER JOIN" in Chapter 7, Listing 7.32), or simulate the subquery in a procedural host language such as Perl, PHP, or Java (not covered in this book).

UNDERSTANDING SUBQUERIES

Subquery Syntax

The syntax of a subquery is the same as that of a normal SELECT statement (see Chapters 4 through 7), except for the following differences:

- You can nest a subquery in a SELECT, FROM, WHERE, or HAVING clause or in another subquery.

- Always enclose a subquery in parentheses.

- Don't terminate a subquery with a semicolon. (You still must terminate the statement that contains the subquery with a semicolon.)

- Don't put an ORDER BY clause in a subquery. (A subquery returns an intermediate result that you never see, so sorting a subquery makes no sense.)

- A subquery comprises a single SELECT statement. (You can't use, say, a UNION of multiple SELECT statements as a subquery.)

- A subquery can use columns in the tables listed in its own FROM clause or in the outer query's FROM clause.

- If a table appears in an inner query but not in the outer query, you can't include that table's columns in the final result (that is, in the outer query's SELECT clause).

- Depending on the situation in which it's used, a subquery may be required to return a limited number of rows or columns. The SQL standard categorizes a subquery by the number of rows and columns it returns (**Table 8.1**). In all cases, the subquery also can return an empty table (zero rows).

In practice, usually you'll see a subquery in a WHERE clause that takes one of these forms:

- WHERE *test_expr op* (*subquery*)

- WHERE *test_expr* [NOT] IN (*subquery*)

- WHERE *test_expr op* ALL (*subquery*)

- WHERE *test_expr op* ANY (*subquery*)

- WHERE [NOT] EXISTS (*subquery*)

test_expr is a literal value, a column name, an expression, or a scalar subquery; *op* is a comparison operator (=, <>, <, <=, >, or >=); and *subquery* is a simple or correlated subquery. I'll cover each of these forms later in this chapter. You can use these subquery forms in a HAVING clause, too.

✔ Tip

- **DBMS** The SQL standard doesn't specify a maximum number of subquery nesting levels, so your DBMS will set its own upper limit. This built-in limit typically far exceeds the natural limit set by human comprehension. **Microsoft SQL Server**, for example, permits 32 levels of nesting.

Table 8.1

Size of Subquery Results

Subquery	Rows	Columns
Scalar subquery	1	1
Row subquery	1	≥ 1
Table subquery	≥1	≥ 1

SUBQUERY SYNTAX

Listing 8.5a This statement uses a subquery to list the authors who live in the same city in which a publisher is located. See Figure 8.5 for the result.

```
listing
SELECT au_id, city
  FROM authors
  WHERE city IN
    (SELECT city FROM publishers);
```

Listing 8.5b This statement is equivalent to Listing 8.5a but uses an inner join instead of a subquery. See Figure 8.5 for the result.

```
listing
SELECT a.au_id, a.city
  FROM authors a
  INNER JOIN publishers p
    ON a.city = p.city;
```

```
au_id city
----- -------------
A03   San Francisco
A04   San Francisco
A05   New York
```

Figure 8.5 Result of Listings 8.5a and 8.5b.

Subqueries vs. Joins

In "Understanding Subqueries" earlier in this chapter, Listings 8.3 and 8.4 showed two equivalent queries: one used a join, and the other used a subquery. Many subqueries can be formulated alternatively as joins. In fact, a subquery is a way to relate one table to another without actually doing a join.

As subqueries can be hard to use and debug, you may prefer to use joins, but you can pose some questions only as subqueries. In cases where you can use subqueries and joins interchangeably, the choice is yours. Usually, no performance difference exists between a statement that uses a subquery and a semantically equivalent version that uses a join (but see "Comparing Equivalent Queries" later in this chapter).

The following syntax diagrams show some equivalent statements that use subqueries and joins. These two statements are equivalent (IN subquery):

```
SELECT *
  FROM table1
  WHERE id IN
    (SELECT id FROM table2);
```

and (inner join):

```
SELECT table1.*
  FROM table1
  INNER JOIN table2
    ON table1.id = table2.id;
```

See **Listings 8.5a** and **8.5b** and **Figure 8.5** for an example.

continues on next page

These three statements are equivalent (NOT IN subquery):

```
SELECT *
  FROM table1
  WHERE id NOT IN
    (SELECT id FROM table2);
```

and (NOT EXISTS subquery):

```
SELECT *
  FROM table1
  WHERE NOT EXISTS
    (SELECT *
      FROM table2
      WHERE table1.id = table2.id);
```

and (left outer join):

```
SELECT table1.*
  FROM table1
  LEFT OUTER JOIN table2
    ON table1.id = table2.id
  WHERE table2.id IS NULL;
```

See **Listings 8.6a**, **8.6b**, and **8.6c** and **Figure 8.6** for an example. I'll describe IN and EXISTS subqueries later in this chapter.

Listing 8.6a This statement uses an IN subquery to list the authors who haven't written (or co-written) a book. See Figure 8.6 for the result.

```
SELECT au_id, au_fname, au_lname
  FROM authors
  WHERE au_id NOT IN
    (SELECT au_id FROM title_authors);
```

Listing 8.6b This statement is equivalent to Listing 8.6a but uses an EXISTS subquery instead of an IN subquery. See Figure 8.6 for the result.

```
SELECT au_id, au_fname, au_lname
  FROM authors a
  WHERE NOT EXISTS
    (SELECT *
      FROM title_authors ta
      WHERE a.au_id = ta.au_id);
```

Listing 8.6c This statement is equivalent to Listings 8.6a and 8.6b but uses a left outer join instead of a subquery. See Figure 8.6 for the result.

```
SELECT a.au_id, a.au_fname, a.au_lname
  FROM authors a
  LEFT OUTER JOIN title_authors ta
    ON a.au_id = ta.au_id
  WHERE ta.au_id IS NULL;
```

```
au_id  au_fname  au_lname
-----  --------  -----------
A07    Paddy     O'Furniture
```

Figure 8.6 Result of Listings 8.6a, 8.6b, and 8.6c.

Listing 8.7a This statement uses a subquery to list the authors who live in the same state as author A04 (Klee Hull). See Figure 8.7 for the result.

```
                     listing
SELECT au_id, au_fname, au_lname, state
  FROM authors
  WHERE state IN
    (SELECT state
      FROM authors
      WHERE au_id = 'A04');
```

Listing 8.7b This statement is equivalent to Listing 8.7a but uses an inner join instead of a subquery. See Figure 8.7 for the result.

```
                     listing
SELECT a1.au_id, a1.au_fname,
    a1.au_lname, a1.state
  FROM authors a1
  INNER JOIN authors a2
    ON a1.state = a2.state
  WHERE a2.au_id = 'A04';
```

```
au_id au_fname au_lname state
----- -------- -------- -----
A03   Hallie   Hull     CA
A04   Klee     Hull     CA
A06            Kellsey  CA
```

Figure 8.7 Result of Listings 8.7a and 8.7b.

✔ Tips

- You also can write a self-join as a subquery (**Listings 8.7a** and **8.7b** and **Figure 8.7**). For information about self-joins, see "Creating a Self-Join" in Chapter 7.

- You always can express an inner join as a subquery, but not vice versa. This asymmetry occurs because inner joins are commutative; you can join tables A to B in either order and get the same answer. Subqueries lack this property. (You always can express an outer join as a subquery, too, even though outer joins aren't commutative.)

continues on next page

- Favor subqueries if you're comparing an aggregate value to other values (**Listing 8.8** and **Figure 8.8**). Without a subquery, you'd need two SELECT statements to list all the books with the highest price: one query to find the highest price, and a second query to list all the books selling for that price. For information about aggregate functions, see Chapter 6.

- Use joins when you include columns from multiple tables in the result. Listing 8.5b uses a join to retrieve authors who live in the same city in which a publisher is located. To include the publisher ID in the result, I'll simply add the column pub_id to the SELECT-clause list (**Listing 8.9** and **Figure 8.9**).

  I can't accomplish this same task with a subquery, because it's illegal to include a column in the outer query's SELECT-clause list from a table that appears in only the inner query:

  ```
  SELECT a.au_id, a.city, p.pub_id
    FROM authors a
    WHERE a.city IN
      (SELECT p.city
        FROM publishers p);   --Illegal
  ```

- **DBMS** **MySQL** 4.0 and earlier versions don't support subqueries. For workarounds, see the DBMS Tip in "Understanding Subqueries" earlier in this chapter.

Listing 8.8 List all books whose price equals the highest book price. See Figure 8.8 for the result.

```
SELECT title_id, price
  FROM titles
  WHERE price =
    (SELECT MAX(price)
      FROM titles);
```

```
title_id price
-------- -----
T03      39.95
```

Figure 8.8 Result of Listing 8.8.

Listing 8.9 List the authors who live in the same city in which a publisher is located, and include the publisher in the result. See Figure 8.9 for the result.

```
SELECT a.au_id, a.city, p.pub_id
  FROM authors a
  INNER JOIN publishers p
    ON a.city = p.city;
```

```
au_id city          pub_id
----- ------------- ------
A03   San Francisco P02
A04   San Francisco P02
A05   New York      P01
```

Figure 8.9 Result of Listing 8.9.

Simple and Correlated Subqueries

You can use two types of subqueries:

◆ Simple subqueries

◆ Correlated subqueries

A *simple subquery,* or *noncorrelated subquery,* is a subquery that can be evaluated independently of its outer query and is processed only once for the entire statement. All the subqueries in this chapter's examples so far have been simple subqueries (except Listing 8.6b).

A *correlated subquery* can't be evaluated independently of its outer query; it's an inner query that depends on data from the outer query. A correlated subquery is used if a statement needs to process a table in the inner query for *each row* in the outer query.

Correlated subqueries have more-complicated syntax and a knottier execution sequence than simple subqueries, but you can use them to solve problems that you can't solve with simple subqueries or joins. In this section, I'll give an example of a simple subquery and a correlated subquery and then describe how a DBMS executes each one. Subsequent sections in this chapter contain more examples of each type of subquery.

Simple subqueries

A DBMS evaluates a simple subquery by evaluating the inner query once and substituting its result into the outer query. A simple subquery executes prior to, and independent of, its outer query.

Let's revisit Listing 8.5a from earlier in this chapter. **Listing 8.10** (which is identical to Listing 8.5a) uses a simple subquery to list the authors who live in the same city in which a publisher is located; see **Figure 8.10** for the result. Conceptually, a DBMS processes this query in two steps as two separate SELECT statements:

1. The inner query (a simple subquery) returns the cities of all the publishers (**Listing 8.11** and **Figure 8.11**).

2. The DBMS substitutes the values returned by the inner query in step 1 into the outer query, which finds the author IDs corresponding to the publishers' cities (**Listing 8.12** and **Figure 8.12**).

Listing 8.12 List the authors who live in one of the cities returned by Listing 8.11. See Figure 8.12 for the result.

```
SELECT au_id, city
  FROM authors
  WHERE city IN
    ('New York', 'San Francisco',
     'Hamburg', 'Berkeley');
```

```
au_id city
----- -------------
A03   San Francisco
A04   San Francisco
A05   New York
```

Figure 8.12 Result of Listing 8.12.

Listing 8.10 List the authors who live in the same city in which a publisher is located. See Figure 8.10 for the result.

```
SELECT au_id, city
  FROM authors
  WHERE city IN
    (SELECT city
      FROM publishers);
```

```
au_id city
----- -------------
A03   San Francisco
A04   San Francisco
A05   New York
```

Figure 8.10 Result of Listing 8.10.

Listing 8.11 List the cities in which the publishers are located. See Figure 8.11 for the result.

```
SELECT city
  FROM publishers;
```

```
city
-------------
New York
San Francisco
Hamburg
Berkeley
```

Figure 8.11 Result of Listing 8.11.

Correlated subqueries

Correlated subqueries offer a more powerful data-retrieval mechanism than simple subqueries do. A correlated subquery's important characteristics are:

◆ It differs from a simple query in its order of execution and in the number of times that it's executed.

◆ It can't be executed independently of its outer query, because it depends on the outer query for its values.

◆ It's executed repeatedly—once for each candidate row selected by the outer query.

◆ It always refers to the table mentioned in the **FROM** clause of the outer query.

◆ It uses qualified column names to refer to values specified in the outer query. In the context of correlated subqueries, these qualified named are called *correlation variables*. For information about qualified names and table aliases, see "Qualifying Column Names" and "Creating Table Aliases with **AS**" in Chapter 7.

◆ The basic syntax of a query that contains a correlated subquery is:

```
SELECT outer_columns
  FROM outer_table
  WHERE outer_column_value IN
    (SELECT inner_column
     FROM inner_table
     WHERE inner_column = outer_column)
```

Execution always starts with the outer query (in black). The outer query selects each individual row of *outer_table* as a candidate row. For each candidate row, the DBMS executes the correlated inner query (in red) once and flags the *inner_table* rows that satisfy the inner **WHERE** condition for the value *outer_column_value*. The DBMS tests the outer **WHERE** condition against the flagged *inner_table* rows and displays the flagged rows that satisfy this condition. This process continues until all the candidate rows have been processed.

continues on next page

Listing 8.13 uses a correlated subquery to list the books that have sales better than the average sales of books of its type; see **Figure 8.13** for the result. `candidate` (following `titles` in the outer query) and `average` (following `titles` in the inner query) are alias table names for the table `titles`, so that the information can be evaluated as though it comes from two different tables (see "Creating a Self-Join" in Chapter 7).

In Listing 8.13, the subquery can't be resolved independently of the outer query. It needs a value for `candidate.type`, but this value is a correlation variable that changes as the DBMS examines different rows in the table `candidate`. The column `average.type` is said to *correlate* with `candidate.type` in the outer query. The average sales for a book type are calculated in the subquery by using the type of each book from the table in the outer query (`candidate`). The subquery computes the average sales for this type and then compares it with a row in the table `candidate`. If the sales in the table `candidate` are greater than or equal to average sales for the type, that book is displayed in the result. A DBMS processes this query as follows:

1. The book type in the first row of `candidate` is used in the subquery to compute an average sales.

   Take the row for book T01, whose type is history, so the value in the column `type` in the first row of the table `candidate` is history. In effect, the subquery becomes:

   ```
   SELECT AVG(sales)
     FROM titles average
    WHERE average.type = 'history';
   ```

Listing 8.13 List the books that have sales greater than or equal to the average sales of books of its type. The correlation variable `candidate.type` defines the *initial* condition to be met by the rows of the inner table `average`. The outer `WHERE` condition (`sales >=`) defines the *final* test that the rows of the inner table `average` must satisfy. See Figure 8.13 for the result.

```
┌────────────────── listing ──────────────────┐
SELECT
    candidate.title_id,
    candidate.type,
    candidate.sales
  FROM titles candidate
  WHERE sales >=
    (SELECT AVG(sales)
       FROM titles average
      WHERE average.type = candidate.type);
```

title_id	type	sales
T02	history	9566
T03	computer	25667
T05	psychology	201440
T07	biography	1500200
T09	children	5000
T13	history	10467

Figure 8.13 Result of Listing 8.13.

This pass through the subquery yields a value of 6,866—the average sales of history books. In the outer query, book T01's sales of 566 are compared to the average sales of history books. T01's sales are lower than average, so T01 isn't displayed in the result.

2. Next, book T02's row in `candidate` is evaluated.

   T02 also is a history book, so the evaluated subquery is the same as in step 1:

   ```
   SELECT AVG(sales)
     FROM titles average
    WHERE average.type = 'history';
   ```

   This pass through the subquery again yields 6,866 for the average sales of history books. Book T02's sales of 9,566 are higher than average, so T02 is displayed in the result.

3. Next, book T03's row in `candidate` is evaluated.

   T03 is a computer book, so this time, the evaluated subquery is:

   ```
   SELECT AVG(sales)
     FROM titles average
    WHFRF average.type = 'computer';
   ```

   The result of this pass through the subquery is average sales of 25,667 for computer books. Because book T03's sales of 25,667 equals the average (it's the only computer book), T03 is displayed in the result.

4. The DBMS repeats this process until every row in the outer table `candidate` has been tested.

continues on next page

SIMPLE AND CORRELATED SUBQUERIES

✔ Tips

- If you can get the same result by using a simple subquery or a correlated subquery, use the simple subquery, because it probably will run faster. **Listings 8.14a** and **8.14b** show two equivalent queries that list all authors who earn 100 percent (1.0) of the royalty share on a book. Listing 8.14a, which uses a simple subquery, is more efficient than Listing 8.14b, which uses a correlated subquery. In the simple subquery, the DBMS reads the inner table `title_authors` once. In the correlated subquery, the DBMS must loop through `title_authors` five times—once for each qualifying row in the outer table `authors`. See **Figure 8.14** for the result.

  Why do I say that a statement that uses a simple subquery *probably* will run faster than an equivalent statement that uses a correlated subquery when a correlated subquery clearly requires more work? Because your DBMS's optimizer may be clever enough to recognize and reformulate a correlated subquery as a semantically equivalent simple subquery internally before executing the statement. For more information, see "Comparing Equivalent Queries" later in this chapter.

- **DBMS** **MySQL** 4.0 and earlier versions don't support subqueries. For workarounds, see the DBMS Tip in "Understanding Subqueries" earlier in this chapter.

  In **PostgreSQL**, convert the floating-point numbers in Listings 8.14a and 8.14b to `DECIMAL`; see "Converting Data Types with `CAST()`" in Chapter 5. To run Listings 8.14a and 8.14b in PostgreSQL, change the floating-point literal in each listing to:

  `CAST(1.0 AS DECIMAL)`

Listing 8.14a This statement uses a simple subquery to list all authors who earn 100 percent (1.0) royalty on a book. See Figure 8.14 for the result.

```
listing
SELECT au_id, au_fname, au_lname
  FROM authors
  WHERE au_id IN
    (SELECT au_id
       FROM title_authors
       WHERE royalty_share = 1.0);
```

Listing 8.14b This statement is equivalent to Listing 8.14a but uses a correlated subquery instead of a simple subquery. This query probably will run slower than Listing 8.14a. See Figure 8.14 for the result.

```
listing
SELECT au_id, au_fname, au_lname
  FROM authors
  WHERE 1.0 IN
    (SELECT royalty_share
       FROM title_authors
       WHERE title_authors.au_id =
             authors.au_id);
```

```
au_id au_fname  au_lname
----- --------- ---------
A01   Sarah     Buchman
A02   Wendy     Heydemark
A04   Klee      Hull
A05   Christian Kells
A06             Kellsey
```

Figure 8.14 Result of Listings 8.14a and 8.14b.

Listing 8.15a The tables publishers and titles both contain a column named pub_id, but you don't have to qualify pub_id in this query because of the implicit assumptions about table names that SQL makes. See Figure 8.15 for the result.

```
                 listing
SELECT pub_name
  FROM publishers
  WHERE pub_id IN
    (SELECT pub_id
      FROM titles
      WHERE type = 'biography');
```

Listing 8.15b This query is equivalent to Listing 8.15a, but with explicit qualification of pub_id. See Figure 8.15 for the result.

```
                 listing
SELECT pub_name
  FROM publishers
  WHERE publishers.pub_id IN
    (SELECT titles.pub_id
      FROM titles
      WHERE type = 'biography');
```

```
pub_name
-------------------
Abatis Publishers
Schadenfreude Press
```

Figure 8.15 Result of Listings 8.15a and 8.15b.

Qualifying Column Names in Subqueries

Recall from "Qualifying Column Names" in Chapter 7 that you can qualify a column name explicitly with a table name to identify the column unambiguously. In statements that contain subqueries, column names are qualified implicitly by the table referenced in the FROM clause at the same nesting level.

In **Listing 8.15a**, for example, the column names are qualified implicitly, meaning:

◆ The column pub_id in the outer query's WHERE clause is qualified implicitly by the table publishers in the outer query's FROM clause.

◆ The column pub_id in the subquery's SELECT clause is qualified implicitly by the table titles in the subquery's FROM clause.

Listing 8.15b shows Listing 8.15a with explicit qualifiers. See **Figure 8.15** for the result.

✔ Tips

■ It's never wrong to state a table name explicitly.

■ You can use explicit qualifiers to override SQL's default assumptions about table names and specify that a column is to match a table at a nesting level outside the column's own level.

■ If a column name can match more than one table at the same nesting level, the column name is ambiguous, and you must qualify it with a table name (or table alias).

■ **DBMS** **MySQL** 4.0 and earlier versions don't support subqueries. For workarounds, see the DBMS Tip in "Understanding Subqueries" earlier in this chapter.

Nulls in Subqueries

Beware of nulls; their presence complicates subqueries greatly. If you don't eliminate them when they're present, you may get an unexpected answer.

A subquery can hide a comparison to a null. Recall from "Nulls" in Chapter 3 that nulls don't equal each other and that you can't determine whether a null matches any other value. I'll use an example that involves a NOT IN subquery (see "Testing Set Membership with IN" later in this chapter.) Consider the following two tables, each with one column. The first table is named table1:

```
col
----
   1
   2
```

The second table is named table2:

```
col
----
   1
   2
   3
```

If I run **Listing 8.16** to list the values in table2 that aren't in table1, I get **Figure 8.16a**, as expected. Now I'll add a null to table1:

```
col
----
   1
   2
NULL
```

If I rerun Listing 8.16, I get **Figure 8.16b** (an empty table), which is correct logically but not what I expected. Why is the result empty this time? The solution requires some algebra. I can move the NOT outside the subquery

Listing 8.16 List the values in table2 that aren't in table1. See Figure 8.16 for the result.

```
SELECT col
  FROM table2
  WHERE col NOT IN
    (SELECT col
       FROM table1);
```

```
col
----

   3
```

Figure 8.16a Result of Listing 8.16 when table1 doesn't contain a null.

```
col
----
```

Figure 8.16b Result of Listing 8.16 when table1 contains a null. This result is an empty table, which is correct logically but not what I expected.

condition without changing the meaning of Listing 8.16:

```
SELECT col
  FROM table2
  WHERE NOT col IN
    (SELECT col FROM table1);
```

The IN clause determines whether a value in table2 matches *any* value in table1, so I can rewrite the subquery as a compound condition:

```
SELECT col
  FROM table2
  WHERE NOT ((col = 1)
         OR (col = 2)
         OR (col = NULL));
```

If I apply DeMorgan's Laws (refer to Table 4.6 in Chapter 4), this query becomes:

```
SELECT col
  FROM table2
  WHERE (col <> 1)
    AND (col <> 2)
    AND (col <> NULL);
```

The final expression, col <> NULL, always is unknown. Refer to the AND truth table (Table 4.3 in Chapter 4) and you'll see that the entire WHERE search condition reduces to unknown, which always is rejected by WHERE.

✔ Tips

■ To fix Listing 8.16 so that it doesn't examine the null in table1, add an IS NOT NULL condition to the subquery (see "Testing for Nulls with IS NULL" in Chapter 4):

```
SELECT col
  FROM table2
  WHERE col NOT IN
    (SELECT col
       FROM table1
       WHERE col IS NOT NULL);
```

■ **DBMS** **MySQL** 4.0 and earlier versions don't support subqueries. For workarounds, see the DBMS Tip in "Understanding Subqueries" earlier in this chapter.

Using Subqueries as Column Expressions

In Chapters 4, 5, and 6, you learned that the items in a SELECT-clause list can be literals, column names, or expressions. SQL also permits you to embed a subquery in a SELECT-clause list.

A subquery that's used as a column expression must be a scalar subquery. Recall from Table 8.1 in "Subquery Syntax" earlier in this chapter that a scalar subquery returns a single value (that is, a one-row, one-column result). In most cases, you'll have to use an aggregate function or restrictive WHERE conditions in the subquery to guarantee that the subquery returns only one row.

The syntax for the SELECT-clause list is the same as you've been using all along, except that you may specify a parenthesized subquery as one of the column expressions in the list, as the following examples show.

Listing 8.17 uses two simple subqueries as column expressions to list each biography, its price, the average price of all books (not just biographies), and the difference between the price of the biography and the average price of all books. The aggregate function AVG() guarantees that each subquery returns a single value. See **Figure 8.17** for the result. Remember that AVG() ignores nulls when computing an average; see "Calculating an Average with AVG()" in Chapter 6.

Listing 8.17 List each biography, its price, the average price of all books, and the difference between the price of the biography and the average price of all books. See Figure 8.17 for the result.

```
SELECT title_id,
    price,
    (SELECT AVG(price) FROM titles)
      AS "AVG(price)",
    price - (SELECT AVG(price) FROM titles)
      AS "Difference"
  FROM titles
  WHERE type='biography';
```

title_id	price	AVG(price)	Difference
T06	19.95	18.3875	1.5625
T07	23.95	18.3875	5.5625
T10	NULL	18.3875	NULL
T12	12.99	18.3875	-5.3975

Figure 8.17 Result of Listing 8.17.

Listing 8.18 List all the authors of each book in one row. See Figure 8.18 for the result.

```
                       listing
SELECT title_id,
    (SELECT au_id
       FROM title_authors ta
      WHERE au_order = 1
        AND title_id = t.title_id)
        AS "Author 1",
    (SELECT au_id
       FROM title_authors ta
      WHERE au_order = 2
        AND title_id = t.title_id)
        AS "Author 2",
    (SELECT au_id
       FROM title_authors ta
      WHERE au_order = 3
        AND title_id = t.title_id)
        AS "Author 3"
  FROM titles t;
```

Listing 8.18 uses correlated subqueries to list all the authors of each book in one row, as you'd view them in a report or spreadsheet. See **Figure 8.18** for the result. Note that, in each WHERE clause, SQL qualifies title_id implicitly with the table alias ta referenced in the subquery's FROM clause; see "Qualifying Column Names in Subqueries" earlier in this chapter. (For a more efficient way to implement this query, see the Tips in this section.)

continues on next page

title_id	Author 1	Author 2	Author 3
T01	A01	NULL	NULL
T02	A01	NULL	NULL
T03	A05	NULL	NULL
T04	A03	A04	NULL
T05	A04	NULL	NULL
T06	A02	NULL	NULL
T07	A02	A04	NULL
T08	A06	NULL	NULL
T09	A06	NULL	NULL
T10	A02	NULL	NULL
T11	A06	A03	A04
T12	A02	NULL	NULL
T13	A01	NULL	NULL

Figure 8.18 Result of Listing 8.18.

USING SUBQUERIES AS COLUMN EXPRESSIONS

In **Listing 8.19**, I revisit Listing 7.30 in "Creating Outer Joins with OUTER JOIN" in Chapter 7, but this time, I'm using a correlated subquery instead of an outer join to list the number of books that each author wrote (or co-wrote). See **Figure 8.19** for the result.

Listing 8.19 List the number of books that each author wrote (or co-wrote), including authors who have written no books. See Figure 8.19 for the result.

```
SELECT au_id,
    (SELECT COUNT(*)
      FROM title_authors ta
      WHERE ta.au_id = a.au_id)
        AS "Num books"
  FROM authors a
  ORDER BY au_id ASC;
```

```
au_id Num books
----- ---------
A01           3
A02           4
A03           2
A04           4
A05           1
A06           3
A07           0
```

Figure 8.19 Result of Listing 8.19.

Listing 8.20 List each author and the latest date on which he or she published a book. See Figure 8.20 for the result.

```
                     listing
SELECT au_id,
    (SELECT MAX(pubdate)
      FROM titles t
      INNER JOIN title_authors ta
       ON ta.title_id = t.title_id
      WHERE ta.au_id = a.au_id)
        AS "Latest pub date"
  FROM authors a;
```

```
au_id Latest pub date
----- ---------------
A01   2000-08-01
A02   2000-08-31
A03   2000-11-30
A04   2001-01-01
A05   2000-09-01
A06   2002-05-31
A07   NULL
```

Figure 8.20 Result of Listing 8.20.

Listing 8.20 uses a correlated subquery to list each author and the latest date on which he or she published a book. You should qualify every column name explicitly in a subquery that contains a join to make it clear which table is referenced (even when qualifiers are unnecessary). See **Figure 8.20** for the result.

continues on next page

Listing 8.21 uses a correlated subquery to compute the running total of all book sales. A *running total,* or *running sum,* is a common calculation: For each book, I want to compute the sum of all sales of the books that precede the book. Here, I'm defining *precede* to mean those books whose `title_id` comes before the current book's `title_id` alphabetically. Note the use of table aliases to refer to the same table in two contexts. The subquery returns the sum of sales for all books preceding the current book, which is denoted by `t1.title_id`. See **Figure 8.21** for the result.

Listing 8.21 Compute the running sum of all book sales. See Figure 8.21 for the result.

```
SELECT t1.title_id, t1.sales,
    (SELECT SUM(t2.sales)
      FROM titles t2
      WHERE t2.title_id < t1.title_id)
        AS "Running total"
  FROM titles t1;
```

title_id	sales	Running total
T01	566	NULL
T02	9566	566
T03	25667	10132
T04	13001	35799
T05	201440	48800
T06	11320	250240
T07	1500200	261560
T08	4095	1761760
T09	5000	1765855
T10	NULL	1770855
T11	94123	1770855
T12	100001	1864978
T13	10467	1964979

Figure 8.21 Result of Listing 8.21.

Listing 8.22 Calculate the greatest number of titles written (or co-written) by any author. See Figure 8.22 for the result.

```
                        listing
SELECT MAX(ta.count_titles) AS "Max titles"
  FROM (SELECT COUNT(*) AS count_titles
          FROM title_authors
          GROUP BY au_id) ta;
```

```
Max titles
----------
         4
```

Figure 8.22 Result of Listing 8.22.

■ **DBMS** **MySQL** 4.0 and earlier versions don't support subqueries. For workarounds, see the DBMS Tip in "Understanding Subqueries" earlier in this chapter.

In **Microsoft Access**, you must increase the precision of the average-price calculation in Listing 8.17. Use the type-conversion function CDbl() to coerce the average price to a double-precision floating-point number; see the DBMS Tip in "Converting Data Types with CAST()" in Chapter 5. To run Listing 8.17 in Access, change both occurrences of AVG(price) to CDbl(AVG(price)).4444

✔ Tips

■ You also can use a subquery in a FROM clause. In the Tips in "Aggregating Distinct Values with DISTINCT" in Chapter 6, I used a FROM subquery to replicate a distinct aggregate function. **Listing 8.22** uses a FROM subquery to calculate the greatest number of titles written (or co-written) by any author. See **Figure 8.22** for the result. Note that the outer query uses a table alias (**ta**) and column label (**count_titles**) to reference the inner query's result.

■ You also can use a subquery as a column expression in UPDATE, INSERT, and DELETE statements (see Chapter 9), but not in an ORDER BY list.

■ Use CASE expressions instead of correlated subqueries to implement Listing 8.18 more efficiently (see "Evaluating Conditional Values with CASE" in Chapter 5):

```
SELECT title_id,
    MIN(CASE au_order WHEN 1
          THEN au_id
        END)
      AS "Author 1",
    MIN(CASE au_order WHEN 2
          THEN au_id
        END)
      AS "Author 2",
    MIN(CASE au_order WHEN 3
          THEN au_id
        END)
      AS "Author 3"
  FROM title_authors
  GROUP BY title_id
  ORDER BY title_id ASC;
```

USING SUBQUERIES AS COLUMN EXPRESSIONS

Comparing a Subquery Value by Using a Comparison Operator

You can use a subquery as a filter in a WHERE clause or HAVING clause by using one of the comparison operators (=, <>, <, <=, >, or >=). The important characteristics of a subquery comparison test are:

◆ The comparison operators work the same way as they do in other comparisons (refer to Table 4.2 in Chapter 4).

◆ The subquery can be simple or correlated (see "Simple and Correlated Subqueries" earlier in this chapter).

◆ The subquery's SELECT-clause list can include only one expression or column name.

◆ The compared values must have the same data type or must be implicitly convertible to the same type (see "Converting Data Types with CAST()" in Chapter 5).

◆ String comparisons may be case-insensitive or case-sensitive, depending on your DBMS; see the DBMS Tip in "Filtering Rows with WHERE" in Chapter 4.

◆ The subquery must return a single value (a one-row, one-column result). A subquery that returns more than one value will cause an error.

◆ If the subquery result contains zero rows, the comparison test will evaluate to false.

The hard part of writing these statements is getting the subquery to return one value, which you can guarantee several ways:

◆ Using an aggregate function on an ungrouped table always returns a single value (see Chapter 6).

◆ Using a join with the outer query based on a key always returns a single value.

Listing 8.23 List the authors who live in the state in which the publisher Tenterhooks Press is located. See Figure 8.23 for the result.

```
SELECT au_id, au_fname, au_lname, state
  FROM authors
 WHERE state =
   (SELECT state
      FROM publishers
     WHERE pub_name = 'Tenterhooks Press');
```

```
au_id au_fname au_lname state
----- -------- -------- -----
A03   Hallie   Hull     CA
A04   Klee     Hull     CA
A06            Kellsey  CA
```

Figure 8.23 Result of Listing 8.23.

Listing 8.24 List the authors who live in the state in which the publisher XXX is located. See Figure 8.24 for the result.

```
SELECT au_id, au_fname, au_lname, state
  FROM authors
 WHERE state =
   (SELECT state
      FROM publishers
     WHERE pub_name = 'XXX');
```

```
au_id au_fname au_lname state
----- -------- -------- -----
```

Figure 8.24 Result of Listing 8.24 (an empty table).

Listing 8.25 List the books with above-average sales. See Figure 8.25 for the result.

```
SELECT title_id, sales
  FROM titles
  WHERE sales >
    (SELECT AVG(sales)
      FROM titles);
```

```
title_id sales
-------- -------
T05        201440
T07       1500200
```

Figure 8.25 Result of Listing 8.25.

Listing 8.26 List the authors of the books with above-average sales by using a join and a subquery. See Figure 8.26 for the result.

```
SELECT ta.au_id, ta.title_id
  FROM titles t
  INNER JOIN title_authors ta
    ON ta.title_id = t.title_id
  WHERE sales >
    (SELECT AVG(sales)
      FROM titles)
  ORDER BY ta.au_id ASC, ta.title_id ASC;
```

```
au_id title_id
----- --------
A02   T07
A04   T05
A04   T07
```

Figure 8.26 Result of Listing 8.26.

To compare a subquery value:

◆ In the WHERE clause of a SELECT statement, type:

WHERE *test_expr op* (*subquery*)

test_expr is a literal value, a column name, an expression, or a subquery that returns a single value; *op* is a comparison operator(=, <>, <, <=, >, or >=); and *subquery* is a scalar subquery that returns exactly one column and zero or one rows.

If the value returned by *subquery* satisfies the comparison to *test_expr,* the comparison condition evaluates to true. The comparison condition is false if the subquery value doesn't satisfy the condition, the subquery value is null, or the subquery result is empty (has zero rows).

The same syntax applies to a HAVING clause:

HAVING *test_expr op* (*subquery*)

Listing 8.23 tests the result of a simple subquery for equality to list the authors who live in the state in which Tenterhooks Press is located. Only one publisher is named *Tenterhooks Press,* so the inner WHERE condition guarantees that the inner query returns a single-valued result. See **Figure 8.23** for the result.

Listing 8.24 is the same as Listing 8.23 except for the name of the publisher. No publisher named XXX exists, so the subquery returns an empty table (zero rows). The comparison evaluates to null, so the final result is empty. See **Figure 8.24** for the result.

Listing 8.25 lists the books with above-average sales. Subqueries introduced with comparison operators often use aggregate functions to return a single value. See **Figure 8.25** for the result.

To list the authors of the books with above-average sales, I've added an inner join to Listing 8.25 (**Listing 8.26** and **Figure 8.26**).

continues on next page

USING SUBQUERIES WITH COMPARISON OPERATORS

Recall from the introduction to this chapter that you can use a subquery almost anywhere an expression is allowed, so this syntax is valid:

```
WHERE (subquery) op (subquery)
```

The left subquery must return a single value. **Listing 8.27** is equivalent to Listing 8.26, but I've removed the inner join and instead placed a correlated subquery to the left of the comparison operator. See **Figure 8.27** for the result.

You can include GROUP BY or HAVING clauses in a subquery if you know that the GROUP BY or HAVING clause itself returns a single value. **Listing 8.28** lists the books priced higher than the highest-priced biography. See **Figure 8.28** for the result.

Listing 8.27 List the authors of the books with above-average sales, by using a two subqueries. See Figure 8.27 for the result.

```
SELECT au_id, title_id
  FROM title_authors ta
  WHERE
    (SELECT AVG(sales)
      FROM titles t
      WHERE ta.title_id = t.title_id)
    >
    (SELECT AVG(sales)
      FROM titles)
  ORDER BY au_id ASC, title_id ASC;
```

```
au_id title_id
----- --------
A02    T07
A04    T05
A04    T07
```

Figure 8.27 Result of Listing 8.27.

Listing 8.28 List the books priced higher than the highest-priced biography. See Figure 8.28 for the result.

```
SELECT title_id, price
  FROM titles
  WHERE price >
    (SELECT MAX(price)
      FROM titles
      GROUP BY type
      HAVING type = 'biography');
```

```
title_id price
-------- -----
T03      39.95
T13      29.99
```

Figure 8.28 Result of Listing 8.28.

Listing 8.29 List the publishers whose average sales exceed the overall average sales. See Figure 8.29 for the result.

```
SELECT pub_id, AVG(sales) AS "AVG(sales)"
  FROM titles
  GROUP BY pub_id
  HAVING AVG(sales) >
    (SELECT AVG(sales)
      FROM titles);
```

```
pub_id AVG(sales)
------ ----------
P03      506744.33
```

Figure 8.29 Result of Listing 8.29.

Listing 8.30 List authors whose royalty share is less than the highest royalty share of any co-author of a book. See Figure 8.30 for the result.

```
SELECT ta1.au_id, ta1.title_id,
    ta1.royalty_share
  FROM title_authors ta1
  WHERE ta1.royalty_share <
    (SELECT MAX(ta2.royalty_share)
      FROM title_authors ta2
      WHERE ta1.title_id = ta2.title_id);
```

```
au_id title_id royalty_share
----- -------- -------------
A04   T04            0.40
A03   T11            0.30
A04   T11            0.30
```

Figure 8.30 Result of Listing 8.30.

Listing 8.29 uses a subquery in a HAVING clause to list the publishers whose average sales exceed overall average sales. Again, the subquery returns a single value (the average of all sales). See **Figure 8.29** for the result.

Listing 8.30 uses a correlated subquery to list authors whose royalty share is less than the highest royalty share of any co-author of a book. The outer query selects the rows of title_authors (that is, of ta1) one by one. The subquery calculates the highest royalty share for each book being considered for selection in the outer query. For each possible value of ta1, the DBMS evaluates the subquery and puts the row being considered in the result if the royalty share is less than the calculated maximum. See **Figure 8.30** for the result.

continues on next page

USING SUBQUERIES WITH COMPARISON OPERATORS

Listing 8.31 uses a correlated subquery to imitate a GROUP BY clause and list all books that have a price greater than the average for books of its type. For each possible value of t1, the DBMS evaluates the subquery and includes the row in the result if the price value in that row exceeds the calculated average. It's unnecessary to group by type explicitly, because the rows for which average price is calculated are restricted by the subquery's WHERE clause. See **Figure 8.31** for the result.

Listing 8.32 uses the same structure as Listing 8.31 to list all the books whose sales are less than the best-selling book of its type. See **Figure 8.32** for the result.

✔ Tips

■ If a subquery returns more than one row, you can use ALL or ANY to modify the comparison operator, or you can introduce the subquery with IN. I'll cover ALL, ANY, and IN later in this chapter.

■ **DBMS** MySQL 4.0 and earlier versions don't support subqueries. For workarounds, see the DBMS Tip in "Understanding Subqueries" earlier in this chapter.

Listing 8.31 List all books that have a price greater than the average for books of its type. See Figure 8.31 for the result.

```
                         listing
SELECT type, title_id, price
  FROM titles t1
  WHERE price >
    (SELECT AVG(t2.price)
      FROM titles t2
      WHERE t1.type = t2.type)
  ORDER BY type ASC, title_id ASC;
```

type	title_id	price
biography	T06	19.95
biography	T07	23.95
children	T09	13.95
history	T13	29.99
psychology	T04	12.99

Figure 8.31 Result of Listing 8.31.

Listing 8.32 List all the books whose sales are less than the best-selling book of its type. See Figure 8.32 for the result.

```
                         listing
SELECT type, title_id, sales
  FROM titles t1
  WHERE sales <
    (SELECT MAX(sales)
      FROM titles t2
      WHERE t1.type = t2.type
        AND sales IS NOT NULL)
  ORDER BY type ASC, title_id ASC;
```

type	title_id	sales
biography	T06	11320
biography	T12	100001
children	T08	4095
history	T01	566
history	T02	9566
psychology	T04	13001
psychology	T11	94123

Figure 8.32 Result of Listing 8.32.

Testing Set Membership with IN

You learned in "List Filtering with **IN**" in Chapter 4 how to use the **IN** keyword in a **WHERE** clause to compare a literal, column value, or expression to a list of values. You also can use a subquery to generate the list. The important characteristics of a subquery set membership test are:

◆ **IN** works the same way with the values in a subquery result as it does with a parenthesized list of values (see "List Filtering with **IN**" in Chapter 4).

◆ The subquery can be simple or correlated (see "Simple and Correlated Subqueries" earlier in this chapter).

◆ The subquery's **SELECT**-clause list can include only one expression or column name.

◆ The compared values must have the same data type or must be implicitly convertible to the same type (see "Converting Data Types with **CAST()**" in Chapter 5).

◆ String comparisons may be case-insensitive or case-sensitive, depending on your DBMS; see the DBMS Tip in "Filtering Rows with **WHERE**" in Chapter 4.

◆ The subquery must return exactly one column and zero or more rows. A subquery that returns more than one column will cause an error.

◆ You can use **NOT IN** to reverse the effect of the **IN** test. If you specify **NOT IN**, the DBMS takes the action specified by the SQL statement if there is *no* matching value in the subquery's result.

To test set membership:

◆ In the WHERE clause of a SELECT statement, type:

WHERE *test_expr* [NOT] IN (*subquery*)

test_expr is a literal value, a column name, an expression, or a subquery that returns a single value, and *subquery* is a subquery that returns one column and zero or more rows.

If the value of *test_expr* equals any value returned by *subquery*, the IN condition evaluates to true. The IN condition is false if the subquery result is empty, if no row in the subquery result matches *test_expr*, or if all the values in the subquery result are null. Specify NOT to negate the condition's result.

The same syntax applies to a HAVING clause:

HAVING *test_expr* [NOT] IN (*subquery*)

Listing 8.33 lists the names of the publishers that have published biographies. The DBMS evaluates this statement in two steps. First, the inner query returns the IDs of the publishers that have published biographies (P01 and P03). Second, the DBMS substitutes these values into the outer query, which finds the names that go with the IDs in the table publishers. See **Figure 8.33** for the result. Here's the join version of Listing 8.33:

```
SELECT DISTINCT pub_name
  FROM publishers p
  INNER JOIN titles t
    ON p.pub_id = t.pub_id
  AND type = 'biography';
```

Listing 8.34 is the same as Listing 8.33, except that it uses NOT IN to list the names of the publishers who haven't published biographies. See **Figure 8.34** for the result. This statement can't be converted to a join. The analogous not-equal join has a different meaning: It lists the names of publishers that have published *some* book that isn't a biography.

Listing 8.33 List the names of the publishers that have published biographies. See Figure 8.33 for the result.

```
SELECT pub_name
  FROM publishers
  WHERE pub_id IN
    (SELECT pub_id
      FROM titles
      WHERE type = 'biography');
```

```
pub_name
------------------
Abatis Publishers
Schadenfreude Press
```

Figure 8.33 Result of Listing 8.33.

Listing 8.34 List the names of the publishers that haven't published biographies. See Figure 8.34 for the result.

```
SELECT pub_name
  FROM publishers
  WHERE pub_id NOT IN
    (SELECT pub_id
      FROM titles
      WHERE type = 'biography');
```

```
pub_name
------------------
Core Dump Books
Tenterhooks Press
```

Figure 8.34 Result of Listing 8.34.

Listing 8.35 List the authors who haven't written (or co-written) a book. See Figure 8.35 for the result.

```
SELECT au_id, au_fname, au_lname
  FROM authors
  WHERE au_id NOT IN
    (SELECT au_id
      FROM title_authors);
```

```
au_id au_fname au_lname
----- -------- -----------

A07   Paddy    O'Furniture
```

Figure 8.35 Result of Listing 8.35.

Listing 8.36 List the names of the authors who have published a book with publisher P03. See Figure 8.36 for the result.

```
SELECT DISTINCT a.au_id, au_fname, au_lname
  FROM title_authors ta
  INNER JOIN authors a
    ON ta.au_id = a.au_id
  WHERE title_id IN
    (SELECT title_id
      FROM titles
      WHERE pub id = 'P03');
```

```
au_id au_fname au_lname
----- -------- ---------

A01   Sarah    Buchman
A02   Wendy    Heydemark
A04   Klee     Hull
```

Figure 8.36 Result of Listing 8.36.

Listing 8.35 is equivalent to Listing 7.31 in Chapter 7, except that it uses a subquery instead of an outer join to list the authors who haven't written (or co-written) a book. See **Figure 8.35** for the result.

Listing 8.36 lists the names of the authors who have published a book with publisher P03 (Schadenfreude Press). The join to the table authors is necessary to include the authors' names (not just their IDs) in the result. See **Figure 8.36** for the result.

continues on next page

A subquery can itself include one or more subqueries. **Listing 8.37** lists the names of authors who have participated in writing at least one biography. The innermost query returns the title IDs T06, T07, T10, and T12. The DBMS evaluates the subquery at the next higher level by using these title IDs and returns the author IDs. Finally, the outermost query uses the author IDs to find the names of the authors. See **Figure 8.37** for the result.

Excessive subquery nesting makes a statement hard to read; often, it's easier to restate the query as a join. Here's the join version of Listing 8.37:

```
SELECT DISTINCT a.au_id, au_fname,
    au_lname
  FROM authors a
  INNER JOIN title_authors ta
    ON a.au_id = ta.au_id
  INNER JOIN titles t
    ON t.title_id = ta.title_id
  WHERE type = 'biography';
```

Listing 8.38 lists the names of all non-lead authors (au_order > 1) who live in California and who receive less than 50 percent of the royalties for a book. See **Figure 8.38** for the result. Here's the join version of Listing 8.38:

```
SELECT DISTINCT a.au_id, au_fname,
    au_lname
  FROM authors a
  INNER JOIN title_authors ta
    ON a.au_id = ta.au_id
  WHERE state = 'CA'
    AND royalty_share < 0.5
    AND au_order > 1;
```

Listing 8.37 List the names of authors who have participated in writing at least one biography. See Figure 8.37 for the result.

```
SELECT au_id, au_fname, au_lname
  FROM authors
  WHERE au_id IN
    (SELECT au_id
      FROM title_authors
      WHERE title_id IN
        (SELECT title_id
          FROM titles
          WHERE type = 'biography'));
```

```
au_id au_fname au_lname
----- -------- ---------
A02   Wendy    Heydemark
A04   Klee     Hull
```

Figure 8.37 Result of Listing 8.37.

Listing 8.38 List the names of all ancillary authors who live in California and who receive less than 50 percent of the royalties for a book. See Figure 8.38 for the result.

```
SELECT au_id, au_fname, au_lname
  FROM authors
  WHERE state = 'CA'
    AND au_id IN
      (SELECT au_id
        FROM title_authors
        WHERE royalty_share < 0.5
          AND au_order > 1);
```

```
au_id au_fname au_lname
----- -------- --------
A03   Hallie   Hull
A04   Klee     Hull
```

Figure 8.38 Result of Listing 8.38.

Listing 8.39 List the names of authors who are co-authors of a book. See Figure 8.39 for the result.

```
                    listing
SELECT au_id, au_fname, au_lname
  FROM authors a
  WHERE au_id IN
    (SELECT au_id
       FROM title_authors
       WHERE royalty_share < 1.0);
```

```
au_id au_fname au_lname
----- -------- ---------
A02   Wendy    Heydemark
A03   Hallie   Hull
A04   Klee     Hull
A06            Kellsey
```

Figure 8.39 Result of Listing 8.39.

Listing 8.40 List the names of authors who are sole authors of a book. See Figure 8.40 for the result.

```
                    listing
SELECT a.au_id, au_fname, au_lname
  FROM authors a
  WHERE 1.0 IN
    (SELECT royalty_share
       FROM title_authors ta
       WHERE ta.au_id = a.au_id);
```

```
au_id au_fname   au_lname
----- ---------  ---------
A01   Sarah      Buchman
A02   Wendy      Heydemark
A04   Klee       Hull
A05   Christian  Kells
A06              Kellsey
```

Figure 8.40 Result of Listing 8.40.

Listing 8.39 lists the names of authors who are co-authors of a book. To determine whether an author is a co-author or the sole author of a book, examine his or her royalty share for the book. If the royalty share is less than 100 percent (1.0), the author is a co-author; otherwise, he or she is the sole author. See **Figure 8.39** for the result.

Listing 8.40 uses a correlated subquery to list the names of authors who are sole authors of a book—that is, authors who earn 100 percent (1.0) of the royalty on a book. See **Figure 8.40** for the result. The DBMS considers each row in the outer-query table **authors** to be a candidate for inclusion in the result. When the DBMS examines the first candidate row in **authors**, it sets the correlation variable a.au_id equal to A01 (Sarah Buchman), which it substitutes into the inner query:

```
SELECT royalty_share
  FROM title_authors ta
  WHERE ta.au_id = 'A01';
```

The inner query returns 1.0, so the outer query evaluates to:

```
SELECT a.au_id, au_fname, au_lname
  FROM authors a
  WHERE 1.0 IN (1.0)
```

The **WHERE** condition is true, so author A01 is included in the result. The DBMS repeats this procedure for every author; see "Simple and Correlated Subqueries" earlier in this chapter.

continues on next page

TESTING SET MEMBERSHIP WITH IN

Listing 8.41 lists the names of authors who are both co-authors and sole authors. The inner query returns the author IDs of sole authors, and the outer query compares these IDs with the IDs of the co-authors. See **Figure 8.41** for the result.

You can rewrite Listing 8.41 as a join or as an intersection. Here's the join version of Listing 8.41:

```
SELECT DISTINCT a.au_id, au_fname,
    au_lname
  FROM authors a
  INNER JOIN title_authors ta1
    ON a.au_id = ta1.au_id
  INNER JOIN title_authors ta2
    ON a.au_id = ta2.au_id
  WHERE ta1.royalty_share < 1.0
    AND ta2.royalty_share = 1.0;
```

Here's the intersection version of Listing 8.41 (see "Finding Common Rows with INTERSECT" in Chapter 7):

```
SELECT DISTINCT a.au_id, au_fname,
    au_lname
  FROM authors a
  INNER JOIN title_authors ta
    ON a.au_id = ta.au_id
  WHERE ta.royalty_share < 1.0
INTERSECT
SELECT DISTINCT a.au_id, au_fname,
    au_lname
  FROM authors a
  INNER JOIN title_authors ta
    ON a.au_id = ta.au_id
  WHERE ta.royalty_share = 1.0;
```

Listing 8.42 uses a correlated subquery to list the types of books published by more than one publisher. See **Figure 8.42** for the result. Here's the self-join version of Listing 8.42:

```
SELECT DISTINCT t1.type
  FROM titles t1
  INNER JOIN titles t2
    ON t1.type = t2.type
    AND t1.pub_id <> t2.pub_id;
```

Listing 8.41 List the names of authors who are both co-authors and sole authors. See Figure 8.41 for the result.

```
SELECT DISTINCT a.au_id, au_fname, au_lname
  FROM authors a
  INNER JOIN title_authors ta
    ON a.au_id = ta.au_id
  WHERE ta.royalty_share < 1.0
    AND a.au_id IN
      (SELECT a.au_id
        FROM authors a
        INNER JOIN title_authors ta
          ON a.au_id = ta.au_id
          AND ta.royalty_share = 1.0);
```

```
au_id au_fname au_lname
----- -------- ---------
A02   Wendy    Heydemark
A04   Klee     Hull
A06            Kellsey
```

Figure 8.41 Result of Listing 8.41.

Listing 8.42 List the types of books common to more than one publisher. See Figure 8.42 for the result.

```
SELECT DISTINCT t1.type
  FROM titles t1
  WHERE t1.type IN
    (SELECT t2.type
      FROM titles t2
      WHERE t1.pub_id <> t2.pub_id);
```

```
type
---------
biography
history
```

Figure 8.42 Result of Listing 8.42.

TESTING SET MEMBERSHIP WITH IN

✔ Tips

- IN is equivalent to = ANY; see "Comparing Some Subquery Values with ANY" later in this chapter.

- NOT IN is equivalent to <> ALL (*not* <> ANY); see "Comparing All Subquery Values with ALL" later in this chapter.

- **DBMS** **MySQL** 4.0 and earlier versions don't support subqueries. For workarounds, see the DBMS Tip in "Understanding Subqueries" earlier in this chapter.

To run Listing 8.41 in **Microsoft Access**, type:

```
SELECT DISTINCT a.au_id, au_fname,
    au_lname
FROM (authors AS a
  INNER JOIN title_authors AS ta1
    ON a.au_id = ta1.au_id)
  INNER JOIN title_authors AS ta2
    ON a.au_id = ta2.au_id
  WHERE ta1.royalty_share < 1.0
    AND ta2.royalty_share = 1.0;
```

In **PostgreSQL**, convert the floating-point numbers in Listings 8.38 through 8.41 to DECIMAL; see "Converting Data Types with CAST()" in Chapter 5. To run Listings 8.38 through 8.41 in PostgreSQL, change the floating-point literals to (Listing 8.38):

CAST(0.5 AS DECIMAL)

and (Listing 8.39):

CAST(1.0 AS DECIMAL)

and (Listing 8.40):

CAST(1.0 AS DECIMAL)

and (Listing 8.41):

CAST(1.0 AS DECIMAL) (in two places)

Some DBMSes permit you to test multiple values simultaneously by using this syntax:

```
SELECT columns
  FROM table1
  WHERE (col1, col2,..., colN) IN
    (SELECT colA, colB,..., colN
      FROM table2);
```

The test expression (left of IN) is a parenthesized list of *table1* columns. The subquery returns the same number of columns as there are in the list. The DBMS compares the values in corresponding columns. The following query, for example, works in **Oracle** and **PostgreSQL**:

```
SELECT au_id, city, state
  FROM authors
  WHERE (city, state) IN
    (SELECT city, state
      FROM publishers);
```

The result lists the authors who live in the same city and state as some publisher:

```
au_id city          state
----- ------------- -----
A03   San Francisco CA
A04   San Francisco CA
A05   New York      NY
```

Comparing All Subquery Values with ALL

You can use the ALL keyword to determine whether a value is less than or greater than *all* the values in a subquery result. The important characteristics of subquery comparisons that use ALL are:

◆ ALL modifies a comparison operator in a subquery comparison test and follows =, <>, <, <=, >, or >=; see "Comparing a Subquery Value by Using a Comparison Operator" earlier in this chapter.

◆ The combination of a comparison operator and ALL tells the DBMS how to apply the comparison test to the values returned by a subquery. < ALL, for example, means less than every value in the subquery result, and > ALL means greater than every value in the subquery result.

◆ When ALL is used with <, <=, >, or >=, the comparison is equivalent to evaluating the subquery result's minimum or maximum value. < ALL means less than every subquery value—in other words, less than the minimum value. > ALL means greater than every subquery value—in other words, greater than the maximum value. **Table 8.2** shows equivalent ALL expressions and column functions. In Listing 8.45 later in this section, I show you how to replicate a > ALL query by using MAX().

◆ The comparison = ALL is valid but isn't often used. = ALL always will be false unless all the values returned by the subquery are identical (and equal to the test value).

◆ The subquery can be simple or correlated (see "Simple and Correlated Subqueries" earlier in this chapter).

◆ The subquery's SELECT-clause list can include only one expression or column name.

◆ The compared values must have the same data type or must be implicitly convertible to the same type (see "Converting Data Types with CAST()" in Chapter 5).

◆ String comparisons may be case-insensitive or case-sensitive, depending on your DBMS; see the DBMS Tip in "Filtering Rows with WHERE" in Chapter 4.

◆ The subquery must return exactly one column and zero or more rows. A subquery that returns more than one column will cause an error.

◆ If the subquery returns no rows, the ALL condition is true. (You may find this result to be counterintuitive.)

Table 8.2

ALL **Equivalencies**	
ALL EXPRESSION	COLUMN FUNCTION
< ALL(*subquery*)	< MIN(*subquery* values)
> ALL(*subquery*)	> MAX(*subquery* values)

Listing 8.43 List the authors who live in a city in which no publisher is located. See Figure 8.43 for the result.

```
SELECT au_id, au_lname, au_fname, city
  FROM authors
  WHERE city <> ALL
    (SELECT city
      FROM publishers);
```

```
au_id au_lname    au_fname city
----- ----------- -------- ---------
A01   Buchman     Sarah    Bronx
A02   Heydemark   Wendy    Boulder
A06   Kellsey              Palo Alto
A07   O'Furniture Paddy    Sarasota
```

Figure 8.43 Result of Listing 8.43.

Listing 8.44 List the nonbiographies that are cheaper than all the biographies. See Figure 8.44 for the result.

```
SELECT title_id, title_name
  FROM titles
  WHERE type <> 'biography'
    AND price < ALL
    (SELECT price
      FROM titles
      WHERE type = 'biography'
        AND price IS NOT NULL);
```

```
title_id title_name
-------- -------------------------------
T05      Exchange of Platitudes
T08      Just Wait Until After School
T11      Perhaps It's a Glandular Problem
```

Figure 8.44 Result of Listing 8.44.

To compare all subquery values:

◆ In the WHERE clause of a SELECT statement, type:

WHERE *test_expr op* ALL (*subquery*)

test_expr is a literal value, a column name, an expression, or a subquery that returns a single value; *op* is a comparison operator (=, <>, <, <=, >, or >=); and *subquery* is a subquery that returns one column and zero or more rows.

The ALL condition evaluates to true if all values in *subquery* satisfy the ALL condition or if the subquery result is empty (has zero rows). The ALL condition is false if any (at least one) value in *subquery* doesn't satisfy the ALL condition or if any value is null.

The same syntax applies to a HAVING clause:

HAVING *test_expr op* ALL (*subquery*)

Listing 8.43 lists the authors who live in a city in which no publisher is located. The inner query finds all the cities in which publishers are located, and the outer query compares each author's city to all the publishers' cities. See **Figure 8.43** for the result.

You can use NOT IN to replicate Listing 8.43:

```
SELECT au_id, au_lname, au_fname, city
  FROM authors
  WHERE city NOT IN
    (SELECT city FROM publishers);
```

Listing 8.44 lists the nonbiographies that are priced less than all the biographies. The inner query finds all the biography prices. The outer query inspects the lowest price in the list and determines whether each nonbiography is cheaper. See **Figure 8.44** for the result. The price IS NOT NULL condition is required because the price of biography T10 is null. Without this condition, the entire query would return zero rows, because it's impossible to determine whether a price is less than null (see "Nulls" in Chapter 3).

continues on next page

Listing 8.45 lists the books that outsold all the books that author A06 wrote (or co-wrote). The inner query uses a join to find the sales of each book by author A06. The outer query inspects the highest sales figure in the list and determines whether each book sold more copies. See **Figure 8.45** for the result. Again, the IS NOT NULL condition is needed in case **sales** is null for a book by author A06. I can replicate Listing 8.45 by using GROUP BY, HAVING, and MAX() (instead of ALL):

```
SELECT title_id
  FROM titles
  GROUP BY title_id
  HAVING MAX(sales) >
    (SELECT MAX(sales)
      FROM title_authors ta
      INNER JOIN titles t
        ON t.title_id = ta.title_id
      WHERE ta.au_id = 'A06');
```

Listing 8.46 uses a correlated subquery in the HAVING clause of the outer query to list the types of books for which the highest sales figure is more than twice the average sales for that type. The inner query is evaluated once for each group defined in the outer query (once for each type of book). See **Figure 8.46** for the result.

✔ Tips

- <> ALL is equivalent to NOT IN; see "Testing Set Membership with IN" earlier in this chapter.

- **DBMS** MySQL 4.0 and earlier versions don't support subqueries. For workarounds, see the DBMS Tip in "Understanding Subqueries" earlier in this chapter.

   In **PostgreSQL**, convert the floating-point numbers in Listing 8.46 to DECIMAL; see "Converting Data Types with CAST()" in Chapter 5. To run Listing 8.46 in PostgreSQL, change the floating-point literal to:

   ```
CAST(2.0 AS DECIMAL)
   ```

Listing 8.45 List the books that outsold all the books that author A06 wrote (or co-wrote). See Figure 8.45 for the result.

```
SELECT title_id, title_name
  FROM titles
  WHERE sales > ALL
    (SELECT sales
      FROM title_authors ta
      INNER JOIN titles t
        ON t.title_id = ta.title_id
      WHERE ta.au_id = 'A06'
        AND sales IS NOT NULL);
```

```
title_id  title_name
--------  --------------------------
T05       Exchange of Platitudes
T07       I Blame My Mother
T12       Spontaneous, Not Annoying
```

Figure 8.45 Result of Listing 8.45.

Listing 8.46 List the types of books for which the highest sales figure is more than twice the average sales for that type. See Figure 8.46 for the result.

```
SELECT t1.type
  FROM titles t1
  GROUP BY t1.type
  HAVING MAX(t1.sales) >= ALL
    (SELECT 2.0 * AVG(t2.sales)
      FROM titles t2
      WHERE t1.type = t2.type);
```

```
type
---------
biography
```

Figure 8.46 Result of Listing 8.46.

Comparing Some Subquery Values with ANY

ANY works like ALL (see the preceding section) but instead determines whether a value is equal to, less than, or greater than *any* (at least one) of the values in a subquery result. The important characteristics of subquery comparisons that use ANY are:

◆ ANY modifies a comparison operator in a subquery comparison test and follows =, <>, <, <=, >, or >=; see "Comparing a Subquery Value by Using a Comparison Operator" earlier in this chapter.

◆ The combination of a comparison operator and ANY tells the DBMS how to apply the comparison test to the values returned by a subquery. < ANY, for example, means less than at least one value in the subquery result, and > ANY means greater than at least one value in the subquery result.

◆ When ANY is used with <, <=, >, or >=, the comparison is equivalent to evaluating the subquery result's maximum or minimum value. < ANY means less than at least one subquery value—in other words, less than the maximum value. > ANY means greater than at least one subquery value—in other words, greater than the minimum value. **Table 8.3** shows equivalent ANY expressions and column functions. In Listing 8.49 later in this section, I show you how to replicate a > ANY query by using MIN().

◆ The comparison = ANY is equivalent to IN; see "Testing Set Membership with IN" earlier in this chapter.

◆ The subquery can be simple or correlated (see "Simple and Correlated Subqueries" earlier in this chapter).

◆ The subquery's SELECT-clause list can include only one expression or column name.

◆ The compared values must have the same data type or must be implicitly convertible to the same type (see "Converting Data Types with CAST()" in Chapter 5).

◆ String comparisons may be case-insensitive or case-sensitive, depending on your DBMS; see the DBMS Tip in "Filtering Rows with WHERE" in Chapter 4.

◆ The subquery must return exactly one column and zero or more rows. A subquery that returns more than one column will cause an error.

◆ If the subquery returns no rows, the ANY condition is false.

Table 8.3

ANY **Equivalencies**	
ANY EXPRESSION	COLUMN FUNCTION
< ANY(*subquery*)	< MAX(*subquery* values)
> ANY(*subquery*)	> MIN(*subquery* values)

To compare some subquery values:

◆ In the WHERE clause of a SELECT statement, type:

WHERE *test_expr op* ANY (*subquery*)

test_expr is a literal value, a column name, an expression, or a subquery that returns a single value; *op* is a comparison operator (=, <>, <, <=, >, or >=); and *subquery* is a subquery that returns one column and zero or more rows.

If any (at least one) value in *subquery* satisfies the ANY condition, the condition evaluates to true. The ANY condition is false if no value in *subquery* satisfies the condition, or if *subquery* is empty (has zero rows) or contains all nulls.

The same syntax applies to a HAVING clause:

HAVING *test_expr op* ANY (*subquery*)

Listing 8.47 lists the authors who live in a city in which a publisher is located. The inner query finds all the cities in which publishers are located, and the outer query compares each author's city to all the publishers' cities. See **Figure 8.47** for the result.

You can use IN to replicate Listing 8.47:

```
SELECT au_id, au_lname, au_fname, city
  FROM authors
  WHERE city IN
    (SELECT city FROM publishers);
```

Listing 8.48 lists the nonbiographies that are priced less than at least one biography. The inner query finds all the biography prices. The outer query inspects the highest price in the list and determines whether each nonbiography is cheaper. See **Figure 8.48** for the result.

Unlike the ALL comparison in Listing 4.44 in the preceding section, the price IS NOT NULL condition isn't required here, even though the price of biography T10 is null. The DBMS doesn't determine whether *all* the price comparisons are true; just whether *at least one* is true, so the null comparison is ignored.

Listing 8.47 List the authors who live in a city in which a publisher is located. See Figure 8.47 for the result.

```
SELECT au_id, au_lname, au_fname, city
  FROM authors
  WHERE city = ANY
    (SELECT city
      FROM publishers);
```

```
au_id au_lname au_fname  city
----- -------- --------- -------------
A03   Hull     Hallie    San Francisco
A04   Hull     Klee      San Francisco
A05   Kells    Christian New York
```

Figure 8.47 Result of Listing 8.47.

Listing 8.48 List the nonbiographies that are cheaper than at least one biography. See Figure 8.48 for the result.

```
SELECT title_id, title_name
  FROM titles
  WHERE type <> 'biography'
    AND price < ANY
      (SELECT price
        FROM titles
        WHERE type = 'biography');
```

```
title_id title_name
-------- --------------------------------
T01      1977!
T02      200 Years of German Humor
T04      But I Did It Unconsciously
T05      Exchange of Platitudes
T08      Just Wait Until After School
T09      Kiss My Boo-Boo
T11      Perhaps It's a Glandular Problem
```

Figure 8.48 Result of Listing 8.48.

Listing 8.49 List the books that outsold at least one of the books that author A06 wrote (or co-wrote). See Figure 8.49 for the result.

```
SELECT title_id, title_name
  FROM titles
  WHERE sales > ANY
    (SELECT sales
      FROM title_authors ta
      INNER JOIN titles t
        ON t.title_id = ta.title_id
      WHERE ta.au_id = 'A06');
```

```
title_id  title_name
--------  ---------------------------------
T02       200 Years of German Humor
T03       Ask Your System Administrator
T04       But I Did It Unconsciously
T05       Exchange of Platitudes
T06       How About Never?
T07       I Blame My Mother
T09       Kiss My Boo-Boo
T11       Perhaps It's a Glandular Problem
T12       Spontaneous, Not Annoying
T13       What Are The Civilian Applications?
```

Figure 8.49 Result of Listing 8.49.

■ **DBMS** **MySQL** 4.0 and earlier versions don't support subqueries. For workarounds, see the DBMS Tip in "Understanding Subqueries" earlier in this chapter.

Listing 8.49 lists the books that outsold at least one of the books that author A06 wrote (or co-wrote). The inner query uses a join to find the sales of each book by author A06. The outer query inspects the lowest sales figure in the list and determines whether each book sold more copies. See **Figure 8.49** for the result.

Again, unlike the ALL comparison in Listing 4.45 in the preceding section, the IS NOT NULL condition isn't needed here. I can replicate Listing 8.49 by using GROUP BY, HAVING, and MIN() (instead of ANY):

```
SELECT title_id
  FROM titles
  GROUP BY title_id
  HAVING MIN(sales) >
    (SELECT MIN(sales)
      FROM title_authors ta
      INNER JOIN titles t
        ON t.title_id = ta.title_id
      WHERE ta.au_id = 'A06');
```

✔ Tips

■ = ANY is equivalent to IN, but <> ANY isn't equivalent to NOT IN. If *subquery* returns the values *x*, *y*, and *z*:

test_expr <> ANY (*subquery*)

is equivalent to:

test_expr <> *x* OR

test_expr <> *y* OR

test_expr <> *z*

But

test_expr NOT IN (*subquery*)

is equivalent to:

test_expr <> *x* AND

test_expr <> *y* AND

test_expr <> *z*

(NOT IN actually is equivalent to <> ALL.)

■ In the SQL standard, the keywords ANY and SOME are synonyms. In many DBMSes, you can use SOME in place of ANY.

COMPARING SOME SUBQUERY VALUES WITH ANY

Testing Existence
with EXISTS

So far in this chapter, I've been using the comparison operators, IN, ALL, and ANY to compare a specific test value to values in a subquery result. EXISTS and NOT EXISTS don't compare values; rather, they simply look for the existence or nonexistence of rows in a subquery result. The important characteristics of an existence test are:

◆ An existence test doesn't compare values, so it isn't preceded by a test expression.

◆ The subquery can be simple or correlated but usually is correlated (see "Simple and Correlated Subqueries" earlier in this chapter).

◆ The subquery can return any number of columns and rows.

◆ By convention, the SELECT clause in the subquery is SELECT * to retrieve all columns. Listing specific column names is unnecessary, because EXISTS simply tests for the *existence* of rows that satisfy the subquery conditions; the actual values in the rows are irrelevant.

◆ All IN, ALL, and ANY queries can be expressed with EXISTS or NOT EXISTS. I'll give equivalent queries in some of the examples later in this section.

◆ If the subquery returns at least one row, an EXISTS test is true, and a NOT EXISTS test is false.

◆ If the subquery returns no rows, an EXISTS test is false, and a NOT EXISTS test is true.

◆ A subquery row that contains only nulls counts as a row. (An EXISTS test is true, and a NOT EXISTS test is false.)

◆ Because an EXISTS test performs no comparisons, it's not subject to the same problems with nulls as tests that use comparison operators (IN, ALL, or ANY; see "Nulls in Subqueries" earlier in this chapter).

Listing 8.50 List the names of the publishers that have published biographies. See Figure 8.50 for the result.

```
SELECT pub_name
  FROM publishers p
  WHERE EXISTS
    (SELECT *
      FROM titles t
      WHERE t.pub_id = p.pub_id
        AND type = 'biography');
```

```
pub_name
-------------------
Abatis Publishers
Schadenfreude Press
```

Figure 8.50 Result of Listing 8.50.

Listing 8.51 List the authors who haven't written (or co-written) a book. See Figure 8.51 for the result.

```
SELECT au_id, au_fname, au_lname
  FROM authors a
  WHERE NOT EXISTS
    (SELECT *
      FROM title_authors ta
      WHERE ta.au_id - a.au_id);
```

```
au_id au_fname  au_lname
----- --------- -----------
A07   Paddy     O'Furniture
```

Figure 8.51 Result of Listing 8.51.

To test existence:

◆ In the WHERE clause of a SELECT statement, type:

WHERE [NOT] EXISTS (*subquery*)

subquery is a subquery that returns any number of columns and rows.

If *subquery* returns one or more rows, the EXISTS test evaluates to true. If *subquery* returns zero rows, the EXISTS test evaluates to false. Specify NOT to negate the test's result.

The same syntax applies to a HAVING clause:

HAVING [NOT] EXISTS (*subquery*)

Listing 8.50 lists the names of the publishers that have published biographies. This query considers each publisher's ID in turn and determines whether it causes the existence test to evaluate to true. Here, the first publisher is P01 (Abatis Publishers). The DBMS ascertains whether any rows exist in the table titles in which pub_id is P01 and type is biography. If so, Abatis Publishers is included in the final result. The DBMS repeats the same process for each of the other publisher IDs. See **Figure 8.50** for the result. If I wanted to list the names of publishers that *haven't* published biographies, I'd change EXISTS to NOT EXISTS. See Listing 8.33 earlier in this chapter for an equivalent query that uses IN.

Listing 8.51 lists the authors who haven't written (or co-written) a book. See **Figure 8.51** for the result. See Listing 8.35 earlier in this chapter for an equivalent query that uses NOT IN.

continues on next page

TESTING EXISTENCE WITH EXISTS

Listing **8.52** lists the authors who live in a city in which a publisher is located. See **Figure 8.52** for the result. See Listing 8.47 earlier in this chapter for an equivalent query that uses = ANY.

Recall from "Finding Common Rows with INTERSECT" in Chapter 7 that you can use INTERSECT to retrieve the rows that two tables have in common. You also can use EXISTS to find an intersection. **Listing 8.53** lists the cities in which both an author and publisher are located. See **Figure 8.53** for the result. See Listing 7.46 in Chapter 7 for an equivalent query that uses INTERSECT. You also can replicate this query with an inner join:

```
SELECT DISTINCT a.city
  FROM authors a
  INNER JOIN publishers p
    ON a.city = p.city;
```

Listing 8.52 List the authors who live in a city in which a publisher is located. See Figure 8.52 for the result.

```
SELECT au_id, au_lname, au_fname, city
  FROM authors a
  WHERE EXISTS
    (SELECT *
      FROM publishers p
      WHERE p.city = a.city);
```

au_id	au_lname	au_fname	city
A03	Hull	Hallie	San Francisco
A04	Hull	Klee	San Francisco
A05	Kells	Christian	New York

Figure 8.52 Result of Listing 8.52.

Listing 8.53 List the cities in which both an author and publisher are located. See Figure 8.53 for the result.

```
SELECT DISTINCT city
  FROM authors a
  WHERE EXISTS
    (SELECT *
      FROM publishers p
      WHERE p.city = a.city);
```

city
New York
San Francisco

Figure 8.53 Result of Listing 8.53.

Listing 8.54 List the cities in which an author lives but a publisher isn't located. See Figure 8.54 for the result.

```
SELECT DISTINCT city
  FROM authors a
  WHERE NOT EXISTS
    (SELECT *
      FROM publishers p
      WHERE p.city = a.city);
```

```
city
---------
Boulder
Bronx
Palo Alto
Sarasota
```

Figure 8.54 Result of Listing 8.54.

Listing 8.55 List the authors who wrote (or co-wrote) three or more books. See Figure 8.55 for the result.

```
SELECT au_id, au_fname, au_lname
  FROM authors a
  WHERE EXISTS
    (SELECT *
      FROM title_authors ta
      WHERE ta.au_id = a.au_id
      HAVING COUNT(*) >= 3);
```

```
au_id au_fname au_lname
----- -------- ---------
A01   Sarah    Buchman
A02   Wendy    Heydemark
A04   Klee     Hull
A06            Kellsey
```

Figure 8.55 Result of Listing 8.55.

Recall from "Finding Different Rows with EXCEPT" in Chapter 7 that you can use EXCEPT to retrieve the rows in one table that aren't also in another table. You also can use NOT EXISTS to find a difference. **Listing 8.54** lists the cities in which an author lives but a publisher isn't located. See **Figure 8.54** for the result. See Listing 7.47 in Chapter 7 for an equivalent query that uses EXCEPT. You also can replicate this query with NOT IN:

```
SELECT DISTINCT city
  FROM authors
  WHERE city NOT IN
    (SELECT city
      FROM publishers);
```

Or with an outer join:

```
SELECT DISTINCT a.city
  FROM authors a
  LEFT OUTER JOIN publishers p
    ON a.city = p.city
  WHERE p.city IS NULL;
```

Listing 8.55 lists the authors who wrote (or co-wrote) three or more books. See **Figure 8.55** for the result.

continues on next page

TESTING EXISTENCE WITH EXISTS

Listing 8.56 uses two existence tests to list the authors who wrote (or co-wrote) both children's and psychology books. See **Figure 8.56** for the result.

Listing 8.56 List the authors who wrote (or co-wrote) a children's book and also wrote (or co-wrote) a psychology book. See Figure 8.56 for the result.

```
SELECT au_id, au_fname, au_lname
  FROM authors a
  WHERE EXISTS
    (SELECT *
      FROM title_authors ta
      INNER JOIN titles t
        ON t.title_id = ta.title_id
      WHERE ta.au_id = a.au_id
        AND t.type = 'children')
  AND EXISTS
    (SELECT *
      FROM title_authors ta
      INNER JOIN titles t
        ON t.title_id = ta.title_id
      WHERE ta.au_id = a.au_id
        AND t.type = 'psychology');
```

```
au_id au_fname au_lname
----- -------- --------
A06            Kellsey
```

Figure 8.56 Result of Listing 8.56.

Listing 8.57 Does the column au_id in the table authors contains duplicate values? See Figure 8.57 for the result.

```
SELECT DISTINCT 'Yes' AS "Duplicates?"
  WHERE EXISTS
    (SELECT *
      FROM authors
      GROUP BY au_id
      HAVING COUNT(*) > 1);
```

```
Duplicates?
-----------
```

Figure 8.57 Result of Listing 8.57.

Listing 8.58 Does the column au_id in the table title_authors contains duplicate values? See Figure 8.58 for the result.

```
SELECT DISTINCT 'Yes' AS "Duplicates?"
  WHERE EXISTS
    (SELECT *
      FROM title_authors
      GROUP BY au_id
      HAVING COUNT(*) > 1);
```

```
Duplicates?
-----------
Yes
```

Figure 8.58 Result of Listing 8.58.

Listing 8.57 performs a uniqueness test to determine whether duplicates occur in the column au_id in the table authors. The query prints *Yes* if duplicate values exist in the column au_id; otherwise, it returns an empty result. See **Figure 8.57** for the result. au_id is the primary key of authors, so of course it contains no duplicates.

Listing 8.58 shows the same query for the table title_authors, which does contain duplicate au_id values. See **Figure 8.58** for the result. You can add grouping columns to the GROUP BY clause to determine whether multiple-column duplicates exist.

continues on next page

✔ Tips

- You also can use COUNT(*) to determine whether a subquery returns at least one row, but COUNT(*) (usually) is less efficient than EXISTS. The DBMS quits processing an EXISTS subquery as soon as it determines whether the subquery returns a row, whereas COUNT(*) forces the DBMS to process the entire subquery. This query is equivalent to Listing 8.52 but runs slower:

```
SELECT au_id, au_lname, au_fname,
    city
  FROM authors a
  WHERE
    (SELECT COUNT(*)
      FROM publishers p
      WHERE p.city = a.city) > 0;
```

- Although SELECT * is the most common form of the SELECT clause in an EXISTS subquery, you can use SELECT *column* or SELECT *constant_value* to speed queries if your DBMS's optimizer isn't bright enough to figure out that it doesn't need to construct an *entire* interim table for an EXISTS subquery. For more information, see "Comparing Equivalent Queries" later in this chapter.

- Although I use SELECT COUNT(*) in some of the DBMS-specific subqueries in the DBMS Tip in this section, you should be wary of using an aggregate function in a subquery's SELECT clause. The existence test in **Listing 8.59**, for example, *always* is true because COUNT(*) always will return a row (with the value zero here). I could argue that the result, **Figure 8.59**, is flawed logically because no publisher ID XXX exists.

Listing 8.59 Be careful when using aggregate functions in a subquery SELECT clause. See Figure 8.59 for the result.

```
SELECT pub_id
  FROM publishers
  WHERE EXISTS
    (SELECT COUNT(*)
      FROM titles
      WHERE pub_id = 'XXX');
```

```
pub_id
------
P01
P02
P03
P04
```

Figure 8.59 The result of Listing 8.59.

■ **DBMS** **MySQL** 4.0 and earlier versions don't support subqueries. For workarounds, see the DBMS Tip in "Understanding Subqueries" earlier in this chapter.

To run Listings 8.57 and 8.58 in **Oracle**, add a `FROM DUAL` clause to the outer query; see the DBMS Tip in "Creating Derived Columns" in Chapter 5.

To run Listings 8.55, 8.57, and 8.58 in **Microsoft Access**, type (Listing 8.55):

```
SELECT au_id, au_fname, au_lname
  FROM authors a
  WHERE EXISTS
    (SELECT COUNT(*)
      FROM title_authors ta
      WHERE ta.au_id = a.au_id
      HAVING COUNT(*) >= 3);
```

and (Listing 8.57):

```
SELECT DISTINCT 'Yes' AS
    "Duplicates?"
  FROM authors
  WHERE EXISTS
    (SELECT COUNT(*)
      FROM authors
      GROUP BY au_id
      HAVING COUNT(*) > 1);
```

and (Listing 8.58):

```
SELECT DISTINCT 'Yes' AS
    "Duplicates?"
  FROM title_authors
  WHERE EXISTS
    (SELECT COUNT(*)
      FROM title_authors
      GROUP BY au_id
      HAVING COUNT(*) > 1);
```

To run Listings 8.55, 8.57, and 8.58 in **PostgreSQL**, type (Listing 8.55):

```
SELECT au_id, au_fname, au_lname
  FROM authors a
  WHERE EXISTS
    (SELECT COUNT(*)
      FROM title_authors ta
      WHERE ta.au_id = a.au_id
      HAVING COUNT(*) >= 3);
```

and (Listing 8.57):

```
SELECT 'Yes' AS "Duplicates?"
  WHERE EXISTS
    (SELECT COUNT(*)
      FROM authors
      GROUP BY au_id
      HAVING COUNT(*) > 1);
```

and (Listing 8.58):

```
SELECT 'Yes' AS "Duplicates?"
  WHERE EXISTS
    (SELECT COUNT(*)
      FROM title_authors
      GROUP BY au_id
      HAVING COUNT(*) > 1);
```

Comparing Equivalent Queries

As you've seen in this chapter and the preceding one, you can express the same query in different ways (different syntax, same semantics). To expand on this point, I've written the same query six semantically equivalent ways. Each of the statements in **Listing 8.60** lists the authors who have written (or co-written) at least one book. See **Figure 8.60** for the result.

The first two queries (inner joins) will run at the same speed as one another. Of the third through sixth queries (which use subqueries), the last one probably is the worst performer. The DBMS can—and probably will—stop processing the other subqueries as soon as it encounters a single matching value. But the subquery in the last statement has to count all the matching rows before it returns either true or false. The inner joins should run at about the same speed as the fastest subquery statement.

You may find this programming flexibility to be attractive, but people who design DBMS optimizers don't, as they are tasked with considering all the possible ways to express a query, figuring out which one performs best, and reformulating your query internally to its optimal form. (Entire careers are devoted to solving these types of optimization problems.) If your DBMS has a (very) intelligent optimizer, it will run all six of the queries in Listing 8.60 at the same speed. But that situation is unlikely, so you'll have to experiment with your DBMS to see which version runs fastest.

Listing 8.60 These six queries are equivalent semantically; they all list the authors who have written (or co-written) at least one book. See Figure 8.60 for the result.

```
┌─────────────────── listing ───────────────────┐
SELECT DISTINCT a.au_id
  FROM authors a
  INNER JOIN title_authors ta
    ON a.au_id = ta.au_id;

SELECT DISTINCT a.au_id
  FROM authors a, title_authors ta
  WHERE a.au_id = ta.au_id;

SELECT au_id
  FROM authors a
  WHERE au_id IN
    (SELECT au_id
      FROM title_authors);

SELECT au_id
  FROM authors a
  WHERE au_id = ANY
    (SELECT au_id
      FROM title_authors);

SELECT au_id
  FROM authors a
  WHERE EXISTS
    (SELECT *
      FROM title_authors ta
      WHERE a.au_id = ta.au_id);

SELECT au_id
  FROM authors a
  WHERE 0 <
    (SELECT COUNT(*)
      FROM title_authors ta
      WHERE a.au_id = ta.au_id);
```

```
au_id
-----
A01
A02
A03
A04
A05
A06
```

Figure 8.60 Each of the six statements in Listing 8.60 returns this result.

INSERTING, UPDATING, AND DELETING ROWS

To this point, I've explained how to use SELECT to retrieve and analyze the data in tables. In this chapter, I'll explain how to use SQL statements to *modify* table data:

- The INSERT statement adds new rows to a table.

- The UPDATE statement changes the values in a table's existing rows.

- The DELETE statement removes rows from a table.

These statements don't return a result, but your DBMS normally will print a message indicating whether the statement ran successfully and, if so, the number of rows affected by the change. To see the actual effect the statement had on a table, type a SELECT statement such as SELECT * FROM *table*.

Unlike SELECT, which only accesses data, these statements change data, so your database administrator may need to grant you permission to run them.

Displaying a Table's Column Definitions

To use INSERT, UPDATE, or DELETE, you'll need to know the column definitions of the table whose data you're modifying, including:

◆ The order of the columns in the table

◆ Each column's name

◆ Each column's data type

◆ Whether a column is a key (or part of a key)

◆ Whether a column's values must be unique within that column

◆ Whether a column permits nulls

◆ Each column's default value (if any)

I gave the column definitions of the sample-database tables in Tables 2.2 through 2.6 in "The Sample Database" in Chapter 2, but you can get the same information by using DBMS tools that describe database objects. In this section, I'll explain how to use those tools to display column definitions.

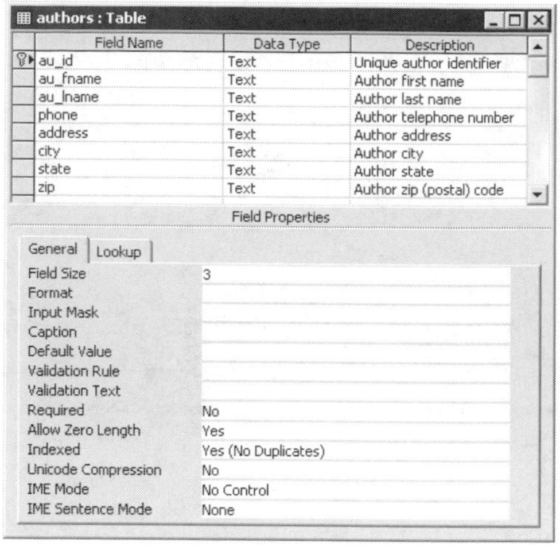

To display a table's column definitions in Microsoft Access:

1. Press F11 to switch to the Database window.

2. Click Tables (below Objects).

3. Click a table in the list.

4. Click Design in the toolbar to open the table in Design View (**Figure 9.1**).

Figure 9.1 Displaying column definitions in Microsoft Access.

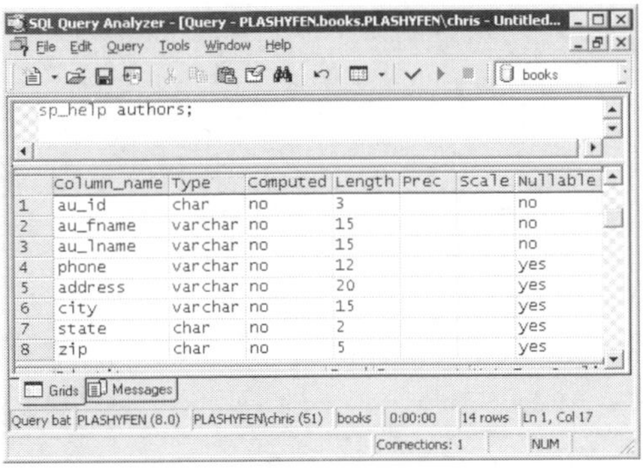

Figure 9.2 Displaying column definitions in Microsoft SQL Server.

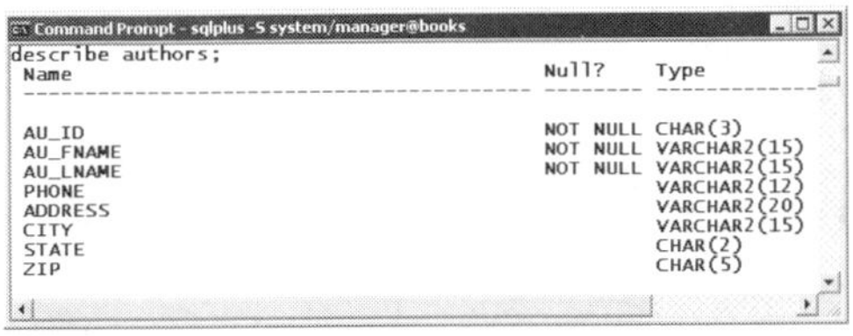

Figure 9.3 Displaying column definitions in Oracle.

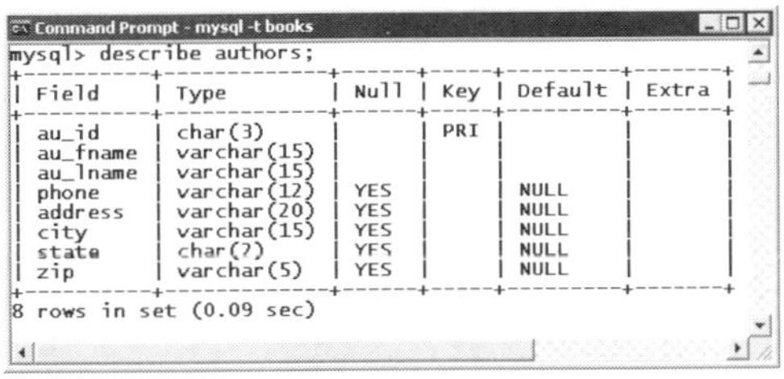

Figure 9.4 Displaying column definitions in MySQL.

To display a table's column definitions in Microsoft SQL Server:

1. Start SQL Query Analyzer or the interactive osql command-line utility (see "Microsoft SQL Server" in Chapter 1).

   The command produces abundant output, so I recommend that you use SQL Query Analyzer and choose Query > Results in Grid.

2. Type sp_help *table*;.

   table is a table name.

3. In SQL Query Analyzer, choose Query > Execute or press F5 (**Figure 9.2**).

   or

   In osql, press Enter, type go, and press Enter.

To display a table's column definitions in Oracle:

1. Start SQL*Plus or the interactive sqlplus command-line utility (see "Oracle" in Chapter 1).

2. Type describe *table*;, and press Enter (**Figure 9.3**).

   table is a table name.

To display a table's column definitions in MySQL:

1. Start the interactive mysql command-line utility (see "MySQL" in Chapter 1).

2. Type describe *table*; and press Enter (**Figure 9.4**).

   table is a table name.

To display a table's column definitions in PostgreSQL:

1. Start the interactive `psql` command-line utility (see "PostgreSQL" in Chapter 1).
2. Type `\d` *`table`*, and press Enter (**Figure 9.5**).

   table is a table name. Note that you don't terminate this command with a semicolon.

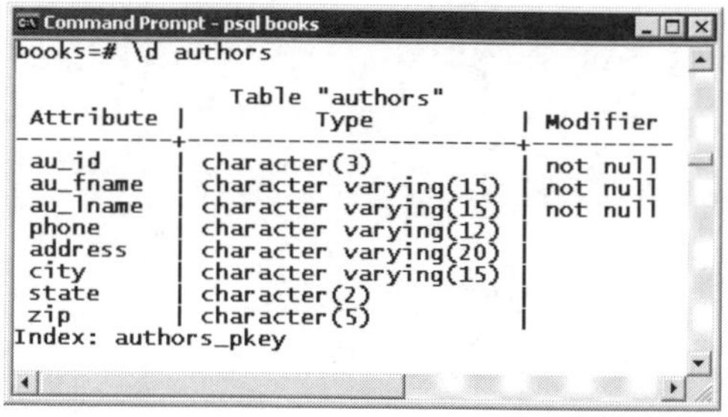

```
books=# \d authors

              Table "authors"
 Attribute |         Type          | Modifier
-----------+-----------------------+----------
 au_id     | character(3)          | not null
 au_fname  | character varying(15) | not null
 au_lname  | character varying(15) | not null
 phone     | character varying(12) |
 address   | character varying(20) |
 city      | character varying(15) |
 state     | character(2)          |
 zip       | character(5)          |
Index: authors_pkey
```

Figure 9.5 Displaying column definitions in PostgreSQL.

✔ Tips

- If you want to list a table's column names and the order in which they appear without listing any of the table's data, type:

  `SELECT * FROM` *`table`* `WHERE 1 = 2;`

  table is a table name, and `1 = 2` represents any condition that always is false.

- For general information about columns, see "Tables, Columns, and Rows" in Chapter 2.

  For information about keys, see "Primary Keys" and "Foreign Keys" in Chapter 2.

  For information about data types, see "Data Types" in Chapter 3.

- I'll explain how to create, alter, and drop column definitions in Chapter 10.

Inserting Rows with INSERT

The INSERT statement adds new rows to a table. In this section, I'll explain how to use several variations of INSERT to:

- Insert a row by using column positions (INSERT VALUES)

- Insert a row by using column names (INSERT VALUES)

- Insert rows from one table into another table (INSERT SELECT)

The important characteristics of INSERT are:

- In a positional insert, you insert ordered values into a new row in the same sequence as the columns appear in a table (see "To insert a row by using column positions" later in this section). In a named-column insert, you name the specific column into which each value is inserted in the new row (see "To insert a row by using column names" later in this section).

  You always should use a named-column insert so your SQL code still will work if someone reorders the table's columns or adds new columns.

- With INSERT VALUES, you specify explicit values to insert into a table. With INSERT SELECT, you choose rows from another table to insert into a table.

- INSERT VALUES adds one row to a table. INSERT SELECT adds zero or more rows to a table.

- Each inserted value must have the same data type or must be implicitly convertible to the same type as its corresponding column (see "Converting Data Types with CAST()" in Chapter 5).

- To preserve referential integrity, an inserted foreign-key value must contain either null or an existing key value from the primary or unique key columns referenced by the foreign key; see "Primary Keys" and "Foreign Keys" in Chapter 2.

- An inserted value can't violate a check constraint; see "Adding a Check Constraint with CHECK" in Chapter 10.

- No expression may cause an arithmetic error (an overflow or divide-by-zero error, for example).

- Recall from "Tables, Columns, and Rows" in Chapter 2 that the order of rows in a table is unimportant and that you have no control over the physical location of rows, so new rows may appear anywhere among a table's existing rows.

To insert a row by using column positions:

◆ Type:

INSERT INTO *table*

    VALUES(*value1, value2,..., valueN*);

table is the name of a table into which a row is inserted, and *value1, value2,...., valueN* is a parenthesized list of comma-separated literals or expressions that provides a value to every column in the new row.

The number of values must equal the number of columns in *table*, and the values must be listed in the same sequence as the columns in *table*. The DBMS inserts each value into the column that corresponds to the value's position in *table*. *value1* is inserted into the first column of *table* in the new row, *value2* into the second column, and so on.

This statement adds one row to *table* (**Listing 9.1**).

Listing 9.1 This INSERT statement adds a new row to the table authors by listing values in the same order in which the columns appear in authors. See Figure 9.6 for the result.

```
                          listing
INSERT INTO authors
   VALUES(
     'A08',
     'Michael',
     'Polk',
     '512-953-1231',
     '4028 Guadalupe St',
     'Austin',
     'TX',
     '78701');
```

Listing 9.2 This INSERT statement adds a new row to the table authors by listing values in the same order in which the column names appear in the column list. See Figure 9.6 for the result.

```
INSERT INTO authors(
    au_id,
    au_fname,
    au_lname,
    phone,
    address,
    city,
    state,
    zip)
VALUES(
    'A09',
    'Irene',
    'Bell',
    '415-225-4689',
    '810 Throckmorton Ave',
    'Mill Valley',
    'CA',
    '94941');
```

Listing 9.3 You don't have to list column names in the same order in which they appear in the table. Here, I've rearranged the column names and their corresponding values. See Figure 9.6 for the result.

```
INSERT INTO authors(
    zip,
    phone,
    address,
    au_lname,
    au_fname,
    state,
    au_id,
    city)
VALUES(
    '60614',
    '312-998-0020',
    '1937 N. Clark St',
    'Weston',
    'Dianne',
    'IL',
    'A10',
    'Chicago');
```

To insert a row by using column names:

◆ Type:

INSERT INTO *table*

  (*column1, column2, ..., columnN*)

  VALUES(*value1, value2, ..., valueN*);

table is the name of the table into which a row is inserted; *column1, column2,..., columnN* is a parenthesized list of comma-separated names of columns in *table*; and *value1, value2,..., valueN* is a parenthesized list of comma-separated literals or expressions that provides values to the named columns in the new row.

The number of values must equal the number of columns in the column list, and the values must be listed in the same sequence as the column names. The DBMS inserts each value into a column by using corresponding list positions. *value1* is inserted into *column1* in the new row, *value2* into *column2,* and so on. An omitted column is assigned its default value or null.

This statement adds one row to *table*.

It's clearer to list column names in the same order as they appear in the table (**Listing 9.2**), but you can list them in any order (**Listing 9.3**). In either case, the values in the VALUES clause must match the sequence in which you list the column names.

continues on next page

You can omit column names if you want to provide values for only some columns explicitly (**Listing 9.4**). If you omit a column, the DBMS must be able to provide a value based on the column's definition. The DBMS will insert the column's default value (if defined) or null (if permitted). If you omit a column that doesn't have a default value or permit nulls, the DBMS will display an error message and won't insert the row. For information about specifying a default value and permitting nulls, see "Specifying a Default Value with **DEFAULT**" and "Forbidding Nulls with **NOT NULL**" in Chapter 10.

Figure 9.6 shows the new rows in table authors after Listings 9.1 through 9.4 have run.

Listing 9.4 Here, I've added a row for a new author but omitted column names and values for the author's address information. The DBMS inserts nulls into the omitted columns automatically. See Figure 9.6 for the result.

```
                        listing
INSERT INTO authors(
    au_id,
    au_fname,
    au_lname,
    phone)
VALUES(
    'A11',
    'Max',
    'Allard',
    '212-502-0955');
```

au_id	au_fname	au_lname	phone	address	city	state	zip
A01	Sarah	Buchman	718-496-7223	75 West 205 St	Bronx	NY	10468
A02	Wendy	Heydemark	303-986-7020	2922 Baseline Rd	Boulder	CO	80303
A03	Hallie	Hull	415-549-4278	3800 Waldo Ave, #14F	San Francisco	CA	94123
A04	Klee	Hull	415-549-4278	3800 Waldo Ave, #14F	San Francisco	CA	94123
A05	Christian	Kells	212-771-4680	114 Horatio St	New York	NY	10014
A06		Kellsey	650-836-7128	390 Serra Mall	Palo Alto	CA	94305
A07	Paddy	O'Furniture	941-925-0752	1442 Main St	Sarasota	FL	34236
A08	Michael	Polk	512-953-1231	4028 Guadalupe St	Austin	TX	78701
A09	Irene	Bell	415-225-4689	810 Throckmorton Ave	Mill Valley	CA	94941
A10	Dianne	Weston	312-998-0020	1937 N. Clark St	Chicago	IL	60614
A11	Max	Allard	212-502-0955	NULL	NULL	NULL	NULL

Figure 9.6 The table authors has four new rows after I run Listings 9.1 through 9.4.

To insert rows from one table into another table:

◆ Type:

```
INSERT INTO table
    [(column1, column2,..., columnN)]
    select_statement;
```

table is the name of table into which rows are inserted. *column1, column2,..., columnN* is an optional parenthesized list of comma-separated names of columns in *table. select_statement* is any valid SELECT statement that returns rows of data to be inserted into *table.*

The number of columns in the *select_statement* result must equal the number of columns in *table* or in the column list. The DBMS ignores the column names in the *select_statement* result and uses column position instead. The first column in the *select_statement* result is used to populate the first column in *table* or *column1,* and so on. An omitted column is assigned its default value or null.

This statement adds zero or more rows to *table.*

The remaining examples in this section use the table new_publishers (**Figure 9.7**), which I created to show how INSERT SELECT works. new_publishers has the same structure as the table publishers and acts only as the source of new rows; it isn't itself changed by the INSERT operations.

continues on next page

```
pub_id pub_name              city        state country
------ --------------------- ----------- ----- ------------
P05    This is Pizza? Press  New York    NY    USA
P06    This is Beer? Press   Toronto     ON    Canada
P07    This is Irony? Press  London      NULL  United Kindom
P08    This is Fame? Press   Los Angeles CA    USA
```

Figure 9.7 This table, named new_publishers, is used in Listings 9.5 through 9.7. new_publishers has the same structure as publishers.

INSERTING ROWS WITH INSERT

289

Listing 9.5 inserts the rows for Los Angeles-based publishers from `new_publishers` into `publishers`. Here, I've omitted the column list, so the DBMS uses the column positions in `publishers` rather than column names to insert values. This statement inserts one row into `publishers`; see Figure 9.8 for the result.

Listing 9.6 inserts the rows for non-U.S. publishers from `new_publishers` into `publishers`. Here, the column names are the same in both the **INSERT** and **SELECT** clauses, but they don't have to match because the DBMS disregards the names of the columns returned by **SELECT** and uses their positions instead. This statement inserts two rows into `publishers`; see Figure 9.8 for the result.

It's legal for the **SELECT** clause to return an empty result (zero rows). **Listing 9.7** inserts the rows for publishers named XXX from `new_publishers` into `publishers`. I can use **SELECT *** instead of listing column names because `new_publishers` and `publishers` have the same structure. This statement inserts no rows into `publishers` because no publisher is named XXX; see Figure 9.8 for the result.

Figure 9.8 shows the table `publishers` after Listings 9.5 through 9.7 are run.

Listing 9.5 Insert the rows for Los Angeles-based publishers from `new_publishers` into `publishers`. See Figure 9.8 for the result.

```
INSERT INTO publishers
  SELECT
      pub_id,
      pub_name,
      city,
      state,
      country
  FROM new_publishers
  WHERE city = 'Los Angeles';
```

```
pub_id  pub_name             city          state  country
------  -------------------- ------------- -----  -------------
P01     Abatis Publishers    New York      NY     USA
P02     Core Dump Books      San Francisco CA     USA
P03     Schadenfreude Press  Hamburg       NULL   Germany
P04     Tenterhooks Press    Berkeley      CA     USA
P06     This is Beer? Press  Toronto       ON     Canada
P07     This is Irony? Press London        NULL   United Kindom
P08     This is Fame? Press  Los Angeles   CA     USA
```

Figure 9.8 The table `publishers` has three new rows after I run Listings 9.5 through 9.7.

Listing 9.6 Insert the rows for non-U.S. publishers from new_publishers into publishers. See Figure 9.8 for the result.

```
INSERT INTO publishers(
    pub_id,
    pub_name,
    city,
    state,
    country)
  SELECT
      pub_id,
      pub_name,
      city,
      state,
      country
    FROM new_publishers
    WHERE country <> 'USA';
```

Listing 9.7 Insert the rows for publishers named XXX from new_publishers into publishers. See Figure 9.8 for the result.

```
INSERT INTO publishers(
    pub_id,
    pub_name,
    city,
    state,
    country)
  SELECT *
    FROM new_publishers
    WHERE pub_name = 'XXX';
```

✔ Tips

■ The process of adding rows to a table for the first time is called *populating the table*.

■ You can use the SELECT INTO statement to create a new table and populate it with the rows of a SELECT statement; see "Creating a New Table from an Existing One with SELECT INTO" in Chapter 10.

■ If you want to be extra-careful before you insert rows, you can test your INSERT statement on a temporary copy of the table; see "Creating a Temporary Table with CREATE TEMPORARY TABLE" and "Creating a New Table from an Existing One with SELECT INTO" in Chapter 10.

■ You also can INSERT rows through a view; see "Updating Data Through a View" in Chapter 12.

■ If you're using transactions, you must use a COMMIT statement after your final INSERT statement to make the changes to the table permanent. For information about transactions, see Chapter 13.

■ If *table1* and *table2* have compatible structures, you can insert all the rows from *table2* into *table1* by typing:

```
INSERT INTO table1
  SELECT * FROM table2;
```

■ **DBMS** According to the SQL standard, the INTO keyword is optional in an INSERT statement. **Microsoft Access**, **Oracle**, and **PostgreSQL** require INTO, however, so I always include it for portability.

Check the documentation to see how your DBMS handles the insertion of values into columns whose data type generates a unique row identifier automatically (see the DBMS Tip in "Primary Keys" in Chapter 2). DBMSes may restrict the insertion of values into these columns.

INSERTING ROWS WITH INSERT

Updating Rows with UPDATE

The **UPDATE** statement changes the values in a table's existing rows. You can use **UPDATE** to update:

◆ All rows in a table

◆ Specific rows in a table

To update rows, you specify:

◆ The table to update

◆ The names of the columns to update and their new values

◆ An optional search condition that specifies which rows to update

The important characteristics of **UPDATE** are:

◆ **UPDATE** takes an optional **WHERE** clause that specifies which rows to update. Without a **WHERE** clause, **UPDATE** changes *all* the rows in the table.

◆ **UPDATE** is dangerous because it's easy to omit the **WHERE** clause mistakenly (and update all rows) or misspecify the **WHERE** search condition (and update the wrong rows). It's wise to run a **SELECT** statement that uses the same **WHERE** clause before running the actual **UPDATE** statement. The **SELECT** displays all rows that the DBMS will modify when you run the **UPDATE**. Use **SELECT COUNT(*)** to display just the number of rows that the DBMS will update.

◆ Each updated value must have the same data type or must be implicitly convertible to the same type as its column (see "Converting Data Types with **CAST()**" in Chapter 5).

◆ To preserve referential integrity, DBMSes allow you define the action the DBMS takes automatically when you try to **UPDATE** a key value to which foreign key values point; see the Tips in "Specifying a Foreign Key with **FOREIGN KEY**" in Chapter 10.

◆ An updated value can't violate a check constraint; see "Adding a Check Constraint with **CHECK**" in Chapter 10.

◆ No expression may cause an arithmetic error (an overflow or divide-by-zero error, for example).

◆ Recall from "Tables, Columns, and Rows" in Chapter 2 that the order of rows in a table is unimportant and that you have no control over the physical location of rows, so an updated row may change position in a table.

Listing 9.8 Change the value of contract to zero in every row. See Figure 9.9 for the result.

```
listing
UPDATE titles
  SET contract = 0;
```

Listing 9.9 Double the price of history books. See Figure 9.9 for the result.

```
listing
UPDATE titles
  SET price = price * 2.0
  WHERE type = 'history';
```

Listing 9.10 For psychology books, set the type to self help and the number of pages to null. See Figure 9.9 for the result.

```
listing
UPDATE titles
  SET type = 'self help',
      pages = NULL
  WHERE type = 'psychology';
```

To update rows:

◆ Type:

```
UPDATE table
  SET column = expr
  [WHERE search_condition];
```

table is the name of a table to update.

column is the name of the column in *table* that contains the data to be changed. *expr* is a literal, an expression, or a parenthesized subquery that returns a single value. The value returned by *expr* replaces the existing value in *column*. To change the values in multiple columns, type a list of comma-separated *column = expr* expressions in the SET clause. You can list the *column = expr* expressions in any order.

search_condition specifies the conditions to be met for the rows that are updated. The *search_condition* conditions can be WHERE conditions (comparison operators, LIKE, BETWEEN, IN, and IS NULL; see Chapter 4) or subquery conditions (comparison operators, IN, ALL, ANY, and EXISTS; see Chapter 8), combined with AND, OR, and NOT. If the WHERE clause is omitted, every row in *table* is updated.

Listing 9.8 changes the value of contract to zero in every row of titles. The lack of a WHERE clause tells the DBMS to update all the rows in the column contract. This statement updates 13 rows; see Figure 9.9 for the result.

Listing 9.9 uses an arithmetic expression and a WHERE condition to double the price of history books. This statement updates three rows; see Figure 9.9 for the result.

Listing 9.10 updates the columns type and pages for psychology books. You use only a single SET clause to update multiple columns, with *column = expr* expressions separated by commas. (Don't put a comma after the last expression.) This statement updates three rows; see Figure 9.9 for the result.

continues on next page

UPDATING ROWS WITH UPDATE

Listing 9.11 uses a subquery and an aggregate function to cut the sales of books with above-average sales in half. This statement updates two rows; see Figure 9.9 for the result.

You can update values in a given table based on the values stored in another table. **Listing 9.12** uses nested subqueries to update the publication date for all the books written (or co-written) by Sarah Buchman. This statement updates three rows; see Figure 9.9 for the result.

Suppose that Abatis Publishers (publisher P01) swallows Tenterhooks Press (P04) in a merger, so now, all the Tenterhooks Press books are published by Abatis Publishers. **Listing 9.13** works in a bottom-up fashion to change the publisher IDs in `titles` from P04 to P01. The `WHERE` subquery retrieves the `pub_id` for Tenterhooks Press. The DBMS uses this `pub_id` to retrieve the books in the table `titles` whose publisher is Tenterhooks Press. Finally, the DBMS uses the value returned by the `SET` subquery to update the appropriate rows in the table `titles`. Because the subqueries are used with an unmodified comparison operator, they must be scalar subqueries that return a single value (that is, a one-row, one-column result); see "Comparing a Subquery Value by Using a Comparison Operator" in Chapter 8. Listing 9.13 updates five rows; see Figure 9.9 for the result.

Figure 9.9 shows the table `titles` after Listings 9.8 through 9.13 are run. Each listing updates values in a different column (or columns) from those in the other listings. The updated values in each column are shown in red.

Listing 9.11 Cut the sales of books with above-average sales in half. See Figure 9.9 for the result.

```
UPDATE titles
  SET sales = sales * 0.5
  WHERE sales >
    (SELECT AVG(sales)
      FROM titles);
```

Listing 9.12 Change the publication date of all of Sarah Buchman's books to January 1, 2003. See Figure 9.9 for the result.

```
UPDATE titles
  SET pubdate = DATE '2003-01-01'
  WHERE title_id IN
    (SELECT title_id
      FROM title_authors
      WHERE au_id IN
        (SELECT au_id
          FROM authors
          WHERE au_fname = 'Sarah'
            AND au_lname = 'Buchman'));
```

Listing 9.13 Change the publisher of all of Tenterhooks Press' books to Abatis Publishers. See Figure 9.9 for the result.

```
UPDATE titles
  SET pub_id =
    (SELECT pub_id
      FROM publishers
      WHERE pub_name = 'Abatis Publishers')
  WHERE pub_id =
    (SELECT pub_id
      FROM publishers
      WHERE pub_name = 'Tenterhooks Press');
```

✔ Tips

- The DBMS will evaluate expressions in a SET or WHERE clause by using the values that the referenced columns had *before* any updates. Consider this UPDATE statement:

```
UPDATE mytable
  SET col1 = col1 * 2,
      col2 = col1 * 4,
      col3 = col2 * 8
  WHERE col1 = 1
    AND col2 = 2;
```

The DBMS sets col1 to 2, col2 to 4 (1 × 4, not 2 × 4), and col3 to 16 (2 × 8, not 4 × 8).

- If you want to be extra-careful before you update rows, you can test your UPDATE statement on a temporary copy of the table; see "Creating a Temporary Table with CREATE TEMPORARY TABLE" and "Creating a New Table from an Existing One with SELECT INTO" in Chapter 10.

- You also can UPDATE rows through a view; see "Updating Data Through a View" in Chapter 12.

- If you're using transactions, you must use a COMMIT statement after your final UPDATE statement to make the changes to the table permanent. For information about transactions, see Chapter 13.

- **DBMS** In **Microsoft Access** date literals, omit the DATE keyword, and surround the literal with # characters instead of quotes. To run Listing 9.12 in Access, change the date literal to #2003-01-01#.

Microsoft Access doesn't support scalar subqueries in the SET clause. To run Listing 9.13 in Access, split the UPDATE statement into two statements: one that SELECTs the pub_id for Abatis Publishers from publishers, and one that uses this pub_id to change the pub_id of all the Tenterhooks Press books in titles.

continues on next page

title_id	title name	type	pub_id	pages	price	sales	pubdate	contract
T01	1977!	history	P01	107	43.98	566	2003-01-01	0
T02	200 Years of German Humor	history	P03	14	39.90	9566	2003-01-01	0
T03	Ask Your System Administrator	computer	P02	1226	39.95	25667	2000-09-01	0
T04	But I Did It Unconsciously	self help	P01	NULL	12.99	13001	1999-05-31	0
T05	Exchange of Platitudes	self help	P01	NULL	6.95	100720	2001-01-01	0
T06	How About Never?	biography	P01	473	19.95	11320	2000-07-31	0
T07	I Blame My Mother	biography	P03	333	23.95	750100	1999-10-01	0
T08	Just Wait Until After School	children	P01	86	10.00	4095	2001-06-01	0
T09	Kiss My Boo-Boo	children	P01	22	13.95	5000	2002-05-31	0
T10	Not Without My Faberge Egg	biography	P01	NULL	NULL	NULL	NULL	0
T11	Perhaps It's a Glandular Problem	self help	P01	NULL	7.99	94123	2000-11-30	0
T12	Spontaneous, Not Annoying	biography	P01	507	12.99	100001	2000-08-31	0
T13	What Are The Civilian Applications?	history	P03	802	59.98	10467	2003-01-01	0

Figure 9.9 The table titles after I run Listings 9.8 through 9.14. The updated values are shown in red

UPDATING ROWS WITH UPDATE

In **Microsoft SQL Server** date literals, omit the DATE keyword. To run Listing 9.12 in SQL Server, change the date literal to `'2003-01-01'`.

MySQL 4.0 and earlier versions don't support subqueries and won't run Listings 9.11, 9.12, and 9.13. For workarounds, see the DBMS Tip in "Understanding Subqueries" in Chapter 8.

In **PostgreSQL**, convert the floating-point numbers in Listings 9.9 and 9.11 to DECIMAL; see "Converting Data Types with CAST()" in Chapter 5. To run Listings 9.9 and 9.11 in PostgreSQL, change the floating-point literal to (Listing 9.9):

```
CAST(2.0 AS DECIMAL)
```

and (Listing 9.11):

```
CAST(0.5 AS DECIMAL)
```

Check the documentation to see how your DBMS handles updating values in columns whose data type generates a unique row identifier automatically (see the DBMS Tip in "Primary Keys" in Chapter 2). DBMSes may restrict updating values in these columns.

Deleting Rows with DELETE

The DELETE statement removes rows from a table. You can use DELETE to remove:

◆ All rows in a table

◆ Specific rows in a table

To delete rows, you specify:

◆ The table whose rows to delete

◆ An optional search condition that specifies which rows to delete

The important characteristics of DELETE are:

◆ Unlike INSERT and UPDATE, DELETE takes no column names because it removes entire rows.

◆ DELETE removes rows from a table, but it never deletes the table's definition. Even if you remove all rows from a table, the table itself still exists. If you want to delete a table definition (and all its associated data, indexes, and so on), see "Dropping a Table with DROP TABLE" in Chapter 10.

◆ DELETE takes an optional WHERE clause that specifies which rows to delete. Without a WHERE clause, DELETE removes *all* the rows in the table.

◆ DELETE is dangerous because it's easy to omit the WHERE clause mistakenly (and remove all rows) or misspecify the WHERE search condition (and remove the wrong rows). It's wise to run a SELECT statement that uses the same WHERE clause before running the actual DELETE statement. The SELECT displays all rows that the DBMS will remove when you run the DELETE. Use SELECT COUNT(*) to display just the number of rows that the DBMS will remove.

◆ To preserve referential integrity, DBMSes allow you define the action the DBMS takes automatically when you try to DELETE a key value to which foreign key values point; see the Tips in "Specifying a Foreign Key with FOREIGN KEY" in Chapter 10.

◆ No expression may cause an arithmetic error (an overflow or divide-by-zero error, for example).

◆ Recall from "Tables, Columns, and Rows" in Chapter 2 that the order of rows in a table is unimportant and that you have no control over the physical location of rows, so a deletion may reorder the positions of the rows remaining in a table.

To delete rows:

◆ Type:

DELETE FROM *table*

  [WHERE *search_condition*];

table is the name of a table from which rows are deleted.

search_condition specifies the conditions to be met for the rows that are deleted. The *search_condition* conditions can be WHERE conditions (comparison operators, LIKE, BETWEEN, IN, and IS NULL; see Chapter 4) or subquery conditions (comparison operators, IN, ALL, ANY, and EXISTS; see Chapter 8), combined with AND, OR, and NOT. If the WHERE clause is omitted, every row in *table* is deleted.

In the following examples, I'm going to ignore referential-integrity constraints—which I wouldn't do in a production database, of course.

Listing 9.14 deletes every row in royalties. The lack of a WHERE clause tells the DBMS to delete all the rows. This statement deletes 13 rows; see **Figure 9.10** for the result.

The WHERE clause in **Listing 9.15** tells the DBMS to remove the authors with the last name Hull from authors. This statement deletes two rows; see **Figure 9.11** for the result.

Listing 9.14 Delete all rows from the table royalties. See Figure 9.10 for the result.

```
DELETE FROM royalties;
```

```
title_id advance royalty_rate
-------- ------- ------------
```

Figure 9.10 Result of Listing 9.14.

Listing 9.15 Delete the rows in which the author's last name is Hull from the table authors. See Figure 9.11 for the result.

```
DELETE FROM authors
  WHERE au_lname = 'Hull';
```

au_id	au_fname	au_lname	phone	address	city	state	zip
A01	Sarah	Buchman	718-496-7223	75 West 205 St	Bronx	NY	10468
A02	Wendy	Heydemark	303-986-7020	2922 Baseline Rd	Boulder	CO	80303
A05	Christian	Kells	212-771-4680	114 Horatio St	New York	NY	10014
A06		Kellsey	650-836-7128	390 Serra Mall	Palo Alto	CA	94305
A07	Paddy	O'Furniture	941-925-0752	1442 Main St	Sarasota	FL	34236

Figure 9.11 Result of Listing 9.15.

Listing 9.16 Delete the rows for books published by publisher P01 or P04 from the table `title_authors`. See Figure 9.12 for the result.

```listing
DELETE FROM title_authors
  WHERE title_id IN
    (SELECT title_id
      FROM titles
      WHERE pub_id IN ('P01', 'P04'));
```

title_id	au_id	au_order	royalty_share
T02	A01	1	1.00
T03	A05	1	1.00
T07	A02	1	0.50
T07	A04	2	0.50
T13	A01	1	1.00

Figure 9.12 Result of Listing 9.16.

■ **DBMS** According to the SQL standard, the FROM keyword is optional in a DELETE statement. **Microsoft Access**, **MySQL**, and **PostgreSQL** require FROM, however, so I always include it for portability.

MySQL 4.0 and earlier versions don't support subqueries and won't run Listing 9.16. For workarounds, see the DBMS Tip in "Understanding Subqueries" in Chapter 8.

You can delete rows in a given table based on the values stored in another table. **Listing 9.16** uses a subquery to remove all the books published by publishers P01 or P04 from `title_authors`. This statement deletes 12 rows; see **Figure 9.12** for the result.

✔ Tips

■ If you want to be extra-careful before you remove rows, you can test your DELETE statement on a temporary copy of the table; see "Creating a Temporary Table with CREATE TEMPORARY TABLE" and "Creating a New Table from an Existing One with SELECT INTO" in Chapter 10.

■ You also can DELETE rows through a view; see "Updating Data Through a View" in Chapter 12.

■ If you're using transactions, you must use a COMMIT statement after your final DELETE statement to make the changes to the table permanent. For information about transactions, see Chapter 13.

■ If you want to delete all the rows in a table, the TRUNCATE statement is faster than DELETE. TRUNCATE isn't part of the SQL standard, but **Microsoft SQL Server**, **Oracle**, **MySQL**, and **PostgreSQL** support it. TRUNCATE functionally is identical to a DELETE statement with no WHERE clause: Both remove all rows in a table. But TRUNCATE is faster and uses fewer system resources than DELETE, because TRUNCATE doesn't scan the entire table and record changes in the transaction log (see Chapter 13). The tradeoff is that with TRUNCATE, you can't recover (roll back) your changes if you make a mistake. The syntax is:

TRUNCATE TABLE *table*;

table is the name of the table to be truncated. For information about TRUNCATE, search your DBMS documentation for *truncate*.

CREATING, ALTERING, AND DROPPING TABLES

10

Many DBMSes have interactive, graphical tools that let you create and manage tables and table properties such as column definitions and constraints. In this chapter, I'll explain how to perform those tasks programmatically by using SQL:

- The CREATE TABLE statement creates a new table.

- The ALTER TABLE statement modifies the structure of an existing table.

- The DROP TABLE statement destroys a table and all its data.

- The CREATE TEMPORARY TABLE statement creates a table that the DBMS destroys automatically when it's no longer in use.

- The SELECT INTO statement creates a new table from an existing one.

These statements don't return a result, but your DBMS normally will print a message indicating whether the statement ran successfully. To see the actual effect the statement had on a table, examine the table's structure by using one of the commands described in "Displaying a Table's Column Definitions" in Chapter 9.

These statements modify database objects (and data, in some cases), so your database administrator may need to grant you permission to run them.

Creating Tables

Database designers spend considerable time normalizing tables and defining relationships and constraints before they write a line of SQL code. If you're going to create tables for production databases, I recommend that you study database design and normalization principles beyond those presented in Chapter 2.

Recall from "Tables, Columns, and Rows" in Chapter 2 that a database is organized around tables. To a user or an SQL programmer, a database appears to be a collection of one or more tables (and nothing but tables). To create a table, you specify the following:

◆ Table name

◆ Column names

◆ Data types of the columns

◆ Constraints

The table name and the column names must conform to the rules for SQL identifiers; see "SQL Syntax" in Chapter 3. (Each DBMS has its own rules.) The data type of each column is a character, numeric, datetime, or other data type; see "Data Types" in Chapter 3. Constraints define properties such as nullability, default values, keys, and permissible values.

You create a new table by using the **CREATE TABLE** statement, whose general syntax is:

```
CREATE TABLE table
  (
  column1 data_type1 [col_constraints1],
  column2 data_type2 [col_constraints2],
  ...
  columnN data_typeN [col_constraintsN]
  [, table_constraint1]
  [, table_constraint2]
  ...
  [, table_constraintN]
  );
```

Each column definition has a column name, a data type, and an optional list of one or more column constraints. Don't separate multiple column constraints with commas. An optional list of table constraints follows the final column definition. A comma follows each column definition and each table constraint (except the final one). For information about constraints, see "Understanding Constraints" later in this chapter.

By convention, I start each column definition and table constraint on its own line.

Table 10.1

Constraints	
CONSTRAINT	DESCRIPTION
NOT NULL	Prevents nulls from being inserted into a column
DEFAULT	Sets the default value of a column
PRIMARY KEY	Sets the table's primary-key column(s)
FOREIGN KEY	Sets the table's foreign-key column(s)
UNIQUE	Prevents duplicate values from being inserted into a column
CHECK	Limits the values that can be inserted into a column by using logical (Boolean) expressions

Understanding Constraints

Constraints allow you to define rules for values allowed in columns (**Table 10.1**). Your DBMS uses these rules to enforce the integrity of the database automatically. Constraints come in two flavors:

◆ A *column constraint* is part of a column definition and imposes a condition on that column only.

◆ A *table constraint* is declared independently of a column definition and can impose a condition on more than one column in a table. You must use a table constraint to include more than one column in a constraint.

You can specify some constraints as either column or table constraints, depending on the context in which they're used. If a primary key contains one column, for example, you can define it as a column constraint or as a table constraint. If the primary key has two or more columns, you must use a table constraint.

Assigning names to constraints allows you manage them efficiently; you easily can change or delete a named constraint by using the **ALTER TABLE** statement, for example. Constraint names are optional, but many SQL programmers and database designers name *all* constraints. It's not uncommon to leave **NOT NULL** and **DEFAULT** constraints unnamed, but you always should name other types of constraints (even if I don't do so in some of the examples).

continues on next page

If you don't name a constraint explicitly, your DBMS will generate a name and assign it to the constraint automatically. System-assigned names often contain strings of random characters and are cumbersome to use; use the CONSTRAINT clause to assign your own name instead. Constraint names also appear in warnings and error messages, which is another good reason to name constraints yourself.

To name a constraint:

◆ Preceding a constraint definition, type:

CONSTRAINT *constraint_name*

constraint_name is the name of the constraint and is a valid SQL identifier. Constraints names must be unique within a table.

I'll give examples of named constraints in subsequent examples in this chapter.

✔ Tip

■ **DBMS** **MySQL** doesn't support the CONSTRAINT clause for column constraints (but you can use it for table constraints).

Listing 10.1 Create the sample-database table `titles`.

```
listing
CREATE TABLE titles
  (
  title_id    CHAR(3)      ,
  title_name  VARCHAR(40)  ,
  type        VARCHAR(10)  ,
  pub_id      CHAR(3)      ,
  pages       INTEGER      ,
  price       DECIMAL(5,2) ,
  sales       INTEGER      ,
  pubdate     DATE         ,
  contract    SMALLINT
  );
```

Listing 10.2 Create the sample-database table `title_authors`.

```
listing
CREATE TABLE title_authors
  (
  title_id      CHAR(3)      ,
  au_id         CHAR(3)      ,
  au_order      SMALLINT     ,
  royalty_share DECIMAL(5,2)
  );
```

Creating a New Table with CREATE TABLE

In this section, I'll show you how to create a new table by using a minimal CREATE TABLE statement. In subsequent sections, I'll show you how to add column and table constraints to CREATE TABLE.

To create a new table:

◆ Type:
  ```
  CREATE TABLE table
    (
    column1 data_type1,
    column2 data_type2,
    ...
    columnN data_typeN
    );
  ```

table is the name of the new table to create.

column1, column2,..., columnN are the names of the columns in *table*. You must create at least one column.

data_type1, data_type2,..., data_typeN specify the SQL data type of each corresponding column. A data type may contain a length, scale, or precision specification, where applicable; see "Data Types" and subsequent sections in Chapter 3.

The table name must be unique within the database, and each column name must be unique within the table.

Listing 10.1 creates the sample-database table `titles`.

Listing 10.2 creates the sample-database table `title_authors`.

✔ Tips

- To see the result of a CREATE TABLE statement, examine the table's structure by using one of the commands described in "Displaying a Table's Column Definitions" in Chapter 9.

- Your DBMS will generate an error if you try to create a table with a name that already exists in the database. To prevent you from overwriting a table accidentally, SQL requires that you destroy a table explicitly with DROP TABLE before creating a new table with the same name; see "Dropping a Table with DROP TABLE" later in this chapter.

- A newly created table is empty (has zero rows). To populate the table with data, use the INSERT statement; see "Inserting Rows with INSERT" in Chapter 9.

- Columns permit nulls by default. If you don't want to allow nulls, see "Forbidding Nulls with NOT NULL" later in this chapter.

- To modify the structure of an existing table, see "Altering a Table with ALTER TABLE" later in this chapter.

- To create a table by using the structure and data of an existing table, see "Creating a New Table from an Existing One with SELECT INTO" later in this chapter.

- **DBMS** **Microsoft SQL Server** doesn't support the data type DATE. To run Listing 10.1 in SQL Server, change the data type of the column pubdate to DATETIME.

  MySQL changes VARCHAR columns with a length less than four characters to CHAR silently.

Forbidding Nulls
with NOT NULL

A column's nullability determines whether its rows can contain nulls—that is, whether values are required or optional in the column. I described nulls and their effects in "Nulls" in Chapter 3, but I'll review the basics here:

◆ A null is not a value but a marker that means no value has been entered.

◆ A null represents a missing, unknown, or inapplicable value. A null in the column price doesn't mean that an item has no price or that its price is zero; it means that the price is unknown or has not been set.

◆ A null isn't the same as zero (0), a blank, or an empty string ("").

◆ Nulls belong to no data type and can be inserted into any column that permits nulls.

◆ In SQL statements, the keyword NULL represents a null.

When you're defining a nullability constraint, some important considerations are:

◆ A nullability constraint always is a column constraint and not a table constraint; see "Understanding Constraints" earlier in this chapter.

◆ You define a nullability constraint by using the keywords NULL or NOT NULL in a CREATE TABLE column definition.

◆ In general, avoid permitting nulls because they complicate queries, insertions, and updates.

◆ Forbidding nulls in a column can help maintain data integrity by ensuring that users entering data must enter a value in the column. The DBMS won't insert or update a row if a non-nullable column contains a null.

◆ Some other constraints, such as a PRIMARY KEY constraint, can't be used with nullable columns.

◆ Nulls affect referential-integrity checks in foreign keys, see "Specifying a Foreign Key with FOREIGN KEY" later in this chapter.

◆ If you INSERT a row but include no value for a column that allows null values, your DBMS supplies a null (unless a DEFAULT constraint exists); see "Inserting Rows with INSERT" in Chapter 9 and "Specifying a Default Value with DEFAULT" later in this chapter.

◆ A user can enter NULL explicitly in a nullable column, no matter what data type or default value the column has.

◆ If you don't specify a NULL or NOT NULL constraint, the column accepts nulls by default.

To specify a column's nullability:

♦ Add the following column constraint to a CREATE TABLE column definition:

[CONSTRAINT *constraint_name*]
  [NOT] NULL

Specify NULL to permit nulls in a column or NOT NULL to forbid nulls. If no nullability constraint is specified, NULL is assumed. For the general syntax of CREATE TABLE, see "Creating Tables" earlier in this chapter.

The CONSTRAINT clause is optional, and *constraint_name* is the name of the column's nullability constraint; see "Understanding Constraints" earlier in this chapter.

Listing 10.3 creates the sample-database table authors and assigns a nullability constraint to each column explicitly. Missing addresses and telephone numbers are common, so I've permitted nulls in those columns. Notice that I've forbidden nulls in both the first-name and last-name columns. If the author's name has only a single word (like author A06, Kellsey), I'll insert the name into au_lname and insert an empty string ('') into au_fname. *Or* I could have allowed nulls in au_fname and inserted a null into au_fname for one-named authors. *Or* I could have allowed nulls in both au_fname and au_lname and added a check constraint that required at least one of the two columns to contain a non-null, non-empty string. The database designer makes these types of decisions *before* creating a table.

Listing 10.4 creates the sample-database table titles. Where omitted, the nullability constraint defaults to NULL.

Listing 10.3 Create the sample-database table authors and assign nullability constraints to each column explicitly.

```
                           listing
CREATE TABLE authors
  (
  au_id    CHAR(3)      NOT NULL,
  au_fname VARCHAR(15)  NOT NULL,
  au_lname VARCHAR(15)  NOT NULL,
  phone    VARCHAR(12)  NULL    ,
  address  VARCHAR(20)  NULL    ,
  city     VARCHAR(15)  NULL    ,
  state    CHAR(2)      NULL    ,
  zip      CHAR(5)      NULL
  );
```

Listing 10.4 Create the sample-database table titles. Where omitted, the nullability constraint defaults to NULL.

```
                           listing
CREATE TABLE titles
  (
  title_id   CHAR(3)       NOT NULL,
  title_name VARCHAR(40)   NOT NULL,
  type       VARCHAR(10)           ,
  pub_id     CHAR(3)       NOT NULL,
  pages      INTEGER               ,
  price      DECIMAL(5,2)          ,
  sales      INTEGER               ,
  pubdate    DATE                  ,
  contract   SMALLINT      NOT NULL
  );
```

✔ Tips

■ To see the result of a CREATE TABLE statement, examine the table's structure by using one of the commands described in "Displaying a Table's Column Definitions" in Chapter 9.

■ When you insert a row into a table, you must provide values explicitly for columns that prohibit nulls (and have no default value). For the table authors created by Listing 10.3, for example, the minimal INSERT statement looks like this:

```
INSERT INTO authors(
    au_id,
    au_fname,
    au_lname)
VALUES(
    'A08',
    'Michael',
    'Polk');
```

The DBMS assigns nulls automatically to the columns in authors that aren't listed in the INSERT column list (phone, address, and so on); see "Inserting Rows with INSERT" in Chapter 9.

■ When inserting a null into a row, don't place the keyword NULL in quotes; if you do, your DBMS will interpret it as the character string 'NULL' rather than as a null.

■ You can detect nulls with IS NULL; see "Testing for Nulls with IS NULL" in Chapter 4.

■ You can use the function COALESCE() to display a specific value instead of a null; see "Checking for Nulls with COALESCE()" in Chapter 5.

■ You can use the function NULLIF() to convert values to nulls in calculations; see "Comparing Expressions with NULLIF()" in Chapter 5.

■ All columns defined within a PRIMARY KEY constraint must be defined as NOT NULL. If you don't specify nullability, the DBMS sets all PRIMARY KEY columns to NOT NULL implicitly; see "Specifying a Primary Key with PRIMARY KEY" later in this chapter.

■ **DBMS** **Microsoft SQL Server** doesn't support the data type DATE. To run Listing 10.4 in SQL Server, change the data type of the column pubdate to DATETIME.

MySQL doesn't support the CONSTRAINT clause for column constraints (but you can use it for table constraints).

Oracle treats an empty string (' ') as null; see the DBMS Tip in "Nulls" in Chapter 3.

For the DBMSes that I consider in this book, the nullability constraint for each column definition is optional (and defaults to NULL), but other DBMSes may require you to specify NULL or NOT NULL for each column explicitly.

Check the documentation to see how your DBMS handles nullability constraints for columns whose data type generates a unique row identifier automatically; see the DBMS Tip in "Primary Keys" in Chapter 2.

Specifying a Default Value with DEFAULT

A *default* specifies a value that your DBMS assigns to a column if you omit a value for the column when inserting a row; see "Inserting Rows with INSERT" in Chapter 9. When you're defining a default constraint, some important considerations are:

◆ A default constraint always is a column constraint and not a table constraint; see "Understanding Constraints" earlier in this chapter.

◆ You define a default constraint by using the keyword DEFAULT in a CREATE TABLE column definition.

◆ A default value can be any expression that evaluates to a constant.

◆ The default must have the same data type or must be implicitly convertible to the same type as its column; see "Converting Data Types with CAST()" in Chapter 5.

◆ The column must be long enough to hold the default value.

◆ If you INSERT a row without specifying a value for a column, that column's default is used. If the column definition has no DEFAULT constraint, the default is null.

◆ If a column has a NOT NULL constraint but no DEFAULT constraint, you must specify the column's value explicitly when you INSERT a row; otherwise, your DBMS will display an error message and refuse to insert the row. See "Inserting Rows with INSERT" in Chapter 9.

To specify a column's default value:

◆ Add the following column constraint to a CREATE TABLE column definition:

```
[CONSTRAINT constraint_name]
  DEFAULT expr
```

expr is an expression that evaluates to a constant, such as a literal, a built-in function, a mathematical expression, or NULL. If no default constraint is specified, NULL is assumed. For the general syntax of CREATE TABLE, see "Creating Tables" earlier in this chapter.

The CONSTRAINT clause is optional, and *constraint_name* is the name of the column's default constraint; see "Understanding Constraints" earlier in this chapter.

Listing 10.5 assigns defaults to some of the columns in the sample-database table titles. The columns title_id and pub_id are NOT NULL and have no default values, so you must provide explicit values for them in an INSERT statement. The pages constraint DEFAULT NULL is equivalent to omitting the DEFAULT constraint. The pubdate and contract defaults show that the defaults can be expressions more complex than plain literals.

Listing 10.6 shows the minimal INSERT statement that you can use to insert a row into the table titles (as created by Listing 10.5). **Figure 10.1** shows the inserted row, with default values highlighted. The title_name default, an empty string (''), is invisible.

Listing 10.5 Set default values for some of the columns in the sample-database table titles.

```
CREATE TABLE titles
 (
 title_id   CHAR(3)       NOT NULL                   ,
 title_name VARCHAR(40)   NOT NULL DEFAULT ''        ,
 type       VARCHAR(10)   NULL     DEFAULT 'undefined' ,
 pub_id     CHAR(3)       NOT NULL                   ,
 pages      INTEGER                DEFAULT NULL       ,
 price      DECIMAL(5,2)  NOT NULL DEFAULT 0.00       ,
 sales      INTEGER       NULL                        ,
 pubdate    DATE          NULL     DEFAULT CURRENT_DATE,
 contract   SMALLINT      NOT NULL DEFAULT (3 * 7) - 21
 );
```

Listing 10.6 The DBMS inserts default values into columns omitted from this INSERT statement. Where no default is specified, the DBMS inserts a null. See Figure 10.1 for the result.

```
INSERT INTO titles(title_id, pub_id) VALUES('T14','P01');
```

title_id	title_name	type	pub_id	pages	price	sales	pubdate	contract
T14		undefined	P01	NULL	0.00	NULL	2002-05-06	0

Figure 10.1 Listing 10.6 inserts this row into the table titles.

✔ Tips

■ To see the result of a `CREATE TABLE` statement, examine the table's structure by using one of the commands described in "Displaying a Table's Column Definitions" in Chapter 9.

■ **DBMS** **Microsoft Access** doesn't permit arithmetic expressions in a `DEFAULT` constraint; use a numeric literal. Use `Date()` instead of `CURRENT_DATE` to return the system date. (See the DBMS Tip in "Getting the Current Date and Time" in Chapter 5.) To run Listing 10.5 in Access, change the default constraint of the column `pubdate` to `DEFAULT Date()` and the default constraint of the column `contract` to `DEFAULT 0`.

Microsoft SQL Server doesn't support the data type `DATE`; use `DATETIME` instead. Use `GETDATE()` instead of `CURRENT_DATE` to return the system date; see the DBMS Tip in "Getting the Current Date and Time" in Chapter 5. To run Listing 10.5 in SQL Server, change the `pubdate` column's data type to `DATETIME`, and change its default constraint to `DEFAULT GETDATE()`.

In **Oracle**, the default constraint follows the data type and precedes all other column constraints, including the nullability constraint. Oracle 9i and later versions support CURRENT_DATE; use SYSDATE instead of CURRENT_DATE in Oracle 8i and earlier versions; see the DBMS Tip in "Getting the Current Date and Time" in Chapter 5. Oracle treats an empty string (' ') as null, so I've changed the title_name default to a space character (' '); see the DBMS Tip in "Nulls" in Chapter 3. See **Listing 10.7** for the Oracle version of Listing 10.5.

Oracle doesn't support the CONSTRAINT clause for the DEFAULT constraint (but you can use it for other column constraints and all table constraints).

In **MySQL**, default values must be literals. You can't set a default to be the result of a function or arithmetic expression, for example. This restriction means that you can't set the default of a date column to

CURRENT_DATE. To run Listing 10.5 in MySQL, delete the default constraint of the column pubdate (or change the default expression to a datetime literal), and change the default constraint of the column contract to DEFAULT 0.

MySQL doesn't support the CONSTRAINT clause for column constraints (but you can use it for table constraints).

If a column has no DEFAULT constraint and is declared NOT NULL, some DBMSes assign a default automatically based on the column's date type. **MySQL**, for example, assigns a default value of zero to numeric, non-nullable columns without explicit defaults.

Check the documentation to see how your DBMS handles default constraints for columns whose data type generates a unique row identifier automatically; see the DBMS Tip in "Primary Keys" in Chapter 2.

Listing 10.7 In Oracle, the default constraint must come before other column constraints.

```
                                        listing
CREATE TABLE titles
(
title_id    CHAR(3)                      NOT NULL,
title_name  VARCHAR(40)  DEFAULT ' '     NOT NULL,
type        VARCHAR(10)  DEFAULT 'undefined'  NULL    ,
pub_id      CHAR(3)                      NOT NULL,
pages       INTEGER      DEFAULT NULL               ,
price       DECIMAL(5,2) DEFAULT 0.00    NOT NULL,
sales       INTEGER                      NULL    ,
pubdate     DATE         DEFAULT SYSDATE  NULL    ,
contract    SMALLINT     DEFAULT (3 * 7) - 21 NOT NULL
);
```

Specifying a Primary Key
with PRIMARY KEY

I described primary keys in "Primary Keys" in Chapter 2, but I'll review the basics here:

◆ A primary key uniquely identifies each row in a table.

◆ No two rows can have the same primary-key value.

◆ Primary keys don't allow nulls.

◆ Each table has exactly one primary key.

◆ A primary key is a column or a set of columns. A simple primary key comprises a single column; a composite primary key comprises multiple columns.

◆ In a composite key, values can be duplicated within one column, but each combination of values from all the key's columns must be unique.

◆ A table can have more than one combination of columns that uniquely identify its rows; each combination is a candidate key. The database designer picks one of the candidate keys to be the primary key.

When you're defining a primary-key constraint, some important considerations are:

◆ A simple key can be a column constraint or a table constraint; a composite key always is a table constraint. See "Understanding Constraints" earlier in this chapter.

◆ You define a primary-key constraint by using the keyword PRIMARY KEY in a CREATE TABLE definition.

◆ As a table constraint, PRIMARY KEY requires you to specify column name(s). As a column constraint, PRIMARY KEY applies to the column in which it's defined.

◆ The SQL standard permits you to create a table without a primary key (in violation of the relational model's requirement). In practice, you always should define a primary key for every table.

◆ No more than one primary-key constraint is allowed in a table.

◆ In practice, primary-key constraints almost always are named explicitly. Use a CONSTRAINT clause to name a constraint; see "Understanding Constraints" earlier in this chapter.

◆ The nullability of all PRIMARY KEY columns must be NOT NULL. If you don't specify a nullability constraint, the DBMS sets all primary-key columns to NOT NULL implicitly; see "Forbidding Nulls with NOT NULL" earlier in this chapter.

◆ You must specify a primary-key value explicitly when you INSERT a row unless the column's data type generates a unique row identifier automatically; see the DBMS Tip in "Primary Keys" in Chapter 2. For information about inserting rows, see "Inserting Rows with INSERT" in Chapter 9.

◆ Primary-key values are stable and seldom change after they're inserted. In general, don't UPDATE a primary-key value; see "Updating Rows with UPDATE" in Chapter 9.

◆ Don't reuse a primary-key value if you DELETE a row; see "Deleting Rows with DELETE" in Chapter 9.

◆ For considerations related to inserting, updating, and deleting primary keys that are referenced by foreign keys, see "Specifying a Foreign Key with FOREIGN KEY" later in this chapter.

Listing 10.8a Define a simple primary key for the sample-database table publishers by using a column constraint.

```
                       listing
CREATE TABLE publishers
  (
  pub_id   CHAR(3)     PRIMARY KEY,
  pub_name VARCHAR(20) NOT NULL  ,
  city     VARCHAR(15) NOT NULL  ,
  state    CHAR(2)     NULL      ,
  country  VARCHAR(15) NOT NULL
  );
```

Listing 10.8b Define a simple primary key for the sample-database table publishers by using an unnamed table constraint.

```
                       listing
CREATE TABLE publishers
  (
  pub_id   CHAR(3)     NOT NULL,
  pub_name VARCHAR(20) NOT NULL,
  city     VARCHAR(15) NOT NULL,
  state    CHAR(2)     NULL    ,
  country  VARCHAR(15) NOT NULL,
  PRIMARY KEY (pub_id)
  );
```

Listing 10.8c Define a simple primary key for the sample-database table publishers by using a named table constraint.

```
                       listing
CREATE TABLE publishers
  (
  pub_id   CHAR(3)     NOT NULL,
  pub_name VARCHAR(20) NOT NULL,
  city     VARCHAR(15) NOT NULL,
  state    CHAR(2)     NULL    ,
  country  VARCHAR(15) NOT NULL,
  CONSTRAINT publishers_pk
    PRIMARY KEY (pub_id)
  );
```

To specify a simple primary key:

◆ To specify a simple primary key as a column constraint, add the following column constraint to a CREATE TABLE column definition:

[CONSTRAINT *constraint_name*]
  PRIMARY KEY

or

To specify a simple primary key as a table constraint, add the following table constraint to a CREATE TABLE definition:

[CONSTRAINT *constraint_name*]
  PRIMARY KEY (*key_column*)

key_column is the name of the primary-key column. No more than one PRIMARY KEY constraint is permitted in a table. For the general syntax of CREATE TABLE, see "Creating Tables" earlier in this chapter.

The CONSTRAINT clause is optional, and *constraint_name* is the name of the primary-key constraint; see "Understanding Constraints" earlier in this chapter.

Listings 10.8a , 10.8b, and 10.8c show three equivalent ways to define a simple primary key for the sample-database table publishers.

Listing 10.8a uses a column constraint to designate the primary-key column. This syntax shows the easiest way to create a simple primary key.

Listing 10.8b uses an unnamed table constraint to specify the primary key. I've added an explicit NOT NULL column constraint to pub_id, but it's unnecessary because the DBMS sets this constraint implicitly (except for MySQL; see the DBMS Tip later in this section).

Listing 10.8c uses a named table constraint to specify the primary key. This syntax shows the preferred way to add a primary key; you can use the name publishers_pk if you decide to change or delete the key later. See "Altering a Table with ALTER TABLE" later in this chapter.

To specify a composite primary key:

◆ Add the following table constraint to a
CREATE TABLE definition:

[CONSTRAINT *constraint_name*]
  PRIMARY KEY (*key_columns*)

key_columns is a list of comma-separated
names of the primary-key columns. No
more than one PRIMARY KEY constraint
is permitted in a table. For the general
syntax of CREATE TABLE, see "Creating
Tables" earlier in this chapter.

The CONSTRAINT clause is optional, and
constraint_name is the name of the primary-key constraint; see "Understanding
Constraints" earlier in this chapter.

Listing 10.9 defines a composite primary
key for the sample-database table
title_authors. The primary-key columns
are title_id and au_id, and the key is
named title_authors_pk.

Listing 10.9 Define a composite primary key for the
sample-database table title_authors by using a
named table constraint.

```
listing
CREATE TABLE title_authors
  (
  title_id      CHAR(3)      NOT NULL,
  au_id         CHAR(3)      NOT NULL,
  au_order      SMALLINT     NOT NULL,
  royalty_share DECIMAL(5,2) NOT NULL,
  CONSTRAINT title_authors_pk
    PRIMARY KEY (title_id, au_id)
);
```

✔ Tips

■ To see the result of a CREATE TABLE statement, examine the table's structure by
using one of the commands described in
"Displaying a Table's Column Definitions"
in Chapter 9.

■ To define a foreign key, see "Specifying a
Foreign Key with FOREIGN KEY" later in
this chapter.

■ To define a column that contains unique
values but isn't a primary key, see
"Forcing Unique Values with UNIQUE"
later in this chapter.

■ To change or delete an existing constraint, see "Altering a Table with ALTER
TABLE" later in this chapter.

■ It's illegal to specify two or more PRIMARY
KEY column constraints in the same table.
You can't use this statement, for example,
to specify the composite key for
title_authors:

```
CREATE TABLE title_authors(
  title_id CHAR(3)  PRIMARY KEY,
  au_id    CHAR(3)  PRIMARY KEY,
  au_order SMALLINT NOT NULL,
  ...
);                        --Illegal
```

■ **DBMS** **MySQL** requires you to set the
nullability constraint to NOT NULL
explicitly for PRIMARY KEY columns specified in table constraints (but not in column constraints); see "Forbidding Nulls
with NOT NULL" earlier in this chapter.
MySQL doesn't support the CONSTRAINT
clause for column constraints (but you
can use it for table constraints).

Oracle treats an empty string ('') as
null; see the DBMS Tip in "Nulls" in
Chapter 3.

Specifying a Foreign Key
with FOREIGN KEY

I described foreign keys in "Foreign Keys" in Chapter 2, but I'll review the basics here:

◆ A foreign key is a mechanism that associates two tables.

◆ A foreign key is a column (or set of columns) in a table whose values relate to, or reference, values in some other table.

◆ A foreign key ensures that rows in one table have corresponding rows in another table, called the *referenced table* or *parent table*.

◆ A foreign key establishes a direct relationship to a primary key or candidate key in the referenced table, so foreign-key values are restricted to parent-key values that already exist. This restriction is called *referential integrity*.

◆ A foreign key, unlike a primary key, can permit nulls.

◆ A table can have zero or more foreign keys.

◆ Foreign-key values generally aren't unique in their own table.

◆ Foreign-key columns in different tables can reference the same column in a parent table.

◆ A simple foreign key comprises a single column; a composite foreign key comprises multiple columns.

When you're defining a foreign-key constraint, some important considerations are:

◆ A simple key can be a column constraint or a table constraint; a composite key always is a table constraint. See "Understanding Constraints" earlier in this chapter.

◆ You define a foreign-key constraint by using the keywords FOREIGN KEY or REFERENCES in a CREATE TABLE definition. FOREIGN KEY and REFERENCES are two variations on the same constraint; I'll use FOREIGN KEY to refer to both of them unless the distinction is important.

◆ A foreign key can have a different column name from its parent key.

◆ The foreign key's data type must have the same data type or must be implicitly convertible to the same type as its parent key; see "Converting Data Types with CAST()" in Chapter 5.

◆ A FOREIGN KEY column doesn't have to reference only a PRIMARY KEY column in another table; it also can reference a UNIQUE column in another table. See "Forcing Unique Values with UNIQUE" later in this chapter.

◆ A table can have any number of foreign-key constraints (or none at all).

continues on next page

- In practice, foreign-key constraints almost always are named explicitly. Use a `CONSTRAINT` clause to name a constraint; see "Understanding Constraints" earlier in this chapter.

- The nullability of each `FOREIGN KEY` column can be `NULL` or `NOT NULL`. If you don't specify a nullability constraint, the DBMS assumes `NULL`; see "Forbidding Nulls with `NOT NULL`" earlier in this chapter.

- Foreign-key constraints simplify updates and deletions and make it difficult to introduce inconsistencies into a database, but the topology of relations in even a medium-size database can become astonishingly complex. Poor design may lead to time-consuming routine queries, circular rules, tricky backup-and-restore operations, and psychotically ambitious cascading deletes.

To preserve referential integrity, your DBMS will prevent the creation of orphan rows (rows in a foreign-key table without an associated row in a parent table). When you `INSERT`, `UPDATE`, or `DELETE` a row with a `FOREIGN KEY` column that references a `PRIMARY KEY` column in a parent table, your DBMS performs the following referential-integrity checks:

- **Inserting a row into the foreign-key table.** The DBMS checks that the new `FOREIGN KEY` value matches a `PRIMARY KEY` value in the parent table. If no match exists, the DBMS won't `INSERT` the row.

- **Updating a row in the foreign-key table.** The DBMS checks that the updated `FOREIGN KEY` value matches a `PRIMARY KEY` value in the parent table. If no match exists, the DBMS won't `UPDATE` the row.

- **Deleting a row in the foreign-key table.** A referential-integrity check is unnecessary.

- **Inserting a row into the parent table.** A referential-integrity check is unnecessary.

- **Updating a row in the parent table.** The DBMS checks that none of the `FOREIGN KEY` values matches the `PRIMARY KEY` value to be updated. If a match exists, the DBMS won't `UPDATE` the row.

- **Deleting a row from the parent table.** The DBMS checks that none of the `FOREIGN KEY` values matches the `PRIMARY KEY` value to be deleted. If a match exists, the DBMS won't `DELETE` the row.

The DBMS skips the referential-integrity check for rows with a null in the `FOREIGN KEY` column.

Listing 10.10 Define a simple foreign key for the sample-database table `titles` by using a column constraint.

```
                    listing
CREATE TABLE titles
  (
  title_id    CHAR(3)      NOT NULL
    PRIMARY KEY,
  title_name VARCHAR(40)  NOT NULL,
  type        VARCHAR(10)  NULL,
  pub_id      CHAR(3)      NOT NULL
    REFERENCES publishers(pub_id),
  pages       INTEGER      NULL,
  price       DECIMAL(5,2) NULL,
  sales       INTEGER      NULL,
  pubdate     DATE         NULL,
  contract    SMALLINT     NOT NULL
  );
```

To specify a simple foreign key:

◆ To specify a simple foreign key as a column constraint, add the following column constraint to a **CREATE TABLE** column definition:

[CONSTRAINT *constraint_name*]
  REFERENCES *ref_table(ref_column)*

or

To specify a simple foreign key as a table constraint, add the following table constraint to a **CREATE TABLE** definition:

[CONSTRAINT *constraint_name*]
  FOREIGN KEY (*key_column*)
  REFERENCES *ref_table(ref_column)*

key_column is the name of the foreign-key column. *ref_table* is the name of the parent table referenced by the **FOREIGN KEY** constraint. *ref_column* is the name of the column in *ref_table* that is the referenced key. Zero or more **FOREIGN KEY** constraints are permitted in a table. For the general syntax of **CREATE TABLE**, see "Creating Tables" earlier in this chapter.

The **CONSTRAINT** clause is optional, and *constraint_name* is the name of the foreign-key constraint; see "Understanding Constraints" earlier in this chapter.

Listing 10.10 uses a column constraint to designate a foreign-key column in the table `titles`. This syntax shows the easiest way to create a simple foreign key. After you run this statement, the DBMS will ensure that values inserted into the column `pub_id` in `titles` already exist in the column `pub_id` in `publishers`. Notice that nulls aren't permitted in the foreign-key column, so every book must have a publisher.

continues on next page

SPECIFYING A FOREIGN KEY WITH FOREIGN KEY

The table `royalties` has a one-to-one relationship with the table `titles`, so **Listing 10.11** defines the column `title_id` to be both the primary key and a foreign key that points to `title_id` in `titles`. For information about relationships, see "Relationships" in Chapter 2.

Listing 10.12 uses named table constraints to create two foreign keys. This syntax shows the preferred way to add foreign keys; you can use the names if you decide to change or delete the keys later. (See "Altering a Table with **ALTER TABLE**" later in this chapter.) Each foreign-key column is an individual key and *not* part of a single composite key. Note that foreign keys together, however, comprise the table's composite primary key.

To specify a composite foreign key:

◆ Add the following table constraint to a `CREATE TABLE` definition:

[CONSTRAINT *constraint_name*]

  FOREIGN KEY (*key_columns*)

  REFERENCES *ref_table*(*ref_columns*)

key_columns is a list of comma-separated names of the foreign-key columns. *ref_table* is the name of the parent table referenced by the **FOREIGN KEY** constraint. *ref_columns* is a list of comma-separated names of the columns in *ref_table* that are the referenced keys. *key_columns* and *ref_columns* must have the same number of columns, listed in corresponding order. Zero or more **FOREIGN KEY** constraints are permitted in a table. For the general syntax of **CREATE TABLE**, see "Creating Tables" earlier in this chapter.

The **CONSTRAINT** clause is optional, and *constraint_name* is the name of the foreign-key constraint; see "Understanding Constraints" earlier in this chapter.

The sample database contains no composite foreign keys, but suppose that I create a table

Listing 10.11 Define a simple foreign key for the sample-database table `royalties` by using a named table constraint.

```
CREATE TABLE royalties
  (
  title_id      CHAR(3)      NOT NULL,
  advance       DECIMAL(9,2) NULL    ,
  royalty_rate  DECIMAL(5,2) NULL    ,
  CONSTRAINT royalties_pk
    PRIMARY KEY (title_id),
  CONSTRAINT royalties_title_id_fk
    FOREIGN KEY (title_id)
    REFERENCES titles(title_id)
  );
```

Listing 10.12 Define simple foreign keys for the sample-database table `title_authors` by using named table constraints.

```
CREATE TABLE title_authors
  (
  title_id      CHAR(3)      NOT NULL,
  au_id         CHAR(3)      NOT NULL,
  au_order      SMALLINT     NOT NULL,
  royalty_share DECIMAL(5,2) NOT NULL,
  CONSTRAINT title_authors_pk
    PRIMARY KEY (title_id, au_id),
  CONSTRAINT title_authors_title_id_fk
    FOREIGN KEY (title_id)
    REFERENCES titles(title_id),
  CONSTRAINT title_authors_au_id_fk
    FOREIGN KEY (au_id)
    REFERENCES authors(au_id)
  );
```

named `out_of_print` to store information about each author's out-of-print books. The table `title_authors` has a composite primary key. This constraint shows how to reference this key from the table `out_of_print`:

```
CONSTRAINT out_of_print_fk
  FOREIGN KEY
    (title_id, au_id)
  REFERENCES
    title_authors(title_id, au_id)
```

✔ Tips

- To see the result of a `CREATE TABLE` statement, examine the table's structure by using one of the commands described in "Displaying a Table's Column Definitions" in Chapter 9.

- To define a primary key, see "Specifying a Primary Key with `PRIMARY KEY`" earlier in this chapter.

- To change or delete an existing constraint, see "Altering a Table with `ALTER TABLE`" later in this chapter.

- You can omit the (`ref_column`) or (`ref_columns`) expression in the `REFERENCES` clause if the referenced column(s) is the primary key of *ref_table*.

- A `FOREIGN KEY` constraint can reference another column in the same table (a self-reference). Recall from "Creating a Self-Join" in Chapter 7 that the table `employees` is self-referencing. (I created `employees` for illustrative purposes; it's not part of the sample database.)

  `employees` has three columns: `emp_id`, `emp_name`, and `boss_id`. `emp_id` is a primary key that uniquely identifies an employee, and `boss_id` is an employee ID that identifies the employee's manager. Each manager also is an employee, so to ensure that each manager ID that is added to the table matches an existing employee ID, `boss_id` is defined as a foreign key of `emp_id`:

```
CREATE TABLE employees
  (
  emp_id   CHAR(3)  NOT NULL,
  emp_name CHAR(20) NOT NULL,
  boss_id  CHAR(3)       NULL,
  CONSTRAINT employees_pk
    PRIMARY KEY (emp_id),
  CONSTRAINT employees_fk
    FOREIGN KEY (boss_id)
    REFERENCES employees(emp_id)
  );
```

- SQL lets you define the action the DBMS takes when you try to `UPDATE` or `DELETE` a key value (in a parent table) to which foreign-key values point. To trigger a referential action, specify an `ON UPDATE` or `ON DELETE` clause in the `FOREIGN KEY` constraint. Support for these clauses varies by DBMS; search your DBMS documentation for *foreign key* or *referential integrity*. I'll explain the SQL standard's definition of these clauses in the next two Tips.

- The `ON UPDATE` *action* clause specifies what the DBMS does if you attempt to `UPDATE` a key value in a row (in a parent table) where the key value is referenced by foreign keys in rows in other tables. *action* takes one of four values:

  `CASCADE` updates the dependent foreign-key values to the new parent-key value.

  `SET NULL` sets the dependent foreign-key values to nulls.

  `SET DEFAULT` sets the dependent foreign-key values to their default values; see "Specifying a Default Value with `DEFAULT`" earlier in this chapter.

continues on next page

NO ACTION generates an error on a foreign-key violation. This action is the default.

- The ON DELETE *action* clause specifies what the DBMS does if you attempt to DELETE a key value in a row (in a parent table) where the key value is referenced by foreign keys in rows in other tables. *action* takes one of four values:

  CASCADE deletes the rows that contain foreign-key values that match the deleted parent-key value.

  SET NULL sets the dependent foreign-key values to null.

  SET DEFAULT sets the dependent foreign-key values to their default values; see "Specifying a Default Value with DEFAULT" earlier in this chapter.

  NO ACTION generates an error on a foreign-key violation. This action is the default.

- **DBMS** **Microsoft SQL Server** doesn't support the data type DATE. To run Listing 10.10 in SQL Server, change the data type of the column pubdate to DATETIME.

  MySQL 4.0 and earlier versions don't support foreign keys. These versions permit FOREIGN KEY and REFERENCES clauses in CREATE TABLE statements for SQL compatibility, but MySQL doesn't actually enforce referential integrity. To enforce foreign-key constraints, use the InnoDB table type. InnoDB is a commercial MySQL add-on; search MySQL documentation for *foreign key* or *InnoDB*, or visit www.innodb.com.

  MySQL doesn't support the CONSTRAINT clause for column constraints (but you can use it for table constraints).

  Oracle treats an empty string (' ') as null; see the DBMS Tip in "Nulls" in Chapter 3.

Forcing Unique Values
with UNIQUE

A unique constraint ensures that a column (or set of columns) contains no duplicate values. A unique constraint is similar to a primary-key constraint, except that a unique column can contain nulls and a table can have multiple unique columns. (For information about primary-key constraints, see "Specifying a Primary Key with PRIMARY KEY" earlier in this chapter.)

Suppose that I add the column isbn to the table titles to hold a book's ISBN. An ISBN is a unique, standardized identification number that marks a book unmistakably. titles already has a primary key (title_id), so to ensure that each ISBN value is unique, I can define a unique constraint on the column isbn.

When you're defining a unique constraint, some important considerations are:

◆ A simple unique constraint comprises a single column; a composite unique constraint comprises multiple columns.

◆ In a composite constraint, values can be duplicated within one column, but each combination of values from all the columns must be unique.

◆ A simple unique constraint can be a column constraint or a table constraint; a composite unique constraint always is a table constraint. See "Understanding Constraints" earlier in this chapter.

◆ You define a unique constraint by using the keyword UNIQUE in a CREATE TABLE definition.

◆ As a table constraint, UNIQUE requires you to specify column name(s). As a column constraint, UNIQUE applies to the column in which it's defined.

◆ A table can have zero or more unique constraints.

◆ In practice, unique constraints almost always are named explicitly. Use a CONSTRAINT clause to name a constraint; see "Understanding Constraints" earlier in this chapter.

◆ The nullability of each UNIQUE column can be NULL or NOT NULL. If you don't specify a nullability constraint, the DBMS assumes NULL; see "Forbidding Nulls with NOT NULL" earlier in this chapter.

To specify a simple unique constraint:

◆ To specify a simple unique constraint as a column constraint, add the following column constraint to a CREATE TABLE column definition:

[CONSTRAINT *constraint_name*]
   UNIQUE

or

To specify a simple unique constraint as a table constraint, add the following table constraint to a CREATE TABLE definition:

[CONSTRAINT *constraint_name*]
   UNIQUE (*unique_column*)

unique_column is the name of the column that forbids duplicate values. Zero or more UNIQUE constraints are permitted in a table. For the general syntax of CREATE TABLE, see "Creating Tables" earlier in this chapter.

The CONSTRAINT clause is optional, and *constraint_name* is the name of the unique constraint; see "Understanding Constraints" earlier in this chapter.

Listings 10.13a and 10.13b show two equivalent ways to define a simple unique constraint for the sample-database table titles.

Listing 10.13a uses a column constraint to designate a unique column. This syntax shows the easiest way to create a simple unique constraint.

Listing 10.13b uses a named table constraint to specify a unique column. This syntax shows the preferred way to add a unique constraint; you can use the name if you decide to change or delete the constraint later. See "Altering a Table with ALTER TABLE" later in this chapter.

Listing 10.13a Define a simple unique constraint on the column title_name for the sample-database table titles by using a column constraint.

```
CREATE TABLE titles
  (
  title_id    CHAR(3)       PRIMARY KEY   ,
  title_name  VARCHAR(40)   NOT NULL UNIQUE,
  type        VARCHAR(10)   NULL          ,
  pub_id      CHAR(3)       NOT NULL      ,
  pages       INTEGER       NULL          ,
  price       DECIMAL(5,2)  NULL          ,
  sales       INTEGER       NULL          ,
  pubdate     DATE          NULL          ,
  contract    SMALLINT      NOT NULL
  );
```

Listing 10.13b Define a simple unique constraint on the column title_name for the sample-database table titles by using a named table constraint.

```
CREATE TABLE titles
  (
  title_id    CHAR(3)       NOT NULL,
  title_name  VARCHAR(40)   NOT NULL,
  type        VARCHAR(10)   NULL    ,
  pub_id      CHAR(3)       NOT NULL,
  pages       INTEGER       NULL    ,
  price       DECIMAL(5,2)  NULL    ,
  sales       INTEGER       NULL    ,
  pubdate     DATE          NULL    ,
  contract    SMALLINT      NOT NULL,
  CONSTRAINT titles_pk
    PRIMARY KEY (title_id),
  CONSTRAINT titles_title_name_unique
    UNIQUE (title_name)
  );
```

Listing 10.14 Define a composite unique constraint on the columns au_fname and au_lname for the sample-database table authors by using a named table constraint.

```
                    listing
CREATE TABLE authors
  (
  au_id    CHAR(3)     NOT NULL,
  au_fname VARCHAR(15) NOT NULL,
  au_lname VARCHAR(15) NOT NULL,
  phone    VARCHAR(12) NULL    ,
  address  VARCHAR(20) NULL    ,
  city     VARCHAR(15) NULL    ,
  state    CHAR(2)     NULL    ,
  zip      CHAR(5)     NULL    ,
  CONSTRAINT authors_pk
    PRIMARY KEY (au_id),
  CONSTRAINT authors_au_name_unique
    UNIQUE (au_fname, au_lname)
);
```

- ■ **DBMS** **Microsoft SQL Server** doesn't support the data type DATE. To run Listings 10.13a and 10.13b in SQL Server, change the data type of the column pubdate to DATETIME.

   MySQL doesn't support the CONSTRAINT clause for column constraints (but you can use it for table constraints).

   Oracle treats an empty string ('') as null; see the DBMS Tip in "Nulls" in Chapter 3.

   The SQL standard permits no more than one null in a nullable, unique column. **Microsoft SQL Server** complies with the standard, but **Microsoft Access**, **Oracle**, **MySQL**, and **PostgreSQL** permit multiple nulls in UNIQUE columns without a NOT NULL constraint.

To specify a composite unique constraint:

- ◆ Add the following table constraint to a CREATE TABLE definition:

   [CONSTRAINT *constraint_name*]
   UNIQUE (*unique_columns*)

   unique_columns is a list of comma-separated names of the columns that forbid duplicate values. Zero or more unique constraints are permitted in a table. For the general syntax of CREATE TABLE, see "Creating Tables" earlier in this chapter.

   The CONSTRAINT clause is optional, and *constraint_name* is the name of the unique constraint; see "Understanding Constraints" earlier in this chapter.

Listing 10.14 defines a multicolumn unique constraint for the sample-database table authors. This constraint forces the combination of each author's first and last name to be unique.

✔ Tips

- ■ To see the result of a CREATE TABLE statement, examine the table's structure by using one of the commands described in "Displaying a Table's Column Definitions" in Chapter 9.

- ■ A foreign-key column can point to a UNIQUE column; see "Specifying a Foreign Key with FOREIGN KEY" earlier in this chapter.

- ■ To change or delete an existing constraint, see "Altering a Table with ALTER TABLE" later in this chapter.

- ■ You can create a unique index instead of a unique constraint; see "Creating an Index with CREATE INDEX" in Chapter 11. To determine whether your DBMS prefers an index or a constraint, search your DBMS documentation for *unique, index,* or *constraint.*

Adding a Check Constraint with CHECK

So far, the only restrictions on an inserted value are that it have the proper data type, size, and range for its column. You can use check constraints to further limit the values that a column (or set of columns) accepts. Check constraints commonly are used to check the following:

- **Minimum or maximum values.** Prevent sales of fewer than zero items, for example.

- **Specific values.** Permit only `'biology'`, `'chemistry'`, or `'physics'` in the column `science`, for example.

- **A range of values.** Make sure that an author's royalty rate is between 2 percent and 20 percent, for example.

A check constraint resembles a foreign-key constraint in that both control values placed in a column (see "Specifying a Foreign Key with FOREIGN KEY" earlier in this chapter). They differ in how they determine which values are allowed. A foreign-key constraint gets the list of valid values from another table, whereas a check constraint determines the valid values by using a logical (Boolean) expression. This check constraint, for example, ensures that no employee's salary exceeds $50,000:

```
CHECK (salary <= 50000)
```

When you're defining a check constraint, some important considerations are:

- A check constraint that applies to a single column can be a column constraint or a table constraint; a check constraint that applies to multiple columns always is a table constraint. See "Understanding Constraints" earlier in this chapter.

- You define a unique constraint by using the keyword CHECK in a CREATE TABLE definition.

- A column can have zero or more check constraints associated with it.

- If you create multiple check constraints for a column, design them carefully so that their purposes don't conflict. Don't assume that the DBMS will evaluate the constraints in any particular order or will verify that the constraints are mutually exclusive.

- In practice, check constraints almost always are named explicitly. Use a CONSTRAINT clause to name a constraint; see "Understanding Constraints" earlier in this chapter.

- The check constraint's condition is any valid WHERE condition, such as a comparison (=, <>, <, <=, >, >=), LIKE, BETWEEN, IN, or IS NULL condition. You can join multiple conditions with AND, OR, and NOT. For information about conditions, see "Filtering Rows with WHERE" and subsequent sections in Chapter 4.

- A check constraint's condition can refer to any column in the table, but it can't refer to columns in other tables.

- Although it's possible to add check constraints after a table has been populated, it's a better practice to impose check constraints before populating the table to detect input errors as early as possible.

Listing 10.15 Define some check constraints for the sample-database table `titles`.

```
                     listing
CREATE TABLE titles
  (
  title_id   CHAR(3)      NOT NULL,
  title_name VARCHAR(40)  NOT NULL,
  type       VARCHAR(10)  NULL
    CONSTRAINT type_chk
      CHECK (type IN ('biography',
        'children','computer',
        'history','psychology'))   ,
  pub_id     CHAR(3)      NOT NULL,
  pages      INTEGER      NULL
    CHECK (pages > 0)               ,
  price      DECIMAL(5,2) NULL    ,
  sales      INTEGER      NULL    ,
  pubdate    DATE         NULL    ,
  contract   SMALLINT     NOT NULL,
  CONSTRAINT titles_pk
    PRIMARY KEY (title_id),
  CONSTRAINT titles_pub_id_fk
    FOREIGN KEY (pub_id)
    REFERENCES publishers(pub_id),
  CONSTRAINT title_id_chk
    CHECK (
    (SUBSTRING(title_id FROM 1 FOR 1) = 'T')
    AND
    (CAST(SUBSTRING(title_id FROM 2 FOR 2)
    AS INTEGER) BETWEEN 0 AND 99)),
  CONSTRAINT price_chk
    CHECK (price >= 0.00
      AND price < 100.00),
  CONSTRAINT sales_chk
    CHECK (sales >= 0),
  CONSTRAINT pubdate_chk
    CHECK (pubdate >= DATE '1950-01-01'),
  CONSTRAINT title_name_contract_chk
    CHECK (title_name <> ''
      AND contract >= 0),
  CONSTRAINT revenue_chk
    CHECK (price * sales >= 0.00)
  );
```

To add a check constraint:

◆ To add a check constraint as a column constraint or table constraint, add the following constraint to a **CREATE TABLE** definition:

```
[CONSTRAINT constraint_name]
  CHECK (condition)
```

condition is a logical (Boolean) condition that the DBMS evaluates each time a **INSERT**, **UPDATE**, or **DELETE** statement modifies the contents of the table. If *condition* evaluates to true or unknown (due to a null) after the modification, the DBMS allows the change. If *condition* evaluates to false, the DBMS undoes the change and returns an error. For the general syntax of **CREATE TABLE**, see "Creating Tables" earlier in this chapter.

The **CONSTRAINT** clause is optional, and *constraint_name* is the name of the primary-key constraint; see "Understanding Constraints" earlier in this chapter.

Listing 10.15 shows various column and table check constraints for the sample-database table **titles**. The constraint **title_id_chk** makes sure the each primary-key value takes the form **'T*nn*'**, in which *nn* represents an integer between 00 and 99, inclusive.

continues on next page

ADDING A CHECK CONSTRAINT WITH CHECK

✔ Tips

■ To see the result of a CREATE TABLE statement, examine the table's structure by using one of the commands described in "Displaying a Table's Column Definitions" in Chapter 9.

■ To change or delete an existing constraint, see "Altering a Table with ALTER TABLE" later in this chapter.

■ According to the SQL standard, the condition generally can't contain a datetime function (CURRENT_DATE, CURRENT_TIME, or CURRENT_TIMESTAMP) or a user function (CURRENT_USER, SESSION_USER, or SYSTEM_USER), but some DBMSes permit them. **Microsoft Access**, **Microsoft SQL Server**, and **PostgreSQL** (but not **Oracle**) permit this check constraint, for example:

CHECK(ship_time >=
CURRENT_TIMESTAMP)

In Access, use Now() instead of CURRENT_TIMESTAMP. See "Getting the Current Date and Time" and "Getting User Information" in Chapter 5.

■ Some DBMSes, such as **Microsoft SQL Server** and **Oracle**, let you create *user-defined data types,* which essentially are standard data types (CHARACTER, INTEGER, and so on) with additional check and other constraints imposed. You can define the data type marital_status, for example, as a single-character CHARACTER data type that permits only the values S, M, W, D, or NULL (for single, married, widowed, divorced, or unknown). The advantage of a custom data type is that you can define it once and use it in multiple tables, rather than repeat its definition in each table in which it's used. Search your DBMS documentation for *data type.*

■ **DBMS** To run Listing 10.15 in **Microsoft Access**, convert the two column constraints (for the columns type and pages) to table constraints by moving them after the last column definition. Change the first substring expression to Mid(title_id, 1, 1); change the CAST expression to CInt(Mid(title_id, 2, 2)); and drop the keyword DATE from the date literal and surround it with # characters instead of quotes (#1950-01-01#).

To run Listing 10.15 in **Microsoft SQL Server**, change the data type of the column pubdate to DATETIME; change the two substring expressions to SUBSTRING(title_id, 1, 1) and SUBSTRING(title_id, 2, 2); and drop the keyword DATE from the date literal ('1950-01-01').

To run Listing 10.15 in **Oracle**, change the two substring expressions to SUBSTR(title_id, 1, 1) and SUBSTR(title_id, 2, 2).

MySQL 4.0 and earlier versions don't support check constraints. These versions permit CHECK clauses in CREATE TABLE statements for SQL compatibility, but MySQL doesn't actually enforce the checks. If you specify a check constraint, it must be a table constraint and not a column constraint.

To run Listing 10.15 in **PostgreSQL**, change the floating-point literals 0.00 and 100.00 to CAST(0.00 AS DECIMAL) and CAST(100.00 AS DECIMAL); see "Converting Data Types with CAST()" in Chapter 5.

In **Microsoft SQL Server**, you can specify the check constraint title_id_chk alternatively as CHECK (title_id LIKE '[T][0-9][0-9]'); search SQL Server Help for *pattern* or *wildcard.*

Oracle treats an empty string ('') as null; see the DBMS Tip in "Nulls" in Chapter 3.

Creating a Temporary Table with CREATE TEMPORARY TABLE

Every table I've created so far has been a permanent table, called a *base table,* which stores data persistently until you destroy (DROP) the table explicitly. SQL also lets you create temporary tables to use for working storage or intermediate results. Temporary tables commonly are used to:

◆ Store the result of a complex, time-consuming query once and use the result repeatedly in subsequent queries, improving performance greatly.

◆ Create an image, or *snapshot,* of a table at a particular moment in time. (You can add a column with the DEFAULT value CURRENT_TIMESTAMP for recording the exact time.)

◆ Hold the result of a subquery; see the DBMS Tip in "Creating Outer Joins with OUTER JOIN" in Chapter 7, Listing 7.32, for example.

A *temporary table* is a table that the DBMS destroys automatically at the end of a session or transaction. (The table's data is destroyed along with the table itself, of course.) A *session* is the time during which you're connected to a DBMS—between login and logoff—and the DBMS accepts and executes your commands. A *transaction* is a set of successive SQL statements that succeeds or fails as a group (see Chapter 13).

When you're creating a temporary table, some important considerations are:

◆ The two types of temporary tables— global and local—are differentiated by their visibility. A *global temporary table* is available to all active sessions; a *local temporary table* is available to only the session that created it.

◆ Temporary tables follow the same rules as base tables with regard to table names, column names, date types, and so on.

◆ You define a temporary table by using a standard CREATE TABLE statement with a bit of extra syntax. Add the keywords GLOBAL TEMPORARY or LOCAL TEMPORARY before the keyword TABLE.

◆ A temporary table has no rows initially. You can INSERT, UPDATE, and DELETE rows as you would in a base table (see Chapter 9).

◆ If you create a large temporary table, you can free memory by destroying it yourself rather than waiting for the DBMS to do it; see "Dropping a Table with DROP TABLE" later in this chapter.

◆ If you create a temporary table that has the same name as a base table, the temporary table hides, or occludes, the base table until the temporary table is destroyed.

◆ CREATE TEMPORARY TABLE provides a way for database administrators to give users working storage space without giving them (potentially disastrous) CREATE TABLE, ALTER TABLE, or DROP TABLE permissions.

To create a temporary table:

◆ Type:

CREATE {LOCAL | GLOBAL} TEMPORARY

→ TABLE *table*

(

column1 data_type1 [constraints1],

column2 data_type2 [constraints2],

...

columnN data_typeN [constraintsN]

[, table_constraints]

);

table is the name of the temporary table to create. LOCAL specifies that *table* is a local temporary table. GLOBAL specifies that *table* is a global temporary table (**Listings 10.16** and **10.17**).

column1, column2,..., columnN are the names of the columns in *table*. *data_type1, data_type2,..., data_typeN* specify the SQL data type of each corresponding column.

The permissible column constraints and table constraints for temporary tables vary by DBMS; search your DBMS documentation for *temporary tables*. For general information about constraints, see "Understanding Constraints" earlier in this chapter.

Listing 10.16 A local temporary table is available to only you. It dematerializes when your DBMS session ends.

```
CREATE LOCAL TEMPORARY TABLE editors
  (
  ed_id    CHAR(3)    ,
  ed_fname VARCHAR(15),
  ed_lname VARCHAR(15),
  phone    VARCHAR(12),
  pub_id   CHAR(3)
  );
```

Listing 10.17 A global temporary table can be accessed by you and other users. It dematerializes when your DBMS session ends and all other tasks have stopped referencing it.

```
CREATE GLOBAL TEMPORARY TABLE editors
  (
  ed_id    CHAR(3)    ,
  ed_fname VARCHAR(15),
  ed_lname VARCHAR(15),
  phone    VARCHAR(12),
  pub_id   CHAR(3)
  );
```

USING CREATE TEMPORARY TABLE

✔ Tips

- To see the result of a `CREATE TEMPORARY TABLE` statement, examine the table's structure by using one of the commands described in "Displaying a Table's Column Definitions" in Chapter 9.

- To modify a temporary table, see "Altering a Table with `ALTER TABLE`" later in this chapter.

- To create a temporary copy of an existing table, see "Creating a New Table from an Existing One with `SELECT INTO`" later in this chapter.

- A global temporary table can be used to pass data among users.

- **DBMS** **Microsoft Access** doesn't support temporary tables.

  In **Microsoft SQL Server,** omit the syntax `{LOCAL | GLOBAL} TEMPORARY` and indicate a local or global temporary table by prefixing the table name with one or two # characters. You must include the # character(s) whenever you refer to a temporary table by name. The SQL Server syntax to create a local temporary table is:

  `CREATE TABLE #table (...);`

  The SQL Server syntax to create a global temporary table is:

  `CREATE TABLE ##table (...);`

In **Oracle**, a temporary table's *definition* is visible to all sessions, but its *data* is visible to only the session that inserts the data into the table. The Oracle syntax to create a temporary table is:

`CREATE GLOBAL TEMPORARY`
`→ TABLE table (...);`

MySQL supports only local temporary tables; omit the keyword `LOCAL`. The MySQL syntax to create a local temporary table is:

`CREATE TEMPORARY TABLE table (...);`

PostgreSQL supports only local temporary tables; the keyword `LOCAL` is optional.

Your DBMS may support the optional `ON COMMIT` clause that is defined by the SQL standard. `ON COMMIT PRESERVE ROWS` preserves any data modifications to the temporary table on a `COMMIT`, whereas `ON COMMIT DELETE ROWS` empties the table after a `COMMIT`. For information about `COMMIT`, see Chapter 13.

DBMSes vary in how they implement temporary tables with respect to visibility, constraints, foreign keys (referential integrity), indexes, and views; search your DBMS documentation for *temporary tables*.

Creating a New Table from an Existing One with
SELECT INTO

The SELECT INTO statement creates a new table and populates it with the result of a SELECT. It's similar to creating an empty table with CREATE TABLE and then populating the table with INSERT SELECT (see "Inserting Rows with INSERT" in Chapter 9). But note that SELECT INTO *exports* rows from an existing table, whereas INSERT SELECT *imports* rows into an existing table. SELECT INTO commonly is used to:

◆ Archive specific rows

◆ Make backup copies of tables

◆ Create a snapshot of a table at a particular moment in time

◆ Quickly duplicate a table's structure but not its data

◆ Create test data

◆ Copy a table to test INSERT, UPDATE, and DELETE operations before modifying production data.

When you're using SELECT INTO, some important considerations are:

◆ You can choose rows for the new table by using the standard SELECT clauses WHERE, JOIN, GROUP BY, and HAVING or any of the SELECT options described in Chapters 4 through 8.

◆ SELECT INTO inserts rows into a single table regardless of how many source tables the SELECT references.

◆ The properties of the columns and expressions in the SELECT-clause list define the new table's structure.

◆ When you include a derived (computed) column in the SELECT-clause list, the values in the new table's corresponding column are the values that were computed at the time SELECT INTO was executed. See "Creating Derived Columns" in Chapter 5.

◆ The new table must have a different name from the existing table.

◆ To use SELECT INTO, you must have CREATE TABLE permission from your database administrator.

Listing 10.18 Copy the structure and data of the existing table authors to a new table named authors2.

```listing
SELECT *
  INTO authors2
  FROM authors;
```

Listing 10.19 Copy the structure (but not the data) of the existing table publishers to a new table named publishers2.

```listing
SELECT *
  INTO publishers2
  FROM publishers
  WHERE 1 = 2;
```

Listing 10.20 Create a global temporary table named titles2 that contains the titles and sales of books published by publisher P01.

```listing
SELECT title_name, sales
  INTO GLOBAL TEMPORARY TABLE titles2
  FROM titles
  WHERE pub_id = 'P01';
```

Listing 10.21 Create a new table named author_title_names that contains the names of the authors who aren't from New York State or California and the titles of their books.

```listing
SELECT a.au_fname, a.au_lname, t.title_name
  INTO author_title_names
  FROM authors a
  INNER JOIN title_authors ta
    ON a.au_id = ta.au_id
  INNER JOIN titles t
    ON ta.title_id = t.title_id
  WHERE a.state NOT IN ('CA', 'NY');
```

To create a new table from an existing table:

◆ Type:

SELECT *columns*
   INTO *new_table*
   FROM *existing_table*
   [WHERE *search_condition*];

new_table is the name of the table to create, *existing_table* is the name of the source table, and *columns* is a list of one or more comma-separated expressions or column names from *existing_table*.

The DBMS evaluates the expressions in *columns* to determine the structure of *new_table*. The columns in *new_table* are created in the order specified by *columns*. Each column in *new_table* has the same name, data type, and value as the corresponding expression in *columns*. The WHERE clause specifies the rows to retrieve from *existing_table* to insert into *new_table*. You also can specify GROUP BY, HAVING, and JOIN clauses. *search_condition* is any valid WHERE search condition; see "Filtering Rows with WHERE" and subsequent sections in Chapter 4.

Listing 10.18 copies the structure and data of the existing table authors to a new table named authors2.

Listing 10.19 uses a WHERE condition that always is false to copy only the structure (but not the data) of the existing table publishers to a new table named publishers2.

Listing 10.20 creates a global temporary table named titles2 that contains the titles and sales of books published by publisher P01; see "Creating a Temporary Table with CREATE TEMPORARY TABLE" earlier in this chapter.

Listing 10.21 uses joins to create a new table named author_title_names that contains the names of the authors who aren't from New York State or California and the titles of their books.

CREATING A NEW TABLE WITH SELECT INTO

✔ Tips

- To see the rows in the table created by SELECT INTO, type a SELECT statement such as SELECT * FROM new_table. To examine the new table's structure, use one of the commands described in "Displaying a Table's Column Definitions" in Chapter 9.

- To modify a table, see "Altering a Table with ALTER TABLE" later in this chapter.

- To insert rows into an existing table, use the INSERT; see "Inserting Rows with INSERT" in Chapter 9.

- Another common use of SELECT INTO is to create a temporary table that contains data for the current date, such as this example:

```
SELECT *
  INTO GLOBAL TEMPORARY TABLE
    todays_sales
  FROM orders
  WHERE order_date = CURRENT_DATE;
```

- **DBMS** The SQL standard defines SELECT INTO usage differently than I present it here. The standard's SELECT INTO selects a value into a scalar variable in a host program rather than creating a new table. In fact, **Oracle's** version of SELECT INTO works in the standard way.

Microsoft Access doesn't support temporary tables. To run Listing 10.20 in Access, delete the keywords GLOBAL TEMPORARY TABLE. To run Listing 10.21 in Access, type:

```
SELECT a.au_fname, a.au_lname,
    t.title_name
  INTO author_title_names
  FROM titles t
  INNER JOIN (authors a
  INNER JOIN title_authors ta
    ON a.au_id = ta.au_id)
    ON t.title_id = ta.title_id
  WHERE a.state NOT IN ('NY','CA');
```

Microsoft SQL Server uses ## to designate a global temporary table. To run Listing 10.20 in SQL Server, replace INTO GLOBAL TEMPORARY TABLE titles2 with INTO ##titles2.

In **Oracle**, the SELECT INTO statement is used only to assign variables in PL/SQL. Oracle's CREATE TABLE AS SELECT statement (also known as CTAS) is equivalent semantically to SELECT INTO, described in this section. The syntax is:

```
CREATE TABLE new_table AS
  SELECT columns
  FROM existing_table
  [WHERE search_condition];
```

To run Listings 10.18 through 10.21 in Oracle, type (Listing 10.18):

```
CREATE TABLE authors2 AS
  SELECT *
  FROM authors;
```

and (Listing 10.19):

```
CREATE TABLE publishers2 AS
  SELECT *
  FROM publishers
  WHERE 1 = 2;
```

and (Listing 10.20):

```
CREATE GLOBAL TEMPORARY TABLE
    titles2 AS
  SELECT title_name, sales
  FROM titles
  WHERE pub_id = 'P01';
```

and (Listing 10.21):

```
CREATE TABLE author_title_names AS
  SELECT a.au_fname, a.au_lname,
    t.title_name
  FROM authors a
  INNER JOIN title_authors ta
    ON a.au_id = ta.au_id
  INNER JOIN titles t
    ON ta.title_id = t.title_id
  WHERE a.state NOT IN ('CA', 'NY');
```

In Oracle 8i, use WHERE syntax instead of JOIN syntax in Listing 10.21:

```
CREATE TABLE author_title_names AS
  SELECT a.au_fname, a.au_lname,
    t.title_name
  FROM authors a, title_authors ta,
    titles t
  WHERE a.au_id = ta.au_id
    AND ta.title_id = t.title_id
    AND a.state NOT IN ('CA', 'NY');
```

MySQL doesn't support SELECT INTO, replicate Listings 10.18 through 10.21 by using CREATE TABLE and INSERT SELECT.

In **PostgreSQL**, delete the keyword GLOBAL to run Listing 10.20. PostgreSQL also supports the statement CREATE TABLE AS, which is equivalent semantically to SELECT INTO.

CREATING A NEW TABLE WITH SELECT INTO

Altering a Table with
ALTER TABLE

Use the **ALTER TABLE** statement to modify a table definition by adding, altering, or dropping columns and constraints.

DBMS Despite the SQL standard, the implementation of **ALTER TABLE** varies greatly by DBMS. To determine what you can alter and the conditions under which alterations are permitted, search your DBMS documentation for *ALTER TABLE*. Depending on your DBMS, some of the modifications that you can make by using **ALTER TABLE** are:

◆ Add or drop a column

◆ Alter a column's data type

◆ Add, alter, or drop a column's nullability or default constraint

◆ Add, alter, or drop column or table constraints such as primary-key, foreign-key, unique, and check constraints

◆ Rename a column

◆ Rename a table

To alter a table:

◆ Type:

ALTER TABLE *table*
  alter_table_action;

table is the name of the table to alter. *alter_table_action* is a clause that specifies the action to take and begins with the keyword **ADD**, **ALTER**, or **DROP**.

Use these actions, for example, to add or drop columns or constraints:

ADD [COLUMN] *column data_type*

DROP COLUMN *column*

ADD *constraint_definition*

DROP CONSTRAINT *constraint_name*

Listing 10.22 Add the column `email_address` to the table `authors`.

```
                    listing
ALTER TABLE authors
    ADD email_address CHAR(25);
```

Listing 10.23 Drop the column `email_address` from the table `authors`.

```
                    listing
ALTER TABLE authors
    DROP COLUMN email_address;
```

Listings 10.22 and **10.23** add and drop the column `email_address` from the table `authors`.

If your DBMS's `ALTER TABLE` statement doesn't support an action that you need (such as, say, dropping or renaming a column or constraint), you can re-create and repopulate the table in its desired state manually.

To re-create and repopulate a table:

1. Use `CREATE TABLE` to create a new table with the new column definitions, column constraints, and table constraints; see "Creating a New Table with `CREATE TABLE`" and subsequent sections earlier in this chapter.

2. Use `INSERT SELECT` to copy rows (from the appropriate columns) from the old table into the new table; see "Inserting Rows with `INSERT`" in Chapter 9.

3. Use `SELECT * FROM new_table` to confirm that the new table has the proper rows; see "Retrieving Columns with `SELECT` and `FROM`" in Chapter 4.

4. Use `DROP TABLE` to drop the old table; see "Dropping a Table with `DROP TABLE`" later in this chapter.

5. Rename the new table to the name of the old table; see the DBMS Tip in this section.

6. Re-create indexes as needed; see "Creating an Index with `CREATE INDEX`" in Chapter 11.

   You also need to re-create any other properties that were dropped along with the old table, such as permissions and triggers.

✔ Tips

- To see the result of an ALTER TABLE statement, examine the table's structure by using one of the commands described in "Displaying a Table's Column Definitions" in Chapter 9.

- To alter or drop a constraint, use the name that you specified in the CONSTRAINT clause when you created the constraint; see "Understanding Constraints" earlier in this chapter. If you didn't name the constraint, use the constraint name that your DBMS generated automatically.

- DBMSes typically enforce fewer modification restrictions on empty tables than they do on populated tables. When you add a new column to a table that already has one or more rows, for example, that column can't have a NOT NULL constraint; whereas a new column in an empty table can be non-nullable.

- **DBMS** In **PostgreSQL**, ALTER TABLE allows you to add or rename a column but not drop a column, so Listing 10.23 doesn't work in PostgreSQL. To drop a column, use the re-create-and-repopulate procedure described earlier in this section.

  Each DBMS has a different procedure for renaming a table. In **Microsoft Access**, right-click the table in the Database window and then click Rename. In **Microsoft SQL Server**, execute the stored procedure EXEC sp_rename 'old_name', 'new_name'. In **Oracle**, run the statement RENAME old_name TO new_name;. In **MySQL**, run the statement RENAME TABLE old_name TO new_name;. In **PostgreSQL**, run the statement ALTER TABLE old_name RENAME TO new_name;.

Listing 10.24 Drop the table `royalties`.

```
listing

DROP TABLE royalties;
```

Dropping a Table with
DROP TABLE

Use the DROP TABLE statement to remove a table from a database. When you're dropping a table, some important considerations are:

◆ You can drop a base table or a temporary table.

◆ A dropped table is gone forever. You can't undo or roll back a DROP TABLE statement.

◆ Dropping a table destroys its structure, data, indexes, constraints, permissions, and so on.

◆ Dropping a table isn't the same as deleting all its rows. You can empty a table of rows, but not destroy it, with DELETE FROM *table*;. See "Deleting Rows with DELETE" in Chapter 9.

◆ Dropping a table doesn't drop views that reference that table; see Chapter 12.

◆ You'll encounter problems with foreign keys or views that reference a dropped table unless they're altered or dropped as well.

To drop a table:

◆ Type:

DROP TABLE *table*

table is the name of the table to drop (**Listing 10.24**).

✔ Tips

- The only way to recover a dropped table is to re-create the table and restore its data from the most recent backup.

- **DBMS** Some DBMSes require you to drop or alter certain other properties before dropping the table itself. In **Microsoft SQL Server**, for example, you can't use DROP TABLE to drop a table referenced by a FOREIGN KEY constraint until the referencing FOREIGN KEY constraint or the referencing table is dropped first.

  Standard SQL lets you specify RESTRICT or CASCADE drop behavior. RESTRICT (which is safe) prevents you from dropping a table that's referenced by views or other constraints. CASCADE (which is dangerous) causes referencing objects to be dropped along with the table. To find out whether your DBMS supports this feature or a similar one, search your DBMS documentation for *DROP TABLE*.

INDEXES

Recall from "Tables, Columns, and Rows" in Chapter 2 that rows stored in a table are unordered, as required by the relational model. This lack of order makes it easy for the DBMS to INSERT, UPDATE, and DELETE rows quickly, but its unfortunate side effect is that it makes searching and sorting inefficient. Suppose that you run this query:

```
SELECT *
  FROM authors
  WHERE au_lname = 'Hull';
```

To execute this query, the DBMS must search the entire table authors sequentially, comparing the value in each row's au_lname column to the string *Hull*. Searching an entire table in a small database is trivial, but production database tables may have millions of rows.

DBMSes provide a mechanism called an index that has the same purpose as its book or library counterpart: speeding data retrieval. At a simplified level, an *index* is a sorted list in which every distinct value in an indexed column (or set of columns) is stored with the disk address (physical location) of the rows containing that value. Instead of reading an entire table to locate specific rows, the DBMS scans only the index for addresses to access directly. Indexed searches typically are orders of magnitude faster than sequential searches but some tradeoffs are involved, as explained in this chapter.

Creating an Index
with CREATE INDEX

Indexes are complex; their design and effects on performance depend on the idiosyncrasies of your DBMS's optimizer. I'll provide guidelines in this section, but search your DBMS documentation for *index* to learn how your DBMS implements and uses indexes. In general, indexes are *appropriate* for columns that are:

◆ Searched frequently

◆ Sorted frequently

◆ Regularly used in joins

In general, indexes are *inappropriate* for columns that:

◆ Accept only a few distinct values (gender or state, for example)

◆ Rarely are used in queries

◆ Are part of a small table with few rows

When you're creating an index, some important considerations are:

◆ SQL's indexing statements modify database objects, so your database administrator may need to grant you permission to run them.

◆ An index never changes data; it's merely a fast access path to the data.

◆ A table can have zero or more indexes.

◆ Ideally, you create all a table's indexes when you create the table. In practice, index creation is an iterative process. Typically, only vital indexes are created along with the table. More indexes are added over time as performance problems arise. Most DBMSes provide testing and benchmarking tools to determine the effectiveness of indexes.

◆ Don't create any more indexes than you absolutely need. The DBMS must update (and possibly reorganize) an index after you INSERT, UPDATE, or DELETE rows in a table (see Chapter 9). As the number of indexes on a table grows, row-modification performance degrades as the DBMS spends more and more time maintaining indexes.

◆ Your DBMS will maintain and use indexes automatically after they're created. No additional actions are required by users or SQL programmers to reflect data changes in all relevant indexes.

◆ Indexes are transparent to the user and SQL programmer. The absence or presence of an index doesn't require a change in the wording of any SQL statement.

◆ An index can reference one or more columns in a table. An index that references a single column is a *simple index;* an index that references multiple columns is a *composite index.* Columns in a composite index need not be adjacent in the table.

◆ The order in which columns appear in a composite index is significant. A composite index applies only to the group of columns on which it's defined, but not to each column individually or the same columns in different order.

- You can create more than one composite index that use the same columns if you specify distinctly different combinations of the columns. The following two statements, for example, specify valid combinations for the same table:

```
CREATE INDEX au_name_idx1
  ON authors (au_fname, au_lname);
CREATE INDEX au_name_idx2
  ON authors (au_lname, au_fname);
```

- In addition to allowing rapid searches, an index can ensure uniqueness. A *unique index* forces the value of the column (or columns) upon which the index is based to be distinct.

- If you try to create a unique index for column(s) in which duplicate values already exist, your DBMS will generate an error and refuse to create the index.

- DBMSes create unique indexes automatically when you define a primary-key or unique constraint.

- A DBMS may or may not create indexes for foreign keys automatically. If not, you should create these indexes yourself, because most joins involve a foreign key.

- All DBMSes implement indexes even though indexes aren't part of the relational model (and don't violate any of the model's rules).

- As indexes aren't covered in the SQL-92 specification, index-related SQL statements vary by DBMS, although the minimal **CREATE INDEX** statement is consistent across many DBMSes.

To create an index:

◆ Type:

```
CREATE [UNIQUE] INDEX index
  ON table (index_columns);
```

index is the name of the index to create and is a valid SQL identifier. Index names must be unique within a table. For **Oracle** and **PostgreSQL**, index names must be unique within a database.

table is the name of the table to create the index for, and *index_columns* is a list of one or more comma-separated names of the columns to index.

Specify UNIQUE to create a unique index. UNIQUE causes the DBMS to check for duplicates in *index_columns*. If *table* already contains rows with duplicates in *index_columns*, the DBMS won't create the index. If you attempt to INSERT or UPDATE duplicate values in *index_columns*, the DBMS generates an error and cancels the operation.

Listing 11.1 creates a simple index named pub_id_idx on the column pub_id for the table titles. pub_id is a foreign key and is a good candidate for an index because:

◆ Changes to PRIMARY KEY constraints are checked with FOREIGN KEY constraints in related tables.

◆ Foreign-key columns often are used in join criteria when the data from related tables is combined in queries by matching the FOREIGN KEY column(s) of one table with the PRIMARY KEY or UNIQUE column(s) in the other table.

Listing 11.2 creates a simple unique index named title_name_idx on the column title_name for the table titles. The DBMS will create this index only if no duplicates already exist in the column title_name. This index also prohibits nondistinct title names from being INSERTed or UPDATEd.

Listing 11.1 Create a simple index on the column pub_id for the table titles.

```
                      listing
CREATE INDEX pub_id_idx
  ON titles (pub_id);
```

Listing 11.2 Create a simple unique index on the column title_name for the table titles.

```
                      listing
CREATE UNIQUE INDEX title_name_idx
  ON titles (title_name);
```

Listing 11.3 Create a composite index on the columns state and city for the table authors.

```listing
CREATE INDEX state_city_idx
  ON authors (state, city);
```

Listing 11.3 creates a composite index named state_city_idx on the columns state and city for the table authors. The DBMS uses this index when you sort rows in state plus city order. This index is useless for sorts and searches on state alone, city alone, or city plus state; you must create separate indexes for those purposes.

✔ Tips

- Don't use the terms *index* and *key* interchangeably (although you'll see them used so in books). An index is a *physical* (hardware-related) mechanism that the DBMS uses to improve performance. A key is a *logical* (based on data) concept that the DBMS uses to enforce referential integrity and update through views.

- You can create a unique constraint instead of a unique index to prevent duplicate values; see "Forcing Unique Values with UNIQUE" in Chapter 10.

- Indexes themselves are files stored on disk and so occupy storage space (sometimes, a lot of space). But when used properly, indexes are the primary means of reducing disk wear and tear by obviating the need to read large tables sequentially.

- Searching a table sequentially (for lack of an index) is called a *table scan*.

- For programmers: Most indexes are implemented as B-trees. Some DBMSes allow you to specify the data structure and algorithm to use when constructing an index.

- **DBMS** **Microsoft SQL Server** considers multiple nulls to be duplicates when UNIQUE is specified and permits no more than one null in columns with a unique index. **Microsoft Access**, **Oracle**, **MySQL**, and **PostgreSQL** permit multiple nulls in such columns.

CREATING AN INDEX WITH CREATE INDEX

Dropping an Index
with DROP INDEX

Use the DROP INDEX statement to destroy an index. As an index is logically and physically independent of the data in its associated table, you can drop the index at any time without affecting the table (or other indexes). All SQL programs and other applications continue to work if you drop an index, but access of previously indexed data will be slower.

The usual reasons for dropping an index are:

◆ The index is no longer needed.

◆ The extra time it takes the DBMS to maintain the index after INSERT, UPDATE, or DELETE operations outweighs the speed improvement in retrieval operations that the index provides.

The SQL-92 standard omits indexes, so index-related SQL statements vary by DBMS. I'll describe how to drop an index for each DBMS covered in this book. If you're using a different DBMS, search the documentation for *index* to learn how to drop an index.

In **Oracle** and **PostgreSQL**, index names must be unique within a database, so you don't specify a table name when you drop an index. In **Microsoft Access**, **Microsoft SQL Server**, and **MySQL**, index names must be unique within a table but may be reused in other tables, so you must specify a table along with the index to be dropped. The examples in this section drop the index created by Listing 11.1 in the preceding section.

Listing 11.4a Drop the index `pub_id_idx` (Microsoft Access or MySQL).

```
                    listing
DROP INDEX pub_id_idx
  ON titles;
```

Listing 11.4b Drop the index `pub_id_idx` (Microsoft SQL Server).

```
                    listing
DROP INDEX titles.pub_id_idx;
```

Listing 11.4c Drop the index `pub_id_idx` (Oracle or PostgreSQL).

```
                    listing
DROP INDEX pub_id_idx;
```

To drop an index in Microsoft Access or MySQL:

◆ Type:

    DROP INDEX *index*

       ON *table*;

index is the name of the index to drop, and *table* is the name of the index's associated table (**Listing 11.4a**).

To drop an index in Microsoft SQL Server:

◆ Type:

    DROP INDEX *table*.*index*;

index is the name of the index to drop, and *table* is the name of the index's associated table (**Listing 11.4b**).

To drop an index in Oracle or PostgreSQL:

◆ Type:

    DROP INDEX *index*;

index is the name of the index to drop (**Listing 11.4c**).

DROPPING AN INDEX WITH DROP INDEX

VIEWS

A *view* is a stored **SELECT** statement that
returns a table whose data is derived from one
or more other tables (called *underlying tables*).
Some important characteristics of a view are:

◆ A view's underlying tables can be base
  tables, temporary tables, or other views.

◆ A view is called a *virtual* or *derived table* to
  distinguish it from a base or temporary table.

◆ The DBMS stores a view as *only* a **SELECT**
  statement, *not* as a set of data values,
  thus preventing data redundancy.

◆ A view materializes dynamically as a
  physical table when referenced by name
  in an SQL statement. It exists only for the
  duration of the statement and vanishes
  when the statement ends.

◆ A view consists of a set of named
  columns and rows of data, so you can use
  it almost anywhere you'd use a real table.

◆ You have no restrictions on querying
  (**SELECT**ing) through views. In some cases,
  views can be updated, causing the data
  changes to be passed through to the
  underlying base tables.

◆ Because of closure, a view always is a single table no matter how many underlying
  tables it references or how those tables
  are combined; see the Tips in "Tables,
  Columns, and Rows" in Chapter 2.

Creating a View with
CREATE VIEW

Think of a view as being a tailored presentation that provides a tabular window into one or more base tables. The window can display an entire base table, part of a base table, or a combination of base tables (or parts thereof). A view also may reflect the data in base tables through other views—windows into windows. Generally, SQL programmers use views to present data to end users in database applications. Views offer these advantages:

- **Simplified data access.** Views hide data complexity and simplify statements, so users can perform operations on a view more easily than on the base tables directly. If you create a complex view— one that involves, say, multiple base tables, joins, and subqueries—users can query this view without having to understand complex relational concepts or even knowing that multiple tables are involved.

- **Automatic updating.** When a base table is updated, all views that reference the table reflect the change automatically. If you insert a row representing a new author into the table authors, for example, all views defined over authors will reflect the new author automatically. This scheme saves disk space and prevents redundancy because, without views, the DBMS would have to store derived data to keep it synchronized.

- **Increased security.** One of the most common uses of views is to hide data from users by filtering the underlying tables. Suppose that the table employees contains the columns salary and commission. If you create a view on employees that omits these two columns,

the database administrator can grant users permission to see the view but not see the underlying table, thereby hiding compensation data from the overcurious.

- **Logical data independence.** Base tables provide a *real view* of a database. But when you use SQL to build a database application, you want to present end users not the real view, but a *virtual view* specific to the application. The virtual view hides the parts of the database (entire tables or specific rows or columns) that aren't relevant to the application. Thus users interact with the virtual view, which is derived from—though independent of—the real view presented by the base tables.

A virtual view immunizes an application from logical changes in the design of the database. Suppose that many applications access the table titles. Books go out of print over time, so the database designer decides to reduce the system load by segregating out-of-print books. He splits titles into two tables: in_print_titles and out_of_print_titles. Consequently, all the applications break because they expect the now-unavailable table titles.

But if those applications had accessed a *view* of titles instead of the real table, that view could be redefined to be the UNION of in_print_titles and out_of_print_titles (see "Combining Rows with UNION" in Chapter 7). The applications transparently would see the two new tables as though they were the one original table and continue to work as though the split never happened. (You can't use views to immunize an application against *all* changes, however. Views can't compensate for dropped tables or columns, for example.)

When you're creating a view, some important considerations are:

- View-related SQL statements modify database objects and data, so your database administrator may need to grant you permission to run them.

- View names follow the same rules that table names do.

- Views names must be unique within the database. (They can't have the same name as any other table or view.)

- The columns in a view inherit the default column names from the underlying tables. You can give view columns different names by using AS; see "Creating Column Aliases with AS" in Chapter 4.

- You must specify a new name for a column in a view that would have the same name as another column in the view (usually because the view definition includes a join, and the columns from two or more different underlying tables have the same name).

- A column defined in a view can be a simple column reference, a literal, or an expression that involves calculations or aggregate functions.

- In some DBMSes, you must specify explicitly the name of a column in a view if the column is derived from an arithmetic expression, a built-in function, or a literal.

- A view column inherits the data type of the column or expression from which it is derived.

- You have no practical limit on the number of views that you can create. Generally, you'll want to create views on subsets of data that are of interest to many users.

- Some DBMSes don't allow views on temporary tables.

- Almost any valid SELECT statement can define a view, though an ORDER BY clause usually is prohibited.

- You can nest views—that is, a view's SELECT statement may retrieve data from another view. Nested views eventually must resolve to base tables (otherwise, you'd be viewing nothing). The maximum number of nesting levels varies by DBMS.

- You can use views as a convenience to save complex queries. By saving a query that performs extensive calculations as a view, you can recalculate each time the view is queried.

- A view can express a query that can't be expressed without using a view. You can define a view that joins a GROUP BY view with a base table, for example, or define a view that joins a UNION view with a base table.

- A view definition can't reference itself, because it doesn't exist yet.

- Views can display data formatted differently from that in the underlying tables.

- Unlike a base table, a view doesn't allow you to use indexes or constraints.

- When you define a view by using SELECT *, SQL converts the * to a list of all columns internally. This conversion occurs only once, at view creation (not at execution), so the definition of your view won't change if someone adds a column to an underlying table (by using ALTER TABLE).

- Because views store no data, the DBMS must execute them every time they're referenced. Complex views—particularly nested views—can degrade performance seriously.

To create a view:

◆ Type:

```
CREATE VIEW view [(view_columns)]
  AS select_statement;
```

view is the name of the view to create. The view name must be unique within the database.

view_columns is an optional, parenthesized list of one or more comma-separated names to be used for the columns in *view*. The number of columns in *view_columns* must match the number of columns in the **SELECT** clause of *select_statement*. (If you name one column this way, you must name them all this way.) Specify *view_columns* when a column in *select_statement* is derived from an arithmetic expression, a function, or a literal; when two or more view columns would otherwise have the same name (usually because of a join); or to give a column in *view* a name different from that of the column from which derived. If *view_columns* is omitted, *view* inherits column names from *select_statement*. Column names also can be assigned in *select_statement* via **AS** clauses. Each column name must be unique within the view.

select_statement is a **SELECT** statement that identifies the columns and rows of the table(s) that the view is based on. *select_statement* can be arbitrarily complex and use more than one table or other views. An **ORDER BY** clause usually is prohibited. For information about the **SELECT** statement, see Chapters 4 through 8. For DBMS-specific restrictions on **SELECT** in views, search your DBMS's documentation for *CREATE VIEW* (**Listings 12.1** through **12.5**).

Listing 12.1 Create a view that hides the authors' personal information (telephone numbers and addresses).

```
CREATE VIEW au_names
  AS
  SELECT au_id, au_fname, au_lname
    FROM authors;
```

Listing 12.2 Create a view that lists the authors who live in a city in which a publisher is located. Note that I use the column names au_city and pub_city in the view. Renaming these columns resolves the ambiguity that would arise if both columns inherited the same column name city from the underlying tables.

```
CREATE VIEW cities
  (au_id, au_city, pub_id, pub_city)
  AS
  SELECT a.au_id, a.city, p.pub_id, p.city
    FROM authors a
    INNER JOIN publishers p
      ON a.city = p.city;
```

Listing 12.3 Create a view that lists total revenue (= price × sales) grouped by book type within publisher. The view will be easier to query later because I name the result of an arithmetic expression explicitly rather than let the DBMS assign a default name.

```
CREATE VIEW revenues
  (Publisher, BookType, Revenue)
  AS
  SELECT pub_id, type, SUM(price * sales)
    FROM titles
    GROUP BY pub_id, type;
```

Listing 12.4 Create a view that makes it easy to print mailing labels for authors. Note that I assigned column names in the SELECT clause rather than in the CREATE VIEW clause.

```
CREATE VIEW mailing_labels
  AS
  SELECT
      TRIM(au_fname || ' ' || au_lname)
        AS "address1",
      TRIM(address)
        AS "address2",
      TRIM(city) || ', ' || TRIM(state) ||
        ' ' || TRIM(zip)
        AS "address3"
    FROM authors;
```

Listing 12.5 Create a view that lists the last names of authors A02 and A05, and the books that each one wrote (or co-wrote). Note that this statement uses a nested view: It references the view au_names created by Listing 12.1.

```
CREATE VIEW au_titles (LastName, Title)
  AS
  SELECT an.au_lname, t.title_name
    FROM title_authors ta
    INNER JOIN au_names an
      ON ta.au_id = an.au_id
    INNER JOIN titles t
      ON t.title_id = ta.title_id
    WHERE an.au_id in ('A02','A05');
```

✔ Tips

- To select rows and columns through a view, see "Retrieving Data Through a View" later in this chapter.

- To change base-table values through a view, see "Updating Data Through a View" later in this chapter.

- To destroy a view, see "Dropping a View with DROP VIEW" later in this chapter.

- You can't SELECT INTO a view; see "Creating a New Table from an Existing One with SELECT INTO" in Chapter 10.

- You can't create temporary views. Views and temporary tables are differentiated by their persistence. A view exists for the duration of an SQL statement; a temporary table exists for the duration of a session. See "Creating a Temporary Table with CREATE TEMPORARY TABLE" in Chapter 10.

- SQL has no ALTER VIEW statement. If the underlying table(s) or view(s) changed since a view was created, drop and re-create the view. (**Microsoft SQL Server** and **Oracle** support a nonstandard ALTER VIEW statement.)

continues on next page

CREATING A VIEW WITH CREATE VIEW

■ **DBMS** When you run a `CREATE VIEW` statement in **Microsoft Access**, the view appears as a query object in the Database window. To run Listing 12.4 in Access, change every occurrence of | | to +; see the DBMS Tip in "Concatenating Strings with | |" in Chapter 5. To run Listing 12.5 in Access, type:

```
CREATE VIEW au_titles
  (LastName, Title)
  AS
  SELECT an.au_lname, t.title_name
    FROM au_names an
    INNER JOIN (titles t
    INNER JOIN title_authors ta
      ON t.title_id = ta.title_id)
      ON an.au_id = ta.au_id
    WHERE an.au_id IN ('A02','A05');
```

Microsoft SQL Server doesn't support the use of a semicolon after a `CREATE VIEW` statement (oddly). To run Listings 12.1 through 12.5 in SQL Server, remove the terminating semicolon from each statement. Additionally, to run Listing 12.4 in SQL Server, change every occurrence of | | to + and every occurrence of `TRIM(x)` to `LTRIM(RTRIM(x))`; see the DBMS Tips in "Concatenating Strings with | |" and "Trimming Characters with `TRIM()`" in Chapter 5.

Oracle 9i will run Listings 12.2 and 12.5 as is. To run Listings 12.2 and 12.5 in Oracle 8i, use `WHERE` syntax instead of `JOIN` syntax. Type (Listing 12.2):

```
CREATE VIEW cities
  (au_id, au_city, pub_id, pub_city)
  AS
  SELECT a.au_id, a.city,
```

```
  p.pub_id, p.city
  FROM authors a, publishers p
  WHERE a.city = p.city;
```

and (Listing 12.5):

```
CREATE VIEW au_titles
  (LastName, Title)
  AS
  SELECT an.au_lname, t.title_name
    FROM title_authors ta,
      au_names an, titles t
    WHERE ta.au_id = an.au_id
      AND t.title_id = ta.title_id
      AND an.au_id in ('A02','A05');
```

MySQL 4.0 and earlier versions don't support views and won't run Listings 12.1 through 12.5. To hide data, use MySQL's privilege system to restrict column access.

Standard SQL lets you specify the optional clause `WITH [CASCADED | LOCAL] CHECK OPTION` when you create a view. This clause applies only to updatable views and ensures that only data that can be read by the view can be inserted, updated, or deleted; see "Updating Data Through a View" later in this chapter. If a view shows authors from only New York State, for example, it would be impossible to insert, update, or delete non-New York authors through that view. The `CASCADED` and `LOCAL` options apply to nested views only. `CASCADED` performs the check for the current view and all the views it references. `LOCAL` performs the check for the current view only, even if it references other views. **Microsoft SQL Server** and **Oracle** support `CHECK OPTION`, search the documentation for *CREATE VIEW* for DBMS-specific details.

Listing 12.6 List all the rows and columns of the view au_titles. See Figure 12.1 for the result.

```
                     listing
SELECT *
  FROM au_titles;
```

```
LastName   Title
---------  -----------------------------
Kells      Ask Your System Administrator
Heydemark  How About Never?
Heydemark  I Blame My Mother
Heydemark  Not Without My Faberge Egg
Heydemark  Spontaneous, Not Annoying
```

Figure 12.1 Result of Listing 12.6.

Listing 12.7 List the distinct cities in the view cities. See Figure 12.2 for the result.

```
                     listing
SELECT DISTINCT au_city
  FROM cities;
```

```
au_city
-------------
New York
San Francisco
```

Figure 12.2 Result of Listing 12.7.

Retrieving Data Through a View

Creating a view displays nothing. All that CREATE VIEW does is cause the DBMS to save the view as a named SELECT statement. To see data through a view, query the view by using SELECT, just as you would query a table. You can:

◆ Rearrange the order of the displayed columns with the SELECT clause

◆ Use operators and functions to perform calculations

◆ Change column headings with AS

◆ Filter rows with WHERE

◆ Group rows with GROUP BY

◆ Filtered grouped rows with HAVING

◆ Join the view to other views or tables with JOIN

◆ Sort the result with ORDER BY

continues on next page

RETRIEVING DATA THROUGH A VIEW

To retrieve data through a view:

◆ Type:

SELECT *columns*

    FROM *view*

    [JOIN *joins*]

    [WHERE *search_condition*]

    [GROUP BY *group_columns*]

    [HAVING *search_condition*]

    [ORDER BY *sort_columns*];

view is the name of the view to query. The clauses work with views the same way that they work with tables. For SELECT, FROM, ORDER BY, and WHERE, see Chapter 4; for GROUP BY and HAVING, see Chapter 6; for JOIN, see Chapter 7.

Listings 12.6 through **12.11** and **Figures 12.1** through **12.6** show how to retrieve data through the views created by Listings 12.1 through 12.5 "Creating a View with CREATE VIEW" earlier in this chapter.

Listing 12.8 List the types of books whose average revenue exceeds $1 million. See Figure 12.3 for the result.

```
SELECT BookType,
    AVG(Revenue) AS "AVG(Revenue)"
  FROM revenues
  GROUP BY BookType
  HAVING AVG(Revenue) > 1000000;
```

```
BookType      AVG(Revenue)
----------    ------------
biography     18727318.50
computer       1025396.65
psychology     2320933.76
```

Figure 12.3 Result of Listing 12.8.

Listing 12.9 List the third line of the mailing address of each author whose name contains the string *Kell*. See Figure 12.4 for the result.

```
SELECT address3
  FROM mailing_labels
  WHERE address1 LIKE '%Kell%';
```

```
address3
-------------------
New York, NY 10014
Palo Alto, CA 94305
```

Figure 12.4 Result of Listing 12.9.

Listing 12.10 List the name of each author who wasn't the lead author of at least one book. See Figure 12.5 for the result.

```
                    listing
SELECT DISTINCT an.au_fname, an.au_lname
  FROM au_names an
  INNER JOIN title_authors ta
    ON an.au_id = ta.au_id
  WHERE ta.au_order > 1;
```

```
au_fname  au_lname
--------  --------
Hallie    Hull
Klee      Hull
```

Figure 12.5 Result of Listing 12.10.

Listing 12.11 List the names of the authors from California. See Figure 12.6 for the result.

```
                    listing
SELECT au_fname, au_lname
  FROM au_names
  WHERE state = 'CA';
```

```
ERROR: Invalid column name 'state'.
```

Figure 12.6 Result of Listing 12.11. The view au_names references authors but hides the column state, so referring to state through the view causes an error.

✔ Tips

- To change base-table values through a view, see "Updating Data Through a View" later in this chapter.

- To destroy a view, see "Dropping a View with DROP VIEW" later in this chapter.

- **DBMS** To run Listing 12.9 in **Microsoft Access**, enclose the view's column names in double quotes and brackets:

  ```
  SELECT ["address3"]
    FROM mailing_labels
    WHERE ["address1"] LIKE '%Kell%';
  ```

  To run Listing 12.9 in **Oracle**, enclose the view's column names in double quotes:

  ```
  SELECT "address3"
    FROM mailing_labels
    WHERE "address1" LIKE '%Kell%';
  ```

  MySQL 4.0 and earlier versions don't support views and won't run Listings 12.6 through 12.11.

Updating Data Through a View

An *updatable view* is a view to which you can apply INSERT, UPDATE, and DELETE operations to modify data in the underlying table(s). Any changes made in an updatable view always pass through to the base table(s) unambiguously. The syntax for the INSERT, UPDATE, and DELETE statements is the same for views as it is for tables; see Chapter 9.

A *nonupdatable view* is one that doesn't support INSERT, UPDATE, and DELETE operations because changes would be ambiguous. Nonupdatable views are said to be *read-only* views. To change the data that appears in a read-only view, you must change the underlying table(s) directly.

Each row in an updatable view is associated with exactly one row in an underlying base table. For a view to be updatable, the ANSI SQL standard requires the SELECT statement that defines the view to adhere to these conditions:

◆ The view must be defined over only one table (that is, no joins).

◆ The SELECT statement can't have GROUP BY or HAVING clauses.

◆ SELECT DISTINCT is prohibited.

◆ UNION, INTERSECT, and EXCEPT queries are prohibited.

◆ The SELECT clause can specify only simple column references, not calculated columns, aggregate functions, and so on.

◆ If the underlying table is itself a view, that view must be updatable.

The ANSI restrictions on updatability are stringent but very safe. Some DBMSes relax the ANSI restrictions because many more types of updatable views exist; a DBMS often can expand the set of updatable views by examining the database's referential integrity constraints. In addition to supporting ANSI's updatable views, your DBMS may let the following types of queries define updatable views:

◆ One-to-one inner joins

◆ One-to-one outer joins

◆ One-to-many inner joins

◆ One-to-many outer joins

◆ Many-to-many joins

◆ UNION and EXCEPT queries

In this section, I'll give examples for an updatable view that references only one underlying table (in compliance with ANSI SQL). See the documentation to find out whether your DBMS supports updatable views that reference multiple underlying tables and, if so, how view updates affect each base table.

Listing 12.12 Create and display the view ny_authors, which lists the IDs, names, and states of only those authors from New York State. See Figure 12.7 for the result.

```
CREATE VIEW ny_authors
  AS
  SELECT au_id, au_fname, au_lname, state
    FROM authors
    WHERE state = 'NY';


SELECT *
  FROM ny_authors;
```

au_id	au_fname	au_lname	state
A01	Sarah	Buchman	NY
A05	Christian	Kells	NY

Figure 12.7 Result of Listing 12.12: the view ny_authors.

Listing 12.13 Insert a new row through the view ny_authors.

```
INSERT INTO ny_authors
  VALUES('A08','Don','Dawson','NY');
```

Listing 12.14 Insert a new row through the view ny_authors. The DBMS would cancel this insertion if WITH CHECK OPTION had been used when ny_authors was created.

```
INSERT INTO ny_authors
  VALUES('A09','Jill','LeFlore','CA');
```

Inserting a row through a view

Consider the view ny_authors, which consists of the IDs, names, and states of only those authors from New York State (**Listing 12.12** and **Figure 12.7**). ny_authors references only the base table authors.

Listing 12.13 inserts a new row through a view. The DBMS inserts a new row into the table authors. The row contains A08 in the column au_id, Don in au_fname, Dawson in au_lname, and NY in state. The other columns in the row—phone, address, city, and zip—are set to null (or their default values, if DEFAULT constraints exist).

Listing 12.14, like Listing 12.13, inserts a new row through a view. But this time, the new author is from California, not New York, which violates the WHERE condition in the view's definition. Does the DBMS insert the row or cancel the operation? The answer depends on how the view was created. In this particular example, the insertion is allowed because the CREATE VIEW statement (see Listing 12.12) lacks a WITH CHECK OPTION clause, so the DBMS isn't forced to maintain consistency with the view's original definition. For information about WITH CHECK OPTION, see the DBMS Tip in "Creating a View with CREATE VIEW" earlier in this chapter. The DBMS would have canceled the insertion if ny_authors were defined as:

```
CREATE VIEW ny_authors
  AS
  SELECT au_id, au_fname, au_lname,
      state
    FROM authors
    WHERE state = 'NY'
  WITH CHECK OPTION;
```

UPDATING DATA THROUGH A VIEW

Updating a row through a view

Listing 12.15 updates an existing row through a view. The DBMS updates the row for author A01 in the table authors by changing the author's name from Sarah Buchman to Yasmin Howcomely. The values in the other columns in the row—au_id, phone, address, city, state, and zip—don't change.

But suppose that Listing 12.15 looked like this:

```
UPDATE ny_authors
  SET au_fname = 'Yasmin',
      au_lname = 'Howcomely',
      state = 'CA'
  WHERE au_id = 'A01';
```

This statement presents the same problem as Listing 12.14: The desired change would cause Yasmin's row to no longer meet the conditions for membership in the view. Again, the DBMS will accept or reject the UPDATE depending on whether the WITH CHECK OPTION clause was specified when the view was created. If WITH CHECK OPTION is used, rows can't be modified in a way that causes them to disappear from the view.

Listing 12.15 Update an existing row through the view ny_authors.

```
UPDATE ny_authors
  SET au_fname = 'Yasmin',
      au_lname = 'Howcomely'
  WHERE au_id = 'A01';
```

Listing 12.16 Delete a row through the view ny_authors.

```
                     listing
DELETE FROM ny_authors
  WHERE au_id = 'A05';
```

Deleting a row through a view

Listing 12.16 deletes a row through a view. The DBMS deletes the row for author A05 in the table **authors**. (Every column in the row is deleted, not just those in the view.) In turn, the row disappears from the view ny_authors.

View updates may have integrity repercussions, of course. The DBMS will disallow a deletion if removing a row violates a referential-integrity constraint; see "Specifying a Foreign Key with FOREIGN KEY" in Chapter 10. If you delete a row, all the underlying FOREIGN KEY constraints in related tables must still be satisfied for the delete to succeed. Some updating may be handled by the CASCADE option (if specified) of a FOREIGN KEY constraint, not by the view definition.

In Listing 12.16, for example, the DBMS will cancel the DELETE if I don't first change or delete the foreign-key values in the table title_authors that point to author A05 in authors.

✔ Tips

- To destroy a view, see "Dropping a View with DROP VIEW" later in this chapter.

- An updatable view must contain a key of the base table to ensure that each view row maps back to only one row in the base table.

- Any column excluded from an updatable view must be nullable or have a DEFAULT constraint in the base table, so that the DBMS can construct the entire row for insertion.

- Updated values must adhere to the base table's column restrictions, such as data type, nullability, and other constraints.

continues on next page

UPDATING DATA THROUGH A VIEW

- Some arithmetically derived columns are (theoretically) updatable. In a view with the derived column bonus = 0.1 * salary, for example, you'd expect to be able to update bonus and have SQL apply the reverse function (bonus/0.1) to update salary in the base table. Your expectations would be dashed, however, as SQL won't back-propagate updates in derived columns.

- As updatable views become more complex, you'll find that one type of view operation may involve other types of operations. A view UPDATE, for example, may involve INSERTing new base rows.

- **DBMS** To run Listing 12.12 in **Microsoft SQL Server**, omit the terminating semicolon from the CREATE VIEW statement and run the two statements separately.

  MySQL 4.0 and earlier versions don't support views and won't run Listings 12.12 through 12.16.

  You must use the **PostgreSQL** rule system to allow view operations. The CREATE RULE statement, which defines rules, is a PostgreSQL language extension and not part of ANSI SQL; search PostgreSQL documentation for *CREATE RULE* or *rule system*.

  Check the documentation to see how your DBMS handles updatable views for columns whose data type generates a unique row identifier automatically; see the DBMS Tip in "Primary Keys" in Chapter 2.

Listing 12.17 Drop the view ny_authors.

```
                       listing
DROP VIEW ny_authors;
```

Dropping a View with
DROP VIEW

Use the DROP VIEW statement to destroy a view. As a view is physically independent of its underlying table(s), you can drop the view at any time without affecting the table(s). All SQL programs, applications, and other views that reference the dropped view will break, however.

To drop a view:

◆ Type:

DROP VIEW *view*;

view is the name of the view to drop (**Listing 12.17**).

✔ Tips

■ Dropping a table doesn't drop the views that reference that table, so you must drop the views with DROP VIEW explicitly; see "Dropping a Table with DROP TABLE" in Chapter 10.

■ SQL has no ALTER VIEW statement. If the underlying table(s) or view(s) changed since a view was created, drop and re-create the view. (**Microsoft SQL Server** and **Oracle** support a nonstandard ALTER VIEW statement.)

■ **DBMS** **MySQL** 4.0 and earlier versions don't support views and won't run Listing 12.17.

TRANSACTIONS

```
UPDATE savings_accounts
  SET balance = balance - 500.00
  WHERE account_number = 1009;


UPDATE checking_accounts
  SET balance = balance + 500.00
  WHERE account_number = 6482;
```

Figure 13.1 Two SQL statements are needed when a banking customer transfers money from savings to checking.

A *transaction* is a sequence of one or more SQL statements executed as a single logical unit of work. The DBMS considers a transaction to be an indivisible, all-or-nothing proposition: It executes all the transaction's statements as a group, or it executes none of them.

Canonical law requires me to illustrate the importance of transactions with a banking example. Suppose that a customer transfers $500 from her savings account to her checking account. This operation consists of two separate actions, executed sequentially:

1. Decrement savings account by $500.

2. Increment checking account by $500.

Figure 13.1 shows the two SQL statements for this transaction. Now imagine that the DBMS fails—power outage, system crash, hardware problem—after it executes the first statement, but not the second. The accounts would be out of balance without your knowledge. Accusations of malfeasance and prison time would soon follow.

To avoid a police record, use a transaction to guarantee that both SQL statements are performed to maintain the accounts in proper balance. When something prevents one of the statements in a transaction from executing, the DBMS undoes (rolls back) the other statements of the transaction. If no error occurs, the changes are made permanent (committed).

Executing a Transaction

To learn how transactions work, you need to acquire a small vocabulary:

◆ **Commit.** Committing a transaction makes all data modifications performed since the start of the transaction a permanent part of the database. After a transaction is committed, all changes made by the transaction become visible to other users and are guaranteed to be permanent if a crash or other failure occurs.

◆ **Roll back.** Rolling back a transaction retracts any of the changes resulting from the SQL statements in the transaction. After a transaction is rolled back, the affected data is left unchanged, as though the SQL statements in the transaction were never executed.

◆ **Transaction log.** The transaction log file, or just *log,* is a serial record of all modifications that have occurred in a database via transactions. The transaction log records the start of each transaction, the changes to the data, and enough information to undo or redo the changes made by the transaction (if necessary later). The log grows continually as transactions occur in the database.

Although it's the DBMS's responsibility to ensure the *physical* integrity of each transaction, it's your responsibility to start and end transactions at points that enforce the *logical* consistency of the data, according to the rules of your organization or business. A transaction should comprise only the SQL statements necessary to make one consistent change—no more and no fewer. Data in

all referenced tables must be in a consistent state before the transaction begins and after it ends.

When you're designing and executing transactions, some important considerations are:

◆ Transaction-related SQL statements modify data, so your database administrator may need to grant you permission to run them.

◆ Transaction processing applies *only* to INSERT, UPDATE, and DELETE statements (see Chapter 9). You can't roll back SELECT, CREATE, ALTER, or DROP statements; if you include them in transaction blocks, they won't be rolled back.

◆ Every INSERT, UPDATE, and DELETE statement should be executed as part of a transaction.

◆ A committed transaction is said to be *durable,* meaning that its changes remain in place permanently, persisting even if the system fails.

◆ A DBMS's data recovery mechanism depends on transactions. When the DBMS is brought back online following a failure, the DBMS checks its transaction log to see whether all transactions were committed to the database. If it finds uncommitted (partially executed) transactions, it rolls them back based on the log. You must resubmit the rolled-back transactions (although some DBMSes complete unfinished transactions automatically).

◆ A DBMS's backup/restore facility depends on transactions. The backup facility takes regular snapshots of the database and stores them with (subsequent) transaction logs on a backup disk. Suppose that a crash damages a production disk in a way that renders the data and transaction log unreadable. You can invoke the restore facility, which will use the most recent database backup and then execute, or *roll forward*, all *committed* transactions in the log from the time the snapshot was taken to the last transaction preceding the failure. This restore operation brings the database to its correct state before the crash. (Again, you'll have to resubmit uncommitted transactions.)

◆ For obvious reasons, you should store a database and its transaction log on separate physical disks.

Concurrency Control

To humans, computers appear to carry out two or more processes at the same time. In reality, computer operations occur not concurrently, but in sequence. The illusion of simultaneity appears because a microprocessor works with much smaller time slices than people can perceive. In a DBMS, *concurrency control* is a group of strategies that prevent loss of data integrity caused by interference between two or more users trying to access or change the same data simultaneously.

DBMSes use locking (the most common strategy) to ensure transactional integrity and database consistency. *Locking* restricts data access during read and write operations; thus, it prevents users from reading data that's being changed by other users and prevents multiple users from changing the same data at the same time. Without locking, data may become logically incorrect, and statements executed against those data may return unexpected results. Locking mechanisms are very sophisticated; search your DBMS documentation for *locking*.

Concurrency transparency is the appearance from a transaction's perspective that it's the only transaction operating on the database. A DBMS isolates a transaction's changes from changes made by any other concurrent transactions. Consequently, a transaction never sees data in an intermediate state; it either sees data in the state it was in before another concurrent transaction changed it, or it sees the data after the other transaction has completed. This level of isolation, called *serializability*, enables you to reload starting data and replay (roll forward) a series of transactions to end up with the data in the same state it was in after the original transactions were executed.

For a transaction to be executed in all-or-nothing fashion, the transaction's boundaries (starting and ending points) must be clear. These boundaries let the DBMS execute the statements as one atomic unit of work. According to the ANSI SQL standard, a transaction always begins *implicitly* with the first executable SQL statement and always ends *explicitly* with a COMMIT or ROLLBACK statement. (A transaction never ends implicitly.)

DBMS **Oracle** is compatible with the ANSI standard. In other DBMSes, you can (or must) begin a transaction explicitly. DBMSes typically use the keyword BEGIN to mark the start of a transaction explicitly. BEGIN isn't part of the ANSI standard, however, so the syntax varies by DBMS; search the documentation for DBMS-specific transaction requirements.

To begin a transaction explicitly:

◆ In **Microsoft Access** or **Microsoft SQL Server**, type:
```
BEGIN TRANSACTION;
```
or

In **MySQL** or **PostgreSQL**, type:
```
BEGIN;
```

To commit a transaction:

◆ Type:
```
COMMIT;
```

To roll back a transaction:

◆ Type:
```
ROLLBACK;
```

The SELECT statements in **Listing 13.1** show that the UPDATE operations are performed by the DBMS and then undone by a ROLLBACK statement. See **Figure 13.2** for the result.

Listing 13.1 Within a transaction block, UPDATE operations (like INSERT and DELETE operations) are never final. See Figure 13.2 for the result.

```
SELECT SUM(pages), AVG(price) FROM titles;


BEGIN;
  UPDATE titles SET pages = 0;
  UPDATE titles SET price = price * 2;
  SELECT SUM(pages), AVG(price) FROM titles;
ROLLBACK;


SELECT SUM(pages), AVG(price) FROM titles;
```

```
SUM(pages) AVG(price)
---------- ----------
      5107    18.3875


SUM(pages) AVG(price)
---------- ----------
         0    36.7750


SUM(pages) AVG(price)
---------- ----------
      5107    18.3875
```

Figure 13.2 Result of Listing 13.1. The results of the SELECT statements show that the DBMS cancelled the transaction.

Listing 13.2 Use a transaction to delete publisher P04 from the table `publishers` and delete its related rows from other tables.

```listing
BEGIN;

  DELETE FROM title_authors
    WHERE title_id IN
      (SELECT title_id
        FROM titles
        WHERE pub_id = 'P04');

  DELETE FROM royalties
    WHERE title_id IN
      (SELECT title_id
        FROM titles
        WHERE pub_id = 'P04');

  DELETE FROM titles
    WHERE pub_id = 'P04';

  DELETE FROM publishers
    WHERE pub_id = 'P04';

COMMIT;
```

Listing 13.2 shows a more practical example of a transaction. I want to delete the publisher P04 from the table `publishers` without generating a referential-integrity error. Because some of the foreign-key values in `titles` point to publisher P04 in `publishers`, I first need to delete the related rows from the tables `titles`, `titles_authors`, and `royalties`. I use a transaction to be certain that *all* the `DELETE` statements are executed. If only some of the statements were successful, the data would be rendered inconsistent. (For information about referential-integrity checks, see "Specifying a Foreign Key with `FOREIGN KEY`" in Chapter 10.)

✔ Tips

- Always end transactions explicitly with either `COMMIT` or `ROLLBACK`. A missing endpoint could lead to huge transactions with unpredictable results on the data or, on abnormal program termination, rollback of the last uncommitted transaction.

- You can nest transactions. The maximum number of nesting levels depends on the DBMS.

- Most DBMSes operate in autocommit mode by default unless overridden by either explicit or implicit transactions. In *autocommit mode*, each statement is executed as its own transaction. If a statement completes successfully, the DBMS commits it; if the DBMS encounters any error, it rolls back the statement.

- For long transactions, you can set arbitrary intermediate markers, called *savepoints*, to divide a transaction into smaller parts. Savepoints allow you to roll back changes made from the current point in the transaction to a location earlier in the transaction (provided that the transaction hasn't been committed). Imagine a

continues on next page

session in which you've made a complex series of uncommitted INSERTs, UPDATEs, and DELETEs and then realize that the last few changes are incorrect or unnecessary. You can use savepoints to avoid resubmitting every statement. **Microsoft SQL Server** and **Oracle** support savepoints.

- **DBMS** To run Listings 13.1 and 13.2 in **Microsoft Access**, change BEGIN to BEGIN TRANSACTION. In Access, you can't execute transactions through the Access SQL View user interface or DAO; you must use the Jet OLE DB provider and ADO.

  To run Listings 13.1 and 13.2 in **Microsoft SQL Server**, change BEGIN to BEGIN TRANSACTION.

  Oracle transactions begin implicitly. To run Listings 13.1 and 13.2 in Oracle, omit the statement BEGIN.

  MySQL 4.0 and earlier versions support transactions in InnoDB and BDB tables but not in native tables; search the MySQL documentation for *transactions*.

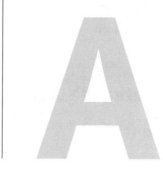

APPENDIX

Most of the examples in this book use the sample database **books**; see "The Sample Database" in Chapter 2. To follow along with the examples, you'll need to create **books** in your DBMS.

In this appendix, I'll describe how to create **books**, build its tables, and populate those tables with data. All the files you'll need are available for download at this book's companion Web site, www.peachpit.com/vqs/sql. The files are compressed into a single zip file. To expand this file, use a free decompression utility such as WinZip (Windows; www.winzip.com), StuffIt (Mac OS; www.stuffit.com), or gunzip or unzip (Unix). After decompression, read the file readme.txt for a description of the distribution.

Creating the Sample Database books

If you're using Microsoft Access, simply open the file books.mdb. If you're using a server DBMS, you must create books and then run an SQL script to build its tables and populate them with data. **Listing A.1** shows an ANSI SQL script named create_books.sql that creates the tables and inserts rows into them. To create the sample database in a server DBMS, you perform these general steps:

1. Create the database books.

2. If necessary, modify create_books.sql to work in your particular DBMS.

3. Run create_books.sql against books.

I'll describe the specific steps for each DBMS that I cover in this book. As usual, I assume that you have the necessary permissions from your database administrator, that you can connect to a database, and that your path is in order (see the Tips in "Running SQL Programs" in Chapter 1).

All the DBMSes support the statement CREATE DATABASE to create a new database, but I'll explain how to use other, easier tools. If you prefer to use CREATE DATABASE, refer to the DBMS's documentation. CREATE DATABASE is not part of the ANSI standard, so its syntax and capabilities vary by DBMS. (The closest SQL-92 gets to CREATE DATABASE is the CREATE SCHEMA statement.)

Listing A.1 The SQL program create_books.sql creates all the tables in the sample database books and populates them with data. This program is written in ANSI SQL for maximum compatibility, but you may have to make some changes to run it on your DBMS.

```
DROP TABLE authors;
CREATE TABLE authors
  (
  au_id    CHAR(3)     NOT NULL,
  au_fname VARCHAR(15) NOT NULL,
  au_lname VARCHAR(15) NOT NULL,
  phone    VARCHAR(12) NULL    ,
  address  VARCHAR(20) NULL    ,
  city     VARCHAR(15) NULL    ,
  state    CHAR(2)     NULL    ,
  zip      CHAR(5)     NULL    ,
  CONSTRAINT authors_pk PRIMARY KEY (au_id)
  );

DROP TABLE publishers;
CREATE TABLE publishers
  (
  pub_id   CHAR(3)     NOT NULL,
  pub_name VARCHAR(20) NOT NULL,
  city     VARCHAR(15) NOT NULL,
  state    CHAR(2)     NULL    ,
  country  VARCHAR(15) NOT NULL,
  CONSTRAINT publishers_pk PRIMARY KEY (pub_id)
  );
```

code continues on next page

Listing A.1 *continued*

```
┌──────────────────────────────── listing ────────────────────────────────┐
DROP TABLE titles;
CREATE TABLE titles
  (
  title_id   CHAR(3)      NOT NULL,
  title_name VARCHAR(40)  NOT NULL,
  type       VARCHAR(10)  NULL    ,
  pub_id     CHAR(3)      NOT NULL,
  pages      INTEGER      NULL    ,
  price      DECIMAL(5,2) NULL    ,
  sales      INTEGER      NULL    ,
  pubdate    DATE         NULL    ,
  contract   SMALLINT     NOT NULL,
  CONSTRAINT titles_pk PRIMARY KEY (title_id)
  );

DROP TABLE title_authors;
CREATE TABLE title_authors
  (
  title_id      CHAR(3)      NOT NULL,
  au_id         CHAR(3)      NOT NULL,
  au_order      SMALLINT     NOT NULL,
  royalty_share DECIMAL(5,2) NOT NULL,
  CONSTRAINT title_authors_pk PRIMARY KEY (title_id, au_id)
  );

DROP TABLE royalties;
CREATE TABLE royalties
  (
  title_id     CHAR(3)      NOT NULL,
  advance      DECIMAL(9,2) NULL    ,
  royalty_rate DECIMAL(5,2) NULL    ,
  CONSTRAINT royalties_pk PRIMARY KEY (title_id)
  );

INSERT INTO authors VALUES('A01','Sarah','Buchman','718-496-7223',
  '75 West 205 St','Bronx','NY','10468');
INSERT INTO authors VALUES('A02','Wendy','Heydemark','303-986-7020',
  '2922 Baseline Rd','Boulder','CO','80303');
INSERT INTO authors VALUES('A03','Hallie','Hull','415-549-4278',
  '3800 Waldo Ave, #14F','San Francisco','CA','94123');
INSERT INTO authors VALUES('A04','Klee','Hull','415-549-4278',
  '3800 Waldo Ave, #14F','San Francisco','CA','94123');
INSERT INTO authors VALUES('A05','Christian','Kells','212-771-4680',
  '114 Horatio St','New York','NY','10014');
INSERT INTO authors VALUES('A06','','Kellsey','650-836-7128',
  '390 Serra Mall','Palo Alto','CA','94305');
INSERT INTO authors VALUES('A07','Paddy','O''Furniture','941-925-0752',
  '1442 Main St','Sarasota','FL','34236');

INSERT INTO publishers VALUES('P01','Abatis Publishers','New York','NY','USA');
INSERT INTO publishers VALUES('P02','Core Dump Books','San Francisco','CA','USA');
INSERT INTO publishers VALUES('P03','Schadenfreude Press','Hamburg',NULL,'Germany');
INSERT INTO publishers VALUES('P04','Tenterhooks Press','Berkeley','CA','USA');
```

code continues on next page

CREATING THE SAMPLE DATABASE BOOKS

Listing A.1 *continued*

```
┌────────────────────────────────── listing ──────────────────────────────────┐
INSERT INTO titles VALUES('T01','1977!','history','P01',
  107,21.99,566,DATE '2000-08-01',1);
INSERT INTO titles VALUES('T02','200 Years of German Humor','history','P03',
  14,19.95,9566,DATE '1998-04-01',1);
INSERT INTO titles VALUES('T03','Ask Your System Administrator','computer','P02',
  1226,39.95,25667,DATE '2000-09-01',1);
INSERT INTO titles VALUES('T04','But I Did It Unconsciously','psychology','P04',
  510,12.99,13001,DATE '1999-05-31',1);
INSERT INTO titles VALUES('T05','Exchange of Platitudes','psychology','P04',
  201,6.95,201440,DATE '2001-01-01',1);
INSERT INTO titles VALUES('T06','How About Never?','biography','P01',
  473,19.95,11320,DATE '2000-07-31',1);
INSERT INTO titles VALUES('T07','I Blame My Mother','biography','P03',
  333,23.95,1500200,DATE '1999-10-01',1);
INSERT INTO titles VALUES('T08','Just Wait Until After School','children','P04',
  86,10.00,4095,DATE '2001-06-01',1);
INSERT INTO titles VALUES('T09','Kiss My Boo-Boo','children','P04',
  22,13.95,5000,DATE '2002-05-31',1);
INSERT INTO titles VALUES('T10','Not Without My Faberge Egg','biography','P01',
  NULL,NULL,NULL,NULL,0);
INSERT INTO titles VALUES('T11','Perhaps It''s a Glandular Problem','psychology','P04',
  826,7.99,94123,DATE '2000-11-30',1);
INSERT INTO titles VALUES('T12','Spontaneous, Not Annoying','biography','P01',
  507,12.99,100001,DATE '2000-08-31',1);
INSERT INTO titles VALUES('T13','What Are The Civilian Applications?','history','P03',
  802,29.99,10467,DATE '1999-05-31',1);

INSERT INTO title_authors VALUES('T01','A01',1,1.0);
INSERT INTO title_authors VALUES('T02','A01',1,1.0);
INSERT INTO title_authors VALUES('T03','A05',1,1.0);
INSERT INTO title_authors VALUES('T04','A03',1,0.6);
INSERT INTO title_authors VALUES('T04','A04',2,0.4);
INSERT INTO title_authors VALUES('T05','A04',1,1.0);
INSERT INTO title_authors VALUES('T06','A02',1,1.0);
INSERT INTO title_authors VALUES('T07','A02',1,0.5);
INSERT INTO title_authors VALUES('T07','A04',2,0.5);
INSERT INTO title_authors VALUES('T08','A06',1,1.0);
INSERT INTO title_authors VALUES('T09','A06',1,1.0);
INSERT INTO title_authors VALUES('T10','A02',1,1.0);
INSERT INTO title_authors VALUES('T11','A06',1,0.4);
INSERT INTO title_authors VALUES('T11','A03',2,0.3);
INSERT INTO title_authors VALUES('T11','A04',3,0.3);
INSERT INTO title_authors VALUES('T12','A02',1,1.0);
INSERT INTO title_authors VALUES('T13','A01',1,1.0);

INSERT INTO royalties VALUES('T01',10000,0.05);
INSERT INTO royalties VALUES('T02',1000,0.06);
INSERT INTO royalties VALUES('T03',15000,0.07);
INSERT INTO royalties VALUES('T04',20000,0.08);
INSERT INTO royalties VALUES('T05',100000,0.09);
INSERT INTO royalties VALUES('T06',20000,0.08);
INSERT INTO royalties VALUES('T07',1000000,0.11);
INSERT INTO royalties VALUES('T08',0,0.04);
INSERT INTO royalties VALUES('T09',0,0.05);
INSERT INTO royalties VALUES('T10',NULL,NULL);
INSERT INTO royalties VALUES('T11',100000,0.07);
INSERT INTO royalties VALUES('T12',50000,0.09);
INSERT INTO royalties VALUES('T13',20000,0.06);
```

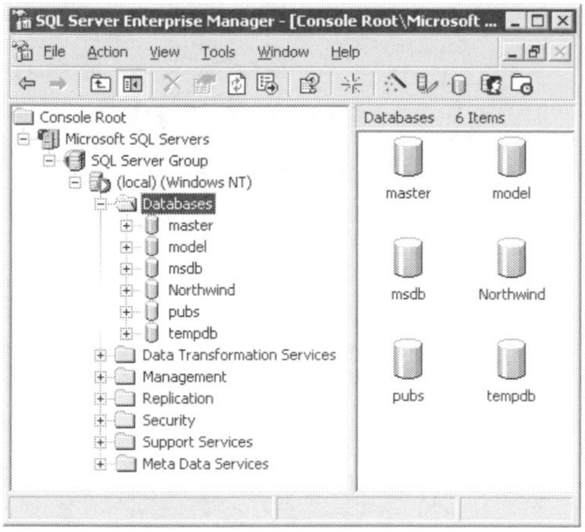

Figure A.1 SQL Server displays a list of databases in the Details pane.

Figure A.2 The Create Database Wizard guides you through the steps needed to create a database.

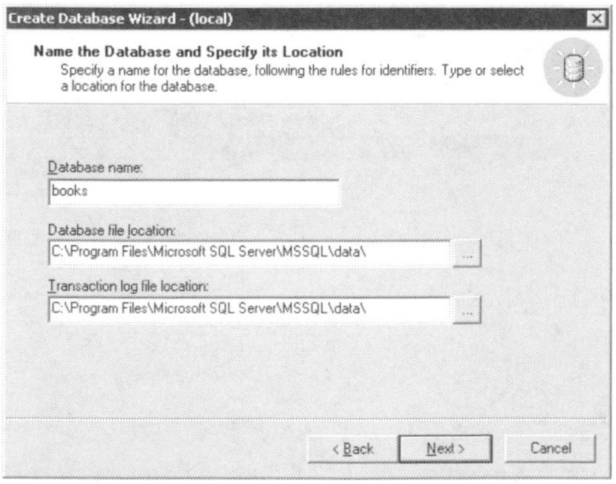

Figure A.3 Name the database *books*.

To open books in Microsoft Access:

1. Choose File > Open, select books.mdb, and then click Open.

2. To inspect the tables, click Tables (below Objects) in the Database window.

   To run SQL statements against books, see "Microsoft Access" in Chapter 1.

To create books in Microsoft SQL Server:

1. Choose Start > Programs > Microsoft SQL Server > Enterprise Manager.

2. Navigate to the Databases folder of the server you're using (**Figure A.1**).

3. Choose Tools > Wizards.

4. Select Create Database Wizard in the Database section and then click OK (**Figure A.2**).

5. Click Next to skip the Welcome screen.

6. Type *books* in the Database Name field, and click Next.

   Click the browse buttons if you want to change the locations of the database and transaction log files (**Figure A.3**).

continues on next page

CREATING THE SAMPLE DATABASE BOOKS

7. Accept the default database file name and initial size (**Figure A.4**), and click Next.

8. Accept the default database file-growth settings (**Figure A.5**), and click Next.

9. Accept the default transaction-log file name and initial size (**Figure A.6**), and click Next.

10. Accept the default transaction-log file-growth settings (**Figure A.7**), and click Next.

11. Click Finish to accept your choices (**Figure A.8**).

12. Click OK to dismiss the confirmation message box.

13. Click No to decline creating a maintenance plan.

The database books now appears in the Details pane of Enterprise Manager.

14. To run create_books.sql in SQL Server, change the data type of the column pubdate in the table titles from DATE to DATETIME, and delete the DATE keyword in the date literals of all the INSERT INTO titles statements. Change DATE '2000-08-01' to '2000-08-01', for example.

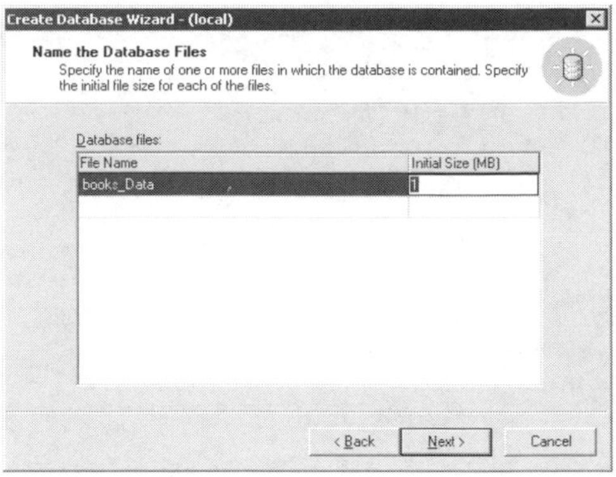

Figure A.4 Accept the default name and initial size of the database file.

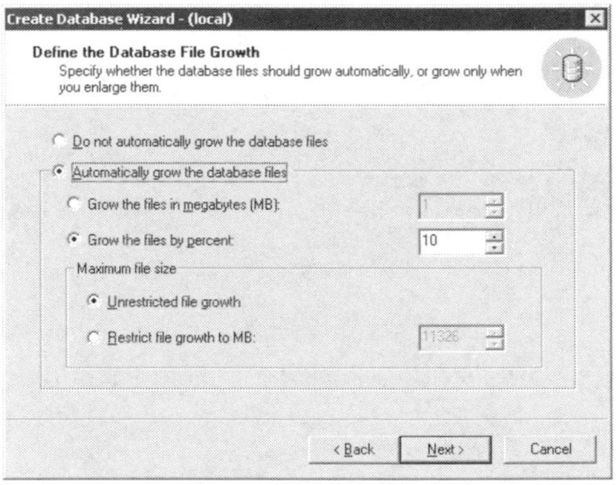

Figure A.5 For this database, let SQL Server grow the database file automatically rather than only when you enlarge it.

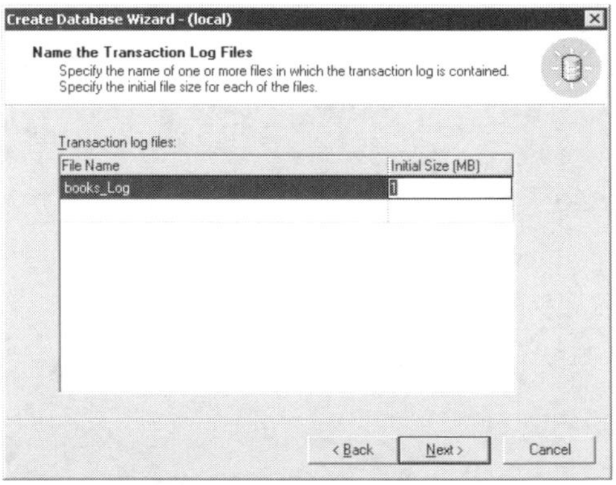

Figure A.6 Accept the default name and initial size of the transaction-log file.

15. Choose Start > Programs > Microsoft SQL Server > Query Analyzer.

16. Select the server and authentication mode, and click OK.

17. Choose the database books from the toolbar combo box.

18. Choose File > Open, select create_books.sql in the Open dialog box, and then click OK.

19. Choose Query > Execute or press F5 (**Figure A.9**).

The bottom pane displays the results. Ignore SQL Server's messages that it can't drop nonexistent tables. The DROP TABLE statements are required if you want to re-run create_books.sql later to restore the tables to their original state.

20. To run SQL scripts and interactive statements against books, see "Microsoft SQL Server" in Chapter 1.

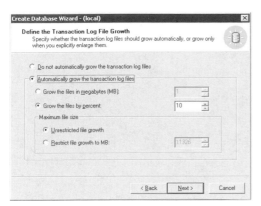

Figure A.7 For this database, let SQL Server grow the transaction-log file automatically rather than only when you enlarge it.

Figure A.8 SQL Server is ready to create the database.

Figure A.9 Use Query Analyzer to create the sample tables and insert data into them. Ignore the warning messages that appear the first time you run the script.

CREATING THE SAMPLE DATABASE BOOKS

To create books in Oracle:

1. Start the Database Configuration Assistant.

   This procedure varies by platform. In Windows, for example, choose Start > Programs > Oracle - OraHome91 > Configuration and Migration Tools > Database Configuration Assistant.

2. Click Next to skip the Welcome screen.

3. Select Create a Database (**Figure A.10**), and click Next.

4. Select General Purpose (**Figure A.11**), and click Next.

5. Type *books* in the Global Database Name and SID fields (**Figure A.12**), and click Next.

6. Select Dedicated Server Mode (**Figure A.13**), and click Next.

Figure A.10 The Database Configuration Assistant guides you through the steps needed to create a database.

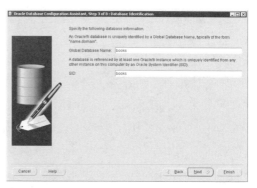

Figure A.12 Name the database *books*.

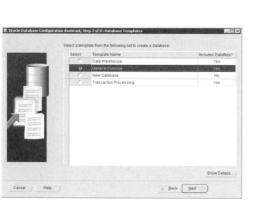

Figure A.11 Here, I've selected General Purpose. You can select New Database instead, but Oracle will take longer to create the database.

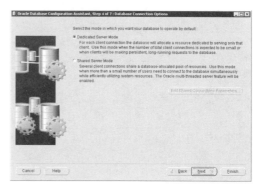

Figure A.13 Dedicated Server Mode is appropriate when the number of clients is expected to be small.

Figure A.14 The Typical setting is appropriate to create a database with minimal user input.

Figure A.15 Accept the default storage settings .

Figure A.16 Oracle is ready to create the database.

7. Select Typical, accept the other default initialization parameters (**Figure A.14**), and click Next.

8. Accept the default Database Storage settings (**Figure A.15**), and click Next.

9. Select Create Database (**Figure A.16**), and click Finish.

10. Click OK to dismiss the Summary screen and create the database.

11. Click Exit in the message box that appears when Oracle finishes creating the database.

12. To run `create_books.sql` in Oracle, change the value in the column `au_fname` in the table `authors` for author A06 from an empty string (`''`) to a space character (`' '`).

This change prevents Oracle from interpreting the first name of author A06 as null; see the DBMS Tip in "Nulls" in Chapter 3.

13. Start SQL*Plus.

This procedure varies by platform. In Windows, for example, choose Start > Programs > Oracle - OraHome91 > Application Development > SQL Plus.

14. Enter your user name, password, and the host string `books`, and then click OK.

continues on next page

CREATING THE SAMPLE DATABASE BOOKS

15. At the SQL prompt, type
`@create_books.sql`,
and press Enter (**Figure A.17**).

You can include an absolute or relative pathname; see the sidebar in "Running SQL Programs" in Chapter 1.

SQL*Plus displays the results. Ignore Oracle's messages that it can't drop non-existent tables. The DROP TABLE statements are required if you want to re-run `create_books.sql` later to restore the tables to their original state.

16. To run SQL scripts and interactive statements against books, see "Oracle" in Chapter 1.

Figure A.17 Use SQL*Plus to create the sample tables and insert data into them. Ignore the warning messages that appear the first time you run the script.

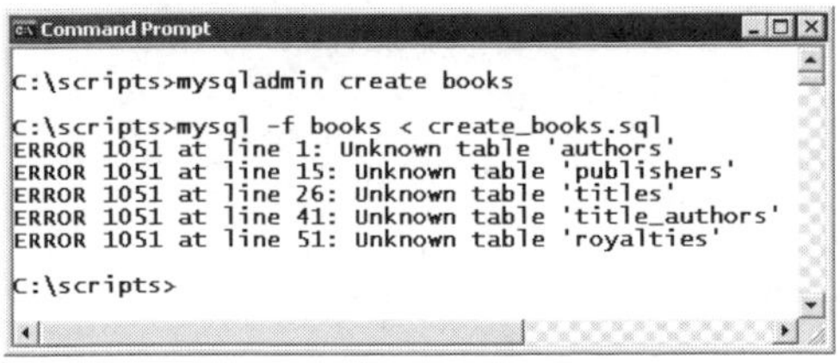

Figure A.18 Creating the database books in MySQL. Ignore the warning messages that appear the first time you run the script.

To create books in MySQL:

1. At an operating-system prompt (shell), type `mysqladmin create books`, and press Enter.

   MySQL creates the database books.

2. At the shell, type:

   `mysql -f books < create_books.sql`

   The `-f` option forces `mysql` to keep running even if it encounters SQL errors (**Figure A.18**). `create_books.sql` needs no changes to run in MySQL. You can include an absolute or relative pathname; see the sidebar in "Running SQL Programs" in Chapter 1.

   `mysql` displays the results. Ignore MySQL's messages that it can't drop nonexistent tables. The `DROP TABLE` statements are required if you want to re-run `create_books.sql` later to restore the tables to their original state.

3. To run SQL scripts and interactive statements against books, see "MySQL" in Chapter 1.

✔ Tip

- If you're running MySQL from a remote computer on a network, you'll need to specify a host, user name, and password to connect to the server. To do so, type:

  `mysql -h host -u user -p dbname`

  host is the host name, *user* is your user name, and *dbname* is the name of the database to use. MySQL will prompt you for a password. Contact your database administrator to find out what connection parameters you should use to connect.

CREATING THE SAMPLE DATABASE BOOKS

To create books in PostgreSQL:

1. At an operating-system prompt (shell), type `createdb books`, and press Enter. PostgreSQL creates the database `books`.

2. At the shell, type:

   `psql -f create_books.sql books`

   The `-f` option specifies the name of the SQL file (**Figure A.19**).

   `create_books.sql` needs no changes to run in PostgreSQL. You can include an absolute or relative pathname; see the sidebar in "Running SQL Programs" in Chapter 1.

   `psql` displays the results. Ignore PostgreSQL's messages that it can't drop nonexistent tables. The `DROP TABLE` statements are required if you want to re-run `create_books.sql` later to restore the tables to their original state.

3. To run SQL scripts and interactive statements against `books`, see "PostgreSQL" in Chapter 1.

✔ Tip

- If you're running PostgreSQL from a remote computer on a network, you'll need to specify a host, user name, and password to connect to the server. To do so, type:

  `psql -h host -U user -W dbname`

  host is the host name, *user* is your user name, and *dbname* is the name of the database to use. PostgreSQL will prompt you for a password. Contact your database administrator to find out what connection parameters you should use to connect.

Figure A.19 Creating the database books in PostgreSQL. Ignore the warning messages that appear the first time you run the script.

Index